THIRD HISTORICAL SURVEY OF EDUCATIONAL DEVELOPMENT IN INDIA

Concepts in Communication
Informatics & Librarianship
(CICIL)

For a list of titles in this series
see pp. 490-93 at the end of the book

ABOUT THE AUTHORS

S.P. Agrawal (*b.* 1929) was Director, National Social Science Documentation Centre, ICSSR, and Member Secretary, Indian Association of Social Science Institutions. He was also the Vice-Chairman of the Asia and Pacific Information Network in Social Sciences (APINESS). In 1988 he was awarded the degree of Doctor of Philosophy in Education (Honoris Causa) by International University Foundation. Presently, he is Member, IFLA Round Table on Research in Reading, and Member, International Committee for Social Science Information and Documentation. He is also Member of Board of Studies of National Archives of India and Hindi Advisory Committee, Ministry of Coal, Government of India. Born and brought up in the cradle of freedom movement which he joined at the tender age of twelve, he gained an insight into political problems and developed a sense of responsibility which bore fruit as an information scientist committed to Gandhiji's philosophy and action-plan in the field and its social concept. He has written extensively on various aspects of Education, Indian Polity and Library and Information Science.

J.C. Aggarwal (*b.* 1928), former Deputy Director of Education/Executive Director of Delhi Bureau of Textbooks, Delhi Administration has a varied experience in the field of education. He has singly/jointly authored about 130 books on Education, Social Sciences and Current Problems. In collaboration with S.P. Agrawal, he has written Documentation Encyclopaedia of UNESCO and Education (in two parts), Women's Education in India, National Policy on Education Agenda for India 2001, Indian Writings on Education, 1979 to 1986, and Vocational Education in India. His other recent publications include : Yearbook of Indian Education, 1991 : World Overview; Ramamurti Report 1990 on National Policy on Education in India; and Survey of Education Documents in the World since 1983, etc.

Concepts in Communication
Informatics & Librarianship-57
General Editor : **S.P. Agrawal**

THIRD HISTORICAL SURVEY OF EDUCATIONAL DEVELOPMENT IN INDIA

Select Documents 1990-1992

S.P. Agrawal
former Member Secretary
Indian Association of Social Science Institutions
New Delhi

J.C. Aggarwal
former Executive Director
Delhi Bureau of Textbooks, Delhi Administration, Delhi

CONCEPT PUBLISHING COMPANY, NEW DELHI 110059

ISBN 81-7022-516-7

First Published 1994

S.P. **Agrawal** (*b*. 1929)
J.C. **Aggarwal** (*b*. 1928)

Published and Printed by
Ashok Kumar Mittal
Concept Publishing Company
A/15-16, Commercial Block
Mohan Garden, New Delhi-110059 (India)

Lasertypeset by
Printing Express
H-13, Bali Nagar
New Delhi-110015

GENERAL EDITOR'S INTRODUCTION

The First Historical Survey of *Development of Education in India* was published in 1986. *The Second Historical Survey* covering the period 1985-1990 was brought out in 1991 under CICIL series which covers a wide range of disciplines – interrelated but at the same time including a very wide stretch of topics for investigations, research and study. It is of great consolation that both these surveys placed in the hands of the discerning educationists as also reviewers have been well received. In all humility, we assume that these surveys are fulfilling a long felt need.

This volume reflects the attempts made in the direction of implementing the National Policy of Education, 1986 and that modified in 1992. The material has been grouped in four parts. Part one presents a historical survey of educational planning with special reference to Eighth Five Year Plan (1992-97) and the formulation of the modified National Policy on Education in 1992. Part two is devoted to Educational Statistics. Part three includes documents covering almost all facets of education. Part four consists of appendices relating to topics not covered earlier.

S.P. AGRAWAL

PREFACE

The survey volume covering the period 1990-1992, is a sequel to *Second Historical Survey of Educational Developments in India : Select Documents, 1985-1990.* A few documents relating to the year 1989, not already covered, have also been included. Main documentation sources are: Ministry of Human Resource Development, Department of Education, Government of India, New Delhi; University Grants Commission, New Delhi; National Council of Educational Research and Training, New Delhi; National Institute of Educational Planning and Administration, New Delhi and Association of Indian Universities, New Delhi. Significant educational statistics covering various facets of educational development have also been incorporated. The authors are grateful to all resource institutions/organizations for using their documents in this publication.

S.P. AGRAWAL
J.C. AGGARWAL

CONTENTS

PART I

EDUCATIONAL PLANNING, POLICIES AND PROGRESS

1

EDUCATION IN EIGHTH FIVE YEAR PLAN (1992-97)*

GENERAL EDUCATION

Introduction

It is now universally acknowledged that the goal of Plan efforts is human development, of which human resource development is a necessary pre-requisite. Education is the catalytic factor, which leads to human resource development comprising better health and nutrition, improved socio-economic opportunities and more congenial and beneficial natural environment for all. There is already enough evidence in India to show that high literacy rates, especially high female literacy rates, are associated with low rates of population growth, infant mortality and maternal mortality, besides a higher rate of life expectancy. Although the country has not so far achieved the goals of universalisation of elementary eduation (UEE) and eradication of adult illiteracy (EAI), the 1991 Census results reveal a literacy rate of over 52 per cent, with a higher rate of growth for female literacy. This is highly encouraging and the country can hope to achieve the broader goal of 'Education for All' (EFA) by AD 2000, which has incidentally received international recognition at the world conference on EFA held at Jomtien in March 1990. The commitment of the Government to the National Policy on Education (NPE), implemented from 1986-87 onwards and reviewed in 1990, has been reaffirmed with revised formulation in respect of a few paras, placed before the Parliament on 7-5-1992. On the eve of Eighth Plan, therefore, the country is poised to make a real breakthrough in achieving its long cherished

* Published by the Planning Commission, Government of India, New Delhi.

educational goals as well as in supporting the drive for higher rate of economic growth.

Plan Performance Review (1985-92)

The development of education in terms of institutions and enrolment from 1984-85 onwards is indicated at the end of this Chapter (Annexure 1.1).

Elementary Education

The Seventh Plan gave overriding priority for the realisation of the objective of UEE by 1990. It was estimated that for achieving the goal, over 5 crore additional children would have to be enrolled. By 1991-92 however about 2.53 crores were actually enrolled in the formal system and even after taking account of 0.72 crore in the non-formal system, the target could not be achieved. At the end of 1991-92 the gross enrolment at the primary and upper-primary stages is likely to have reached 10.09 crores and 3.44 crores respectively. The details of enrolment at the elementary stage are given in Table 1.1.

TABLE 1.1: Enrolment in Elementary Education : Additional and Cumulative Achievement during 1985-92

(Figures in Crores)

Sl. No.	System/Stage	7th Plan (1985-90) additional achievement	Annual Plans (1990-91 and 1991-92) additional achievement	Cumulative enrolment at the end of 1991-92
1.	Formal :	1.95	0.58	13.53
	(a) Primary	1.34	0.36	10.09
	(b) Upper primary	0.61	0.22	3.44
2.	Non-formal	0.64	0.08	0.72
	Total	2.59	0.66	14.25

The latest data show that in 1990-91, the gross enrolment ratio (GER) had reached 101.03 per cent at the primary stage and 60.4 per cent at the upper primary stage. Considering that the number of overage and underage children in the GER data was in the range of

16.23 per cent and the dropout rate for primary stage in 1987-88 was 46.97 per cent and for elementary stage as a whole 62.29 per cent, we are clearly far away from the goal of universal enrolment and retention much less achievement.

The strategies of the Seventh Plan underwent a change in the middle of the Plan period with the adoption of the NPE in 1986. The new thrust in elementary education emphasized the aspects of : (i) universal enrolment and universal retention, and (ii) substantial improvement in the quality of education. As part of implementation of NPE, the new scheme of 'Operation Blackboard' (OB) was launched. Besides, the scheme of Non-Formal Education (NFE) was revised and a number of schemes for teacher education were also taken up. By March 1992, the scheme of OB covered about 80 per cent of the blocks and 49 experimental, innovative NFE projects were sanctioned. There were 27,342 NFE centres run by 419 voluntary agencies and there were 2.72 lakh State-run NFE centres.

Teacher Education

In 1987-88 a Centrally-Sponsored Scheme (CSS) for restructuring and reorganisation of teacher education was started, which included Mass Orientation of School Teachers (MOST), strengthening of Secondary Teacher Education Institutions (STEIs), State Councils of Educational Research and Training (SCERT), setting up of District Institutes of Education and Training (DIETs) and establishment and strengthening of Institutes of Advanced Studies in Education (IASE) in Universities. Between 1987-88 and 1991-92, 12.96 lakh teachers were covered under the scheme of MOST and Central assistance was extended to set up 287 DIETs, 25 STEIs and 12 IASEs. The scheme of strengthening SCERTs did not, however, make headway.

Adult Education

The NPE and the Programme of Action (POA) envisaged that the Adult Education Programme (AEP) would cover 4 crore illiterates by 1990 and another 6 crores by 1995. With the launching of the National Literacy Mission (NLM) in 1988, the targets were reformulated and strategies recast. Accordingly, 3 crore illiterates were expected to be covered by 1990 and 5 crore by 1995. While Rural Functional Literacy Programme (RFLP), the post literacy and the teaching-learning process were modified, new strategies like area specific and time bound approach to achieve 100 per cent total literacy (TL), massive participation of non-governmental organisations (NGOs) and students and effective utilisation of traditional and folk theatre forms in literacy work were evolved. By 1991-92, the post-literacy programme was institutionalised in the form of 32,000 Jan Shikshan Nilayams (JSNs). Apart from the introduction of Improved Pace and Content of Learning (IPCL) method, which reduced the duration of learning from 500 to 200 hours, technology demonstration programmes were initiated in 42 selected districts. The scheme of Shramik Vidyapeeths (SVs) was reviewed, suggesting a need for expansion. The number of State Resources Centres (SRCs) increased from 19 to 20. A National Institute of Adult Education (NIAE) was set up in January 1991 to augment the technical and academic resource support to adult education and to undertake quality research and evaluation studies.

Area-specific and time-bound mass campaigns for TL first launched in Kottayam town and Ernakulam district in Kerala in 1989 with the active participation of students and voluntary agencies have been extended to other districts. By March 1992, 25 districts had achieved total literacy (in the sense of 85 per cent literacy) and TL campaigns were at different stages of progress in 80 districts in Andhra Pradesh, Bihar, Gujarat, Haryana, Himachal Pradesh, Karnataka, Madhya Pradesh, Maharashtra, Orissa, Punjab, Rajasthan, Uttar Pardesh and West Bengal covering over 3 crore illiterates with the help of about 30 lakh volunteers.

Secondary Education

As part of NPE, new CSSs for vocationalisation of higher secondary stage, improvement of science education and environmental orientation to school education were started. The new Central schemes of Navodaya Vidyalayas (NVs) and National Open School (NOS) were also initiated. The existing schemes of Integrated Education, Educational Technology and Computer Literacy Studies (CLASS) Project were strengthened.

By the end of 1991-92 about 8.7 per cent of the higher secondary students (5.85 lakhs) would have been diverted to vocational stream. The Open School affiliated to Central Board of Secondary Education (CBSE) was converted into an autonomous NOS in 1989 and by 1991-92, the total enrolment was in the neighbourhood of 1.50 lakhs.

Under the CLASS Project, 2,598 schools were equipped with computers, with 60 institutes providing resource support to these schools. As many as 275 NVs designed to provide good quality school education to talented rural children have been established in 29 States/Union Territories. As on 31 March, 1991, there were 64,517 students in the NVs and the pass percentage of the first batch, which took Class X examination was 95.77. The National Council of Educational Research and Training (NCERT) brought out the National Curriculum Framework for all stages of education and undertook a massive revision of text books for classes I-XII on the basis of the revised syllabi designed as per the framework.

Other Programmes

The Central language institutions relating to Hindi, Indian Languages, English, Urdu, Sanskrit and Foreign Languages implemented a variety of schemes relating to training of language teachers, publication of language teaching materials, assistance to voluntary organisations, support for Urdu Calligraphy Centres etc. The National Book Trust (NBT) was involved in the work relating to preparation of literature for neo-literates under the NLM and preparation of a Central list of books for the libraries of 5.5 lakhs primary schools under the OB Scheme. The NBT's Nehru Bal Pustakalya and Adan-Pradan Schemes have also made a mark. Besides continuing the schemes relating to national scholarships and scholarships for the talented children from the rural areas, in 1988-89 a new scheme for upgradation of merit of SC/ST students through remedial and special coaching was started as part of NPE.

Eighth Plan Thrust Areas

Universalisation of elementary education, eradication of illiteracy in the age group of 15 to 35 and strengthening of vocational education (VE) so as to relate it to the emerging needs in the urban and rural settings are the major thrust areas of the Eighth Plan in the Education Sector. Utilisation of formal, non-formal and open channels of learning would be the strategy for this purpose. The changed approach, improved methodology of teaching, increased participation of NGOs and student volunteers have infused a new vitality into the literacy programme and have given it a fresh momentum. The aim would be to impart a similar vitaliy and momentum to the universal primary educa tion programme with a definite edge in its favour. The programmes c AE and UEE are complementary and there are situations where th Elementary Education (EE) programmes may benefit from the spin-of effect of the AE programmes. The improvement in the literacy percent age in the decade 1981-91, after allowing for statistical adjustment du to the exclusion of age group 0 to 6 is as much due to the highe literacy rate of school-age cohorts and attrition of old-age cohorts wit low level of literacy as to the special efforts on the AE front. The nee for according the highest priority to UEE is, therefore, wel established. Within the overall school-age population, the focus woul be on girls, who account for two-thirds of target, and among adults th focus would be on women's literacy which has a beneficial impact o children's literacy as well as other national objectives like populatio control and family welfare.

So far as UEE is concerned, the NPE stress on retention, particip tion and achievement, rather than mere enrolment, would be rei forced. Enrolment data are easily available and enrolment is a pr condition for any further action. However, special attention would b paid to increase retention, improvement of quality, specification minimum levels of learning (MLL) and their attainment by the lea ners.

In regard to literacy the emphasis would be on sustainability literacy skills gained and on the achievement of goals of remediatio continuation and application of skills to actual living and working co ditions.

In view of the employment orientation of the Plan and the need establish meaningful linkages between the world of work and th world of learning, VE would be another priority area. This would n be confined to higher secondary stage but permeate the whole arena secondary education and non-formal education/training. A combinati of vocational and academic courses would be offered at seconda stage with open education (OE) as an important channel, preparing th students for wage employment and self-employment. In the servi sector, expansion of health-related courses having a rural orientati would be emphasised. In the rural areas, agro-based and technolo based vocational courses would be developed by combining t strengths of existing institutional structures with OE institutions.

Targets

It is estimated that additional enrolment to be achieved during the Eighth Plan to reach universalisation is approximately 5.61 crores children. These data are based on the assumption of 15 per cent incidence of overage/underage phenomenon both at the primary and the upper primary stages. Enrolment of about 4.38 crores would be achieved through formal schools, about one crore through non-formal centres and the rest through the open learning channel of upper primary stage. These targets are much higher than the Seventh Plan achievement. They are, however, within the realm of possibility, if the requisite will and mobilisation of organisational and financial resources are brought to bear on the task and innovative schemes like voluntary primary schools and OE at the upper primary stage are introduced. The NDC Committee on Literacy recently appointed is expected to give a lead in this regard. Working targets in relation to retention and achievement based on institutional capabilities and consultations with State Governments need to laid down. The details of enrolment targets are given in Table 1.2 and State-wise targets of formal system in Annexure 1.6.

TABLE 1.2: Elementary Education : Projected Enrolment for Eighth Plan (1992-97)

(Figures in Crores)

Sl. No.	Stage	Population by 1997		Population with overage/under-age children		Enrolment achieved upto 1991-92		Addnl. Population to be enrolled by 1997	
		Total	Female	Total	Female	Total	Female	Total	Female
1	2	3	4	5	6	7	8	9	10
1.	Elem. Edn	16.64	8.09	19.14	9.30	13.53	5.54	5.61 (67%)	3.76
(a)	Primary(I-V)	10.53	5.12	12.11	5.89	10.09	4.24	2.02 (82%)	1.65
(b)	Upper Primary (VI-VIII)	6.11	2.97	7.03	3.41	3.44	1.30	3.59 (59%)	2.11

According to the 1991 census, the number of illiterates in all age-groups is 33.6 crores. It is estimated that there will be 11.2 crores illiterates in the 15-35 age group of whom 70 lakhs would have become literate by the end of March, 1992. Thus, the target to be covered during the Eighth Plan will be about 10.5 crores, compared to achievement of 2.65 crores during the Seventh Plan. In the context of the emphasis on sustainability of literacy and on continuing education, suitable targets in this regard need to be laid down after consulting State Governments.

In the VE, the target is to cover 15-20 per cent of students of higher secondary stage by the end of Eighth Plan.

Strategies

The main strategy for achieving the targets would be : (a) adoption of the decentralised approach at educational planning and management at all levels through Panchayati Raj (PR) institutions; (b) combining this approach with a convergence model of rural development involving integrated utilisation of all possible resources available at Panchayat, Block and District level for activities relating to elementary education/literacy, child care/development, women's socio-economic empowerment and rural health programmes; (c) large scale participation of voluntary agencies; and (d) development of innovative and cost-effective complementary programmes including open learning system (OLS) supported by distance education techniques.

In specific terms, the following measures will be adopted :

(1) The formal school system will be expanded and improved.

(2) The non-formal system mainly catering to the needs of children working for wages, children working whole time in domestic or household duties and children in schoolless habitations will be expanded, improved and strengthened in the matter of supply of teaching learning materials, instructional delivery and achievements.

(3) A voluntary school scheme will be introduced. At present, elementary education is considered a responsibility of State and local bodies. However, there is scope for providing part time non-formalised education to a large number of learners who are not able to avail of the facility of formal full time school or non-formal education centres. Voluntary agencies would be encouraged in a big way to start non-formal part time schools, thus catering to the learning needs of urban working children and children in the tribal, hilly and inaccessible areas.

(4) A well-defined open learning system will be developed with a network of educational opportunities relevant to the needs and circumstanes of learners, especially girls, women, SCs/STs and the poor, the unemployed and the untrained. The major thrust of OLS would be on the acquisition of life-skills, vocational skills, directly contributing to productivity and inculcation of habits of self-learning.

(5) The MLL with reference to class III, V and VIII will be laid down for improving learning achievement. The educational system will be required to ensure that every child who completes any of these stages of learning reaches the minimum level of achievement. Measures for improving class-room teaching like introduction of a comprehensive evaluation system and a continuous inservice training of teachers will be taken up simultaneously. The MLL approach will be decentralised, each planning unit being able to determine its present levels of achievement, adopt appropriate MLLs and define a realistic timeframe within which to achieve the mastery level, through additional efforts and inputs where necessary.

(6) District Boards of Education (DBEs) would be set up. They are conceived as the nodal agency for planning and management of education at the district level comprising formal education, AE, NFE and teacher training, vertically linked to Block/or Mandal Education Committees and Village Education Committees (VECs) in a decentralised framework.

(7) The school complexes would be developed as the basic unit for educational planning, mobilisation and supervision, building organic linkages between educational institutions, DBEs and the Panchayati Raj Institutions.

(8) The involvement of the people in school management would be operationalised by giving VECs a more prominent role in planning and management of educational programmes at local level so that VECs, which know the micro-level problems, needs and expectations of the local community, will be accountable for the enrolment, retention and achievement of children and teachers.

(9) The methodology of Mahila Samakhya (MS) project of mobilising women's groups to voice their needs would be extended in conjunction with the involvement of local community to create a favourable environment to serve as a monitoring mechanism for promoting UEE and adult literacy.

(10) The district will be treated as a unit of educational planning in the Eighth Plan. For grant of Central assistance under CSSs during Sixth and Seventh Plans, a number of States were characterised as educationally backward. The Gross Enrolment Ratio (GER) was considered as a benchmark for the identification of backwardness. It was considered that there is a need for special assistance to the educationally backward States to overcome the historically obtaining disadvantages and also for reduction of regional disparities in educational development. The district-wise data of various indicators of educational development, however show that the inter-district variations are more significant than the inter-State variations. Moreover, the State is too large and variegated an area to serve as a homogeneous unit for educational planning. Therefore, educationally backward districts would be identified and special inputs would be provided in proportion to the degree of backwardness. The Working Group on early childhood and elementary education had ranked the districts in terms of a composite indicator giving equal weight to four parameters of general/female literacy and general/female GER – primary. Although, almost all districts in the top 200 backward districts were from backward States, there is no guarantee that assistance to backward States will necessarily flow to backward districts within them. During the Eighth Plan, accordingly the backward districts irrespective of the State where they are located, will be targeted. A more systematic study to identify the criteria for educational backwardness of districts and the ranking of the districts in terms of the selected indices on the basis of latest Census data, as a basic tool for investment decision, would also be initiated.

(11) Special efforts will be made to bring down construction cost of school buildings and other educational structures using available materials and adopting locally relevant architectural styles. Attention will be given as much to full utilisation of resources as to larger allocation e.g. more intensive use of buildings by operation of double shifts in schools and of equipment by inter-institutional sharing.

(12) In the case of teacher education, the stress will be on improving the standard of pre-service teacher education institutions and the quality of its programmes, providing continuing education

of a suitable kind to every teacher educator and to a substantial number of teachers and on creation of a system to discourage setting up of substandard institutions and phasing out of existing sub-standard ones.

(13) Time-bound, area-specific and cost-effective TL campaigns by involving all sections of society, specially students and non-governmental organisations would be expanded. While the whole adult education programme will be debureaucratised, the strategies of ensuring continued political commitment, strong administrative support, use of traditional and non-traditional media and cultural and art forms will be adopted. Students and teachers of universities, colleges and schools would be involved in a big way not only by awarding marks to students for their literacy work but also by making literacy work as a part of curriculum.

(14) Apart from consolidation, and expansion of secondary education increasingly through the open channel, the stress during the Eighth Plan will be on qualitative upgradation of secondary education through reorientation of its content and process, examination reform, diversification by way of vocationalisation and modernisation by way of technological inputs.

N.B.: The revised policy formulation relating to the NPE, 1986 which was placed before Parliament on 7th May, 1992 should be kept in view while working out details of programmes under General Education, University and Higher Education and Technical Education.

Programmes

The Eighth Plan is being launched in the backdrop of acceptance by the NDC of the recommendations of the Report of the Narasimha Rao Committee which has removed the uncertainties regarding the continuance of CSSs in Education Sector. All the existing CSSs will be continued. Introduction of new CSSs would require approval of full Planning Commission but they may be taken up in the priority areas when justified.

Elementary Education

Early Childhood Education (ECE) would be expanded by attaching pre-primary classes to selected primary schools. Voluntary agencies and other NGOs would be encouraged and provided financial assistance by reorganising the scheme of ECE. Integrated Child Development Scheme (ICDS) model would be supplemented by Balwadis, Creches and Vikas Wadis.

Primary schools or alternatives to primary schools like non-formal centres etc. would be provided to every child within a walking distance of one kilometre, with suitable adjustment for special cases. Voluntary agencies, factories, cooperatives etc. would be encouraged to set up part time primary schools to serve several groups of children belonging to hilly, desert, marshy, forest areas and nomadic tribes, seasonal migrants, urban poor etc. with freedom to adjust the number of school days, instructional hours and appoint teachers on contract basis.

Innovative programmes like Shiksha Karmi which have given good results in an experimental project in Rajasthan would be expanded. Besides, a range of activities that suit the requirements of specific groups of learners, who are usually left out of the ambit of large scale projects, would be taken up. Opening of night schools in urban areas, pre-primary and lower primary centres for children of 3-9 years of age, 'half-time' instructors and special projects to tackle educational problems of areas with concentration of child labour would be tried out.

Open schools would involve themselves in the post-primary stage education on an experimental basis to provide wider access to children who are working or not in a position to attend regular schools due to socio-economic or any other reasons.

Special efforts will be made to increase enrolment rates and improve participation rates at the upper primary stage especially in respect of girls. Hence, while ensuring effective universal access to all children at the primary stage, the infrastructure at the upper primary stage will have to be considerably expanded.

Besides expansion of school facilities, there will be need to improve the quality of education by providing existing schools with sufficient facilities. Therefore, the "Operation Blackboard" scheme will not only be continued and completed during the Eighth Plan in relation to primary schools but also extended to upper primary schools. The eventual aim would be to move towards a situation where every class has a classroom and a teacher.

In order to expedite universalisation of middle stage education and increase the enrolment of girls, the ratio between primary and upper primary schools would be brought down from the existing 1 : 4 to at least 1 : 3 with the ultimate aim of 1 : 2.

Apart from expanding Tribal Sub-Plan (TSP) and Special Component Plan (SCP), special measures are required for promotion of education of SCs/STs. Certain sub-castes, tribes and communities need particular attention because literacy rates among them are extremely low. The existing scheme of residential ashram schools will be expanded to cover classes from I to X and scolarship schemes for talented children at the secondary level would be expanded. This will be supplemented by the scheme of voluntary schools wherever possible. Suitable incentives will be provided to all educationally backward sections of society, particularly in rural areas. Hill and desert districts, remote and inaccessible areas and islands will be provided adequate institutional infrastructure. Greater attention will be paid to the educationally backward minorities keeping in view the recommendations of the Empowered Committee on Minority Education (1991).

Incentives and Support Services

A system of incentives to overcome social, economic and educational handicaps, which lead to high incidence of dropout has been an integral part of educational planning for universalisation since long. A recent evaluation of these schemes has made a positive assessment but has also emphasised the need for paying adequate attention to management aspects of the system so that they yield the desired results. A comprehensive package of incentives and support services for girls, SCs, STs and children of the economically weaker sections of society will be provided. The emphasis will be on provision of facilities that have special relevance for retention of girls, such as establishment of Day Care Centres for pre-school children and infants, provision of free uniforms, textbooks and stationery, attendance allowance and coordination of support services such as drinking water, fodder and fuel to release children, especially girls as well as women from related domestic chores.

Evaluation

A National Evaluation Organisation (NEO) will be set up to undertake assessment of student learning on national scale on a sample basis to implement the strategy of MLL.

Monitoring of the Progress of UEE

Annual sample studies to estimate the completion rates as envisaged in NPE, viz. "number of children of about 11 years of age completing five years of schooling or its equivalent through the formal/non-formal stream" will be undertaken. The data of completion rates and MLL will be used to set targets for the States under the 20-Point Programme also.

A comprehensive computerised institutional and related data base at the district level will be developed so that information, relevant not only to monitor the internal efficiency of the educational system, both formal and non-formal, but also to improve the planning and management at the district level, is available in time. Computerisation would be extended to all districts of the country in phases.

Teacher Education

Statutory status will be accorded to the National Council for Teacher Education (NCTE) to lay down and maintain standards in institutions and courses. The schemes of DIETs, STEIs and IASEs would be continued and their coverage expanded with a view to strengthening the institutional infrastructure and programmes of teacher education. The scheme for strengthening of SCERTs would be sanctioned and implemented and suitable measures for selection and professional development of staff in SCERTs, DIETs and IASEs will be undertaken. A large number of teachers will be çovered through in-service programmes, both institutional and distance education, and reputed professional organisations will be encouraged to conduct in-service and refresher courses for teachers. Open Universities at the national and State level will be encouraged to introduce induction teacher training courses to supplement the efforts of the existing training institutions. The bulk of seats in tachers' training colleges would be reserved for rural women.

Adult Education

Literacy programmes will be launched in districts/regions which are educationally backward or have high concentration of SC/ST population or have low female literacy. By the close of the Eighth Plan, 345 districts including about two-thirds of all districts in the educationally backward States would be covered by the TL campaigns, while the centre based approach would be gradually phased out and confined to hilly, tribal and sparsely populated regions. The strategy for backward districts would be two-fold. First, a few blocks would be selected where the literacy campaign can achieve success within a reasonable period. The demonstration effect of the blocks would influence the backward blocks which, in course of time, could develop appropriate literacy programmes. Secondly, the voluntary base in educationally backward districts being somewhat weak, ways and means of identification, strengthening and expansion of the same would be evolved in consultation with the respective State Governments. It is also necessary to develop technical comptence among voluntary agencies so that the partnership between the Government and the operating agencies becomes meaningful.

The possibility of further enhancing contributions from the community especially in urban areas and industrial towns would be explored so that apart from voluntary service, at least 20 per cent of the total expenditure on the campaign may be met.

In States, where library movement is strong, rural libraries should be integrated with the JSNs which are envisaged as innovative post-literacy and continuing education centres. Reputed NGOs, educational institutions, distinguished individuals, ex-servicemen, war widows, award winning teachers etc. will be encouraged to set up and run JSNs. Particular attention would be paid to the availability of a variety of quality matrials in adequate quantity to the neo-literates. Reputed printing presses and publishers would be motivated to print gratis literacy materials, posters and charts.

The academic and technical support to Adult Education programmes would be provided by the newly set up NIAE, which would be involved to a greater extent in various aspects of training, action research and monitoring, so that the Directorate of Adult Education can be phased out by the end of the Eighth Plan. At the State level, the State Resource Centres will be strengthened.

The scheme of SVs, which provide a variety of training programmes to the industrial workers and their families would be extended to cover workers in unorgnised sector and would also experiment with a variety of training models including distance education.

The contents of adult education would also include inculcation of values like secularism, national integration, scientific temperament, small family norm, concern for environmental conservation, cultural appreciation and so on. Even a soceity with a literate population is required to provide many avenues for continuing education in the context of the march towards a learning society, in which open schools and Open universities would play an important role.

Secondary Education

The expansion of secondary schools would be regulated and new schools opened on selective basis, particularly to cater to the needs of deprived sections like girls and SCs/STs and in rural areas generally. Quality improvement and the raising of the internal efficiency of the existing (10+2) system would be emphasised. While an increasing number of students may like to discontinue their formal studies either temporarily or permanently after 10 + 2, there would be provision for their re-entry into the education system at a later stage. For this purpose, education would be linked to the world of work by expanding the facilities and improving the quality of vocational education (VE) as also provision of subjective examination credits.

For widening the reach, an open channel of education would be provided to those who do not have access to regular institutions because of socio-economic and locational constraints and those who have already entered the world of work but are keen to improve their skills and income generating capacity. Open education programmes will be imparted with the help of multi-media packages and contact centres.

National Open School (NOS)

The NOS will continue its existing programmes and revise the syllabi and textbooks for the secondary/senior secondary courses and bring out a fresh set of instructional materials for the bridge course. It will develop and introduce vocational courses, especially in the areas of health, agriculture and rural development in collaboration with the concerned departments. The coverage is expected to increase progressively with registration of more and more accredited institutions, which now number 191. It should also coordinate and standardise the work of similar State-level mechanisms. The idea of starting State level open schools in all the States as recommended by the Conference of Boards of Secondary Education should be pursued. The NOS is expected to provide programme and resource support to State-level Open Schools. The setting up of a National Consortium of Open Education to facilitate accreditation of courses and of maintenance of quality through a process of networking and evaluation should be pursued by NOS in cooperation with the Indira Gandhi National Open University (IGNOU).

Vocational Education

The courses which have already been started would be consolidated. Special attention will be given to paramedical vocational courses to meet the needs of health manpower in the Eighth Plan. In addition to vocational courses forming part of the higher secondary courses, efforts would be made to offer varied courses of suitable duration to women, rural and tribal students and deprived sections of society. These courses may be coordinated with the working of Krishi Vigyan Kendras/organisations which offer training for self-employment. Non-formal, flexible and need-based vocational programmes would be made available to neo-literate youth who have completed primary education, to the school drop-outs, or persons engaged in work and to the unemployed or partially employed persons. Institutions of Open Education will be actively involved in this area. Suitable programmes would also be started for the handicapped.

Candidates who have completed vocational courses should have ample opportunities for career improvement and professional growth. For this purpose, bridge courses which would give them an opportunity to take up higher technical and professional courses should be a necessary component.

It is essential that experimental projects with other vocational education models are also tried out, e.g. pre-vocational education at the lower secondary level, exposure to various occupations right from the primary level for attitudinal change etc. It is also proposed to involve major industrial houses in all large projects and to prevail on them to include human resource development as part of project cost. The services of commercial agencies and NGOs will also be utilised.

Other Programmes

The target for the Eighth Plan would be to cover about 200 blocks by following the composite area approach to the planning and implementation of the integrated education for the disabled. Crucial areas like health, physical and art education should be made an integral part of school curriculum and accorded parity with other subjects. It is necessary that the work of NCERT in the area of Value Education is supplemented by work at the State level by SCERTs and measures to enrich teacher education. The CSS for introduction of Yoga in schools should be implemented more effectively and comprehensively. The activities of the National Population Education Project would be directed, in addition to the formal schools, towards the non-formal sector for which the curriculum, material development and facilitator orientation would have to be specially developed. It is proposed to continue assistance to State Institutes of Educational Technology (SIET) and to extend in a phased manner facilities for Educational TV programme production. The government is committed to the establishment of Navodaya Vidyalayas in each of the districts of the country. The construction work for the existing 275 Vidyalayas would be completed. The possibilities of reducing the cost of construction and expenditure towards infrastructure will be explored. The setting up of new NVs in all the remaining districts will be appropriately programmed, keeping in view the stipulated target date. In view of the key role of computers in modernisation of Secondary Education, the CLASS Project will be continued in a modified form and would cover 15,000 higher secondary schools by 1997. The project will be implemented with the collaboration of private agencies, with the elements of accountability and monitoring built in. The physical facilities and characteristics of the selected schools will be ascertained prior to the launching of the project. Full time teachers will be provided for computer literacy by the private organisation and this subject will be taught during the normal school hours unlike the earlier practice of teaching it beyond school hours. The existing schemes of improvement of science education and environmental orientation to school education would be stengthened by improving teacher training inputs. A new scheme for improvement of teaching of Mathematics at school level is being started. The NCERT would undertake Sixth Education Survey and a scheme for examination reforms apart from watching implementation of National Curricular Framework and MLL.

Language Development Scholarships and Book Promotion

For the implementation of the Three Language Formula in a uniform manner, 100 per cent financial assistance for appointment and training of modern Indian language teachers in Hindi-speaking States is envisaged. The Bureau for Promotion of Urdu would be accorded an autonomous status as per the recommendations of Jafri Committee. The long pending Sindhi Vikas Board would be established. The Education Department would collaborate with the Department of Electronics (DoE) in the project 'Technological Development in Indian Languages'. For promotion of classical languages, a national level body is proposed to be set up for maintaining, coordinating and improving teaching of Sanskrit and classical languages as also Arabic and Persian. The potentialities of voluntary Sanskrit organisations for promoting Sanskrit learning would be fully utilised by reorganising and developing the existing ones. Vedic learning and its linkage with modern scientific development under the Rashtriya Veda Vidya Prathisthan (Vedic Endowment) will be strengthened. The scheme of scholarships to upgrade the merit of SC/ST students would be revised with respect to number of awards and amount in consultation with State Governments. The number of awards under other schemes would be suitably enhanced so as to increase coverage and make them attractive. To foster book mindedness in the country, a Readers' Club Movement would be introduced. The National Book Trust intends to set up a National Centre for Children's Literature with the aim of producing 3000 titles every year. Under its Adan Pradan Scheme, translations of a large number of significant books from various Indian languages would be brought out. Besides developing manuscripts for neoliterates in various States, the NBT would provide assistance to publishers and voluntary agencies for production of books. The school Library Programme under OB would continue. A National Society of Authors is envisaged to oversee the interests and needs of authors.

Planning and Management and Information and Monitoring

The Eighth Plan would focus on decentralisation of planning and management activities; providing autonomy to educational institutions; building capabilities for the involvement and participation of the stake-holders in the educational process and building up of capabilities and professional competence among the administrators and voluntary associations and NGOs. The State Advisory Board of Education (SABE) would provide strong advisory support for training, research and dissemination of information on methodologies of planning and management strategies appropriate to the State level and to the district level bodies, namely the DBEs referred to earlier. The existing bodies like Central Advisory Board of Education (CABE), UGC, NCERT and

NIEPA would be strengthened. The CABE needs to be reorganised and should have a number of sub-committees to continuously review and monitor the progress in specific areas of education. A Standing Committee of CABE on Open Education is proposed to be set up. For streamlining the flow of information and developing the planning capacity at the district level, an Educational Management Information System (EMIS) covering all the districts in the country needs to be operationalised by the end of the Eighth Plan. The National Informatic Centre (NIC) has already developed a comprehensive computer network linking all the districts with computers. There is need to coordinate the working of educational management information system with NIC network. Following steps are also necessary to improve the system of educational statistics:

(1) Compulsory registration of non-recognised educational institutions; (2) More extensive use of sample surveys to monitor the progress in respect of some critical indicators of educational development; (3) Continuation of educational surveys conducted by NCERT by clearly defining their frequency and objectives *vis-a-vis* other sources of data; (4) Construction of composite indicators of educational development of various States/districts and periodical monitoring of their behaviour; (5) Coordination between various sub-sectoral agencies for sharing of information; and (6) Development of a comprehensive methodology and a sound data base on private costs of education to rationalise and to improve the efficiency in the use of financial resources.

Resources and Financial Allocations

The NPE statement that from the Eighth Plan onwards, the outlay on education would uniformly exceed 6 per cent of the national income would be treated as a guideline for allocation of resources during the Eighth Plan. The present public sector allocation is much lower and requires to be appropriately stepped up. A conscious effort to tap various avenues for raising resources for education needs to be made. In view of the paucity of domestic resources, vigorous efforts to attract external assistance for financing educational programmes, especially priority programmes without compromising country's basic educational policies is necessary. While the external funding would be an additionality to the resources for education, the externally aided projects would be in total conformity with the national policies, strategies and programmes and drawn up on innovative lines emphasising people's participation, improvement of quality, equality of education and substantial upgradation of facilities. The project formulation would be the responsibility of implementation agencies. At present, India is availing of bilateral assistance for Shiksha Karmi Project in Rajasthan and Mahila Samakhya Project in Uttar Pradesh, Gujarat and Karnataka. Within the broad objectives of the Eighth Plan, it is proposed to take up externally-aided projects, both bilateral and multi-lateral in various educationally backward States for promotion of basic education which includes: primary schooling, non-formal education, adult literacy, women's education and development and post-literacy and continuing education. Such projects are at various stages of development in respect of Bihar, Rajasthan, U.P. and South Orissa.

The actual expenditure on general education sector in the Seventh Plan was Rs. 6549.57 crores, of which Rs. 2294.57 crores were in the Central Plan and Rs. 4255.00 crores in the State Plan. The outlays and expenditure for Seventh Plan and approved outlays for the Eighth Plan are shown in Annexures 1.3 and 1.7. The requirements of UEE, AE, Vocationalisation and OLS would be the first charge on the outlays.

UNIVERSITY AND HIGHER EDUCATION

Review of the Seventh Plan and Annual Plans (1985-92)

Improvement of quality and consolidation continued to be the main concerns in the field of higher education during the Seventh Plan. The enrolment of students in 1991-92 was 44.25 lakhs, 36.93 lakhs in affiliated colleges and 7.32 lakhs in university departments. Women students were 14.37 lakhs (34.2 per cent) and the enrolment of SCs/STs was about 10 per cent. The growth of student enrolment which was 5 per cent per annum up to 1985-86, declined from 1986-87 onwards to around 4.1 per cent. The enrolment in the Correspondence Courses and Open Universities at the end of the Seventh Plan was approximately 5 lakh students, out of which the Indira Gandhi National Open University alone accounted for more than one lakh students. The number of universities rose to 177, including 29 "deemed" universities (Annexure 1.1)

The NPE had suggested: (1) creation of autonomous university departments and colleges; (2) State Councils of Higher Education (SCHE); (3) enhanced support to research; (4) strengthening of Open

Universities (OUs) and Distance Education (DE); (5) consolidation of existing institutions and improvement of quality of teachers and teaching; (6) mechanism for delinking degrees from jobs; (7) establishment of a new pattern of Rural Universities; and (8) establishment of an apex body covering higher education in all areas.

Eleven more colleges were granted autonomous status, thus bringing the total number of such colleges to 106 till December 1991. Under the Academic Staff College Scheme for orientation of newly recruited and in-service college/university teachers, 48 academic staff colleges have been established, which organised 464 Orientation and Refresher Courses covering 12,970 teachers upto December 1991. An SCHE was established in Andhra Pradesh. The University Grants Commission (UGC) provided development grants to Central Universities and 95 State Universities, besides assisting more than 3000 colleges for general development programmes and for implementation of special programmes. About 295 departments received special assistance under different programmes such as Centres of Advanced Study (CAS), Departments of Special Assistance (DSAs) and Departmental Research Support. Under the Programme of Coordinated Strengthening of Infrastructure in Science and Technology (COSIST), 112 departments were assisted. To support educational broadcasts, the UGC has set up 7 audio-visual research centres and 7 education media research centres for production of softwares. As many as 2,323 programmes, popularly known as country-wide classroom programmes, have already been produced. A new organisation called Inter-University Consortium of Educational Communication (IUCEC) is being set up. Programmes like Teacher Fellowships and Research Fellowships for SC/ST candidates and remedial teaching for weaker sections including minorities were continued. The UGC provided assistance for installation of mini/macro-computer systems to 110 universities and 1216 colleges. In collabroation with the Department of Electronics (DoE), several courses in Computer Science were run. An information and library network called "INFLIBNET" has also been proposed. With a view to providing common research facilities and services of the highest quality, inter-university centres in Nuclear Science, Astronomy and Astrophysics and Atomic Energy were established. The IGNOU widened the access to higher education by providing opportunities to learners from disadvantaged groups like women, people living in backward regions and hilly areas with an enrolment of 1.64 lakh by March, 1992. The Research Councils – Indian Council of Social Science

Research (ICSSR), Indian Council of Historical Research (ICHR) and Indian Council of Philosophical Research (ICPR) – continued their activities relating to support of research in respective areas.

Thrust Areas during the Eighth Plan

The higher education system at present suffers from several weaknesses, such as proliferation of substandard institutions, failure to maintain academic calendar, outdated curriculum, disparities in the quality of education and lack of adequate support for research. Recent consultations including the "Brain-Storming" session organised by the Planning Commission to consider future directions have underlined the following thrust areas :

(1) Integrated approach to higher education;
(2) Excellence in higher education;
(3) Expansion of education in an equitable and cost-effective manner, in the process making the higher education system financially self-supporting;
(4) Making higher education relevant in the context of changing socio-economic scenario;
(5) Promotion of value education; and
(6) Strengthening of management system in the universities.

The strategy for achieving the goals in these thrust areas would be as follows :

1. At present the higher education system comprising general, technical, medical and agricultural streams, is fragmented in terms of structures and policies. Greater cooperation among the streams should be encouraged by promoting networking, sharing of facilities and development of manpower including teachers' training/orientation facilities. There should be greater coherence in policy and planning. To adequately meet these requirements, the NPE had envisaged the establishment of a National Council of Higher Education (NCHE). This has however, not made progress so far and a coordination mechanism should be constituted during the Plan period.
2. Several measures will be taken to promote excellence. The

NPE/POA proposal for establishment of a National Accreditation Council (NAC) would be followed up. Apart from continuting the existing programmes of CAS/DAS, COSIST and the inter-university centres, IUCEC and the proposed INFLIBNET, new inter-university centres would be established to provide facilities in the emerging areas like Biotechnology, Atmospheric Science, Oceanography, Electronics and Computer Sciences. Facilities for computer education would be further strengthened in collaboration with the Department of Electronics. Model curricula for all disciplines have already been prepared but their implementation needs to be monitored. The suggestions of the Working Group constituted by the Planning Commission to improve undergraduate courses in science and the teaching of mathematics at Indian universities/colleges would be implemented in a phased manner.

3. The additional enrolment in higher education during the Eighth Plan is estimated to be around 10 lakhs of which 9 lakhs will be at the undergraduate level. This expansion in higher education, keeping in view the present resource crunch has to be accommodated in an equitable and cost-effective manner mainly by large scale expansion of Distance Education system and providing opportunities to larger segments of population, particularly the disadvantaged groups like women and people living in backward and hilly areas and by measures for resource generation. The programmes of Distance Education should absorb at least 50 per cent of the additional enrolment during the Eighth Plan and their cumulative enrolment should reach 15 lakhs, including 5 lakhs adult learners beyond the normal age-group 17-23 who have left school long back. Open Universities should also start innovative programmes of a vocational nature for meeting the learning needs of rural areas. Opening of new conventional universities and colleges should not be encouraged. Simultaneously, involvement of voluntary agencies and private sector participation in the opening and conduct of higher education institutions would be encouraged with proper checks to ensure maintenance of standards and facilities to make higher education as far as possible self-financing. However, the quality of education is not to be compromised at any cost. Upward revision of fee structure has to be considered but at the same time, the fees charged should not be exhorbitant and should be

supplemented by the provision of scholarships and other financial assistance to SCs/STs and students below the poverty line and loans to other students.

4. The tremendous potential of 44.25 lakhs students enrolled in higher education has to be utilised by actively involving them in the programmes of adult literacy, continuing education, population education and other constructive activities. Such extension activities of the universities and colleges would be expanded to cover 95 universities and 2500 colleges during the Eighth Plan.
5. The significance of Value Education has been highlighted by several committees and commissions on education. The Planning Commission has recently constituted a Core Group on value orientation in education. The recommendations of the Group will be considered for implementation in consultation with the Ministry of Human Resource Development, UGC, Association of Indian Universities (AIU) and NCERT.
6. Stress would also be laid on modernisation and restructuring of the management of university system which entails vigorous pursuit of the programmes of autonomous colleges and autonomous university departments. Facilities in universities and colleges, including research facilities, would be consolidated and strengthened. The schemes of redesigning and restructuring of courses to meet the development needs of the country, examination reforms and teachers' training would be expanded.

Other Programmes

The research activities of ICSSR, ICHR, ICPR and Indian Institute of Advanced Study (IIAS), Shimla will receive specific attention for promotion of inter-disciplinary research. Action to support research in humanities which at present is neglected, would be taken up.

With a view to delinking degrees as a requirement for recruitment to services, the NPE visualised establishing a National Testing Service (NTS) to conduct tests on a voluntary basis and evolving norms of comparable competence across the nation to determine the suitability of candidates for specified jobs. Towards this end, the idea of setting up of an appropriate national organisation will be pursued.

A strong need has also been felt for providing training to personnel dealing with university administration, for which the existing infrastructure will be further strengthened rather than creating a separate organisation.

Financial Allocations

The Seventh Plan's actual expenditure on higher education was Rs. 1201.13 crores of which Rs. 659.96 crores was in Central Sector and Rs. 541.17 crores in State Sector. The Eighth Plan outlays are shown in Annexure 1.7.

Conclusion

Strategies, thrust areas and programmes as highlighted above, represent the priorities for implementation during the Eighth Plan. They are by no means exhaustive. Higher education is a vast sector and its significance as a source of new knowledge, research and manpower for preceding stages of education namely, elementary and secondary, should not be minimised. Adequate resources should be mobilised and provided to support the higher education sector so that the nation is fully equipped to face the challenge of the future, which is incrasingly becoming information and knowledge intensive.

TECHNICAL EDUCATION

Introduction

Technical education including Management education is one of the most potent means for creating skilled manpower required for developmental tasks of various sectors of the economy. Technical education incorporates the technological dimension which is a vehicle for development. While this implies high costs of construction, laboratory equipment, library books and journals and high rate of obsolescence, such high cost, being directly related to development, should be viewed as an essential productive investment yielding valuable returns to the society and contributing to socio-economic development.

Plan Performance Review (1985-92)

The Seventh Plan emphasised consolidation and optimum utilisation of existing infrastructural facilities, their upgradation and modernisation identification of critical areas and creation of infrastructure in new areas of emerging technology, effective management of the overall system and institutional linkages between technical education and other development sectors.

Under the thrust areas programme of technical education 510 projects with a grant of Rs. 53.43 crores were supported for strengthening of facilities in the crucial areas of technology where weaknesses exist, 685 projects involving a grant of Rs. 76.84 crores were supported for creation of infrastructure in areas of emerging technologies and 202 projects involving of Rs. 27.1 crores were supported for programme of new technologies. A comprehensive report of requirement of instrumentation engineers at national level for the period 1990-2000 has been prepared by the National Technical Manpower Information System (NTMIS). The number of Community Polytechnics (CPs) inreased to 159 with an annual training coverage of 20,000 rural youth and women.

The following new schemes were started as part of the implementation of NPE :

(i) *Continuing Education*: The scheme envisaged preparation and dissemination of course material packages suited to the needs of industry. Under the scheme implemented by 5 Indian Institutes of Technology (IITs), 4 Technical Training Teachers' Institutes (TTTIs), one Indian Society of Technical Education (ISTE), 4 engineering colleges/university departments and 4 polytechnics, more than 30,000 working professionals have undergone training;

(ii) *Institution-Industry Interaction*: Under the scheme, proposals of 21 engineering colleges and 11 polytechnics have been approved for interaction with the industry; and

(iii) *Research and Development in Technical Education*: One hundred and twenty six R&D Projects were supported.

Eighth Plan Perspective

The perspective of development of technical education for the Eighth Plan would have to take into account the following imbalances and distortions :

(i) During the past four decades, there has been a phenomenal expansion of technical education in the country. Today, we have over 200 recognised technical education institutions (TEIs) at the first degree level and more than 560 polytechnics at the diploma level with annual admission capacities of 40,000 and 80,000 students, respectively. About 140 institutions offer facilities for postgraduate studies and research in several specialised areas with an annual capacity of 9,400 students;

(ii) The quantitative expansion has resulted in the lowering of the standards and there exists a structural imbalance of skill requirement of the business sector and the traditional curriculum followed by the educational institutes. These factors give rise to problems of unemployment and under-employment. The wastage in the system is enormous, being 30 per cent at degree level, 35 per cent at diploma level and 45 per cent at post-graduate level. The situation in unrecognised institutions is still worse. A related phenomenon is that of brain-drain involving migration abroad of those trained in emerging areas in excellent institutes;

(iii) The infrastructural facilities available in the vast majority of TEIs are extremely inadequate. There is an acute shortage of faculty with about 25 to 40 per cent of faculty positions remaining unfilled. In most of the institutions, there is hardly any R&D activity;

(iv) The TEIs are functioning in isolation. Linkage and interaction between TEIs and user-agencies, such as industries, R&D and design organisations and development sectors are not sufficiently strong. Neither is there a strong interaction among institutions by way of sharing of facilities like equipments, libraries, teaching faculty and other resources; and

(v) There has been an enormous increase in public expenditure on education but little attention has been paid to the strategies for raising non-budgetary resources and maximising people's participation.

Eighth Plan Strategy and Thrust

The thrust areas for the Eighth Plan have therefore, been identified as follows :

(1) Modernisation and upgradation of infrastructural facilities;

(2) Quality improvement in technical and management education;
(3) Responding to new industrial policy and industry institution R&D labs interaction;
(4) Resource mobilisation; and
(5) Institutional thrusts.

The strategy to be adopted to achieve these objectives would be on the following lines :

Modernisation and Upgradation of Infrastructural Facilities

Modernisation relates both to technical equipments and teaching methods. Technology development is a capital-intensive process. The country cannot afford to go on changing the technology every year. It is, therefore, imperative to adopt futuristic approaches for achieving modernisation and self-reliance in a sustained manner. Coordinated and concerted efforts would have to be made to upgrade and consolidate the infrastructural facilities in the existing institutions. The process of removal of obsolescence would include enhancement of computer facilities and establishment and interlinking of large computer systems with educational and research institutions through appropriate telecommunication facilities. Steps would be taken to strengthen and create the facilities in crucial areas of technology where weaknesses exist, in areas of emerging technologies and in new specialised fields. Upgradation of insfrastructure would also include a crash programme for recruitment of about 10,000 teachers in polytechnics and colleges and strengthening of arrangement for teacher training.

Upgradation of Polytechnics

Central Government has launched a massive project with the assistance of the World Bank to enable the State Governments upgrade their polytechnics in capacity, quality and efficiency for the period 1990 to 1999. The project is being taken up in two phases with a total outlay of Rs. 1,892 crores. The first phase would cover 296 polytechnics recognised by the AICTE in eight States – Bihar, Gujarat, Karnataka, Kerala, Madhya Pradesh, Orissa, Rajasthan and Uttar Pradesh. The second phase would cover 262 polytechnics in Andhra Pradesh, Assam, Haryana, Himachal Pradesh, Maharashtra, Punjab, Tamil Nadu,

West Bengal and Delhi. The project has also a Central Sector component for establishment of a national project implementation unit. Corresponding outlay is being provided vide Annexure 1.8

Quality Improvement in Technical and Management Education

A holistic and need-based approach would be adopted to reorient the Technical and Management Education (TME). A more broad-based flexible system with provision for multi-point entry is required to enable a better response to the unspecified demands of the future. At the micro-level, the curriculum would be developed to encourage creativity and innovation in experimental work by introducing problem/process-oriented laboratory exercises. New technology-oriented entrepreneurship and management courses would be introduced in selected institutions having adequate infrastructural facilities. There would be greater emphasis on production engineering towards design and product development.

Technology Watch

The Government has recently established a Technology Information Forecasting and Assessment Council (TIFAC). Its objectives include : Evaluation of existing technologies, preparation of technology forecast reports and estimates of the nature and quantum of likely demands for goods and services in future. It would be desirable to couple the tehnology forecasting system with the system of manpower forecasting and planning. Universities and IITs are familiar with the frontiers of knowledge and hence should play an important role in technical forecast and technological assessment with the fruitful involvement of TIFAC, Institute of Applied Manpower Research (IAMR) and the Indian trade and industries associations. It should be possible to develop the right type of indigenous technologies to assess the related manpower requirements and to produce such trained manpower.

The existing facilities for continuing education and retraining are inadequate. There is a need to formalise the retraining programme for engineering and technology pesonnel engaged in all sectors and to make them mandatory. Increasing use of modern communication devices should be made. Programme learning packages need to be created and distance learning methodologies employed to enable self-development and training of all scientific and technical personnel.

Responding to New Industrial Policy

There is a need to establish linkage between industry, national laboratories, developmental sectors, professional bodies, technical education, vocational education and craftsmen training and to bring about metworking among institutions. In the context of the new industrial policy, the priority may be assigned to interaction with industry as it holds the key to industrial competitiveness in a global market. A strategy may be evolved for effective interaction between industry and institutions and for promotion of interaction through apprenticeship opportunities, consultancy and sponsored research, continuing education programmes for industry personnel adjunct professorships in institutions for willing and capable personnel, from industry, seconding of institutional faculty to industry, involvement of industry in the development of curricula and courses etc. For this purpose, organisational mechanisms such as Industrial Liaison Board, Industry-Institution Cells, Industrial Foundation etc., will have to be set up. The R&D activities may be taken up through the support of industry.

In this context, a reference may be made to a model for university-industry symbiosis conceived and implemented at Jawaharlal Nehru Technological University, Hyderabad for bringing about a greater and more effective interaction between technological university and industry. The model envisaged the setting up of a Bureau for Industrial Consultancy and Research and Development (BICARD) in universities/technological institutes of higher education, preparation of a comprehensive directory of technology experts to operationalise various aspects of interaction like orientation of university curriculum, exchange of experts between teaching institutions and industries, inolvement of teaching staff in industry, technological database and self-reliance of institutions etc. This model was recently revised by its author to include the loop of R&D organisations. A national cell to promote and coordinate the linkages between the promotional agencies, university industry and R&D organisations has also been suggested. The revised model could be adopted/adapted with benefit by other TEIs.

Resource Mobilisation

Since technical education is inherently expensive, concrete steps to ensure cost-effectiveness as an aspect of resource mobilisation are of vital importance. These include :

(i) Avoidance of duplication of investment in TEIs located close to each other and proper maintenance of available facilities and instruments;

(ii) Developing institution-wise specialisation in respect of courses and technical manpower so that the institutions can have the most sophisticated and modern library and laboratory facilities in their chosen fields;

(iii) Weeding out of outdated and stereotyped courses and introduction of relevant courses in emerging areas;

(iv) Multiple use of infrastructural facilities through part-time courses, continuing education programmes and consultancy and testing services;

(v) Marginal increase in intake capacities in areas of scarce manpower and decrease in intake of low demand areas. In this connection, an increase in the intake in better institutions by 10 per cent should receive urgent attention;

(vi) Introduction of multiple or at least double shifts in TEIs;

(vii) Maximum use of non-monetary inputs, like better planning, advanced technologies and practices, better system of supervision and administration, monitoring and review etc; and

(viii) Commercialisation of research work of the institutions.

The Task Force appointed by AICTE to go into the question of laying down tuition and other fees and to suggest other sources of mobilisation of resources for technical education has suggested raising of fees in relation to Government, Government aided and unaided institutions on a graduated scale. A beginning has been made by raising fees in the IIMs. The IITs and other TEIs are also required to raise the fees. The measure of raising fees, however, should be coupled with scholarships for SCs/STs and for students below poverty line and a loan scheme for other students.

Creation of a corpus fund can be another way of mobilising resources for an institution, especially in the case of IITs. Contributions to the corpus fund will have to come from various sources viz. industry, alumni, charitable trusts etc. as well as Government.

Another way of enhancing investment is to implement NPE/POA idea of requiring development departments to allocate a fixed percentage of their annual budgets for development of TEIs. The question of collection of education cess from industry, which can thus share the cost of educating technical manpower and of giving tax exempton to industry for contributions made by it to development of technical education should also receive serious consideration.

INSTITUTIONAL THRUSTS

All-India Council of Technical Education (AICTE)

The AICTE was given statutory status in 1988 in view of the need for maintaining and developing standards. It would be further stengthened to ensure coordinated development with its four regional committees located at Kanpur, Madras, Bombay and Calcutta. A Board of Accreditation is expected to be set up shortly and most of the schemes implemented by the Technical Education Bureau of the Department of Education are expected to be taken over by AICTE.

Technical Institutions in the University Sector

The UGC provides financial assistance to 32 institutions in engineering and technology for their overall development. Although some of the institutions in this sector like Indian Institute of Science, Bangalore, are centres of excellence and this sector as a whole accounts for 1,600 M.E./M. Tech students, the financial allocations tend to be limited, as they are part of the overall UGC allocations. A separate mechanism may be set up which would advise UGC regarding the financial needs and priorities of these institutions and the Planning Commission should allocate appropriate earmarked outlays for this sector covering not only post-graduate education as in the past but also under graduate education on a selective basis.

Other Post-graduate Institutes

Sixteen State Governments and 24 non-Government post-graduate institutions are being assisted by the Central Government with a view to developing specialised fields of engineering/technology having national relevance. The intake for post-graduate courses per year in engineering and technology is proposed to be increased from 10,000 to 11,000 by the end of Eighth Plan.

Indian Institutes of Technology (IITs)

The new Industrial Policy has created an environment which requires IITs to adopt a new role as leaders in current and futuristic technology development. The following four areas for futher action have been identified in the light of consultations held by Planning Commission:

(1) Thrust areas of technology development,
(2) International consultancy,
(3) Resource mobilisation and setting up of Corpus Fund, and
(4) Industrial Foundation.

Technology Development

The technology development through innovation and its subsequent transfer to industry by five IITs would be the first step towards the identification of project mission and creation of appropriate environment. These project missions are conceived in three groups:

(i) Areas where gains are likely to be visible in the long-term, such as biotechnology, fuel efficient engines, microelectronics, photonics;
(ii) Areas where short-term gains can be planned, such as communication and software technology, food processing instrumentation and central integrated production engineering and design, non-conventional energy, remote sensing and transportation; and
(iii) Areas where results in the intermediate-term are possible like coal, computer, integrated manufacturing, natural hazard mitigation and new materials technology. It is expected that each of the IITs would select a few areas from among those to work on during the Eighth Plan.

International Consultancy

The IITs have a potential to offer educational and industrial consultancy services at international level. The consultancy would cover : institution building, establishment of specialised laboratory facilities, development of curricula, organising continuing education/joint research projects and faculty development etc. There is a good scope for international consultancy assignments for IITs in South East Asian and other countries. This can be a source of additional resource mobilisation.

Resource Mobilisation and Corpus Fund

Resource mobilisation measures would be taken up on the lines mentioned earlier, including corpus fund to which Government could contribute a block grant annually over a period of years subject to contributions from other sources. Two ideas specific to IITs are: permitting them to charge from foreign students a full cost tuition fee in foreign exchange and obtaining an endowment grant from countries with an explicit commitment to training specified manpower for that country.

Industrial Foundation

In order to facilitate interaction and collaboration with industry and other user organisations in programmes of mutual interest an industrial foundation needs to be set up in each IIT. The foundation would function as a registered society/corporate body linked to the parent-IIT, with financial and administrative automony and adopt industrial culture and methods. Resource generation of these foundations would be through Government grants/corporate membership fees/overheads on projects and services/donation and gifts etc. These foundations would render technical support to small-scale industry and engineering entrepreneurs and develop products and processes at the request of industry. There would also be manpower exchange between IITs and industry.

Regional Engineering Colleges (RECs)

There are 17 regional engineering colleges in the country which are joint ventures between Government of India and State Governments. They are expected to be pace-setting institutions in their regions. They need acadamic autonomy and their funding should be from one source, preferably Central Government. The ultimate aim should be to make them deemed universities. A proposal involving assistance of 6 million pound sterling to develop collaboration between RECs and some British Universities in the emerging areas such as design, materials, energy, informatics etc. is being worked out.

Indian Institutes of Management (IIMs)

The four Indian Institutes of Management set up as pace-setting and premier centres of excellence in management education and research have been instrumental in producing highly qualified managerial manpower. Their activities need to be revamped, particularly keeping in view the changing scenario both at the national and international level. A consultation held by Planning Commission led to the suggestion that there should be links between management institutes and training institutes in specific sectors like health, rural development, agricultural extension etc. It was also suggested that there should be an integrated view of management education and there should be resource mobilisation, corpus fund, mutual sharing of facilities and division of labour in the matter of thrust areas etc. A plan of action is being prepared in this regard.

Community Polytechnics (CPs)

It is proposed to cover all the remaining polytechnics under the scheme of CPs by suitably reorganising and strengthening them in the light of the recommendations of the National Expert Committee set up to appraise them. The Community Polytechnics are expected to play a major role in rural manpower development and their outreach should be expanded by resorting to distance education methods.

Financial Allocations

The actual expenditure on technical education in the Seventh Plan was Rs. 1083.34 crores of which Rs. 610.96 crores was in the Central Sector and Rs. 472.38 crores in the State Sector. The outlays and expenditure for the Seventh Plan and approved outlays for the Eighth Plan are shown in Annexures 1.3 and 1.7. The Eighth Plan outlays in the State Sector are required to be higher to reflect the implementation of the World Bank assisted Technician Education Project.

ANNEXURE 1.1

Progress of General Education During 7th Plan (1985-90)

Institutions = Numbers
Enrolment = Thousands

Sl. No.		1984-85 (6th Plan ending)		1989-90 (7th Plan ending)	
		Institutions	Enrolment	Institutions	Enrolment
1	2	3	4	5	6
1.	Primary Edn. (Class-I V, age 6-10)	519701	83933	550700	97318
2.	Middle (Classes VI-VII age 11-14)	129879	26153	143747	32188
3.	Elementary Edn. (Classes I-VIII age 6-14)	649580	110086	694447	129506
4.	Non-Formal Edn. (Classes I-VIII age 6-14)	Nil	Nil	27087 (Centres)	6400
5.	Total Elementary items (3+4)	649580	110086	694447 +27087	135906
6.	High/Hr. Secondary Edn. (Classes IX-XII)	58834	13828	76119	19970
7.	Colleges (Art, Science, Commerce)	4005	2577	4755	3814
8.	Universities (Including deemed universities)	135	347	174	388
9.	Engineering colleges	198	145	278	733
10.	Polytechnics	389	148	840	284

Source: *Selected Educational Statistics*, 1984-85 and 1989-90, Department of Education, Ministry of Human Resource Development, Government of India.

ANNEXURE 1.2

Achievement of Additional Enrolment at Elementary Stage (classes I-VIII) and Adult Education in the Seventh Plan

(Fig. in Lakhs)

Sl. No.	States/UT's	Primary Classes I-V		Upper Primary Classes I-VIII		Elementary Classes I-VIII		Adult Education
		Girls	Total	Girls	Total	Girls	Total	
1.	Andhra Pradesh	4.12	9.09	1.47	3.78	5.59	12.87	11.12
2.	Arunachal Pradesh	0.15	0.29	0.05	0.09	0.20	0.38	0.92
3.	Assam	1.80	11.42	0.96	3.74	2.76	15.16	5.99
4.	Bihar	2.40	5.66	0.72	1.52	3.12	7.18	39.99
5.	Goa	0.04*	0.06*	-0.01	-0.04	0.03	0.02	0.017
6.	Gujarat	3.71	6.60	1.69	3.90	5.40	10.50	19.32
7.	Haryana	1.43	1.63	0.89	1.28	2.32	2.91	5.21
8.	Himachal Pradesh	0.40	0.70	0.47	0.71	0.87	1.41	1.43
9.	Jammu and Kashmir	0.48	0.99	0.31	0.72	0.79	1.71	2.88
10.	Karnataka	6.72	13.69	1.19	2.79	7.91	16.48	11.88
11.	Kerala	0.27	0.53	0.50	0.95	0.77	1.48	5.08
12.	Madhya Pradesh	7.39	16.35	3.26	8.65	10.65	25.00	26.02
13.	Maharashtra	5.07	7.66	4.30	8.70	9.37	16.36	20.90
14.	Manipur	0.15	0.23	0.04	0.04	0.19	0.27	1.17
15.	Meghalaya	0.20	0.39	0.06	0.10	0.26	0.49	0.89
16.	Mizoram	0.12	0.27	0.04	0.35	0.16	0.62	0.21
17.	Nagaland	0.07	0.13	-0.08	-0.18	-0.01	-0.05	0.65
18.	Orissa	2.55	5.83	2.03	2.87	4.58	8.70	8.22
19.	Punjab	0.64	1.07	0.58	1.05	1.22	2.12	4.86
20.	Rajasthan	3.19	7.20	0.83	3.34	4.02	10.54	14.46
21.	Sikkim	0.07	0.10	0.02	0.02	0.09	0.12	0.41
22.	Tamil Nadu	3.05	6.34	3.52	7.14	6.57	13.48	26.76
23.	Tripura	0.19	0.38	0.14	0.32	0.33	0.70	0.63
24.	Uttar Pradesh	10.32	17.89	2.25	4.26	12.57	22.15	39.72
25.	West Bengal	8.44	17.24	1.59	3.10	10.03	20.34	12.42
	Total (States)	**62.97**	**131.74**	**26.82**	**59.20**	**89.79**	**190.94**	**261.157**
26.	A and N Islands	0.02	0.05	0.03	0.05	0.05	0.10	0.13
27.	Chandigarh	0.07	0.15	0.04	0.07	0.11	0.22	0.17
28.	D and N Haveli	0.02	0.02	0.01	0.01	0.03	0.03	0.11
29.	Daman and Diu	0.05	0.10	0.04	0.08	0.09	0.18	0.001
30.	Delhi	0.72	1.63	0.56	1.16	1.28	2.79	3.60
31.	Lakshadweep	0.00	0.00	0.00	0.00	0.00	0.00	0.011
32.	Pondicherry	0.08	0.15	0.06	0.10	0.14	0.25	0.45
	Total (UTs)	**0.96**	**2.10**	**0.74**	**1.47**	**1.70**	**3.57**	**4.472**
	Total (States & UTs)	**63.93**	**133.84**	**27.56**	**60.67**	**91.49**	**194.51**	**265.629**

* Including Daman and Diu

Source: 1. *Elementary Education: Selected Educational Statistics of 1984-85 and 1989-90*, Department of Education, Ministry of Human Resource Development, Government of India.

2. Adult Education Directorate of Adult Education.

ANNEXURE 1.3

Outlay and Expenditure on Education – Seventh Plan and Annual Plans: 1990-91 and 1991-92 Central and State Sector

(Rs. in Crores)

Sl. No.	Sub-head	7th Plan 1985-90 Approved Outlay	7th Plan 1985-90 Actual Expdr.	Annual Plan 1990-91 Actual Expdr.	Annual Plan 1991-92 Antic. Expdr.
1	2	3	4	5	6
1.	Elementary Education	1963.70	2854.69	805.77	937.50
2.	Adult Education	360.00	469.57	173.84	195.08
3.	General Education	4775.30	6549.51	1797.82	2120.21
4.	Technical Education	681.79	1083.34	314.63	537.45
5.	Art and Culture	482.13	450.89	103.90	132.41
6.	Sports and Youth Affairs	443.43	484.51	113.01	170.78
	(Total Col. 3 to 6)	6382.65	8568.31	2329.36	2960.85

ANNEXURE 1.4

Outlay and Expenditure on Education – Seventh Plan and Annual Plans: 1990-91 and 1991-92 – Central Sector

(Rs. in Crores)

Sl. No.	Sub-head	7th Plan 1985-90 Approved Outlay	7th Plan 1985-90 Actual Expdr.	Annual Plan 1990-91 Actual Expdr.	Annual Plan 1991-92 Antic. Expdr.
1	2	3	4	5	6
1.	Elementary Education	233.25	658.49	218.75	283.50
2.	Adult Education	130.00	313.04	131.15	129.19
3.	Secondary Education	667.75	596.01	195.21	209.90
4.	University and Hr. Education	420.00	659.96	131.55	171.592
5.	Language Development	38.64	43.58	10.78	14.00
6.	Planning and Admn.	29.00	23.49	3.46	6.78
7.	*Other Educational Programmes*				
8.	Total General Education	1518.64	2294.57	690.90	814.96
9.	Technical Education	220.00	610.96	157.60	188.25
10.	Art and Culture	350.00	268.73	60.41	74.20
11.	Sports and Youth Affairs	300.00	248.67	47.56	76.16
	Total Education (Col. 8 to 11)	2388.64	3422.93	956.47	1153.57

ANNEXURE 1.5

Outlay and Expenditure on Education – Seventh Plan and Annual Plans: 1990-91 and 1991-92 – State Sector

(Rs. in Crores)

Sl. No.	Sub-head	7th Plan 1985-90		Annual Plan 1990-91	Annual Plan 1991-92
		Approved Outlay	Actual Expdr.	Actual Expdr.	Antic. Expdr.
1	2	3	4	5	6
1.	Elementary Education	1730.45	2190.92	588.41	644.12
2.	Adult Education	230.00	156.53	43.52	71.44
3.	Secondary Education	N.A.	1235.50	326.16	315.99
4.	University and Higher Education	N.A.	541.17	159.37	154.93
5.	Language Development	N.A.	13.48	6.71	10.10
6.	Planning and Admn.	N.A.	10.05	7.15	9.72
7.	Other Educational programmes	N.A.	107.35	26.89	29.88
8.	Total General Education	3256.66	4255.00	1158.21	1296.18
9.	Technical Education	461.79	472.38	157.03	349.20
10.	Art and Culture	132.13	182.16	43.49	58.21
11.	Sports and Youth Affairs	143.43	235.84	65.45	94.62
	Total Education (Col. 8 to 11)	3994.01	5154.38	1424.18	1798.21

ANNEXURE 1.6

Eighth Plan (1992-97) Targets – Additional Enrolment – Elementary and Adult Education

(Figures in 000's)

Sl. No.	States/UTs	Primary (I-V Classes)		Upper Primary (VI-VIII Classes)		Elementary (I-VIII Classes)		Adult Education age 15-35 year
		Girls	Total	Girls	Total	Girls	Total	
1.	Andhra Pradesh	1475	2588	840	1400	2315	3988	7778
2.	Arunachal Pradesh	12	27	14	36	26	63	175
3.	Assam	244	500	384	800	628	1300	4500
4.	Bihar	4032	8400	1008	2100	5040	10500	9400
5.	Goa	3	6	5	9	8	15	100
6.	Gujarat	72	108	475	1100	547	1208	4300
7.	Haryana	173	275	180	300	353	575	5711
8.	Himachal Pradesh	58	125	29	66	87	191	800
9.	Jammu and Kashmir	62	150	85	227	147	377	600
10.	Karnataka	215	434	98	197	313	631	6000
11.	Kerala	129	252	42	80	171	332	980
12.	Madhya Pradesh	2310	3460	1796	2396	4106	5856	5500
13.	Maharashtra	600	1400	300	750	900	2150	9200
14.	Manipur	12	29	36.70	68.20	48.70	97.20	23
15.	Meghalaya	15	30	22	51	37	81	262
16.	Mizoram	12	25	12	29	24	54	32
17.	Nagaland	16	32	17.50	34	33.50	66	23
18.	Orissa	247	600	142	416	389	1016	130
19.	Punjab	80	190	54	127	134	317	5000
20.	Rajasthan	2180	2647	621	1565	2729	4212	11000
21.	Sikkim	5	11	7	16	12	27	4
22.	Tamil Nadu	215	425	491	1142	706	1567	7800
23.	Tripura	13	25	36	89	49	114	400
24.	Uttar Pradesh	866	2480	530	1930	1396	4410	16700
25.	West Bengal	801	1638	1359	2788	2160	4426	8559
	Total (States)	**13775**	**25857**	**8584.20**	**17716.20**	**22359.20**	**43573.20**	**104977**
26.	A and N Island	4.00	9.00	2.00	6.00	6.00	15.00	10
27.	Chandigarh	4.80	10.10	3.80	8.10	8.60	18.20	26
28.	D and N Haveli	0.05	0.11	0.03	0.13	0.08	0.24	15
29.	Daman and Diu	0.50	1.00	0.50	1.00	1.00	2.00	20
30.	Delhi	38.00	96.00	24.00	85.00	62.00	181.00	750
31.	Lakshadweep	0.05	0.20	0.05	0.10	0.10	0.30	12
32.	Pondicherry	3.00	6.00	1.80	4.00	4.80	10.00	30
	Total (UTs)	**50.40**	**122.41**	**32.18**	**104.33**	**82.58**	**226.74**	**863**
	Total (States & UTs)	**13825.40**	**25979.41**	**8616.38**	**17820.53**	**22441.78**	**43799.94**	**105840**

Source : Plan documents of States/UTs and summary records of Working Groups on Education.

ANNEXURE 1.7

Eighth Plan Outlay for Major Heads of Education

(Rs. in Crores)

Sl. No.	Major Head	Centre	States	UTs	Total
1.	General Education	6619.00	9607.19	587.16	161813.35
2.	Technical Education	824.00	1804.66	157.72	2786.38
3.	(Total 1 and 2)	**7443.00**	**11411.85**	**744.88**	**19599.73**
4.	Art and Culture	385.00	324.76	17.92	727.68
5.	Youth Affairs and Sports	350.00	509.06	30.54	889.60
	Grand Total (3 to 5)	**8178.00**	**12245.67**	**793.34**	**21217.01**

ANNEXURE 1.8

State-wise Coverage of World Bank Assisted Projects for Technician Education (Polytechnics)

(Rs. in Crores

States	Project Base Cost*	No. of Schemes	Proposed No. of Institutions to be covered	Annual Plan 1990-91		Annual Plan 1991-92		8th Plan (1992-97) Recommend Outlay
				Budgeted Outlay	Actual Expdr.	Budgeted Outlay	Antici- Expdr.	
1	2	3	4	5	6	7	8	9
Phase I								
Bihar	88.08	21	26	11.97	1.07	20.16	20.54	79.05
Gujarat	65.08	21	32	9.76	0.52	16.27	16.27**	50.00
Karnataka	52.78	21	43	6.00	1.00	7.50	7.50**	42.50
Kerala	34.10	21	24	5.20	0.58	10.60	10.60	36.67
Madhya Pradesh	100.13	21	49	10.29	8.56	16.90	16.90	74.50
Orissa	56.79	21	13	8.15	8.14	7.00	7.00	43.93
Rajasthan	44.61	21	23	3.80	2.88	8.17	8.17	41.10
Uttar Pradesh	200.00	21	86	6.58	0.65	45.00	45.00	188.00
Sub Total	**641.57**	**168**	**296**	**61.75**	**23.4**	**131.60**	**131.98**	**555.75**

Contd.)

ANNEXURE 1.8 (*Contd.*)

1	2	3	4	5	6	7	8	9
Phase II								
Andhra Pradesh	79.55	21	59	-	-	9.70	5.90	74.04
Assam	30.00	21	9	-	-	2.86	1.00	29.00
Haryana	80.87	21	18	-	-	10.00	10.00	72.00
Himachal Pradesh	20.24	21	5	-	-	2.10	2.10	21.43
Maharashtra	122.68	21	54	-	-	30.00	0.30	120.00
Punjab	79.48	21	19	-	-	12.31	12.31**	75.81
Tamil Nadu	68.00	21	55	-	-	19.96	2.00	76.00
West Bengal	86.16	21	34	-	-	6.00	6.00**	80.00
UT of Delhi	23.60	21	9	-	-	3.20	3.20**	23.60
Sub Total	**590.58**	**189**	**262**	**0**	**0**	**96.13**	**42.81**	**571.88**
Total	**1232.15**	**357.00**	**558.00**	**61.75**	**23.40**	**227.73**	**174.79**	**1127.63**

Notes: 1. Does not include 10 new Women's Wings to be converted as Polytechnics in both phases.
2. Does not include the Central component of Rs. 40.00 Crores
3. Out of Rs. 1892 Crores (US $ 745 million) the World Bank Assistance would be Rs. 1318 Crores (US $ 18.88 million).
* The Base Cost excludes the price escalation due to inflation and increase due to physical contingencies.
** Represents budgeted outlay as anticipated expenditure not specified.

Source : Department of Education, Ministry of Human Resource Development, Government of India, and Plan Documents of States/UTs.

2

NPE 1986 REVIEW RAMAMURTI COMMITTEE (1990)

Introduction

National Front Government headed by Shri V.P. Singh, in pursuance of its election manifesto, appointed on 7th May, 1990, a Committee with Acharya Ramamurti as its Chairman, to review the National Policy on Education (NPE), 1986. The Committee submitted its report to the Minister of State in the Ministry of Human Resource Development on 26th December, 1990. The report was tabled in the Parliament on 9th January, 1991.

The report is entitled *Towards an Enlightened and Humane Society*.

Terms of Reference of the Committee for Review

(a) to review the National Policy on Education, 1986 and its implementation;
(b) to make recommendations regarding revision of the Policy; and
(c) to recommend action necessary for implementation of the revised policy within a time frame.

Text of Government of India Resolution No. F.-1-6/90 PN (D.I.) dated 7th May, 1990

Despite efforts at social and economic development since attainment of Independence, a majority of our people continue to remain deprived of education, which is one of the basic needs for human development. It is also a matter of grave concern that our people comprise 50 per cent of the world's illiterate and large sections of children have to go without acceptable level of primary education. Government accords the highest priority to education – both as a human right and as the means for bringing about a transformation towards a more humane and enlightened society. There is need to make education an effective instrument for securing a status of equality for women, and persons belonging to the backward classes and minorities. However, it is essential to give a work and employment orientation to education and to exclude from it the elitist aberrations which have become the glaring characteristic of the educational scene. Educational institutions are increasingly being influenced by casteism, communalism and obscurantism and it is necessary to lay special emphasis on struggle against this phenomenon and to move towards a genuinely egalitarian and secular social order. The National Policy on Education, 1986 (NPE), needs to be reviewed to evolve a framework which would enable the country to move towards this perspective of education.

Government have, therefore, decided to set up NPE Review Committee.

Members of the NPE Review Committee

Acharya Ramamurti, *Chairman*, NPE Review Committeee, P.O. Khadigram-811313, Dist. Munger, Bihar.

Members: Dr. C.N.R Rao, Director, Indian Institute of Science, Bangalore-560011; Dr. Sukhdev Singh, 5, Sector 11-A, Chandigarh-160001; Dr. M. Santappa, Scientific Adviser, Tamil Nadu Pollution Control Board, 25, Dr. Radhakrishnan Salai, Madras-600004; Dr. Obaid Siddiqi, Molecular, Biology Unit, Tata Institute of Fundamental Research, Homi Bhabha Road, Bombay-400005; Dr. Bhaskar Ray Chaudhuri, Vice-Chancellor, University of Calcutta, Calcutta-700001; Dr. M.G. Bhatawadekar, 41, Sangram Colony, Jaipur-302001; Prof. Usha Mehta, Mani Bhavan, Gandhi Museum, 19, Laburnum Road, Gamdevi, Bombay-400007; Prof. K. Satchidananda Murty, 'Aparajita; Sangam, Jagarlamudi-522213. Guntur District, Andhra Pradesh; Prof. Mrinal Miri, Deptt. of Philosophy, North-Easthern Hill University (NEHU), Shillong-793003 (Meghalaya); Shri Veda Vyasa, 64, Golf Links, New Delhi-110003; Dr. Vidya Niwas Misra, Vice-Chancellor, Sampurnanand Sanskrit University, Varanasi-221002; Dr. S.Z. Qasim, Vice-Chancellor, Jamia Millia Islamia, Jamia Nagar, New Delhi-110025; Father T.V. Kunnunkal, Chairman, National Open School, 39, Community Centre, Wazirpur Industrial Area, Ring Road, Ashok

Vihar Turn, Delhi-110052; Dr. Anil Sadgopal Kishore Bharati, P.O. Bankhedi, Distt. Hoshangabad-461990, Madhya Pradesh; Shri Manubhai Pancholi, Lok Bharati, Sanosara-364230, Distt. Bhavanagar, Gujarat.

Member Secretary: Shri S. Gopalan, Additional Secretary, Department of Education, Ministry of H.R.D., Shastri Bhawan, New Delhi.

Approach

2.1.1 The approach of the Committee in reviewing the National Policy on Education, 1986 and its implementation has been guided by the following principal concerns:

* Equity and social justice.
* Decentralisation of educational management at all levels.
* Establishment of participative educational order.
* Inculcation of values indispensable for creation of an enlightened and humane society.
* Empowerment for work.

2.1.2 The above concerns have been built into the recommendations of the Committee as underlying and all pervasive perceptions so as to realise the constitutional and cultural goals of education.

2.2.1 In order to achieve equity and social justice and thereby remove elitist aberrations, education has been viewed by the Committee in the overall context of social economic, regional and gender based disparities. For example, any effort at vocationalising education will carry no meaning unless, concurrently, the Government lays down an appropriate Income and Wages Policy. Likewise national policies concerning removal of economic disparities such as for land reforms, employment, health and nutrition etc. have to be concurrently established/reviewed. Of course, it is not for this Committee to give recommendations in regard to policies concerning other major sectors. However, mention is made of this only to bring home the point that an educational order based on considerations of equity and social justice cannot autonomously come about without interlinkages with these policies.

Note: Para numbers refer to para of the Report.

2.2.2 A very vital component of the overall strategy for securing equity and social justice in education is the development of the Common School System. The Committee is fully aware that this is no new innovation but has been with us for over quarter of a century since the report of the Education Commission, 1964-66 and the essential point is that this has just remained a concept and its non-implementation has only contributed to the accentuation of the existing educational disparities. Concerete steps for translating this concept into action have to be taken. In order to achieve this objective, the existing Government, Local Body and Government-aided schools have to be transformed through quality improvement into genuine neighbourhood schools. Private schools also should be similarly transformed in course of time by making them freely accessible.

2.2.3 It is particularly in the context of the need for establishing the Common School System that some of the members of the Committee have found it difficult to go along with the Navodaya Vidyalaya Scheme. It is, *inter alia* for this reason that the Committee as a whole has advocated against establishment of more Navodaya Vidyalayas, not to speak of the inequity in nurturing talent only in a few. It is on account of the unfairness in judging a scheme for the implementation of which adequate resources as originally envisaged were not provided, and of the need for a fair and total review of the scheme that the Committee has made alternative recommendations on its future. The Committee, of course, has also taken into account the practical difficulties in abrupty discontinuing a scheme which involves about 50,000 students and 3,000 teachers.

2.2.4 The rural areas in general, and the tribal areas in particular, have suffered in terms of resources, personnel and infrastructure facilities. This phenomenon of regional disparities in educational development has acquired a major political dimension in the current Indian scene. It is reflected in the regional and sub-regional movements. Therefore, the need of the hour is planning for and implementation of, educational development programmes in terms of disaggregated targets and area, community and gender specific activities. This would mean concrete programmes being established on ground for the disadvantaged groups – Scheduled Castes and Scheduled Tribes, women, the educationally backward minorities and the handicapped with appropriate budgeting for the same. No doubt, there have been special component plans for the SCs and sub-plans for the Tribes. But these plans have largely remained exercises on paper, not concretely provided for in the budget documents. The consequence has been that these plans have not had any impact on the educational standards of the SCs and STs in terms of enrolment, retention and reduction in drop out rates. Excepting for the implementation of a small scheme, "The Integrated Education for the Disabled", the handicapped do not significantly feature in the educational programmes of the Centre or the States. The programmes for the educationally backward minorities have not been significant, having been construed as the almost exclusive domain of the States.

2.2.5 In order to promote participation of the girls and women in education at al levels, there is need for an integrated approach in designing and implementing the Schemes that would address all the factors that inhibit their education. Mere implementation of disaggregated schemes such a Opening of Non-formal Education Centres for Girls, Adult Education Centres for Women etc. by themselves are not adequate. In this context special mention may be made of interaction of Early Childhood Care and Education (ECCE) with primary education. Education of women is not to be construed of a question of mere access but of empowering them through education of all on equality of sexes.

2.2.6 The modifications suggested in the case of vocationalisation of school education have been construed in the context of equity and social justice as well. The Scheme, as it is now implemented, though unintendedly, has come to be viewed by the students as well as the parents, as one meant for the less fortunate. It is also on account of this that a single stream of school education with vocational as well as non-vocational components of different mixes becomes relevant and important.

2.2.7 Examination reforms also have their justification from the point of view of equity and social justice. The examination system tilts heavily in favour of the privileged who have access to certain facilities such as special teaching learning material, special coaching etc. It is *inter alia*, to rectify this inequitable tilt that examination reforms have been suggested.

2.2.8 One of the factors seriously inhibiting access for the rural students to higher education is the continuing sway of English. Hence, equity demands that education in the media of regional languages is encouraged at all levels. This would call not merely for political and academic commitment for the switch over to the regional languages media but a package of other measures including conscious efforts at organising tests for recruitments in the public and private services in the regional languages, at least options, for taking university examinations in these languages and incentives for the same, apart from production of appropriate teaching learning materials, reference literature etc.

2.3.1 The fundamental justification for decentralised planning and management of education is the sheer size and diversity of the country. In the sphere of education, the size and diversity of the country get reflected in the magnitude of the population to be provided education, number of the educational institutions to be established from the primary to the university level, the number of languages in which delivery services have to be organised, the cultural and regional diversities which have to be linked to the content and process of education etc. Decentralisation is the only solution to these problems. There is need for decentralisation of educational planning and management all the way down at all levels, from the Centre to the States, from the States to the districts, from the districts to the blocks, from the blocks to the panchayats/villages and habitations. The Committee does realise that a further complexity is added to the dimensions of decentralisation by the uneven status of establishment of the Panchayat Raj system in the country. But this does not detract from the need for decentralisation.

2.3.2 Decentralisation in the university system would mean autonomy for the universities and colleges as well as for the respective faculties and individual teachers. Examination reforms including establishment of continuous, comprehensive internal evaluation cannot come about unless delegation of authority and decentralisation of functions becomes real down to the level of teachers. Educational complexes recommended by the Committee are construed as an instrument of bringing about decentralisation.

2.3.3 Side by side with emphasising decentralisation as the cornerstone of planning and implementation of educational programmes, the Committee would lay much store by convergence of services already available through the parallel infrastructure created in several departments vitally connected with the education. This would call for institutionalised coordination mechanisms to be evolved and to be set into operation as a rule of practice.

2.4.0 The Committee has envisaged the concept of participative educational order as being relevant to every stage of education as only involvement through participation can bring about the environment for genuine reform. Important modalities contemplated in this regard are involvement of the colleges and universities in issues of regional development and improvement of school education; creation of school complexes, bringing about mutual coordination between primary schools, middle schools, high schools, colleges and universities (the universities affiliating themselves, as it were, with these complexes so that management of education becomes a job of the professional); forging education-industry interactions for the purpose of bringing about cost effective and practice oriented vocationalisation of school education; involvement of the village communities in working for the goal of universal elementary education; non-formalising the formal school system so that the system itself reaches out to the door-steps of those who are out of school, apart from being attractive to and also be capable of retaining them; assignment of meaningful role to genuine voluntary agencies engaged in educational development programmes; and of course, the teachers being placed centre-stage in educational reform at all levels with careful attention devoted to their status, recruitment modalities, service conditions and training.

2.5.1 NPE, 1986 as a whole reflects that educational development was construed in the background of human resource development. In fact, the Policy called for new designs of human resource development for availing of the unprecedented opportunities that would be thrown up by the ensuing decades. In the view of the Committee, the human being is to be valued as more than a resource. Mere emphasis on the resource aspect has over-tones of utalitatrian connotations.

While utilitarian aspects are important, the human being has to be developed with accent on character building, dignity of labour and value to the society at the national and international levels.

2.5.2 In the view of the Committee value education is to be construed as a continuous process which is to be sustained throughout the process of growth of the individual from childhood to adolescence, then to adulthood and so on. Inculcation of values has to be seen as distinct from the output of individual schemes and programmes of school

* In order to de-emphasise the utilitarian over-tones of the expression Human Resource Development, the Committee is of the opinion that the nomenclature of the Ministry namely, Ministry of Human Resource Development should be changed into Ministry of Education. The term Education is broad enough to encompass the aspects of Culture and Arts, Youth Affairs and Sports and Women and Child Development.

regimen. The hidden curriculum, as distinct form the explicit ones obtaining in the class-room situation, is much more important for the development of balanced personality amongst the students. It is also the role of value education to bring about integration of the hand, head and heart to ensure that education does not alienate the student from the family, community and life. One of the key roles of education should be creation of a work culture at all stages of education so that the individual develops into a socially and economically useful human being with respect for the welfare of all living beings (*Sarva bhootha hitha*). Above all else, critical appreciation and concern for the cultural and artistic heritage of the country has to be instilled amongst the students. It is this package of values which will help the creation and sustenance of an enlightened and humane society in the country.

2.6.0 It has been clearly within the perception of the Committee that much of what is contained in its report has already been dealt with by different Commissions and Committees which were called upon to go into educational policy from time to time from the 19th century onwards. However, it is a fact that many of the ideas and concepts have remained as such without being translated into action and much impact has not been brought to bear upon the educational development of the country in the desired lines. The Committee's effort has, therefore, largely been one of advising on possible alternative modalities of implementation.

EQUITY, SOCIAL JUSTICE AND EDUCATION

Education and Women's Equality

Access to Water, Fuel and Fodder

1. There is a crucial link between the easy access to water, fuel and fodder and schooling of girls. This understanding needs to be *explicitly* reflected in the policy of Government and be concretised in operational designs. (4.1.10)*

2. 'Local Area Planning', as envisaged in the 'Approach to the Eighth Five Year Plan' document must take into account the above

* The number given in brackets at the end of each recommendation is the paragraph number of the Report of the Review Committee under which that recommendation appears.

linkage while planning for programmes relating to forestry, drinking water and greening of common lands. (4.1.10)

3. The Department of Education should coordinate with the other concerned departments and secure adequate resource allocation for the above-mentioned programmes based on parameters which indicate the status of girls' education in a given habitation/village. For instance, priority needs to be given to the habitations/villages having enrolment and retention rates for girls in schools below the average rates of the States. (4.1.10)

4. To achieve the above purpose, planning for educational development of any given region would have to be necessarily conducted at the Block or sub-Block level. This task would be facilitated if it is undertaken through the proposed Educational Complexes in which there will be Block-level representatives of the various agencies/departments concerned with social welfare and development, along with teachers, *Anganwadi* workers and representatives of poor women's groups and Panchayati Raj institutions. (4.1.10)

5. Teachers, *Anganwadi* workers, village-level functionaries of other departments, and representatives of women's groups and community-level organisations should play an important role in making micro-level information available to the Educational Complex for prioritisation of action in this regard. (4.1.10)

Early Childhood Care and Education (ECCE)

6. The policy framework on women's education must bring out the criticality of the link between ECCE and girls' accessibility to elementary education. (4.1.13)

7. Comprehensive and effective ECCE services should be provided in proximity to every primary and middle school and be programmatically linked with elementary education. (4.1.13)

8. Priority should be given to child-care programmes catering to the 0-3 age group, particularly among the underprivileged sections of society. (4.1.13)

9. The timings of the ECCE centres should include the school hours so that the girls in the 6-14 age group are relieved from the responsibility of sibling care. (4.1.13)

10. While the *Anganwadis* (ICDS) should continue to be given importance, other models which are sensitive to local needs should also be encouraged. (4.1.13)

11. The management of *Anganwadis* and other ECCE programmes should be decentralised and be made participative, as recommended in the chapter on ECCE. (4.1.13)

12. In order that child-care facilities and pre-school and primary education of girls are prioritised in the village and the community, the Anganwadi workers and poor women's groups should be represented on the Village Education Committees. (4.1.13)

Regional Disparities

13. The issue of regional disparities needs to be incorporated into the operational design for universalising girls' access to elementary education. (4.1.16)

14. Any effective strategy for raising the educational status of women in India would have to give priority to the educationally backward districts. (4.1.16)

15. Educational planning at the level of Educational Complexes will depend on block-level or sub-block level profiles. These profiles should be based on micro-level information collected from habitations/villages. Teachers, Anganwadi workers, other village-level functionaries and representatives of poor women and other community level organisations should be involved in making such information available. (4.1.16)

16. Decentralised and participative mode of planning and management offer an effective basis for responding to the challenge of regional disparities in education, including girls' education. Diverse strategies and disaggregated time-frames, worked out locally, constitute the twin instrumentalities to achieve the goal of universalisation. (4.1.16)

Content of Education and the Gender Bias

17. The curriculum in schools should include:

- Increase in the visibility of women and projection of a positive image of the role of women in history, their contribution to society in general and the Indian context in particular. For instance, social history should project the contribution that women have made in the national movement. All such issues should be carefully incorporated in the training and orientation of teachers, educators and administrators.

- Special efforts should be made to strengthen mathematics and science education among girls. Girls' schools should give greater importance to mathematics and science than at present.
- Undifferentiated curriculum for boys and girls.
- Elimination of negative stereotypes and biological and social concepts which have a sexist bias. This has been dealt with in greater detail in the Section that follows.
- Outmoded traditions and myths that hinder positive development of women and their role in national life should be objectively discussed in the class-room in a gender perspective. Similarly the portrayal of women in our epics and mythology needs to be critically examined in the class-room.
- Basic legal information including protective laws regarding women and children and extracts from the Constitution to make the children aware of the fundamental rights and other basic concepts therein.
- Specific measures to improve the participation of girls in physical training and sports should be undertaken. (4.1.19)

Stereotypes in Text-books and the 'Hidden Curriculum'

18. It is recommended that all school text-books, both by NCERT/SCERTs and other publishers, be reviewed to eliminate the invisibility of women and gender stereotypes, and also for the proper incorporation of a women's perspective in the teaching of all subjects. This review should also cover all the supplementary reading material and library books being recommended for schools, particularly those supplied by Operation Blackboard. (4.1.22)

19. As an immediate step such an exercise should seek the active participation of different groups and individuals, such as Women's Studies experts, Women's Studies Centres of the Universities and Research Institutes, and women's organisations working at grass-root level rather than exclusive dependence on NCERT/SCERTs. (4.1.22)

20. A similar exercise should be undertaken for the university curriculum and text-books in all disciplines. This should be initiated by University based Women's Studies Centres and individuals already working on these issues. (4.1.22)

Role of the Media

21. All media channels, both in the public and private sectors, should take serious note of the crucial role that the media can play in promoting gender equality and empowerment of women as enunciated in NPE. (4.1.23)

22. In the specific context of gender, advertisements displaying women as sex symbols and using them for sales promotion should be seriously dealth with. (4.1.23)

23. Media should project positive images of women. Women should also be shown in professional roles, for instance as doctors, engineers and scientists, so that they can serve as role models. (4.1.23)

24. An awareness of the need for women's education, especially elementary and vocational education, should also be spread. (4.1.23)

25. The Information and Broadcasting Ministry should evolve a network to monitor the projection of women, and evolve a code of ethics with regard to the presentation of women in all types of media (similar recommendations are also made in the Shramshakti Report, 1988). (4.1.23)

26. An Inter-Ministerial Committee, comprising representatives of the Departments of Education, Women and Child Development, Culture and Information and Broadcasting, should be constituted to monitor and ensure that the policy guidelines emerging from NPE and POA are being supported, rather than being violated, by the media, particularly Radio and TV. Representatives of women's organisations and Women's Study Centres may also be included in this Committee. (4.1.23)

27. A National Policy on Communication, giving a gender perspective to all forms and processes of mass communications, should be formulated urgently. The National Commission on Women should play an active role in this exercise. (4.1.23)

Vocational Education

28. Vocational Training for women should be planned and implemented at the State level, through the proposed Educational Complexes. (4.1.27)

29. Vocational Training for women should be encouraged in non-traditional occupations, following an undifferentiated curriculum. (4.1.27)

30. Concerted efforts should be made towards discouraging the existing biases in vocational courses for women. (4.1.27)

31. Vocational training courses for girls at 'Plus Class VIII' level (i.e. secondary stage) in order to expand the social base of vocational education. Opportunities should be especially given to dropouts after middle school. (4.1.27)

32. Diversification of courses and trades to match with the job potential at local level is important. For encouraging access to technical or craft-and skill-training institutions, increased stipends, fellowships, and a system of placement is recommended. There should be at least one women's polytechnic in each District. (4.1.27)

Training of Teachers and Other Educational Personnel

33. Teacher training programmes in general require a critical evaluation and re-orientation within which the incorporation of the women's perspective should be a key dimension. This would include sensitivity to women's issues and awareness of the problems in the education of girls. (4.1.30)

34. Teacher educators, Women's Studies researchers in universities and institutes including those in the Women's Cells, as well as representatives of women's organisations and development groups, and not just a handful of Central or State level agencies, should be involved in this process of evaluation and re-orientation of teacher training programmes. (4.1.30)

35. The *core* elements of a restructured teachers' training programme should emerge from the above exercise. Subsequently at the level of the State (or region), the DIETs and Educational Complexes along with educational institutions, Women's Study Centres, educators and grass-root level organisations should participate in evolving the actual curriculum of the teachers' training programme. This kind of decentralisation in curriculum planning, and later even in its implementation, allows for greater flexibility and meaningfulness. (4.1.30)

36. Teachers' training institutes should adopt the revised curriculum so that all teacher trainees, male and female, are exposed to the restructured training programme. (4.1.30)

37. A separate training and sensitisation programme for the teacher educators would have to be undertaken on a prioirty basis. (4.1.30)

38. Simultaneously in-service training programmes should be con-

ducted to sensitize teachers who are already in schools. The DIETs in consultation with the Education Complexes should take the initiative in organising these in-service programmes. (4.1.30)

39. The actual form that the in-service training programmes will take, should be left to the DIETs in consultation with the Education Complexes. For instance, one school can serve as the training school where teachers' training will include practice teaching. The 'internship model' referred to elsewhere can be explored. (4.1.30)

40. Administrators and planners in education (including Heads of institutions) can be sensitised to women's issues through the diffusion of information, holding of workshops and frequent interaction with resource persons in the area of Women's Studies. This is particularly crucial when exercises involving decision-making in education are undertaken. (4.1.30)

Research and Development of Women's Studies

41. Women's Study Centres should be organised in all the Universities and recognised social science research institutions within the Eighth Plan. (4.1.32)

42. Women's Studies research findings should be incorporated into curriculum revision and development, and teacher training programmes at all levels of education. At the university level, representatives of the Women's Study Centres should be included in all official bodies concerned with curriculum and syllabus development in all disciplines. (4.1.30)

43. A close linkage in the work of the University-based Women's Study Centres and Educational Complexes should be encouraged with a view to widen participation, decentralise and diversify training, sensitisation and curriculum evaluation. This will also enrich the work of the Women's Study Centres themselves through feedback from the field. The Women's Study Centres of a university should play a key role in introducing a gender perspective in school education within the Education Complexes of the region that they serve. (4.1.32)

Women's Studies Courses

44. The foundation courses introduced by the UGC should be reviewed and revised to incorporate women's dimensions. This should be part of the students' overall assessment at the undergraduate level.

The course should be carefully structured with the active involvement of Women's Studies research and development organisations and women's organisations working at the grass-roots level. Adequate representation of women's issues, from all sections of society, their concerns and living conditions should be incorporated. (4.1.33)

45. Existing courses should also incorporate the gender perspective, as suggested in the POA. This must apply to all courses, including science and technology, medicine, law, agriculture and veterinary sciences. (4.1.33)

46. All issues related to curricular revision and development on Women's Studies should be extended to the orientation of teachers as well. (4.1.33)

Extension Services

47. Women's Development Centres, such as the ones existing in some University Colleges should be extended to all colleges and higher educational institutions. (4.1.34)

48. These Centres should also be given funds to conduct awareness workshops/seminars etc. at both the school and community levels. (4.1.34)

Representation of Women in the Educational Hierarchy

49. The proportion of women teachers in Primary, Middle and High Schools should be increased to at least 50 per cent. For the success of this measure it would be desirable if the woman teacher is selected from within or near the habitation where she is to teach. In case a local woman teacher cannot be found, it would then be necessary to–

(a) provide living quarters with certain minimum amenities to women teachers on a priority basis;
(b) locate the living quarters within the habitation in order to ensure security; and
(c) wherever possible provide living quarters to all women functionaries, apart from women teachers, in close proximity to each other. (4.1.36)

50. While an increasing number of women should be recruited at different levels of education, there should be promotional avenues also

within the educational hierarchy. Special measures would have to be devised to ensure that women are fairly represented in decision-making bodies in teaching and educational administration. (4.1.36)

51. Special provisions to take care of women's needs should be built into the recruitment and service procedure, evaluation criteria, guidelines for promotion, etc. An example of such procedures is association of women in Selection Committees and Departmental Promotion Committees. This will ensure that women are not prevented by socio-cultural factors from rising in educational hierarchy. (4.1.36)

52. Women and men in positions of planning and decision-making within the educational hierarchy and public administration should be sensitised to women's issues so as to adequately discharge their leadership roles. (4.1.36)

Empowerment of Women

53. Develop *Mahila Samakhya* in a decentralised and participative mode of management, with the decision-making powers devolved to the district or block-level, and ultimately to the poor women's groups themselves. (4.1.40)

54. Implement *Mahila Samakhya* in such a way as to establish organic linkages with the ECCE programme and the efforts towards universalisation of girls' elementary education. (4.1.40)

55. Build a component of closely working with men in the community also, as part of the process of women's empowerment. (4.1.40)

56. Along with the means for economic independence for women, the issues of women's health, including reproductive health and sexuality, should be included in the parameters for empowerment of women. (4.1.40)

Adult Education

57. For imparting adult education to women and thereby empower them, the *Mahila Samakhya* model should be tried out. (4.1.41)

Resources

58. Fifty per cent of the elementary sector allocation for measures to increase girls' participation be earmarked and this allocation be made non-divertible. (4.1.42)

59. A share of all developmental allocations for secondary, vocational and higher education be earmarked for measures to improve girls' access thereto and the quality of education in these sectors be improved. (4.1.42)

60. There should be special earmarking for girls within the Special Component Plan for Scheduled Castes and Tribal Sub-Plan. (4.1.42)

Management

61. Continuance of all Centrally-sponsored Schemes relating, in part or in full, to women's education may be treated in terms of the detailed recommendation given by the Committee in regard to Centrally-sponsored Schemes as a whole in the chapter on Decentralisation and Participative Management. (4.1.44)

62. The responsibility for planning, implementing and internal monitoring of all school-based programmes for women's education be handed over to the Educational Complexes in the Panchayati Raj framework. At the institutional level, the Head of the institution (Primary/Middle/Higher Secondary Schools) should be made fully responsible for micro-level planning and ensuring universalisation (not just enrolment) of girls' education and their access to high school or vocational education, according to disaggregated strategies and time frames. (4.1.44)

EDUCATION FOR THE SCHEDULED CASTES, SCHEDULED TRIBES AND OTHER EDUCATIONALLY BACKWARD SECTIONS

Incentive Schemes

63. A series of studies should be instituted to investigate into the impact that the various incentive schemes implemented in different States have had on enrolment and retention of SC/ST children in the schools. Community profiles of educationally backward communities should also be prepared based on study of their current educational status. With reference to these profiles and the findings of the impact studies, on a disaggregated basis, appropriate and logical strategies should be established for the educational development of the backward communities. (4.2.5)

Status of Access to Education

64. The Fifth All India Education Survey shows that a number of habitations predominantly populated by SCs and STs are not served by schools within walking distance. There should be a programme for the coverage of these unserved habitations with schools as per norms before the end of the Eighth Five-Year Plan. (4.2.6)

Improvement of Capability and Educational Environment

65. The scheme of remedial coaching should be re-organised such that on a phased basis, majority of the schools introduce the same. Instead of coaching being confined to two or three months of pre-examination periods, the same should be offered in a sustained way throughout the academic session in the concerned classes. (4.2.7)

66. A strategy to enrich learning environment and the socio-economic conditions in the tribal regions as distinct from mere remedial coaching should be evolved and brought under implementation. (4.2.7)

67. In the backward areas including SC, ST habitats, a network of school linked libraries should be established. For reaching out to smaller habitation without schools, a dynamic programme of bicycle-borne mobile libraries or para-school-based libraries should be brought under implementation. These libraries need to be enriched with creative children's literature. While the children's literature would be primarily in the regional languages, efforts should be made to increase the availability of children's books in the local dialects or languages spoken in educationally backward areas. (4.2.7)

68. In order to nurture all kinds of talents and aptitudes in children, ranging from academic subjects to co-curricular and socio-cultural spheres as may be identifiable, Educational Complexes should organise a wide-ranging programme of specific theme based workships/work camps, using the best available resource persons in the area. This programme should *encourage school drop outs* as well to join and contribute in this collective endeavour towards excellence. (4.2.7)

69. In the curriculum of the educationally backward the following should be emphasised at all stages of education:

(a) Science and Mathematics;
(b) Expression, both oral and written, and creative writing;

(c) History and sociology of the Scheduled Castes, the Scheduled Tribes and other backward sections of society;
(d) Contribution of these communities to national life and development including the freedom struggle; and
(e) Role played by women belonging to these communities in national life and development.

(In fact, matters covering under (c), (d) and (e) above should also be included in the National Core Curriculum) (4.2.7)

70. Above all else, in order to bring about universalisation of Elementary education among girls in backward areas, including those belonging to SC/ST communities, a network of ECCE centres should be established on a priority basis with linkage to primary schools. (This has also been dealt with in the Chapter on ECCE). (4.2.7)

Recruitment of SC/ST Teachers

71. It should be ensured that in Government and Government-aided schools teachers from SC/ST communities are invariably in the order of 15 per cent and 7.5 per cent respectively. Recruitment to reach these levels should also be closely monitored. (4.2.8)

Curriculum and Tribal Culture

72. The rich diversity of the tribal cultural identities should be included in the common cultural heritage which is one of the elements of the Core Curriculum envisaged in NPE/POA. (4.2.8)

Special Component Plan and Tribal Sub-Plan

73. Special Component Plan and Tribal Sub-Plan should be specifically exhibited in the budget document, schemewise. (4.2.9)

74. To the extent feasible, schemes meant exclusively for the Scheduled Castes and Scheduled Tribes should be prepared and included under SCP/TSP. (4.2.9)

75. Wherever exclusive schemes cannot be formulated, specific physical targets for coverage of Scheduled Castes/Scheduled Tribes under the schemes generally applicable to all should be indicated. (4.2.9)

76. A more effective monitoring mechanism should be established

in the Department of Education itself for the purpose of periodically following up the progress of implementation of SCP/TSP. (4.2.9)

Intensive Area Approach

77. The Ministry of Welfare, according to the Business Rules, is expected to do coordination in the implementation of programmes relating to SCs/STs. While they have given a list of blocks identified as tribal blocks, they have not given, with reference to 1981 census, a list of blocks identified as those of Scheduled Caste concentration. This Ministry should, therefore, provide lists of blocks with SC concentration. With reference to such lists the Department of Education should get feedback from the States regarding their coverage under the various educational programmes. (4.2.10)

78. All the educational programmes should be implemented to the extent feasible conveniently in the same blocks of SC concentration/tribal blocks so that impact of educational development is felt in a demonstrable and balanced way in the respective areas. (4.2.10)

Monitoring

79. A single focal agency in each State should be identified for the purpose of reporting to the Government of India comprehensively on all the educational programmes. (4.2.11)

Minorities

80. Government of India should establish a standing machinery to closely monitor issue of detailed guidelines by the States for the purpose of granting recognition to minority managed educational institutions; to review the pace of disposal of applications for recognition of these institutions; and thereby to secure quality of education in institutions so recognised. (4.2.12)

81. All the educational programmes that are now under implementation should be concurrently implemented, to the extent feasible, in these districts on a priority basis after conduct of bench-mark surveys as enivsaged in POA.* (There is no evidence of implementation of

* The forty-one districts are identified in the POA as being of minority concentration.

education programmes in these districts based on initial bench mark surveys to assess the status of literacy therein and to build programmes thereon for further improvements). (4.2.12)

82. The twenty-five districts which have not yet been covered under the community polytechnics should also be brought under their coverage before the end of the Eighth Five Year Plan. (4.2.12)

83. The orientation programmes for the Principals/Managers and teachers of minority managed educational institutions should be organised on a decentralised basis through SCERTs at the State level and DIETs, CTEs and IASEs at the sub-State levels. (4.2.12)

84. Special coaching should be organised through reputed and progressive voluntary organisations, particularly those operating for the benefit and welfare of the minority communities. (4.2.12)

85. Open Universities including the IGNOU should establish distance education programmes for imparting special coaching. (4.2.12)

Education of the Handicapped

86. People should be made aware of the problems of the handicapped, in terms of the magnitude and types of handicaps. The media should be effectively used for this purpose. (4.3.6)

87. Every family with a handicapped child should be provided support through incentives, dialogue and periodic training and evaluation. Parents' groups and community education groups should be formed. (4.3.6)

88. The educational system for the handicapped should be flexible. It should offer a range of education provisions – special schools for those who cannot be educated in general schools, special classes in general schools, and integrated education for the disabled of the type already in existence. Education should be through different options–formal, non-formal, open schools, home day schools, vocational centres etc. (4.3.6)

89. Educational packages should be offered for hearing impaired children in a differentiated way–

* Pure orally oriented programmes for profoundly deaf children.
* Combined oral-manual programmes for some of the profoundly deaf children for the education of whom pure oral programmes will not be adequate.
* Segregated programmes for those children for whom such

programmes are essential.

* Integrated programmes for those whom this modality promises better emotive, cognitive, social and linguistic development. (4.3.6)

90. For making the boys and girls of impaired hearing economically independent, vocational training has to be specially organised. Vocational training which is job-oriented and matched to the abilities and aptitudes of the hearing imparied, should be organised in a significantly diversified way making a departure from the earlier practice of confining to a limited number of vocational training programmes like in drawing, painting, tailoring, knitting, embroidery, book-binding, etc. These diversified courses also relate to industrial operations such as sheet metal works, printing, turning, fitting, welding, electrician's trade, carpentry, etc. (4.3.6)

91. Bharati Braille has been developed, thanks, *inter alia* to the special effort made by the National Institute for the Visually Handicapped. Based on this, teacher training and book production programmes have also been launched. These production programmes should be intensified by their scales of operation being enlarged and diversified to cover wide range of subjects and in school and out of school needs. (4.3.6)

92. While work has been initiated for development of Braille notations for mathematics and science, not much progress has been made. On account of the growing emphasis on science and mathematics teaching, a comprehensive and effective code for use in the area of mathematics and science should be developed. (4.3.6)

93. For the moderately mentally retarded, special curricula should be developed and standardised – not merely for the purpose of basic education in 3 R's but for training in self-care skills like motor integration, perceptual and motor skills, language, communication and conceptual skills. It should be clearly understood that for the mentally handicapped, academic achievements are relatively unimportant in comparison to social adaptation and vocational training. (4.3.6)

94. Vocational schools for the mentally retarded adults are not too many. For their benefit jobs in sheltered workshops, farms and industries should be provided as they are not capable of receiving open employment. The idea is that after receiving training they can work on sub-contract basis. (4.3.6)

95. In pre-service teacher training programme, education of the

handicapped, should be made part and parcel of the pedagogy and methodology. (4.3.6)

96. A programme of sensitization should be implemented for in-service teachers as well. This should include various components, namely, Non-Formal Education, vocationalisation of education and distance education. (4.3.6)

97. Teachers' training colleges should have special courses for teaching the handicaped children, a special component on the education of the handicapped should be included in the B.Ed. courses as well. (4.3.6)

98. At least one resource faculty should be provided in each DIET to provide teacher training inputs in the context of education for the handicapped. (4.3.6)

99. The role of the special schools should be clearly redefined as spelt out below :

(i) Early identification of children with handicaps and formulation of stimulation programmes for them and the community in their catchment areas;
(ii) Education of the handicapped children who cannot be educated in general schools up to the point when they can be integrated–thus breaking the isolation between the general and special schools;
(iii) Service as resource agencies for implementing the integrated education programmes in general schools so that they feel as a part and parcel of the educational system; and
(iv) Bringing about mutual reinforcement of the pedagogies of special and general education. (4.3.6)

100. A lot of development is taking place in the application of technology for the benefit of the handicapped. Several technological aids are already available like for example, Brailleix produced by Federal Republic of Germany which facilitates recording of whole encyclopaedia on cassettes, printing conversion devices like 'tactacon' which facilitates presentation of printed material in vibro-tactile form so as to enable the blind persons to read, devices facilitating mobility of the blind persons etc. The technologies and techno-aids available for meeting the special needs of the handicapped children should be reviewed and measures for dissemination of information should be formulated. (4.3.6)

101. Sustained researches should be undertaken to determine the needs of the physically handicapped and produce technological aids capable of helping in overcoming handicaps. The Indian Institute of Technology and other technological institutions in the area of higher education should be given specific responsibilities for undertaking these researches. (4.3.6)

Common School System

102. The first step in securing equity and social justice in education is the building up of a Common School System. Specific actions required in this context are the following :

- Provision of significantly increased outlay for elementary (particularly primary) education. This would help in the building up of the required level of infrastructure and quality of education, thereby transforming Government, local-body and aided schools into genuine Neighbourhood Schools.
- Provision of special allocations for improvement of school system in backward areas, urban slums, tribal areas, hilly tracts, desert and marshy areas, drought and flood-prone zones, coastal belts and islands.
- Ensuring instruction for all in the medium of mother tongue at the primary level, particularly for linguistic minorities; active encouragement of teaching in the regional languages at the secondary level; and discontinuance of State aid to the schools imparting education otherwise than in the medium of mother tongue/regional languages.
- Phased implementation of the Common School System within a ten-year time frame; and essential minimum legislation, particularly to dispense with early selection process, tuition fee, capitation fee etc.
- Exploring ways of including the expensive private schools into the Common School System through a combination of incentives, disincentives and legislation. (4.4.8)

Navodaya Vidyalayas

103. The Committee, having considered the strong views expressed by the members for and against the Navodaya Vidyalaya Scheme and

after taking into account all aspects of the scheme in terms of the concept, philosophy, design, its implementation and future, recommends that the Government may decide from out of the following three alternatives:

(i) NO FURTHER NAVODAYA VIDYALAYA NEED BE OPENED. The existing 261 Navodaya Vidyalayas may be restructured and continued with provision of adequate resources. The scheme may also be reviewed at the end of 1992-93. The terms of reference for this review may be –

- Whether the objectives for which the scheme was established have been achieved – in terms of nurturing of talents, reservations for the SCs/STs, girls, representation for rural children, pace setting functions and national integration through migration of children.
- If the objectives have not been achieved what are the reasons for the same?
- Restructuring if any, of the scheme with reference to:

  * redefinition of the concept of special talent or aptitude such that the selection takes into account the entire cognitive and effective domain as well as the psychomotor skills;
  * broadening the process and canvas of selection with a view to make provision for the vast potential of talent in different attributes of life that exists among rural children, but is not identifiable by conventional academic tools; and
  * changing the present life style and value orientation of the Navodaya Vidyalayas such that the alienation of the campuses from rural life, particularly that of the underprivileged sections, is guarded against.

(ii) All the existing 261 Navodaya Vidyalayas may be transferred to the State Sector for the States to run them as residential centres on the Andhra Pradesh model; and

(iii) The Navodaya Vidyalaya scheme may be transformed into a Navodaya Vidyalaya programme of broad based talent nurturing and pace-setting. (A day-school each under the Common

School System can function in the premises of the Navodaya Vidyalayas). (4.5.10)

EARLY CHILDHOOD CARE AND EDUCATION

Scope of Article 45 of the Constitution

104. The scope of the Constitutional directive (Article 45) of providing within a specified time-frame, free and compulsory education for all children until they complete the age of fourteen years, should be enlarged to include ECCE. (5.1.6)

Operational Design

105. Since ECCE is a cross-sectoral programme, addressing the intersecting needs of children, women and girls, ECCE as a component should receive due attention in all dimensions and stages of education, such as women's education, education of Scheduled Castes and Scheduled Tribes, elementary education, vocational education, content and process, teacher training, higher education etc. (5.2.0)

Priority

106. ECCE should be included in the Minimum Needs Programme. (5.3.0)

Role and Responsibility of Various Departments

107. The Department of Women and Child Development in the Ministry of HRD at the Centre (and the Departments of Social Welfare in the States) should be held accountable for the implementation of ECCE *in all aspects* of its operational design, as recommended in the POA. (5.4.4)

108. This Department must also accept the nodal role of stimulating, co-ordinating and monitoring the ECCE work undertaken by other agencies/departments such as Labour, Works and Housing, Tribal Welfare, Irrigation, Rural Development, Forest etc. (5.4.4)

109. The Department of Women and Child Development (and its counterparts in the States) should seek the setting up of an Inter-Ministerial Committee.

Strategies and Measures for Achieving UEE

169. Make each school, primary or middle, fully responsible accountable or formulating and implementing strategies for UEE in villages/habitations/*mohallas* in the area under its coverage. For this purpose, vest the school with the necessary authority and autonomy to decide upon their mix of strategies and measures (e.g. adult education, para-schools, Operation Blackboard). Provide each school through the avenue of the Educational Complex adequate funds and intellectual resources to implement its programme of universalisation. (6.13.0)

170. Authorise the school Head Master/Head Mistress to recruit para-teacher (*Shiksha Karmis*) for reaching out either to unserved habitations or to those children who cannot attend the school in the day hours. The issues of emoluments, rules governing their probationary period and eventual absorption in the school, and their training in an 'Internship Model' have already been dealt with in this chapter. (6.13.0)

171. Encourage innovation by teachers themselves in building up diverse models of child-centred approach to education and create mechanisms of collating, integrating and disseminating the growing experience of the teaching community within and among Educational Complexes. (6.13.0)

172. In order to increase the relevance of education from the standpoint of working children, especially girls, it would be necessary to emphasise vocationalisation of the entire educational process up to Class VIII level. (6.13.0)

173. The goal of universalisation of education may be viewed in two phases – the first phase of Universalisation of Primary Education (UPE) and the second phase of UEE. While the school shall be expected to undertake micro-planning for UPE in association with the Educational Complex in the first phase itself, UEE may be allowed to grow organically out of the development of Primary Education. In the second phase, after achieving the goal of UPE, micro-planning for UEE would also become necessary and viable. (6.13.0)

174. Adopt the principle of differentiated or disaggregated targets and pluralistic educational strategies for achieving UEE. This mode of decentralised and participative planning provides scope for gender specific, community-wise, Block-level and District-level, and regional parameters to inform the planning process. The National and State targets of UEE as well as resource allocation shall emerge from collection

and integration of the disaggregated targets. (6.13.0)

175. Monitoring of the move towards UEE shall be integral to the planning process and may operate at three independent but co-ordinated levels–

(a) Within the Educational Complex, of individual schools;
(b) Within the district, of individual Educational Complexes; and
(c) Within the State, of individual District Boards of Education.

HIGHER EDUCATION

Maintenance of Standards in Higher Education

198. Pressures for opening new colleges and universities being very intense, and the political system reacting to such pressures in different ways, in different States, it would only be appropriate for the Government to re-examine the feasibility of national level statutory mechanism for strongly discouraging non-standard/sub-standard colleges and universities being established. In the process of this examination, no doubt, the Central Government should have necessary prior consultations with the State Governments (9.4.0)

199. After NPE, 1986 was formulated and brought under implementation and though discouragement of proliferation of universities has been specifically mentioned in the Programme of Action, Government of India themselves have passed laws in May 1989 and October 1989 respectively for establishing Assam and Nagaland Universities. Steps of this nature may not help in the process of bringing about discipline in the establishment of universities at the State level and these should be avoided. Therefore, Government of India should themsleves set an example by not establishing more Central Universities without genuine justification for the same. (9.4.0)

Restructuring of UGC

200. The UGC has not been able to function effectively in the face of expansion of the higher education system in terms of increasing number of colleges and universities. Workload in terms of development programmes of the universities to be scrutinised by the Commission has been on the increase and their scrutiny and clearance by the Commission suffer in quality as well as on account of delays.

Therefore, restructuring of the UGC is called for. In the opinion of the Committee, the Commission should consist of at least five full time members apart from the Chairman and Vice-chairman, with specialisation in specific areas – teaching, research, extension, management and finance. The Commission should also have regional offices for decentralised disposal of the problems relating to higher educational institutions in the respective regions. Structural decentralisation would be meaningless unless adequate decentralisation of authority and functions is effected and accordingly this should also be effected. (9.6.0)

Selectiveness in Admission

201. The universities have come under severe strain on account of the load of administering examinations at the bachelor's level. They should be relieved of the responsibility of holding these examinations so that they can concentrate on post-graduate, doctoral and post-doctoral studies, apart from research. (This matter has also been separately dealt with under the subject of Examination Reforms). (9.6.0)

202. If in a college M.A. and M.Sc. teaching is to be continued it must be made mandatory that there are adequate facilities for research in those subjects. (9.6.0)

Autonomous Colleges

203. The UGC has already appointed a Committee to review the programme for establishing autonomous colleges. This review should be expedited and modalities should be evolved in this review for introducing a regime of autonomy by securing the participation of all. (9.7.2)

New Management for Universities

204. Government should facilitate early decisions on the report of the Gnanam Committee, the same having been received as early as January 1990. (9.7.3)

Curriculum Development

205. For the redesigning of courses the UGC has set up 27 Cur-

riculum Development Centres in different disciplines. The emphasis is on modernising and restructuring courses in modular form. Reportedly, 22 Curriculum Development Centres have given the reports.

Agricultural Universities

218. Agricultural Universities may diversify their education programmes, particularly in areas closely connected with agriculture. The State Agricultural Universities should be encouraged to set up centres/institutes for rural development. (9.14.3)

National Council of Higher Education

219. The Programme of Action under NPE, 1986, envisages establishment of a National Apex Body. Action has been initiated by the Department of Education, in this context, for the establishment of a National Council of Higher Education to bring about coordination between the UGC, the All India Council for Technical Education, Indian Council of Agricultural Research, Medical Council of India and Bar Council of India. In specific terms, the objective of establishing this body, as reflected by the POA, is to deal with policy aspects of higher education and to undertake integrated planning and to reinforce programmes of post-graduate education and inter-disciplinary research. Functions envisaged are tendering of advice to Government on policy, coordination of activities of the various bodies in different fields, encouragement of inter-disciplinarity and promotion of interfaces amongst different areas, allocation of resources, establishment and management of common infrastructure and coordination of policy concerning external academic relations.

Going by these objectives and functions of the apex body, it does not seem necessary to create another institution at the national level to function as a super body, as it were. These objectives can be achieved and functions performed by an appropriate coordination mechanism that could be brought into existence by a mere Resolution of Government. This mechanism in the opinion of the Committee, could have a two-tier structure – (i) a Council of Ministers of Higher Education, the Ministers being those holding portfolios relating to education, agriculture, health, law and science and technology; and (ii) a Council of Secretaries dealing with these subjects and Heads of the concerned insituations apart from Finance Secretary to Government of India and

Secretary, Planning Commission. Being a high powered body the former Council may be presided over by the Prime Minister. One of the concerned Ministers may be the Vice-Chairman by rotation. The Council of Secretaries and Heads of institutions together may basically formulate the policies and submit the same to the Council of Ministers for approval. (9.15.0)

Grievance Redressal

220. The recommendation of the Law Commission in regard to tribunalisation of justice in centres of higher education is pending decision. Early decision on this may be taken by the Government. (9.17.0)

RESOURCES FOR EDUCATION

Strategies for Raising Resources

313. The first step therefore, should be to provide for at least 6 per cent of the GNP for Education which has not so far been provided, though this has been repeatedly urged for over quarter of a century. (The figure of 6 per cent of GNP was suggested by the Education Commission (1964-66) on the basis that, that was the level of investment which had already been reached even by certain developing countries of Asia. An estimate of investment required for implementing the recommendations of the report of Education Commission (1964-66) was made. Coincidentally, it was noted that this amount approximated to 6 per cent of GNP. It had also been noted that the economic growth rate per annum for 20 years since then was envisaged at 6 per cent. A quarter of a century has since passed and considerable changes have come about in the economy. Therefore, in the changed context, there is need for reviewing the proportion of GNP that should go into Education as on date). Even providing 6 per cent of GNP means substantially larger allocations for Education in the budgets of the Central and State Governments. (15.13.5)

314. All teachnical and professional education should be made self-financing, education being viewed as involving the use of resources (inputs) that should be necessarily paid for by the beneficiaries as it confers on them greater employability (output). (15.13.5)

Increase in Fees

315. The tuition fees now prevalent in educational institutions, by and large, are those fixed many years ago. In 1950-51, income from fees accounted for 20 per cent of the total expenditure on education. This proportion has now come down to 5 per cent. In the circumstances, a justifiable strategy is bringing about an appropriate increase in the fees payable by students going in for Higher Education. This increase should be appropriately linked to at least the cost of recurring expenditure and levels of income of the parents of the beneficiaries. The richest quartile of the people can bear 75 per cent of the cost of the education; the next richest quartile 50 per cent of the cost; and the next richest quartile 25 per cent. The last quartile of the economically weak (to be appropriately defined) need not bear any part of the cost. (15.13.5)

316. Besides tuition fees, fees charged for specific purposes in the Higher Educational Institutions like laboratory fees, library fees, magazine fees, games fees etc. also have to be increased on a rational basis with reference to the cost of providing the relevant facilities/services. (15.13.5)

Institutional Loans

317. With the ever increasing number of examines, examination fee can also be an important means of raising internal resources to meet the cost of Higher Education. (15.13.5)

318. While student loans have the advantage of bringing down government investment in Higher Education, they do involve certain problems. They are : Psychologically, people are against loans. Credit markets are not developed. There are difficulties in securing repayment of loans even as the government experience of operating loan scholarship shows. (Reference has been made to this later). The poor could face difficulties in having access to loans.

However, institutional loans as a strategy for releasing the pressure on government resources and as a means of putting resources in possession of those aspiring for Higher Education is indispensable. Problems in administration of loans should not result in the easy solution of opting out of them. (15.13.5)

Financing Education by Nationalised Banks and Financial Institutions

319. Nationalised banks and financial institutions as a rule of practice generally concentrate on industrial financing and financing of commercially viable activities. However, there are examples like the State Bank of India advancing loans for Higher Education.

Therefore, there is need for a committed programme of the nationalised banks for providing loans for recipients of Higher Education. (15.13.5)

320. Term lending institutions like the Industrial Development Bank of India (IDBI), Industrial Finance Corporation of India (IFCI) and Industrial Credit and Investment Corporation of India (ICICI) should launch programmes for promoting research in universities. This could ease the burden on the University Grants Commission which, in turn, is provided funds by the Government of India. The IDBI has to its credit several promotional activities with a view to helping the process of industrialisation. It has, for example, set up the Entrepreneurship Development Institute of India. It has also provided assistance to voluntary agencies engaged in imparting production and vocational training. Assistance has also been provided to the National Association for the Blind to set up a polytechnic at Bombay. The IDBI and ICICI have had chairs instituted for specific projects in various universities. This activity could be expanded in an organised way with reference to the merits of individual programmes of the respective Higher Educational Institutions. (15.13.5)

321. Institutional finance for infrastructure needs to be raised in the circumstances. Housing Finance Institutions, therefore, could take up programmes for creation of capital assets in the educational sector i.e. for building for schools, colleges, universities as also hostels for the students, staff and teachers. Repayment of loans may have to be guaranteed by the appropriate Governments. (It is worthy of mention, in this context that Housing Development Finance Corporation (HDFC) has already financed schemes for construction of staff quarters and ownership houses for University staff in Gulbarga, Karnataka. The Universities and Educational Societies, on their part, could consider investment of their provident fund money in the bonds of Housing Finance Institutions approved under Section 36 (i) (VIII) of the Income Tax Act. (15.13.5)

322. There is a strong case for LIC's investment in the area of

housing going for hostel facilities for the students, staff and teachers in the educational institutions. However, diversion of these resources for the education sector would mean doing so at the expense of other development schemes, 90 per cent of the accretions of the LIC already being committed to socially oriented sectors. Therefore, this is a matter on which the Government as well as Planning Commission will have to take a conscious decision regarding the reallocation of the LIC's investible resources with substantive priority for the Education sector (15.13.5)

Scholarships

323. Economically weaker sections of the people going for Higher Education who cannot afford the enhanced fees or loans from financial institutions could be provided appropriate scholarships. (15.13.5)

324. Funds provided in the Central sector for scholarships during the Seventh Plan period was of the order of Rs. 22.26 crores. This would have to be considerably enhanced for the benefit of the economically weaker sections in the interest of equity and providing access to Higher Education for them. There is also need for rationalisation of the whole programme of awarding scholarships. (15.13.5)

325. The Government of India scheme of scholarships in approved residential secondary schools benefit only a small number of 500 students per annum in the whole country. Serious malpractices in the selection of scholars have also reportedly come to the notice of the Government, the benefits, of late, being cornered apparently by manipulations on the part of those hailing from a very few centres in India. This scheme could as well be discontinued and the number of scholarships enhanced for meaningful programmes like for upgradation of merit of SC/ST students. (15.13.5)

326. One of the modalities for securing better implementation of scholarship schemes with more direct and responsible involvement on the part of the States, no doubt, would be for the administration of the scholarships being left totally to the States themselves, necessary outlays being provided to the States as part of the State Plan Outlays on an earmarked basis. (15.13.5)

Other Means of Raising Resources

327. Certain other means of raising resources for education are presented below:

- A sustained programme to be implemented every year right down to the Panchayat levels for raising community contribution (Rules for grants in aid provided to the educational institutions could be modified to provide for built-in incentives such that Government assistance is related to contributions raised from the community on matching basis. In the course of interactions with the Ministers and Secretaries of States, a suggestion was made that there could be funds created for educational development. Like relief funds created in the names of Prime Minister of India and the State Chief Ministers, there could be Prime Minister's and Chief Minister's Educational Funds into which the community contributions, educational cess (about which reference is made later) etc. could be credited. These funds could be operated for the purpose of building up infrastructure for educational institutions up to the elementary levels).
- Institution of innovative programmes like the Phule Foster Parent Scheme of Maharashtra for promoting primary education of girls under which registered foster parents pay Rs. 25 p.m. in cash or kind to the needy girls from weaker sections.
- Removal of restrictions on the investment of surplus income of educational institutions like the stipulation that such income should be invested in low yielding Government securities/bonds etc.
- Collection of educational cess related to revenue sources such as land revenue, excise duties, charges on cash drops, charges on buildings in urban areas etc. (The sources on which cess could be charged naturally will be quite diversified and different for different States. It would be for the respective States to identify the sources on which cess is to be levied).
- Educational institutions being permitted to let out on rent their facilities like conference rooms, auditoriums etc.
- Consultancy services being rendered by higher, general and technical institutions.
- Levying of a direct assessment on developed host countries which utilise the services of professionals from the country. This assessment could be related to the total number of professional personnel migrating, the amount of their income and the taxes they pay to the host countries. In fact, this is one of the suggestions made in the U.N. Report on 'The Reverse Transfer

of Technology' (1979). This strategy would naturally involve entering into bilateral or multilateral tax treaties with the beneficiary developed countries.

- Broad basing distance education.
- Introduction of shift systems in schools, so that the existing infrastructure can be utilised better.
- Identification or surplus teachers in schools and colleges and their deployment otherwise. (15.13.5)

3

THE CENTRAL ADVISORY BOARD OF EDUCATION 1991-1992

FORTY-SIXTH MEETING (1991)*

Introduction

The 46th meeting of the Central Advisory Board of Education (CABE) was held at New Delhi on March 8-9, 1991 under the chairmanship of Shri Rajmangal Pandey, The Minister of Human Resurce Development. The following agenda was discussed –

I. *Elementary Education*

1. Universalisation of Elementary Education
2. Minimum Levels of Learning
3. External Funding for Education for All
4. Teacher Education
5. Teachers' Constituencies in Legislative Council Election : Need and Composition.

II. *Adult Literacy*

6. Review of Literacy Scene
7. Programmes for Universal Literacy (age group 15 to 35)
8. Post-Literacy and Continuing Education

III. *Secondary Education*

9. Vocationalisation of Secondary Education
10. Programmes for Qualitative Improvement
11. Secondary Education

---

* Broughtout by Ministry of Human Resource Development, New Delhi, 1992.

IV. *Technical Education*

11. Regulation of Fees and Admission (Prohibition of Capitation Fees, Self Financing, Provision of Financial Support to Needy and Talented Students.
12. Making AICTE more effective.
13. Review of the Implementation/Formulation of the World Bank Assisted project on Technician (Polytechnic)

V. *Higher Education*

14. Report of the Gnanam Committee on 'Towards New Educational Management: UGC's Recommendations Thereon
15. Measures to Promote Distance Education
16. Formulation and Observance of Academic calendar by Universities and Colleges.
17. Measures to Improve Quality of Education in Colleges.

VI. *Education for SCs/STs/Minorities in Colleges*

18. Programmes for Equalisation of Education Opportunities

VII. *Policy and Planning*

19. Management and Resources
20. Consideration of the Manner in which the Report of the NPE Review Committee (Acharya Ramamurti Committee) is to be processed.
21. Eighth Five Year Plan Formulation–Approach Paper.

Proceedings and Recommendations

1. The report of the Review Committee on NPE was considered. The consensus that emerged after discussion was to constitute a CABE committee to examine the report.

2. The Board considered the reports of the Working Groups formed by it on the first day of the meeting:

(a) Working Group on Secondary Education;
(b) Working Group on Higher Education;
(c) Working Group on Adult Education and Literacy;
(d) Working Group on Technical Education;
(e) Working Group on Elementary Education;
(f) Working Group on Education of Women and Other Disadvan-

taged Groups like SC, ST, Minorities, etc.; and

(g) Working Group on Policy and Planning.

Arrangement of Working Groups

Sl. No.	Name of the Group	Name of the person	Name of rapporteur
1	2	3	4
Group-I	Elementary Education	Dr. (Smt.) Kamla Das, Minister of State for Education, Orissa.	Shri L.P. Pande, Director (Basic Education), Uttar Pradesh.
Group-II	Adult Education and Literacy	Dr. Malcolm S. Adiseshiah, Director, Madras Institute of Development Studies, Madras	Shri A.J. Shukla, Director (AE&PE), Gujarat.
Group-III	Secondary Education	Shri Kanti Biswas, Education Minister, West Bengal	Ms. Sushma Choudhary, Education Secretary, Jammu and Kashmir.
Group-IV	Technical Education	Prof. D. Swaminathan, Member Planning Commission.	Prof. B.B. Chopane, Director (Technical Education), Maharashtra
Group-V	Higher Education	Shri Vikram Verma, Education Minister, Madhya Pradesh	Shri C.T. Benjamin Education Secretary, Karnataka.
Group-VI	Education of Women and other Disadvantaged Groups like SC, ST, Minorities etc.	Shri H.S. Lyngdoh, Education Minister, Meghalaya.	Shri Ashok Kumar Mishra, Education, Secretary Orissa.
Group-VII	Policy and Planning	Shri K. Chandrasekaran, Education Minister, Kerala	Shri Ashok Saikia Commissioner and Secretary, Education, Assam

In the afternoon of 9th March, 1991 the Board met in its plenary session to consider the reports of the various working groups that had been formed the previous day.

Secondary Education: Ms. Sushma Chaudhary, Rapporteur presented the report of the working group on secondary education. While considering the Report, Prof. Ramlal Parikh was of the view that the vocational education should not continue as a distinct stream at the +2 level. The consensus, however, was that the report as prepared by the Group may be adopted. It was also pointed out that in any case this matter will again come up for consideration in the context of examination of Acharya Ramamurti Committee Report. Dr. Anandalakshmi suggested that in the report the terms 'deaf', 'dumb' and 'blind' should be replaced by the terms persons suffering from 'auditory' and 'visual' handicaps. This suggestion was accepted. With this modification the report was adopted.

Higher Education: The report of the working group on Higher Education was presented by Shri C.T. Benjamin, Rapporteur of the group. In the course of discussion, the following decisions were taken:

(a) In regard to the Gnanam Committee Report, the State Governments should formulate their views and send them to the Ministry within three months. The Chairman, CABE should set up a CABE Committee to consider the recommendations of the Gnanam Committee Report keeping in view the comments of the State Governments and have the Report of the Committee placed before CABE at the next meeting; and

(b) The Chairman may also set up a CABE Committee on Distance Education to examine steps to be taken for promotion of distance education in the country including the role of IGNOU *vis-a-vis* the State Open Universities as well as the need for greater use of radio and TV for promotion of distance education.

The CABE approved the Report of the working group with the additional decisions as above.

Adult Education: The report of the working group on adult education and literacy was presented by the Chairman of the group Dr. Malcolm Adiseshiah. The following points were made in course of discussion:

(a) The initiative taken by Prof. Yash Pal, former Chairman, UGC and a number of like-minded persons to involve school and college students in national issues like eradication of illiteracy was welcome;

(b) Concrete steps should be taken to revive the Vidyapeethas set up in Karnataka under the auspices of Karnataka Adult Education Council;

(c) There is need for greater linkage of the adult education programme with the system of libraries. Systematic programmes need to be undertaken for ensuring that neo-literates do not relapse into illiteracy; and

(d) In the planning of literacy and post-literacy programmes special attention should be paid to habitations with SC/ST concentration.

With these observations the CABE adopted the working group report.

Technical Education: The report of the working group on technical education was presented by its Rapporteur, Prof. B.B. Chopne. In the course of discussion some members drew attention towards the urgent need to attract and retain qualified teachers in engineering. Steps need to be taken to improve the general quality of engineering teachers and to provide them better avenues for career advancement. The Board noted that the All India Council for Technical Education was already seized of this matter and that necessary action is being taken by it. The report of the working group was adopted by the CABE.

Elementary Education: The working group report on elementary education was presented by Dr. L.P. Pandey, the Rapporteur of the group.

Education Minister, Karnataka said the CABE should recommend adoption of mid-day meal programme for improving enrolment and retention. He said that the experience of the States which had adopted such a programme had been very positive. In response to this, Shri Anil Bordia explained that CABE had always endorsed the idea of provision of mid-day meals to children but had also consistently taken the stand that the responsibility for this should not lie with the school system, as the work relating to procurement of foodgrains, their storage, cooking, distribution, accounting, monitoring, etc., greatly interfered with the task of teaching/learning in schools.

Prof. D.S. Kothari said that while he fully agreed with the MLL approach and concept, there was need for a re-examination of the recommendations of the R.H. Dave Committee in regard to specific skills and competencies before adopting them. He also advised that inculcation of values and other non-cognitive and affective areas should also be emphasised.

Some other members also made observations on different aspects of the report of the working group. CABE adopted the Report of the working group with the following additional observations:

(a) The specific levels of skills and competencies recommended by the R.H. Dave Committee should be got thoroughly re-examined by the Ministry before accepting the Report;

(b) Operation Blackboard should continue in the Eighth Plan and expanded to the upper primary stage. Funds for appointment of teachers provided by the Central Government during the Seventh Plan should continue to form part of the Centrally-sponsored Schemes during the Eighth Plan. A time-bound programme should be taken up for provision of infrastructure and basic facilities for primary education based on well laid down norms; and

(c) The Central and State Governments should be called upon to fully implement the law relating to child labour, while efforts are made to provide education to all working children.

At this juncture the Chairman (Shri Rajmangal Pande) had to leave due to exigencies of work and the meeting proceeded under the chairmanship of Shri Kanti Biswas, Education Minister, West Bengal.

SC, ST and Women : Report of the working group on women's education and on disadvantaged groups like SC, ST, minorities, etc., was presented by Shri A.K. Misra, Rapporteur of the working group.

Dr. Adiseshiah criticised the clubbing of women with SCs, STs and other disadvantaged groups. It was agreed that in future women's education would be deliberated upon by a separate working group. The CABE noted that the report of the working group had endorsed several recommendations (1 to 102) of the Report of the Acharya Ramamurti Committee. As the Board had not yet considered the Acharya Ramamurti Committee and a CABE Committee is being set up to go into the recommendations of Ramamurti Committee, it was considered inappropriate at this stage to endorse the recommendations of the Review Committee and thereby pre-empt due consideration of the Report. Hence the working group's report was adopted with the deletion of those portions which endorsed the recommendations of the Ramamurti Committee.

Policy and Planning : The report of the working group was presented by Shri Ashok Saikia, Rapporteur of the group. In the course of discussion, Education Minister, Karnataka said that the Central Government should set up some specialised institutions in the States as deemed universities. He added that he would send a detailed note on the subject to the Union Education Minister. Education Minister, Bihar pressed for a CABE Resolution in favour of establishment of a Central University in Bihar. It was decided that a group may be set up by the Chairman, CABE to go into the whole matter of setting up of Central Universities. Dr. Saraswati Swain expressed disagreement with the recommendations of the group in regard to securing external funds for basic education. Education Minister, West Bengal (Shri Kanti Biswas) and Dr. M.S. Adiseshiah also expressed reservation in this behalf. CABE took note of these observations but adopted the report of the working group on policy and planning as presented.

Wrap up of the discussions: Shri Anil Bordia mentioned that the CABE had made valuable recommendations in several areas of education including resources for education, Centrally-sponsored Schemes, processing of the reports of the Ramamurti Committee and the Gnanam Committee, micro planning for universalisation of elementary education, restoration of academic calendar, adult literacy and equalisation of educational opportunities. The recommendations of CABE were relevant not only to the Central Government but also to the State Governments as well as to all persons and organisations engaged in the field of education.

4

JANARDHANA COMMITTEE ON NATIONAL POLICY ON EDUCATION

REVIEW RAMAMURTI COMMITTEE (1991)*

Introduction

Appointment of the Committee

The National Policy on Education (NPE) was adopted by Parliament in May 1986. The Policy was followed up by an elaboration through the Programme of Action (PoA) which was adopted by Parliament in August 1986. Para 11.5 of NPE envisages a review of the implementation of various parameters of the Policy every five years. The Central Government had in May 1990, appointed a Committee to review NPE, 1986 (NPERC), under the chairmanship of Acharya Ramamurti. The Committee submitted its report on 26th December, 1990. The report was tabled in both the Houses of Parliament on 9th January, 1991. The Central Advisory Board of Education (CABE) in its meeting held on 8-9 March, 1991 examined the procedure to be adopted for consideration of the report of the NPERC and decided that a CABE Committee be constituted by the Chairman, viz., Union Minister of Human Resource Development, to consider the recommendations of the NPERC.

In pursuance of the above decision, the Chairman of the CABE appointed a Committee on 31st July, 1991, to review the implementation of various parameters of NPE taking into consideration the report of the NPERC and other relevant developments since the Policy was for-

* Report of the CABE Committee on Policy, Department of Education, Ministry of Human Resource Development, Government of India, New Delhi, 1992.

mulated and to recommend modifications to be made in NPE. Following is the composition of the Committee:

Chairman

Shri N. Janardhana Reddy
CM and Minister of
Education, AP.

Members

1. Shri Vikram Verma
Minister of Education, MP.
2. Shri Geegong Apang
CM and Minister of
Education,
Arunachal Pradesh
3. Dr. Ram Chandra Purve
Minister (SE and PE), Bihar
4. Shri R.M. Veerappan
Minister of Education,
Tamil Nadu
5. Shri S.S. Chakraborty
Minister (Higher Education)
West Bengal
6. Shri E.T. Mohammad
Basheer
Minister of Education,
Kerala
7. Dr. (Smt.) Chitra Naik
Member (Education)
Planning Commission
8. Prof. G. Ram Reddy
Chairman
University Grants
Commission
9. Dr. M.S. Adiseshiah
Chairman
Madras Institute of
Development Studies
79, Second Main Road,
Gandhi Nagar Adyar
Madras : 600 020
10. Dr. Radhika Herzberger
Director
Rishi Valley School
PO Madahapalli, Distt.
Chittoor,
Andhra Pradesh
11. Dr. A.P. Mitra
Bhatnagar Fellow
New Delhi
12. Smt. Jaggannathan
Krishnammal
Secretary
Land for Tillers Freedom
(LAFTI)
Kilvelur : 611104
Tanjore District,
Tamil Nadu
13. Dr. Ram Dayal Munda
Professor of Regional
Languages
Ranchi University, Ranchi
14. Shri Habib Tanvir
Director, Naya Theatre
DDA Staff Quarters
Bar Sarai,
New Delhi-110016

Member Secretary

15. Dr. R.V. Vaidyanatha
Ayyar
Joint Secretary (Planning)

Union Education Secretary (Shri Anil Bordia), Director of NCERT (Dr. K. Gopalan) and Director of NIEPA (Prof. Satya Bhushan), were permanent invitees to the meetings of the Comittee. A copy of the order is attached with Appendix I.

SUMMARY OF RECOMMENDATIONS

Overview

1. The concept of participatory educational order should go beyond involvement of education institutions and should extend to the community itself. (Para 2.2)

2. While very little of policy requires reformulation, the PoA needs to be revised considerably. (Para 2.3)

Education and Women's Equality

3. While the NPERC had rightly reiterated the importance of women's education, the NPE policy frame is adequate and the Programme of Action (PoA) should be revised to take into account the recommendations of the NPERC. (Para 3.5)

Education of the Scheduled Castes, Scheduled Tribes and Other Educationally Backward Sections

4. A single focal agency should be identified in each State for the purpose of monitoring the programmes and reporting to the Central Government. (Para 4.4)

5. A standing CABE Committee on education of SCs, STs and other educationally backward sections should be constituted; educationists from these groups should have representatives in that Committee. (Para 4.4)

6. While instruction should be child-centred and cater to individual differences, it is not advisable to differentiate students in the matter of syllabus and curriculum. (Para 4.5)

7. Monitoring of the implementation of the guidelines for recognition of minority-managed educational institutions is better left to the State Governments, as they are deeply conscious of the need for proper monitoring and many organisations like the Minority Commission already exist for the purpose of monitoring. (Para 4.6)

8. No policy reformulation is necessary; all recommendations of the NPERC on education of the SCs, STs and other educationally backward sections, except R. Nos. 69 and 80, should be taken into account while revising the PoA. (Para 4.8)

Education of the Handicapped

9. No policy reformulation is necessary; the recommendations of the NPERC on education of the handicapped should be built into the revised PoA. (Para. 5.3)

Common School System

10. Effective measures need to be taken to implement the provision of NPE 68 and NPE in regard to Common School System. To this end, disparities between schools should be ended as early as possible by upgrading the quality of ordinary schools and providing amenities for achieving minimum levels of learning. Both the Centre and the States should take determined action in this regard. The privileged schools should accept social accountability by sharing their facilities and resources with other institutions, taking up community activities, and facilitating access to children of the disadvantaged groups. (Para 6.6)

Navodaya Vidyalayas

11. The scheme should continue and a NV should be set up in each district as originally envisaged. Further, the following measures are suggested:

(i) constant review to keep the scheme as cost effective as possible;
(ii) ensuring the continued validity and reliability of the admission tests by periodic evaluation and appropriate modification of admission procedure; and
(iii) more particular attention to the pace-setting role of these institutions. (Para 7.5)

12. It is also necessary to begin thinking about the future course of the scheme after NVs have been established in all districts with the requisite facilities and investment. A choice has to be made between

establishment of new institutions and expansion of facilities in the existing institutions. Planning has also to begin for catering to the higher educational needs of students who pass out of NVs. A scheme needs to be formulated for central financial support to residential schools. In this scheme priority should be given to ST areas and areas predominantly inhabited by SCs. (Para 7.9)

Early Childhood Care and Education

13. The scope of Article 45 of the Constitution need not be enlarged. (Para 8.8)

14. ICDS and other CSS relating to ECCE should continue as Centrally-sponsored Schemes during the Eighth Five Year Plan. The *Anganwadi* workers should play an expanded role and should be the focal point for a number of activities and support services for women and children, such as child care, family welfare, nutrition and health. The recruitment and training of Anganwadi workers should be so organised as to ensure that they have the necessary skills and motivation to discharge the expanded role. (Para 8.8)

15. The other recommendations of the NPERC which broadly relate to implementation modalities should be taken into account for reviweing PoA. (Para 8.8)

Universalisation of Elementary Education

16. What is needed is not so much a Constitutional amendment as suggested by the NPERC as the manifestation of a national will to achieve UEE. The Central and State Governments should bestow overriding priority to adult literacy and UEE, and provide the programmes in these two areas total support – financial, administrative and political – a support which is commensurate with the priority. (Para 9.2)

17. No further refinement of the policy relating to access and enrolment is required; what needs to be done is large scale operationalisation of important components of the strategy outlined by NPE/PoA such as community mobilisation, school mapping and micro-planning. (Para 9.5)

18. MLL should be a thrust area. (Para 9.6)

19. The NPE approach to non-formal education is more practical and realistic than that of the NPERC. (Para 9.13)

20. Expeditious and effective action is required to tone up the management system and the learning environment of NFE so as to ensure that the quality of NFE is comparable with that of formal system in all respects. The Centre and the States should closely and continuously monitor NFE programmes in order that the programmes are effective. (Para 9.13)

21. Operation Blackboard, being one of the priority strategies for UEE, should continue during the Eighth Plan, in an expanded and extended form. (Para. 9.15)

22. Till operational models of an educational complex are developed, tested and tried out, it is not feasible to link the Scheme of Operation Blackboard with the educational complex; nor is it feasible to entrust the planning and minitoring of UEE to the educational complex, as suggested in R.Nos. 169, 171, 173 and 175 by the NPERC. (Para 9.15)

23. Para 5.12 of NPE, which laid the targets for UPE and UEE, needs to be revised. Every effort should be made to ensure that the constitutional obligation of providing free and compulsory education up to the age of 14 years becomes a reality before we enter the twenty-first century. (Paras 2.6 and 9.17)

24. The following points deserve priority during the Eighth Five Year Plan in the area of UEE :

(i) Universal enrolment of all children, including girls and persons belonging to SC/ST;

(ii) Provision of primary school for all children within one kilometer of walking distance. and of facility of non-formal education for school drop-outs; working children and girls who cannot attend schools;

(iii) Improvement of ratio of primary school to upper primary schools from the existing 1:4 to 1:2, this being a pre--condition for larger opportunity for widening girls' participation at upper primary stage;

(iv) Reduction of drop-out rates between Classes I to V and I to VIII from the existing 45 per cent and 60 per cent to 20 per cent and 40 per cent respectively;

(v) Improvement of school facilities by revamed Operation Blackboard, to be extended to upper primary level also;

(vi) Achievement of minimum levels of learning by approximately all children at the primary level and introduction of this concept at the upper primary stage on a large scale;

(vii) Local level committee, with due representation to women and teachers, to assist in the working of primary education and to oversee its functioning; and

(viii) Improvement of the monitoring system for universalisation of elementary education to see to the achievement of above-mentioned goals.

NPE and PoA may be revised accordingly. (Para 9.18)

Adult and Continuing Education

25. The "dual-track approach" of promoting simultaneously UEE and adult literacy should continue to inform educational planning; the special needs of women and of disadvantaged groups like SCs and STs should be specially attended to. (Para 10.1)

26. The NPERC's perception of Mahila Samakhya (MS) as an alternative model is not valid. (Para 10.4)

27. Events since December 1990, when the NPERC submitted its report, have established that NPERC had underestimated the significance of the "Ernakulam experiment". The TLC approach is a potent and viable model which could help achieve a significant breakthrough in the literacy scene in the Eighth Five Year Plan. (Para 10.6)

28. Programmes of post-literacy and continuing education should be planned for neo-literates and youth passing out of primary education system (through the school system or non-formal education programme) and these programmes should be planned simultaneously with literacy campaigns and be made effective as soon as large number of persons complete literacy courses. (Para 10.9)

Secondary Education

29. The policy should be reformulated to bring about the new initiatives that are required in secondary education. (Para 2.7)

30. It would be necessary to bring about a planned expansion of secondary education facilities all over the country in order to cope with new demands for secondary education. (Para 11.3)

31. Efforts should be made to bring about uniformity in the management structure for secondary education in all the States. (Para 11.4)

32. It is necessary to reorganise the Boards of Secondary Education and vest them with autonomy so that their ability to provide academic inputs to secondary education is enhanced. (Para 11.5)

33. Time-bound measures should be taken by the Central and State Governments to implement the directions contained in Para 10.7 of NPE and to empower the Headmasters with administrative, academic and financial powers. Training of the heads of institutions requires particular attention. (Paras 11.6 and 17.15)

34. Teacher training in secondary education requires no less importance than in primary education. (Para 11.8)

35. The ongoing programme of CLASS needs to be revamped. (Para 11.9)

36. Open learning should be given utmost encouragement and that the National Open School should play the same lead role within the open school system as IGNOU with open universities. (Para 11.11)

Vocationalisation of Education

37. The existing vocational stream at the +2 level may be suitably strengthened and wherever possible the vocational courses may be started from class IX also. (Para 12.12)

38. The idea of a core vocational course, mooted by the NPERC, is attrative. Generic vocational courses may be introduced on a selective basis; to begin with generic vocational courses may be tried out in about ten per cent of the schools. (Paras 2.5 and 12.12)

39. The Work Experience programme may be systematically implemented by allocating 12.5 per cent to 20 per cent of the school time for these activities; the activities should have a practical orientation in relation to various subjects under this programme. The vocational "core" would find place at the secondary and higher secondary stages; Work Experience/SUPW would relate to elementary education. (Para 12.12)

40. The other recommendations of the NPERC relating to implementation of the scheme of vocationalisation of education may be taken note of while revising PoA. (Para 12.12)

41. Greater rigour should be brought to bear on the planning and implementation of the scheme. (Para 12.12)

Higher Education

42. It is not advisable to set up a national level statutory mechanism

to regulate the opening of non-standard and sub-standard universities and colleges. The proliferation of colleges without adequate facilities can be curbed to a large extent if the universities exercise rigorous control and insist on creation of necessary infrastructure and if the State Governments respect the decision of the univesities in these matters. The establishment and operationalisation of State Councils of Higher Education will go a long way in the planned development of higher education. (Para 13.3)

43. Efforts should be made to secure involvement of teachers and students in extension work such as literacy. Adequate facilities should be provided to ensure that all students participate in one or the other existing schemes, particularly National Services Scheme (NSS), and National Cadet Corps (NCC). Specific schemes should be formulated to encourage out of school youth to participate in national service and development. The feasibility and financial implications of a two-year composite programme for students who complete the +2 stage, comprising paramilitary service, development of vocational and professional skills, and extension work in rural areas be studied. An important feature of the programme would be that the students would be required to participate in these programmes outside their home state with a view to promoting national integration. (Para 13.4)

44. NTS should undertake the conduct of tests so that it acquires the required expertise and develops into a competent resource centre. (Para 13.5)

45. A Central Council of Rural Institutes is necessary to provide the much needed fillip to rural education on Gandhian lines; it should be set up immediately. (Para 13.6)

46. The recommendation of the NPERC (R. No. 219) on NCHE is sound and Para 5.34 of NPE should be reformulated. (Paras, 2.5 and 13.7)

47. There is no need for appointment of full-time members in the UGC. (Para 13.10)

48. Regional offices of the UGC should be set up at the earliest, with adequate authority and functions. (Para 13.11)

49. Since most of the universities are affiliating universities, R.No. 201 of the NPERC can be implemented only when most of the colleges become autonomous or when a system of internal evaluation gradually replaces a terminal examination or when an independent State level examining body is set up to conduct common examinations for all undergraduate courses. (Para 13.12)

50. The UGC may consider augmenting research facilities in selected colleges within the available resources. (Para 13.13)

51. The Scheme of Curriculum Development Centres should be continued; however, to allay any misgivings the UGC may reiterate that the universities have full freedom to adapt model curricula. The UGC should also consider specific requests from the universities for curriculum development. (Para 13.15)

52. The UGC may closely monitor the implementation of the Scheme of Academic Staff Colleges. (Para 13.16)

Technical and Management Education

53. It is not advisable to regulate through a statute the emigration of graduates of IITs and RECs. All efforts should be made to ensure that environment for science and technology in the country is attractive enough for talented persons. (Para 14.2)

54. A detailed evaluation of the thrust area schemes should be taken up in 1994-95, the third year of the Eighth Plan (1992-97). (Para 14.3)

55. The Department of Education, Government of India (GoI), should take early decisions on the report of the Kalbagh Committee on Community Polytechnics. (Para 14.4)

56. The Department of Education, GoI, should take early decisions on the report of the IIT Review Committee. (Para 14.5)

57. The AICTE Act should be amended and Para 6.19 of NPE should be reformulated. The Regional Committees of the AICTE should be adequately staffed and that the Chairman of the Regional Committee should be an Education Minister of a State from the region by rotation. The Regional Committee should have the power to make recommendations on the opening of new institutions, starting of new courses and enhancing the intake within the framework of the guidelines laid down by the AICTE. The State Governments and the universities should issue the necessary approvals based on the recommendations of the Regional Committees only. (Para 14.6)

58. The recommendations of NPERC relating to improvement of quality and standard, upgradation of infrastructure facilities, industry-institution linkages, technology watch and manpower planning, promotion of R&D, special programme for the disadvantaged entrepreneurship development and continuing education and retraining programmes should be given due consideration in the revision of PoA. (Para 4.7)

Languages in Education

59. All the recommendations of the NPERC in the area, except R. Nos. 239 and 246 are useful and should be taken into account in the revision of POA. (Para 15.3)

60. The merger of KHS, CHD and CSTT is not desirable. (Para 15.4)

61. A fresh linguistic survey is not desirable. (Para. 15.5)

Content and Process of Education

62. The recommendations of the NPERC on value education should be taken into account while revising the PoA. (Para. 16.3)

63. The recommendation of the NPERC on educational technology should be followed up by the Central and State Governments and it be taken into account while revising the PoA. (Para 16.4)

64. There is need to progressively expand facilities for computer education in schools, particularly at the secondary stage. (Para 16.5)

65. The suggestions on Youth and Sports may be taken into account, while revising the PoA. Students should be required to participate in one or the other existing schemes, such as NSS and NCC, as envisaged in Para 8.22 on NPE. (Para 16.7)

66. Rather than leaving examination reforms to the individual initiatives and inclinations of the examining bodies, a strong and coordinated effort should be made by the Centre and the State Governments in this area. *Inter alia* the following measures are suggested:

(i) Preparation of a status report of examination reform measures undertaken by the examining bodies;
(ii) Preparation of a National Examination Reform Framework to serve as a set of guidelines to the examining bodies which would have the freedom to innovate and adopt the framework to suit the specific situation;
(iii) Developing an effective mechanism for coordination, monitoring and evaluation of the implementation of the examination reforms by the different examining bodies; and
(iv) Documentation and dissemination of innovations and measures for examination reforms. (Para 16.11)

67. While the load of the school bag is a valid concern, one cannot

afford to ignore the requirements of modernisation and relevance. (Para 16.12)

68. The NPE provision and the National Curricular Framework should be followed faithfully so that the problem of the load of the school bag will be mitigated. The teachers of the expensive private schools in urban areas should be reoriented so that they give up the habit of prescribing unnecessarily a large number of books. (Para 16.13)

Teachers and Students

69. Licensing of teachers as suggested by the NPERC is not desirable. (Para 17.2)

70. The selection system, whether for teachers or teacher trainees, should be objective and immune from undue inducements, thereby fostering the credibility of the selection process. (Para 17.3)

71. The suggestion of the NPERC on the content and process of teacher education are commended to NCTE, NCERT and SCERTs for consideration whenever the curriculum is reviewed or renewed. (Para 17.4)

72. First degree in teacher education should not be given through correspondence courses. (Para. 17.5)

73. The NCTE should be immediately provided, as envisaged in the NPE/PoA, with necessary resources and capability. (Para. 17.5)

74. An expert body like the NCTE should study the internship model of teacher training as suggested by the NPERC and guide the SCERTs and teacher education institutions. (Para. 17.6)

75. Regarding NPERC's recommendation on the syllabus for the B. Ed. courses NCTE may take necessary action in consultation with States/UTs. (Para 17.6)

76. The attributes of teacher education identified by the NPERC may be kept in mind by the NCERT while preparing special programme for teacher educators. (Para 17.8)

77. Training and management of in-service training programmes for elementary teachers should be the responsibility of the DIETs only. (Para 17.9)

78. State Governments should give emergent attention to fill up all the posts in the teacher training institutions and to frame recruitment rules for them. (Para 17.10)

79. Emergent steps should be taken for operationalising the teacher

education institutions for which financial assistance was provided by the GoI; further financial assistance should be denied to those States in which the physical progress and utilisation of funds are unsatisfactory. (Para 17.11)

80. Every DIET should be a distinct identity with enough operational flexibility. (Para 17.12)

81. The State Governments and universities may take appropriate action on the recommendations of the NPERC on students, taking into account the specific situations. (Para 17.15)

Management of Education

82. The idea of educational complex may be tried on an experimental basis in selected areas. (Para 18.2)

83. The District Boards of Education should be set up and operationalised expeditiously. (Para. 18.3)

84. It would be necessary to hasten the process of consultation with States and to give concrete shape to the idea of IES with due regard to the views and concerns of the States. (Para. 18.4)

85. On Centrally-sponsored Schemes the decisions of the 43rd meeting of the NDC held on 23-24 December, 1991, are reiterated. Launching of new CSSs in some priority areas not so far covered, such as advancement of educationally backward minorities, are also suggested after due process of consultations with the States. (Para 18.7)

86. Constitution of specialised State Level Educational Tribunals is desirable. The details of setting up of these tribunals may be worked out in consultation with the State Governments. (Para 18.8)

87. "Making the System Work" has to be treated as non-negotiable. Formulation and implementation of an Action Plan to put into practice the strategy outlined in Para 7.3 of NPE is strongly recommended. (Para. 18.10)

Resources for Education

88. The practice of treating education as a residual sector in the matter of allocation of resources should be reversed; Para 11.4 of NPE should be implemented forthwith. Need-based financing requires to be provided for priority areas like Universalisation of Elementary Education, Adult Litracy and Vocationalisation. (Para 19.4)

89. Higher budgetary allocation for education should be complemented by other measures such as–

(i) Prioritisation within the Education Sector in the matter of allocation of governmental resources;

(ii) Progressively making higher education and technical and management education largely self-financing by revising the fee structure with appropriate support to the needy students by way of student loans;

(iii) Institutional finances for development of educational infrastructure;

(iv) Incentives to academic institutions to augment income by way of consultancy and other studies;

(v) Encouraging community and the cooperative sectors to financially support education. The time and effort given by thousands of unpaid volunteers in the Total Literacy Campaigns is a concrete demonstration of the possibility of raising social capital without any cost; and

(vi) Efficiency and effectiveness of expenditure which would imply that programmes should be judged not only with reference to the financial expenditure or coverage in terms of geographical area or number of beneficiaries but also in terms of outcomes. (Para. 19.5)

Note: The numbers given in parentheses at the end of each recommendation is the para number of the Report of the Committee under which that recommendation appears.

5

REVISED NATIONAL POLICY ON EDUCATION (1992)

Introduction

In pursuance of its election manifesto, the National Front Government appointed on 7th May, 1990 a Committee with Acharya Ramamurti as its Chairman, to reivew the National Policy on Education (NPE), 1986. The Committee submitted its report to the Minister of State in the Ministry of Human Resource Development on 26th December, 1990. The report was tabled in Parliament on 9th January, 1991. During this period political changes of far reaching consequences took place. Shri V.P. Singh's Government was voted out on 7th November, 1990 and Shri Chandra Shekhar became Prime Minister on 10th November, 1990. Shri Chandra Shekhar's Government lasted for a very brief period between 10th November, 1990 to 6th March, 1991. Thereafter he worked as a caretaker Prime Minister till 20th June, 1991. Shri P.V. Narasimha Rao assumed office of the Prime Minister of India on 21st June, 1991, after the victory of his party at the polls. It was, therefore, natural that under the changed situation, the Ramamurti Report could not receive government patronage.

The recommendations of the Ramamurti Review Committee Report were examined by the Janardhana Committee appointed by the Central Advisory Board of Education in July 1991. The Janardhana Committee submitted its recommendations in January 1992. The CABE considered the Janardhana Committee Report in the first week of May 1992 and finalised the revised NPE.

The Revised NPE was presented in both Houses of Parliament on 7th May, 1992 by the Human Resource Development Minister Arjun Singh. In his statement the Minister said the NPE, 1986 has stood the test of time and enunciated a comprehensive framework to guide the development of education. He further observed that while the framework continues to the relevant, the development during the past few years and the experience in implementation of the policy has necessitated certain modifications.

With a view to have a clear perception of the revised policy 1992, it will be quite in the fitness of things if broad outlines of both policies i.e. 1986 and 1992 are given. Table 5.1 in a nutshell provides the changes incorporated in the two policies. It is observed that only two paragraphs are added and 34 paragraphs are modified.

TABLE 5.1: Modifications at a Glance

Part	Title	Total No. of Paragraphs	Paragraphs Modified
I	Introductory	15	No Change
II	The Essence and Role of Education	4	No Change
III	National System of Education	13	3, 12
IV	Education for Equality	14	4, 5 (vii), 6 (i), 11, 12 13, 14 New Para
V	Reoganisation of Education at Different Stages	41	5, 7, 8, 9, 11, 12, 13 15, 16, 17, 23, 33, 35, 36, 37, 41
VI	Technical and Management Education	20	12, 19
VII	Making the System Work	3	No change
VIII	Reorienting the Content and Process of Education	25	16, 17, 20, 21, 25
IX	The Teacher	6	No Change
X	The Management of Education	10	New para
XI	Resources and Review	5	4
XII	The Future	2	No Change
	Total	158	

TEXT OF THE POLICY*

PART I

Introduction

1.1 Education has continued to evolve, diversify and extend its reach and coverage since the dawn of human history. Every country

* Ministry of Human Resource Development, Government of India, New Delhi, 1986 and 1992.

Note: The modified paragraphs are given in italics.

develops its system of education to express and promote its unique socio-cultural identity and also to meet the challenges of the times. There are moment in history when a new direction has to be given to an age-old process. That moment is today.

1.2 The country has reached a stage in its economic and technical development when a major effort must be made to derive the maximum benefit from the assets already created and to ensure that the fruits of change reach all sections. Education is the highway to that goal.

1.3 With this aim in view, the Government of India (GoI) announced in January 1985 that a new Education Policy would be formulated for the country. A comprehensive appraisal of the existing educational scene was made, followed by a countrywide debate. The views and sugges-tions received from different quarters were carefully studied.

The 1968 Education Policy and After

1.4 The National Policy of 1968 marked a significant step in the history of education in post-Independence India. It aimed to promote national progress, a sense of common citizenship and culture and to strengthen national integration. It laid stress on the need for a radical reconstruction of the educational system, to improve its quality at all stages, and gave much greater attention to science and technology, the cultivation of moral values and a closer relation between education and the life of the people.

1.5 Since the adoption of the 1968 Policy, there has been considerable expansion in educational facilities all over the country at all levels. More than 90 per cent of the country's rural habitations now have schooling facilities within a radius of one kilometre. There has been sizeable augmentation of facilities at other stages also.

1.6 Perhaps the most notable development has been the acceptance of a common structure of education throughout the country and the introduction of the 10+2+3 systems by most States. In the school curricula, in addition to laying down a common scheme of studies for boys and girls, science and mathematics were incorporated as compulsory subjects and work experience assigned a place of importance.

1.7 A beginning was also made in restructuring of courses at the undergraduate level. Centres of Advanced Studies were set up for post-graduate education and research, and we have been able to meet our requirements of educated manpower.

1.8 While these achievements are impressive by themselves, the general formulations incorporated in the 1968 Policy did not, however, get translated into a detailed strategy of implementation, accompanied by the assignment of specific responsibilities and financial and organisational support. As a result, problems of access, quality, quantity, utility and financial outlay, accumulated over the years, have now assumed such massive proportions that they must be tackled with the utmost urgency.

1.9 Education in India stands at the cross roads today. Neither normal linear expansion nor the existing pace and nature of improvement can meet the needs of the situation.

1.10 In the Indian way of thinking, a human being is a positive asset and a precious national resource which needs to be cherished, nurtured and developed with tenderness and care, coupled with dynamism. Each individual's growth presents a different range of problems and requirements, at every stage – from the womb to the tomb. The catalytic action of education in this complex and dynamic growth process needs to be planned meticulously and executed with great sensitivity.

1.11 India's political and social life is passing through a phase which poses the danger of erosion to long accepted values. The goals of secularism, socialism, democracy and professional ethics are coming under increasing strain.

1.12 The rural areas, with poor infrastructure and social services, will not get the benefit of trained and educated youth, unless rural-urban disparities are reduced and determined measures are taken to promote diversification and dispersal of employment opportunities.

1.13 The growth of our population needs to be brought down significantly over the coming decades. The largest single factor that could help achieve this is the spread of literacy and education among women.

1.14 Life in the coming decades is likely to bring new tensions together with unprecedented opportunities. To enable the people to benefit in the new environment will require new designs of human resource development. The coming generations should have the ability to internalise new ideas constantly and creatively. They have to be imbued with a strong commitment to humane values and to social justice. All this implies better education.

1.15 Besides, a variety of new challenges and social needs make it imperative for the Government to formulate and implement a New

Education Policy for the country. Nothing short of this will meet the situation.

PART II

The Essence and Role of Education

2.1 In our national perception education is essential for all. This is fundamental to our all-round development, material and spiritual.

2.2 Education has an acculturating role. It refines sensitivities and perceptions that contribute to national cohesion, a scientific temper and independence of mind and spirit – thus furthering the goals of socialism, secularism and democracy enshrined in our Constitution.

2.3 Education develops manpower for different levels of the economy. It is also the substract on which research and development flourish, being the ultimate guarantee of national self-reliance.

2.4 In sum, education is a unique investment in the present and the future. This cardinal principle is the key to the National Policy on Education.

PART III

National System of Education

3.1 The Constitution embodies the principles on which the National System of Education is conceived of.

3.2 The concept of a National System of Education implies that up to a given level, all students, irrespective of caste, creed, location or sex, have access to education of a comparable quality. To achieve this, the Government will initiate appropriately funded programmes. Effective measures will be taken in the direction of the Common School System recommended in the 1968 Policy.

3.3 (Revised Para) *The National System of Education envisages a common educational structure. The 10+2+3 structure has now been accepted in all parts of the country. Regarding the further break-up of the first 10 years efforts will be made to move towards an elementary system comprising 5 years of primary education and 3 years of upper primary, followd by 2 years of High School. Efforts will also be made to have the +2 stage accepted as a part of school education throughout the country.*

3.3 (NPE 1986) The National System of Education envisages a common educational structure. The 10+2+3 structure has now been accepted in all parts of the country. Regarding the further break up of the first 10 years efforts will be made to move towards an elementary system comprising 5 years of primary education and 3 years of upper primary, followed by 2 years of High School.

3.4 The National System of Education will be based on a national curricular framework which contains a common core along with other components that are flexible. The common core will include the history of India's freedom movement, the constitutional obligations and other content essential to nurture national identity. These elements will cut across subject areas and will be designed to promote vaules such as India's common cultural heritage, egalitarianism, democracy and secularism, equality of the sexes, protection of the environment, removal of social barriers, observance of the small family norm and inculcation of the scientific temper. All educational programmes will be carried on in strict conformity with secular values.

3.5 India has always worked for peace and understanding between nations, treating the whole world as one family. True to this hoary tradition, education has to strengthen this world view and motivate the younger generations for international cooperation and peaceful coexistence. This aspect cannot be neglected.

3.6 To promote equality, it will be necessary to provide for equal opportunity to all not only in access, but also in the conditions for success. Besides awareness of the inherent equality of all will be created through the core curriculum. The purpose is to remove prejudices and complexes transmitted through the social environment and the accident of birth.

3.7 Minimum levels of learning will be laid down for each stage of education. Steps will also be taken to foster among students an understanding of the diverse cultural and social systems of the people living in different parts of the country. Besides the promotion of the link language, programmes will also be launched to increase substantially the translation of books from one language to another and to publish multilingual dictionaries and glossaries. The young will be encouraged to undertake the rediscovery of India, each in his own image and perception.

3.8 In higher education in general, and technical educatiom in particular steps will be taken to facilitate inter-regional mobility by providing equal access to every Indian of requisite merit, regardless of his origin. The universal character of universities and other institutions of higher education is to be underscored.

3.9 In the areas of research and development and education in science and technology, special measures will be taken to establish net-work arrangements between different institutions in the country to pool their resources and participate in projects of national importance.

3.10 The Nation as a whole will assume the responsibility of providing resource support for implementing programmes of educational transformation, reducing disparities, universalisation of elementary education, adult literacy, scientific and technological research etc.

3.11 Life-long education is a cherished goal of the educational process. This presupposes universal literacy. Opportunities will be provided to the youth, housewives, agricultural and industrial workers and professionals to continue for education of their choice at the pace suited to them. The future thrust will be in the direction of open and distance learning.

3.12 (Revised Para) *The institutions which will be strengthened to play an important role in giving shape to the National System of Education are the University Grants Commission, the All India Council of Technical Education, the Indian Council of Agricultural Research and the Indian Medical Council. Integrated planning will be instituted among all these bodies so as to establish functional linkages and reinforce programmes of research and post-graduate education. These, together with the National Council of Educational Research and Training, the National Institute of Educational Planning and Administration, the National Council of Teacher Education and the National Institute of Adult Education will be involved in implementing the Education Policy.*

3.12 (NPE 1986) The institutions which will be strengthened to play an important role in giving shape to the National System of Education are the University Grants Commission, the All India Council of Technical Education, the Indian Council of Agricultural Research and the Indian Medical Council. Integrated planning will be instituted among all these bodies so as to establish functional linkages and reinforce programmes of research and post-graduate education. These, together with the National Council of Educational Research and Training, the National Institute of Educational Planning and Administration and the International Institute of Science and Technology Education will be involved in implementing the Education Policy.

A Meaningful Partnership

3.13 The Constitutional Amendment of 1976, which includes Education in the Concurrent List was a far reaching step whose implications – substantive financial and administrative require a new sharing of responsibility between the Union Government and the States in respect of this vital area of national life. While the role and responsibility of the States in regard to education will remain essentially unchanged, the Union Government would accept a larger responsibility to reinforce the national and integrative character of education, to maintain quality and standards (including those of the teaching profession at all levels), to study and monitor the educational requirements of the country as a whole in regard to manpower for development, to cater to the needs of research and advanced study, to look after the international aspects of education, culture and Human Resource Development and, in general, to promote excellence at all levels of the educational pyramid throughout the country. Concurrency signifies a partnership which is at once meaningful and challenging; the National Policy will be oriented towards giving effect to it in letter and spirit.

PART IV

Education for Equality

Disparities

4.1 The new Education Policy will lay special emphasis on the removal of diparities and to equalise educational opportunity by attending to the specific needs of those who have been denied equality so far.

Education for Women's Equality

4.2 Education will be used as an agent of basic change in the status of women. In order to neutralise the accumulated distortions of the past, there will be a well conceived edge in favour of women. The National Education System will play a positive, interventionist role in the empowerment of women. It will foster the development of new values through redesigned curricula, textbooks, the training and orientation of teachers, decision-makers and administrators, and the active involvement of educational institutions. This will be an act of faith and social engineering. Women's studies will be promoted as a part of various courses and educational institutions encouraged to take up active programmes to further women's development.

4.3 The removal of women's illiteracy and obstacles inhibiting their access to, and retention in, elementary education will receive overriding priority, through provision of special support services, setting of time targets, and effective monitoring. Major emphasis will be laid on women's participation in vocational, technical and professional education at different levels. The policy of non-discrimination will be pursued vigorously to eliminate sex stereotyping in vocational and professional courses and to promote women's participation in non-traditional occupations, as well as in existing and emergent technologies.

The Education of Scheduled Castes

4.4 The central focus in the SCs' educational development is their equalisation with the non-SC population at all stages and levels of education, in all areas and in all the four dimensions – rural male, rural female, urban male and urban female.

4.5 The measures contemplated for this purpose include:

- (i) Incentives to indigent families to send their children to school regularly till they reach the age of 14;
- (ii) Pre-matric Scholarship scheme for children of families engaged in occupations such as scavenging, flaying and tanning to be made applicable from Class I onwards. All children of such families, regardless of incomes, will be covered by this scheme and time-bound programmes targeted on them will be undertaken;
- (iii) Constant micro-planning and verification to ensure that the enrolment, retention and successful completion of courses by SC students do not fall at any stage, and provision of remedial courses to improve their prospects for further education and in employment;
- (iv) The recruitment of teachers from Scheduled Castes;
- (v) Provision of facilities for SC students in hostels at district headquarters, according to a phased programme;
- (vi) Location of school buildings, Balwadis and Adult Education Centres in such a way as to facilitate full participation of the Scheduled Castes.

4.5 [Revised Para (vii)] *The utilisation of Jawahar Rozgar Yojna resources so as to make substantial educational facilities availabe to the Scheduled Castes;* and

4.5 [NPE 1986 Para (vii)] The utilisation of NREP and RLEGP resources so as to make substantial educational facilities available to the Scheduled Castes; and

(viii) Constant innovation in finding new methods to increase the participation of the Scheduled Castes in the educational process.

The Education of Scheduled Tribes

4.6 The following measures will be taken urgently to bring the Scheduled Tribes on par with others:

4.6 **[Revised Para (i)]** *Priority will be accorded to opening primary schools in tribal areas. The construction of school buildings will be undertaken in these areas on a priority basis under the normal funds for education, as well as under the Jawahar Rozgar Yojna, Tribal Welfare schemes, etc.*

4.6 **[NPE 1986 Para (i)]** Priority will be accorded to opening primary school in tribal areas. The construction of school buildings will be undertaken in these areas on a priority basis under the normal funds for education, as well as under the NREP, RLEGP, Tribal Welfare schemes, etc.;

(ii) The socio-cultural milieu of the ST has its distinctive characteristics including, in many cases, their own spoken languages. This underlines the need to develop the curricula and devise institutional materials in tribal languages at the initial stages, with arrangements for switching over to the regional languages;

(iii) Educated and promising Scheduled Tribe youths will be encouraged and trained to take up teaching in tribal areas;

(iv) Residential schools, including Ashram Schools, will be established on a large scale;

(v) Incentive schemes will be formulated for the Scheduled Tribes, keeping in view their special needs and life styles. Scholarships for higher education will emphasise technical, professional and para-professional courses. Special remedial courses and other programmes to remove psycho-social impediments will be provided to improve their performance in various courses;

(vi) *Anganwadis,* Non-formal and Adult Education Centres will be opened on a priority basis in areas prodominantly inhabited by the Scheduled Tribes; and

(vii) The curriculum at all stages of education will be designed to create an awareness of the rich cultural identity of the tribal people as also of their enormous creative talent.

Other Educationally Backward Sections and Areas

4.7 Suitable incentives will be provided to all educationally backward sections of society, particularly in the rural areas. Hill and desert districts, remote and inaccessible areas and islands will be provided adequate institutional infrastruture.

Minorities

4.8 Some minority groups are educationally deprived or backward. Greater attention will be paid to the education of these groups in the interests of equality and social justice. This will naturally include the Constitutional guarantees given to them to establish and administer their own educational institutions and protection to their languages and culture. Simultaneously objectivity will be reflected in the preparation of textbooks, and in all school activities, and all possible measures will be taken to promote an integration based on appreciation of common national goals and ideals, in conformity with the core curriculum.

The Handicapped

4.9 The objective should be to integrate the physically and mentally handicapped with the general community as equal partners, to prepare them for normal growth and to enable them to face life with courage and confidence. The following measures will be taken in this regard:

(i) Wherever it is feasible, the education of children with major handicaps and other mild handicaps will be common with that of others;

(ii) Special schools with hostels will be provided as far as possible at district headquarters for the severely handicapped children;

(iii) Adequate arrangements will be made to give vocational training to the disabled;

(iv) Teachers' training programmes will be reoriented, in particular for teachers of primary classes, to deal with the special difficulties of the handicapped children; and

(v) Voluntary effort for the education of the disabled, will be encouraged in every possible manner.

Adult Education

4.10 Our ancient scriptures define education as that which liberates, i.e., provides the instruments for liberation from ignorance and oppression. In the modern world, it would naturally include the ability to read and write, since that is the main instrument of learning. Hence the crucial importance of adult education including adult literacy.

4.11 (Revised Para): *The whole nation has pledged itself, through the National Literacy Mission, to the eradication of illiteracy, particularly in the 15-35 age group through various means, with special emphasis on total literacy campaigns. The Central and State Governments, political parties and their mass organisations, the mass media and educational institutions, teachers, students, youth, voluntary agencies, social activist groups, and employers, must reinforce their commitment to mass literacy campaigns, which include literacy and functional knowledge and skills and awareness among learners about the socio-economic reality and the possibility to change it.*

4.11 (NPE, 1986): The critical development issue today is the continuous upgradation of skills so as to produce manpower resources of the kind and the number required by the society. Since participation by beneficiaries in the developmental programmes is of crucial importance, systematic programmes of adult education linked with national goals such as alleviation of proverty, national integration, environmental conservation, energisation of the cultural creativity of the people, observance of small family norm, promotion of women's equality, etc. will be organised and the existing programmes reviewed and strengthened.

4.12 (Revised Para): *Since involvement of the participants of the literacy campaigns in the development programmes is of crucial importance, the National Literacy Mission will be geared to the national goals such as alleviation of poverty, national integration environmental conservation, obervance of the small family norm, promotion of women's equality, universalisation of primary education, basic health-care, etc. It will also facilitate energisation of the cultural creativity of the people and their active participation in development processes.*

4.12 (NPE, 1986): The whole Nation must pledge itself to the eradication of illiteracy, particularly in the 15-35 age group. The Central and State Governments, political parties and their mass organisations, the mass media and educational institutions must commit themselves to mass literacy programmes of diverse nature. It will also have to involve on a large scale teachers, students, youth, voluntary agencies, employees, etc. Concerted efforts will be made to harness various research agencies to improve the pedagogical aspects of adult literacy. The mass literacy programme would include, in addition to literacy, functional knowledge and skills, and also awareness among learners about the socio-economic reality and the possibility to change it.

4.13 (Revised Para): *Comprehensive programmes of post-literacy and continuing education will be provided for neo-literate and youth who have received primary education with a view to enabling them to retain and upgrade their literacy skills, and to harness it for the improvement of their living and working conditions. These programmes would include:*

(a) establishment of continuing education centres of diverse kind to enable adults to continue their education of their choice;
(b) workers' education through the employers, trade unions and government;
(c) wider promotion of books, libraries and reading rooms;
(d) use of ratio, TV and films – as mass as well as group learning media;
(e) creation of learners' groups and organisations; and
(f) programmes of distance learning.

4.13 (NPE 1986): A vast programme of adult and continuing education will be implemented through various ways and channels, including:

(a) establishment of centres in rural areas for continuing education;
(b) workers' education through the employers, trade unions and concerned agencies of Government;
(c) post-secondary education institutions;
(d) wider promotion of books, libraries and reading rooms;
(e) use of radio, TV and films, as mass and group learning media;
(f) creation of learners' groups and organisations;

(g) programmes of distance learning;
(h) organising assistance in self-learning; and
(i) organising need and interest based vocational training programmes.

4.14 (New Para): *A critical development issue today is the continuous upgradation of skills so as to produce manpower resources of the kind and the number required by the society. Special emphasis will, therefore, be laid on organisation of employment/self-employment oriented, and need and interest based vocational and skill training programmes.*

PART V

REORGANISATION OF EDUCATION AT DIFFERENT STAGES

Early Childhood Care and Education

5.1 The National Policy on Children specially emphasises investment in the development of the young child, particularly children from sections of the population in which first generation learners predominate.

5.2 Recognising the holistic nature of child development, viz., nutrition, health and social, mental, physical, moral and emotional development. Early Childhood Care and Education (ECCE) will receive high priority and be suitably integrated with the Integrated Child Development Services programme, wherever possible. Day-care centres will be provided as a support service for universalisation of primary education, to enable girls engaged in taking care of siblings to attend school and as a support service for working women belonging to poorer sections.

5.3 Programmes of ECCE will be child-oriented, focused around play, and the individuality of the child. Formal methods and the introduction of the 3 R's will be discouraged at this stage. The local community will be fully involved in these programmes.

5.4 A full integration of child care and pre-primary education will be brought about, both as a feeder and a strengthening factor for primary education and for human resource development in general. In continuation of this stage, the School Health Programme will be strengthened.

Elementary Education

5.5 (Revised Para) *The new thrust in elementary education will emphasise three aspects : (i) universal access and enrolment, (ii) universal retention of children up to 14 years of age; and (iii) a substantial improvement in the quality of education to enable all children to achieve essential levels of learning.*

5.5 (NPE, 1986) The new thrust in elementary education will emphasise two aspects: (i) universal enrolment and universal retention of children up to 14 years of age, and (ii) a substantial improvement in the quality of education.

Child-Centred Approach

5.6 A warm, welcoming and encouraging, approach, in which all concerned share a solicitude for the needs of the child, is the best motivation for the child to attend school and learn. A child-centred and activity-based process of learning should be adopted at the primary stage. First generation learners should be allowed to set their own pace and be given supplementary remedial instruction. As the child grows, the component of cognitive learning will be increased and skills organised through practice. The policy of non-detention at the primary stage will be retained, making evaluation as disaggregated as feasible. Corporal punishment will be firmly excluded from the educational system and school timings as well as vacations adjusted to the convenience of children.

5.7 (Revised Para) *Provision will be made of essential facilities in primary schools. The scope of Operation Blackboard will be enlarged to provide three reasonably large rooms that are usable in all weather, and blackboards, maps, charts, toys, other necessary learning aids and school library. At least three teachers should work in every school, the number increasing, as early as possible, to one teacher per class. At least 50 per cent of teachers recruited in future should be women. The Operation Blackboard will be extended to upper primary stage also. Construction of school buildings will be a priority charge on JRY funds.*

5.7 (NPE, 1986) Provision will be made of essential facilities in primary schools, including at least two reasonably large rooms that are usable in all weather, and the necessary toys, blackboards, maps, charts, and other learning material. At least two teachers, one of whom a woman, should work in every school, the number increasing as early as possible to one teacher per class. A phased drive, symbolically called *Operation Blackboard* will be undertaken with immediate effect to improve Primary schools all over the country. Government, local bodies, voluntary agencies and individuals will be fully involved. Construction of school buildings will be first charge on NREP and RLEGP funds.

5.8 (**Revised Para**) *Modern technological aids will be used to improve the learning environment of NFE-Centres. Talented and dedicated young men and women from the local community will be chosen to serve as instructors, and particular attention paid to their training. All necessary measures will be taken to ensure that the quality of non-formal education is comparable with the formal education. Steps will be taken to facilitate lateral entry into the formal system of children passing out of the non-formal system.*

5.9 (**NPE, 1986**) Modern technological aids will be used to improve the learning environment of NFE centres. Talented and dedicated young men and women from the local community will be chosen to serve as instructors and particular attention paid to their training. Steps will be taken to facilitate their entry into the formal system in deserving cases. All necessary measures will be taken to ensure that the quality of non-formal education is comparable with formal education.

5.10 Effective steps will be taken to provide a framework for the curriculum on the lines of the national core curriculum, but based on the needs of the learners and related to the local environment. Learning material of high quality will be developed and provided free of charge to all pupils. NFE programmes will provide participatory learning environment, and activities such as games and sports, cultural programmes, excursions, etc.

5.11 (**Revised Para**) *The Government will take over-all responsibility for this vital sector. Voluntary agencies and Panchayati Raj institutions will take much of the responsibility of running NFE programmes. The provision of funds to these agencies will be adequate and timely.*

5.11 (**NPE, 1986**) Much of the work running of NFE centres will be done through voluntary agencies and panchayati raj institutions. The provision of funds to the agencies will be adequate and timely. The Government will take over-all responsibility for this vital sector.

A Resolve

5.12 (Revised Para) *The New Education Policy will give the highest priority to solving the problem of children dropping out of school and will adopt an array of meticulously formulated strategies based on micro planning and applied at the grass roots level all over the country, to ensure children's retention at school. This effort will be fully coordinated with the network of non-formal education. It shall be ensured that free and compulsory education of satisfactory quality is provided to all children up to 14 years of age before we enter the twenty-first century. A national mission will be launched for the achievement of this goal.*

5.12 (NPE 1986) The New Education Policy will give the highest priority to solving the problem of children dropping out of school and will adopt an array of meticulously formulated strategies based on micro planning, and applied at the grass-roots level all over the country, to ensure children's retention at school. This effort will be fully coordinated with the network of non-formal education. It shall be ensured that all children who attain the age of about 11 years by 1990 will have had five years of schooling, or its equivalent through the non-formal stream. Likewise, by 1995 all children will be provided free and compulsory education up to 14 years of age.

Secondary Education

5.13 (Revised Para) *Secondary education begins to expose students to the differentiated roles of science, the humanities and social sciences. This is also an appropriate stage to provide children with a sense of history and national perspective and give them opportunities to understand their constitutional duties and rights as citizens. Access to secondary education will be widened with emphasis on enrolment of girls, SCs and STs, particularly in science, commerce and vocational streams. Boards of Secondary Education will be reorganised and vested with autonomy so that their ability to improve the quality of secondary education is enhanced. Effort will be made to provide computer literacy in as many secondary level institutions as possible so that the children are equipped with necessary computer skills to be effective in the emerging technical world. A proper understanding of the work ethos and of the values of a humane and composite culture will be brought about through appropriately formulated curricula.*

Vocationalisation through specialised institutions or through the refashioning of secondary education will, at this stage, provide valuable manpower for economic growth.

5.13 (NPE, 1986) Secondary education begins to expose students to the differentiated roles of science, the humanities and social sciences. This is also an appropriate stage to provide children with a sense of history and national perspective and give them opportunities to understand their constitutional duties and work ethos and of the values of a humane and composite culture will be brought about through appropriately formulated curricula. Vocationalisation through specialised institutions or through the refashioning of secondary education can, at this stage, provide valuable manpower for economic growth. Access to secondary education will be widened to cover areas unserved by it at present. In other areas the main emphasis will be on consolidation.

Pace-Setting Schools

5.14 It is universally accepted that children with special talent or aptitude should be provided opportunities to proceed at a faster pace, by making good quality education available to them, irrespective of their capacity to pay for it.

5.15 (Revised Para) *Pace-setting residential schools, Navodaya Vidyalayas, intended to serve this purpose have been established in most parts of the country on a given pattern, but with full scope for innovation and experimentation. Their broad aim will continue to be to serve the objective of excellence coupled with equity and social justice (with reservation for the rural areas, SCs and STs), to promote national integration by providing opportunities to talented children from different parts of the country, to live and learn together, to develop their full potential, and, most importantly, to become catalysts of a nationwide programme of school improvements.*

5.15 (NPE, 1986) Pace-setting schools intended to serve this purpose will be established in various parts of the country on a given pattern, what with full scope for innovation and experimentation. Their broad aims will be to serve the objective of excellence, coupled with equity and social justice (with reservation for SCs and STs), to promote national integration by providing opportunities to talented children largely rural, from different parts of the country to live and learn together, to develop full potential, and, most importantly, to become catalysts of a nationwide programme of school improvement. The schools will be residential and free of charge.

5.16 (Revised Para) *The introduction of systematic, well planned and rigorously implemented programmes of vocational education is crucial in the proposed educational reorganisation. These elements are meant to develop a healthy attitude amongst students towards work and life, to enhance individual employability, to reduce the mismatch between the demand and supply of skilled manpower, and to provide an alternative for those intending to pursue higher education without particular interest or purpose. Efforts will be made to provide children at the higher secondary level with generic vocational courses which cut across several occupational fields and which are not occupation specific.*

5.16 (NPE, 1986) The introduction of systematic, well-planned and rigorously implemented programmes of vocational education is crucial in the proposed educational reorganisation. These elements are meant to enhance individual employability, to reduce the mismatch between the demand and supply of skilled manpower, and to provide an alternative for those pursuing higher education without particular interest or purpose.

5.17 (Revised Para) *Vocational Education will also be a distinct stream, intended to prepare students for identified occupations spanning several areas of activity. These courses will ordinarily be provided after the secondary stage, but keeping the scheme flexible, they may also be made available after Class VIII.*

5.17 (NPE, 1986) Vocational education will be a distinct stream, intended to prepare students for identified occupations, spanning several areas of activity. These courses will ordinarily be provided after the secondary stage, but keeping the scheme flexible, they may also be made available after Class VIII. In the interests of integrating vocational education better with their facilities the Industrial Training Institutes will also conform to the larger vocational pattern.

5.18 Health planning and health service management should optimally interlock with the education and training of appropriate categories of health manpower through health-related vocational courses. Health education at the primary and middle levels will ensure the commitment of the individual, to family and community health, and lead to health-related vocational courses at the +2 stage of higher secondary education. Efforts will be made to devise similar vocational courses based on Agriculture, Marketing, Social Services, etc. An emphasis in vocational education will also be on development of attitudes, knowledge, and skills for entrepreneurship and self-employment.

5.19 The establishment of vocational courses or institutions will be the responsibility of the Government as well as employers in the public and private sectors; the Government will, however, take special steps to cater to the needs of women, rural and tribal students and the deprived sections of society. Appropriate programmes will also be started for the handicapped.

5.20 Graduates of vocational courses will be given opportunities, under predetermined conditions, for professional growth, career improvement and lateral entry into courses of general, technical and professional education through appropriate bridge courses.

5.21 Non-formal, flexible and need-based vocational programmes will also be made available to neoliterates, youth who have completed primary education, school dropouts, persons engaged in work and unemployed or partially employed persons. Special attention in this regard will be given to women.

5.22 Tertiary level courses will be organised for the young who graduate from the higher secondary courses of the academic stream and may also require vocational courses.

5.23 (Revised Para) *It is proposed that vocational courses cover 10 per cent of higher secondary students by 1995 and 25 per cent by 2000. Steps will be taken to see that a substantial majority of the products of vocational courses are employed or become self-employed. Review of the courses offered would be regularly undertaken. Government will also review its recruitment policy to encourage diversification at the secondary level.*

5.23 (NPE, 1986) It is proposed that vocational courses cover 10 per cent of higher secondary students by 1990 and 25 per cent by 1995. Steps will be taken to see that a substantial majority of the products of vocational courses are employed or become self-employed. Review of the courses offered would be regularly undertaken. Government will also review its recruitment policy to encourage diversification at the secondary level.

Higher Education

5.24 Higher education provides people with an opportunity to reflect on the critical social, economic, cultural moral and spiritual issues facing humanity. It contributes to national development through dissemination of specialized knowledge and skills. It is therefore, a crucial factor for survival. Being at the apex of the educational pyramid, it has also a key role in producing teachers for the education system.

5.25 In the context of the unprecedented explosion of knowledge, higher education has to become dynamic as never before, constantly entering uncharted areas.

5.26 There are around 150 universities and about 5,000 colleges in India today. In view of the need to effect an all-round improvement in these institutions, it is proposed that, in the near future, the main emphasis will be on the consolidation of and expansion of facilities in existing institutions.

5.27 Urgent steps will be taken to protect the system from degradation.

5.28 In view of mixed experiences with the system of affiliation, autonomous colleges will be helped to develop in large numbers until the affiliating system is replaced by a freer and more creative association of universities with colleges. Similarly, the creation of autonomous departments, within universities on a selective basis will be encouraged. Autonomy and freedom will be accompanied by accountability.

5.29 Courses and programmes will be redesigned to meet the demands of specialisation better. Special emphasis will be laid on linguistic competence. There will be increasing flexibility in the combination of courses.

5.30 State level planning and coordination of higher education will be done through Councils of Higher Education. The UGC and these Councils will develop coordinative methods to keep a watch on standards.

5.31 Provision will be made for minimum facilities and admission will be regulated according to capacity. A major effort will be directed towards the transformation of teaching methods. Audio-visual aids and electronic equipment will be introduced; development of science and technology, curricula and material, research and teacher orientation will receive attention. This will require preparation of teachers at the beginning of the service as well as continuing education thereafter. Teacher's performance will be assessed systematically. All posts will be filled on the basis of merit.

5.32 Research in the universities will be provided enhanced support and steps will be taken to ensure its high quality. Suitable mechanisms will be set up by the UGC for coordinating research in the universities, particularly in thrust areas of science and technology, with research undertaken by other agencies. An effort will be made to encourage the setting up of national research facilities within the university system, with proper forms of autonomous management.

5.33 (**Revised Para**) *Research in Indology, the humanities and social sciences will receive adequate support. To fulfil the need for the synthesis of knowledge, inter-disciplinary research will be encouraged. Efforts will be made to delve into India's ancient fund of knowledge and to relate it to contemporary reality. This effort will imply the development of facilities for the intensive study of Sanskrit and other Classical languages. An autonomous commission will be established to foster and improve teaching study and research in Sanskrit and other Classical languages.*

5.33 (**NPE, 1986**) Research in Indology, the humanities and social sciences will receive adequate support. To fulfil the need for the synthesis of knowledge, inter-disciplinary research will be encouraged. Efforts will be made to delve into India's ancient fund of knowledge and to relate it to contemporary reality. This effort will imply the development facilities for the intensive study of Sanskrit and other Classical languages.

5.34 In the interest of greater coordination and consistency in policy, sharing of facilities and developing inter-disciplinary research, a national body covering higher education in general, agricultural medical, technical, legal and other professional fields will be set up.

5.35 (**Revised Para**) *The open learning system has been initiated in order to augment opportunities for higher education, as an instrument of democratising education and to make it a lifelong process. The flexibility and innovativeness of the open learning system are particularly suited to the diverse requirements of the citizens of our country, including those who had joined the vocational stream.*

5.35 (**NPE, 1986**) The Open University system has been initiated in order to augment opportunities for higher education and as an instrument of democratising education.

5.36 (**Revised Para**) *The Indira Gandhi National Open University, established in 1985 in fulfilment of these objectives, will be strengthened. It would also provide support to establishment of open universities in the States.*

5.36 (**NPE, 1986**) The Indira Gandhi National Open University, established in 1985 in fulfilment of these objectives, will be strengthened.

5.37 (**Revised Para**) *The National Open School will be strengthened and open learning facilities extended in a phased manner at the secondary level in all parts of the country.*

5.37 (**NPE, 1986**) This powerful instrument will have to be developed with care and extended with caution.

De-linking Degrees from Jobs

5.38 A beginning will be made in de-linking degrees from jobs in selected areas.

5.39 The proposal cannot be applied to occupation – specific courses like Engineering, Medicine, Law, Teaching, etc. Similarly, the services of specialists with academic qualifications in the humanities, social sciences, sciences, etc. will continue to be required in various jobs positions.

5.40 The de-linking will be applied to services for which university degree need not be a necessary qualification. Its implementation will lead to a re-fashioning of job-specific courses and afford greater justice to those candidates who, despite being equipped for a given job, are unable to get it because of an unnecessary preference for graduate candidates.

5.41 (Revised Para) *Concomitant with de-linking an appropriate machinery, such as a National Testing Service, will be established, in appropriate phases, to conduct tests on a voluntary basis to determine the suitability of candidates for specified jobs, and to pave the way for the emergence of norms of comparable competence across the nation.*

PART VI

TECHNICAL AND MANAGEMENT EDUCATION

6.1 It is essential to look at technical and management education together, in view of their close relationship and complementary concerns. The reorganisation of Technical and Management Education should take into account the anticipated scenario by the turn of the century, with specific reference to the likely changes in the economy, social environment, production and management process, the rapid expansion of knowledge and the great advances in science and technology.

6.2 The infrastructure and services sectors as well as the unorganised rural sector also need a greater introduction of improved technologies and a supply of technical and managerial manpower. This will be attended to by the Government.

6.3 In order to improve the situation regarding manpower information, the recently set up Technical Manpower Information System will be further developed and strengthened.

6.4 Continuing education, covering established as well as emerging technologies, will be promoted.

6.5 As computers have become important and ubiquitous tools, a minimal exposure to computers and a training in their use will form part of professional education. Programmes of computer literacy will be organised on a wide scale from the school stage.

6.6 In view of the present rigid entry requirements to formal courses restricting the access of a large segment of people to technical and managerial education, programmes through a distance learning process, including use of the mass media, will be offered. Technical and management education programmes, including polytechnics, will also be on a flexible modular pattern based on credits, with provision for multipoint entry. A strong guidance and counselling service will be provided.

6.7 In order to increase the relevance of management education, particularly in the non-corporate and under-managed sectors, the management education system will study and document the Indian-experience and create a body of knowledge and specific educational programmes suited to these sectors.

6.8 Appropriate formal and non-formal programmes of technical education relevant to their skills will be devised for the benefit of women, the economically and socially weaker sections, and the physically handicapped.

6.9 The emphasis on vocational education and its expansion will need a large number of teachers and professionals in vocational education, educational technology, curriculum development, etc. Programmes will be started to meet this demand.

6.10 To encourage students to consider 'self-employment' as a career option, training in entrepreneurship will be provided through modular or optional course, in degree or diploma programmes.

6.11 In order to meet the continuing needs of updating curriculum, renewal should systematically phase out obsolescence and introduce new technologies or disciplines.

6.12 (**Revised Para**) *Some polytechnics in the rural areas have started training weaker groups in those areas for productive occupations through a system of community polytechnics. The community polytechnic system will be appropriately strengthened to increase its quality and coverage.*

6.12 (**NPE, 1986**) Some polytechnics in the rural areas have started training weaker groups in those areas for productive occupations through a system of community polytechnics. The community polytechnic system will be appraised and and appropriately strengthened to increase its quality and coverage.

Innovation, Research and Development

6.13 Research as a means of renovation and renewal of educational processes will be undertaken by all higher technical institutions. It will primarily aim at producing quality manpower will focus on improving present technologies, developing new indigenous ones and enhancing production and productivity. A suitable system for watching and forecasting technology will be set up.

6.14 The scope for cooperation, collaboration and networking relationships between institutions at various levels and with the user systems will be utilised. Proper maintenance, and an attitude of innovation and improvement will be promoted systematically.

Promoting Efficiency and Effectiveness at all Levels

6.15 As technical and management education is expensive, the following major steps will be taken for cost-effectiveness and to promote excellence:

(i) High priority will be given to modernisation and removal of obsolescence. However, modernisation will be undertaken to enhance functional efficiency and not for its own sake or as a status symbol;

(ii) Institutions will be encouraged to generate resources using their capacities to provide services to the community and industry. They will be equipped with up-to-date learning resources, library and computer facilities;

(iii) Adequate hostel accommodation will be provided, specially for girls. Facilities for sports, creative work and cultural activities will be expanded;

(iv) More effective procedures will be adopted in the recruitment of staff. Career opportunities, service conditions, consultancy norms and other perquisites will be improved;

(v) Teachers will have multiple roles to perform: teaching, research and development of learning resource material, extension and administration or managing the institution. Initial and in-service training will be made mandatory for faculty members and adequate training reserves will be provided. Staff Development Programmes will be integrated at the State and coordinated at Regional and National levels;

(vi) The curricula of technical and management programmes will be targetted on current as well as the projected needs of industry or user systems. Active interaction between technical or management institutions and industry will be promoted in programme planning and implementation, exchange of personnel, training facilities and resources, research and consultancy and other areas of mutual interest;

(vii) Excellence in performance of institutions and individuals will be recognised and rewarded. The emergence of substandard institutions will be checked. A climate conducive to excellence will be checked. A climate conducive to excellence will be promoted with full involvement of the faculty;

(viii) Select institutions will be awarded academic, administrative and financial autonomy of varying degrees, building in safeguards with respect to accountability; and

(ix) Networking systems will have to be established between technical education and industry, R&D organisations, programmes of rural and community development and with sectors of education with complementary characteristics.

Management Function and Change

6.16 In view of the likely emergence of changes in management systems and the need to equip students with the ability to cope with them, effective mechanisms will be devised to understand the nature and direction of change per se and to develop the important skill of managing change.

6.17 In view of the integrated nature of task, the Ministry of Human Resource Development will coordinate the balanced development of engineering, vocational and management education as well as the education of technicians and craftsmen.

6.18 Professional societies will be encouraged and enabled to perform their due role in the advancement of technical and management education.

6.19 (**Revised Para**) *The All India Council for Technical Education, which has been given statutory status, will be responsible for planning, formulation and the maintenance of norms and standards, accreditation, funding of priority areas, monitoring and evaluation, maintaining parity of certification and awards and ensuring the coordinated and integrated development of technical and management education. Mandatory periodic evaluation will be carried out by a duly constituted Accreditation Board. The Council will be strengthened and it will function in a decentralised manner with greater involvement of State governments and technical institutions of good quality.*

6.19 (**NPE, 1986**) The All India Council for Technical Education will be vested with statutory authority for planning, formulation and the maintenance of norms and standards, accreditation, funding of priority areas, monitoring and evaluation, maintaining parity of certification and awards and ensuring the coordinated and integrated development of technical and management education. Mandatory periodic evaluation will be carried out by a duly constituted Accreditation Board.

6.20 In the interests of maintaining standards and for several other valid reasons, the commercialisation of technical and professional education will be curbed. An alternative system will be devised to involve private and voluntary effort in this sector of education, in conformity with accepted norms and goals.

PART VII

MAKING THE SYSTEM WORK

7.1 It is obvious that these and many other new tasks of education cannot be performed in a state of disorder. Education needs to be managed in an atmosphere of utmost intellectual rigour, seriousness of purpose and, at the same time, of freedom essential for innovation and creativity. While far-reaching changes will have to be incorporated in the quality and range of education, the process of introducing discipline into system will have to be started, here and now, in what exists.

7.2 The country has placed a boundless trust in the educational system. The people have a right to expect concrete results. The first task is to make it work. *All teachers should teach and all students study.*

7.3 The strategy in this behalf will consist of:

(a) a better deal to teachers with greater accountability;
(b) provision of improved student's services and insistence on observance of acceptable norms of behaviour;
(c) provision of better facilities to institutions; and
(d) creation of a system of performance appraisals of institutions according to standards and norms set at the National or State levels.

PART VIII

REORIENTING THE CONTENT AND PROCESS OF EDUCATION

The Cultural Perspective

8.1 The existing schism between the formal system of education and the country's rich and varied cultural traditions needs to be bridged. The preoccupation with modern technologies cannot be allowed to sever new generations from the roots in India's history and culture. De-culturisation, de-humanisation and alienation must be avoided at all costs. Education can and must bring about the fine synthesis between change-oriented technologies and the country's continuity of cultural traditions.

8.2 The curricula and processes of education will be enriched by cultural content in as many manifestations as possible. Children will be enabled to develop sensitivity to beauty, harmony and refinement. Resource persons in the community, irrespective of their formal educational qualifications, will be invited to contribute to the cultural enrichment of education, employing both the literate and oral traditions of communication. To sustain and carry forward the cultural tradition, the role of old masters, who train pupils through traditional modes will be supported and recognised.

8.3 Linkages will be established between the university system and institutions of higher learning in art, archaeology, oriental studies etc. Due attention will also be paid to the specialised disciplines of Fine Arts, Musicology, Folklore etc. Teaching, training and research in these disciplines will be strengthened so as to replenish specialised manpower in them.

Value Education

8.4 The growing concern over the erosion of essential values and an increasing cynicism in society has brought to focus the need for readjustments in the curriculum in order to make education a forceful tool for the cultivation of social and moral values.

8.5 In our culturally plural society education should foster universal and eternal values, oriented towards the unity and integration of our people. Such value education should help, eliminate obscurantism, religious fanaticism, violence, superstition and fatalism.

8.6 Apart from this combative role, value education has a profound positive content, based on our heritage, national goals and universal perceptions. It should lay primary emphasis on this aspect.

Languages

8.7 The Education Policy of 1968 had examined the question of the development of languages in great details; its essential provisions can hardly be improved upon and are as relevant today as before. The implementation of this part of the 1968 Policy has, however, been uneven. The Policy will be implemented more energetically and purposefully.

Books and Libraries

8.8 The availability of books at low prices is indispensable for a people's education. Efforts will be made to secure easy accessibility to books for all segments of the population. Measures will be taken to improve the quality of books, promote the reading habit and encourage creative writing. Author's interests will be protected. Good translations of foreign books into Indian languages will be supported. Special attention will be paid to the production of quality books for children, including textbooks and workbooks.

8.9 Together with the development of books, a nationwide movement for the improvement of existing libraries and the establishment of new ones will be taken up. Provision will be made in all educational institutions for library facilities and the status of librarians improved.

Media and Educational Technology

8.10 Modern communication technologies have the potential to bypass several stages and sequences in the process of development encountered in early decades. Both the constraints of time and distance at once become manageable. In order to avoid structural dualism, modern educational technology must reach out to the most distant areas and the most deprived sections of beneficiaries simultaneously with the areas of comparative affluence and ready availability.

8.11 Educational technology will be employed in the spread of useful information, the training and retraining of teachers, to improve quality, sharpen awareness of art and culture, inculcated abiding values, etc., both in the formal and non-formal sectors. Maximum use will be made of the available infrastructure. In villages without electricity, batteries or solar packs will be used to run the programme.

8.12 The generation of relevant and culturally compatible educational programmes will form an important component of educational technology, and all available resources in the country will be utilised for this purpose.

8.13 The media has profound influence on the minds of children as well as adults; some of it had encouraged consumerism, violence etc., and thus had a deleterious effect. Radio and TV, programmes which clearly militate against proper educational objectives will be prevented. Steps will be taken to discourage such trend in the films and other media also. An active movement will be started to promote the production of children's films of high quality and usefulness.

Work Experience

8.14 Work experience, viewed as purposive and meaningful manual work, organised as an integral part of the learning process and resulting in either goods or services useful to the community, is considered as an essential component at all stages of education, to be provided through well-structured and graded programmes. It would comprise activities in accord with the interests, abilities and needs of students, the level of skills and knowledge to be upgraded with the stages of education. This experience would be helpful on his entry into the workforce. Prevocational programmes provided at the lower secondary stage will also facilitate the choice of the vocational courses at the higher secondary stage.

Education and Environment

8.15 There is a paramount need to create a consciousness of the environment. It must permeate all ages and all sections of society, beginning with the child. Environmental consciousness should inform teaching in schools and colleges. This aspect will be integrated in the entire educational process.

Population Education

8.16 (**Revised Para**) *Population education must be viewed as an important part of the nation's strategy to contain the growth of population. Starting at the primary and secondary levels with inculcation of consciousness about the looming crisis due to expansion of population, educational programmes should actively motivate and inform youth and adults about family planning and responsible parenthood.*

8.17 (**Revised Para**) *Mathematics should be visualised as the vehicle to train a child to think, reason, analyse, and to articulate logically. Apart from being a specific subject, it should be created as a concomitant to any subject involving analysis and reasoning. With the recent introduction of computers in schools, education computing and the emergence of learning through the understanding of cause-effect relationships and the interplay of variables, the teaching of mathematics will be suitably redesigned to bring it in line with modern technological devices.*

Mathematical Teaching

8.16 (**NPE, 1986**) Mathematics should be visualised as the vehicle to train a child to think, reason, analyse and to articulate logically. Apart from being a specific subject, it should be treated as a concomitant to any subject involving analysis and reasoning.

8.17 (**NPE, 1986**) With the recent introduction of computers in schools, educational computing and the emergence of learning through the understanding of cause-effect relationships and the interplay of variables, the teaching of mathematics will be suitably redesigned to bring it in line with modern technological devices.

Science Education

8.18 Science education will be strengthened so as to develop in the child well defined abilities and values such as the spirit of inquiry, creativity, objectivity, the courage to question, and an aesthetic sensibility.

8.19 Science education programmes will be designed to enable the learner to acquire problem solving and decision-making skills and to discover the relationship of science with health, agriculture, industry and other aspects of daily life. Every effort will·be made remained outside the pale of formal education.

Sports and Physical Education

8.20 (Revised Para) *Sports and physical education are an integral part of the learning process, and will be included in the evaluation of performance. A nationwide infrastructure for physical education, sports and games will be built into the educational edifice. The infrastructure will consist of playfields, equipment, coaches and teachers of physical education as part of the School Improvement Programme. Available open spaces in urban areas will be reserved for playgrounds, if necessary by legislation. Efforts will be made to establish sports institutions and hostels where specialised attention will be given to sports activities and sports-related studies, along with normal education. Appropriate encouragement will be given to those talented in sports and games. Due stress will be laid on indigenous traditional games.*

8.20 (NPE, 1986) Sports and physical education are an integral part of the learning process, and will be included in the evaluation of performance. A nation-wide infrastructure for physical education, sports and games will be built into the educational edifice.

Yoga

8.21 (Revised Para) *As a system which promotes an integrated development of body and mind, Yoga will receive special attention. Efforts will be made to introduce Yoga in all schools. To this end, it will be introduced in teacher training courses.*

8.21 (NPE, 1986) The infrastructure will consist of playfields, equipment, coaches and teachers of physical education as part of the School Improvement Programme. Available open spaces in urban areas will be reserved for playgrounds, if necessary by legislation. Efforts will be made to establish sports institutions and hostels where specialised attention will be given to sports activities and sports-related studies, along with normal education. Appropriate encouragement will be given to those talented in sports and games. Due stress will be laid on indigenous traditional games. As a system, which promotes integrated development of body and mind, Yoga will receive special attention. Efforts will be made to introduce Yoga in all schools; to this end, it will be introduced in teacher training courses.

The Role of Youth

8.22 Opportunities will be provided for the youth to involve themselves in national and social development through educational institutions and outside them. Students will be required to participate in one or the other of existing schemes, namely, the National Service Scheme, National Cadet Corps, etc. Outside the institutions, the youth will be encouraged to take up programmes of development, reform and extension. The National Service Volunteer Scheme will be strengthened.

The Evaluation Process and Examination Reform

8.23 Assessment of performance is an integral part of any process of learning and teaching. As part of sound educational strategy, examinations should be employed to bring about qualitative improvement in education.

8.24 The objective will be to re-cast the examination system so as to ensure a method of assessment that is a valid and reliable measure of student development and a powerful instrument for improving teaching and learning. In functional terms, this would mean:

(i) The elimination of excessive element of chance and subjectivity;
(ii) The de-emphasis of memorisation;
(iii) Continuous and comprehensive evaluation that incorporates both scholastic and non-scholastic aspects of education, spread over the total span of instructional times;
(iv) Effective use of evaluation process by teachers, students and parents;
(v) Improvement in the conduct of examinations;
(vi) The introduction of concomitant changes in introductional material and methodology;

(vii) The introduction of the semester system from the secondary stage in a phased manner; and

(viii) The use of grades in place of marks.

8.25 (**Revised Para**) *The above goals are relevant both for external examinations and evaluations within educational institutions. Evaluation at the institutional level will be streamlined and the predominance of external examinations reduced. A National Examination Reform Framework would be prepared to serve as a set of guidelines to the examining bodies which would have the freedom to innovate and adapt the framework to suit the specific situations.*

8.25 (**NPE, 1986**) The above goals are relevant both for external examinations and evaluations within educational institutions. Evaluation at the institutional level will be streamlined and the predominance of external examinations reduced.

PART IX

THE TEACHER

9.1 The status of the teacher reflects the socio-cultural ethos of a society; it is said that no people can rise above the level of its teachers. The Government and the community should endeavour to create conditions which will help motivate and inspire teachers on constructive and creative lines. Teacher should have the freedom to innovate, to devise appropriate methods of communication and activities relevant to the needs and capabilities of and the concerns of the community.

9.2 The methods of recruiting teachers will be reorganised to ensure merit, objectivity and conformity with spatial and functional requirements. The pay and service conditions of teachers have to be commensurate with their social and professional responsibilities and with the need to attract talent to the profession. Efforts will be made to reach the desirable objective of uniform emoluments, service conditions and grievance-removal mechanisms for teachers throughout the country. Guidelines will be formulated to ensure objectivity in the postings and transfers of teachers. A system of teacher evaluation — open, participative and data-based-will be created and reasonable opportunities of promotion to higher grades provided. Norms of accountability will be laid down with incentives for good performance and disincentives for non-performance. Teachers will continue to play a crucial role in the formulation and implementation of educational programmes.

9.3 Teachers' associations must play a significant role in upholding professional integrity and enhancing the dignity of teachers in curbing professional misconduct. National level associations of teachers could prepare a National Code of Professional Ethics for Teachers and see to its observance.

Teacher Education

9.4 Teacher education is a continuous process and its pre-service and in-service components are inseparable. As the first step, the system of teacher education will be overhauled.

9.5 The new programmes of teacher-education will emphasise continuing education and the need for teachers to meet the thrusts envisaged in this Policy.

9.6 District Institutes of Education and Training (DIET) will be established with the capability to organise pre-service and in-service course for elementary school teachers and for the personnel working in non-formal and adult education. As DIETs get established, sub-standard institutions will be phased out. Selected Secondary Teacher Training Colleges will be upgraded to complement the work of State Council of Educational Research and Training. The National Council of Teacher Education will be provided the necessary resources and capability to accredit institutions of teacher-education and provide guidance regarding curricula and methods. Networking arrangements will be created between institutions of teacher education and university department of education.

PART X

THE MANAGEMENT OF EDUCATION

10.1 An overhaul of the system of planning and the management of education will receive high priority. The guiding considerations will be:

(a) Evolving a long-term planning and management perspective of education and its integration with the country's developmental and manpower needs;

(b) Decentralisation and the creation of a spirit of autonomy for educational institutions;
(c) Giving pre-eminence to people's involvement, including association of non-government agencies and voluntary effort;
(d) Inducting more women in the planning and management of education; and
(e) Establishing the principle of accountability in relation to given objectives and norms.

National Level

10.2 The Central Advisory Board of Education will play a pivotal role in reviewing educational development, determining the changes required to improve the system and monitoring implementation. It will function through appropriate Committees and other mechanisms created to ensure contact with, and coordination among the areas of Human Resource Development. The Departments of Education at the Centre and in the States will be strengthened through the involvement of professionals.

Indian Education Service

10.3 A proper management structure in education will entail the establishment of the Indian Education Service as an All-India Service. It will bring a national perspective to this vital sector. The basic principles, functions and procedures of recruitment to this service will be decided in consultation with the State Governments.

State Level

10.4 State Governments may, establish State Advisory Boards of Education on the lines of CABE. Effective measures should be taken to integrate mechanisms in the various State departments concerned with Human Resource Development.

10.5 Special attention will be paid to the training of educational planners, administrators and heads of institutions. Institutional arrangements for this purpose should be set up.

District and Local Level

10.6 District Boards of Education will be created to manage education up to the higher secondary level. State Governments will attend to this aspect with all possible expedition. Within a multi-level framework of educational development, Central, State, District and Local level agencies will participate in planning, coordination, monitoring and evaluation.

10.7 A very important role must be assigned to the head of an educational institution. Heads will be specially selected and trained. School complexes will be promoted on a flexible pattern so as to serve as networks of institutions and synergic alliances to encourage professionalism among teachers, to ensure observance of norms of conduct and to enable the sharing of experiences and facilities. It is expected that a developed system of school complexes will take over much of the inspection functions in due course.

10.8 Local communities, through appropriate bodies, will be assigned a major role in programmes of school improvement.

Voluntary Agencies and Aided Institutions

10.9 Non-Government and voluntary effort including social activist groups will be encouraged, subject to proper management, and financial assistance provided. At the same time, steps will be taken to prevent the establishment of institutions set up to commercialise education.

Redress of Grievances

10.10 *Educational tribunals, fashioned after Administrative Tribunals, will be established at the national and state levels.*

PART XI

RESOURCES AND REVIEW

11.1 The Educational Commission of 1964-66, the National Educational Policy of 1968 and practically all others concerned with education have stressed that the egalitarian goals and the practical development-oriented objectives of Indian society can only be realised by making investments in education of an order commensurate with the nature and dimensions of the task.

11.2 Resources, to the extent possible, will be raised by mobilising donation, asking the beneficiary communities to maintain school building and supplies of some consumables, raising fees at the higher levels of education and effecting some savings by the efficient use of facilities. Institutions involved with research and the development of technical and scientific manpower should also mobilize some funds by levying a cess or charge on the user agencies, including Government departments, and entrepreneurs. All these measures will be taken not only to reduce the burden on State resources but also for creating a greater sense of responsibility with the educational system. However, such measures will contribute only marginally to the total funding. The Government and the community in general will find funds for such programmes as: the universalisation of elementary education; liquidating illiteracy; equality of access to educational opportunities to all sections throughout the country; enhancing the social relevance, quality and functional effectiveness, of educational programmes; generating knowledge and developing technologies in scientific fields crucial to self-sustaining economic development; and creating a critical consciousness of the values and imperatives of national survival.

11.3 The deleterious consequences of non-investment or inadequate investment in education are indeed very serious. Similarly, the cost of neglecting vocational and technical education and of research is also unacceptable. Sub-optimal performance in these fields could cause irreparable damage to the Indian economy. The network of institutions set up from time to time since Independence to facilitate the application of science and technology would need to be substantially and expeditiously updated, since they are fast becoming obsolete.

11.4 (**Revised Para**) *In view of these imperatives, education will be treated as a crucial area of investment for national development and survival. The National Policy on Education, 1968, had laid down that the investment on education be gradually increased to reach a level of 6 per cent of the national income as early as possible. Since the actual level of investment has remained far short of that target, it is important that greater determination is shown now to find the funds for the programmes laid down in this Policy. While the actual requirements will be computed from time to time on the basis of monitoring and review, the outlay will be stepped up to ensure that during the Eighth Five Year Plan and onwards it will uniformly exceed 6 per cent of the national income.*

11.4 (**NPE, 1986**) In view of these imperatives, education will be treated as a crucial area of investment for national development and survival. The National Policy on Education, 1968, had laid down that the investment on education be gradually increased to reach a level of expenditure of 6 per cent of the national income as early as possible. Since the actual level of investment has remained far short of that target, it is an important that greater determination be shown now to find the funds for the programmes laid down in this policy. While the actual requirements will be computed from time to time on the basis of monitoring and review, the outlay on education will be stepped up to the extent essential for policy implementation in the Seventh Plan. It will be ensured that from the Eighth Five Year Plan onwards it will uniformly exceed 6 per cent of the National Income.

Review

11.5 The implementation and parameters of the New Policy must be reviewed every five years. Appraisals of short intervals will also be made to ascertain the progress of implementation and the trends emerging from time to time.

PART XII

THE FUTURE

12.1 The future shape of education in India is too complex to envision with precision. Yet, given our tradition which has almost always put a high premium on intellectual and spiritual attainment, we are bound to succeed in achieving our objectives.

12.2 The main task is to strengthen the base of the pyramid, which might touch a billion people at the turn of the century. Equally, it is important to ensure that those at the top of the pyramid are among the best in the world. Our cultural well-springs had taken good care of both ends in the past; the skew set in with foreign domination and influence. It should now be possible to further intensify the nationwide effort in Human Resource Development, with education playing its multi-faceted role.

6

PROGRAMME OF ACTION ON NPE (1992)*

Introduction

The Revised Policy Formulations (RPF) which set forth the modifications to the National Policy on Education, 1986 (NPE, 1986), were placed in both Houes of Parliament on 7th May, 1992. These modifications were evolved through the same consensual process through which the NPE, 1986 was evolved. In July 1991, a Central Advisory Board of Education (CABE) Committee on Policy (Janardhana Reddy Committee) under the chairmanship of the Chief Minister of Andhra Pradesh, and comprising six other Education Ministers belonging to the major political parties and eight educationists, was constituted to review the implementation of the various parameters of the NPE, 1986, taking into consideration the report of the Committee for Review of the NPE (NPERC) and other relevant development since the Policy was formulated. The Janardhan Reddy Committee (JRC), in its report submitted in January, 1992, came to the conclusion that while very little of the NPE, 1986 required reformulation the Programme of Action (PoA) needed to be revised considerably. At its 47th meeting held on 5-6th May, 1992, the CABE, the historic forum for forging a national consensus on educational issues, considered the JRC report and formulated the RPF. While replying to the discussion on the RPF in the Rajya Sabha, on 12th May, 1992, the Minister of Human Resource Development gave an assurance to present a revised PoA (hereafter referred to as PoA, 1992) in the Monsoon Session.

The PoA, 1992 was evolved through the same consensual process through which the Policy was reviewed. Twenty-two task forces were constituted on different subject areas comprising educationists and

* Broughtout by Department of Education, Ministry of Human Resource Development, Government of India, New Delhi, 1992.

officials of the Union and State Governments. A Steering Committee was also set up. In spite of the time constraint, the Task Forces and the Steering Committee accomplished their work with great care.

The draft Programme of Action was discussed at a Conference of State Secretaries and Directors of Education, held on 3-4 August, 1992. Suggestions received during this meeting were carefully considered and incorporated in the document. The Central Advisory Board of Education (CABE) met on 8th August, 1992 and endorsed the document after detailed consideration. The valuable suggestions made by the State Education Ministers and educationists were also taken into account in finalizing this document.

The Policy review had established that the policy framework of the NPE, 1986 enunciated is robust and can guide the educational development of the country for a long time to come. Likewise, many of the strategies outlined in PoA continue to be relevant and should be acted upon. There are, however, many exceptions, the best example of which is adult literacy. The Total Literacy Campaign approach is a post-PoA innovation which has emerged as a viable model and has transformed the perception of universal adult literacy from one of the hopeless dreams to an achievable prospect. The wisdom of hindsight as well as the evaluation of major programmes launched after the PoA, and the recommendations of NPERC and JRC facilitated the revision. The constant endeavour of the Task Forces and the Steering Committee was to make the PoA, 1992 more practical and action-oriented.

The NPE, 1986 has the distinction of giving an operational meaning to concurrency. Given that Education is a concurrent subject, the PoA, 1992 can be implemented only if the Union and the States/Union Territories (UTs) work together in meaningful partnership. The PoA, 1992 has to be perceived as a charter for action of the nation as a whole requiring a co-operative effort of the Union, States/UTs, the education community and the community at large. Given the rich diversity of our continental nation it would be in the fitness of things if each State and UT formulates a State PoA which is in line with the situational imperative as well as within the PoA, 1992. This process has to be carried to its logical conclusion with each district and educational institution formulating a PoA of its own. In this context it is necessary to stress that what is presented here is not an inflexible structure but only a projection of the direction with varying degrees of detail. A certain amount of flexibility is assumed which will help the implementing agencies in tailoring the PoA, 1992 to suit their contexts and emerging scenarios.

In the ultimate, resources and management would define implementation. In developing this document the resource availability indicated for the Eighth Five Year Plan (1992-97) was kept at the back of the mind; but at the same time the long-term perspective has not been lost sight of. Many actions envisaged by the PoA, 1992 span not only the Eighth Five Year Plan but also the 9th and even beyond. Phasing has, therefore, to be left somewhat flexible so that the pace of implementation can match the mobilisation of resources.

The national resolve of raising the outlay on education to 6 per cent of the national income should be translated into practice at the earliest possible. As envisaged by the NPE, 1986 and through the modalities it outlined, the nation as whole, should assume responsibility of providing the resource support for education. The logical corollary of this proposition is that an ethos of cost-effectiveness and accountability should permeate every part of the education system. To say the least, unplanned proliferation of sub-standard institutions should stop here and now; programmes should cease to be driven by budgets and instead should stress processes and outcomes; efficiency should be rated not by the ability to consume budget and demand more but by performance and delivery. All this calls for extraordinary attention to the management of education which is often neglected. It is obvious that the many tasks which the NPE, 1986 and PoA, 1992 envisage cannot be performed in a state when even routine tasks like supply of textbooks, conduct of examinations and operation of academic calendar leave much to be desired. Reform of management in its entirety should be the first and foremost task of the education community.

While the Union and State Governments will fully shoulder these responsibilities it is people's involvement in the educational reconstruction which will make the real difference. The total literacy campaigns have demonstrated that, given the will, and the right strategy and appropriate structures, people's involvement can be elicited on a large scale. The management challenge in education lies in creating appropriate arrangements for a similar involvement to take on long-standing problems like the Universalisation of Elementary Education (UEE). There is no better way to ensure accountability than an awakened and "demanding" community.

Another important challenge is establishing linkages between education and other related services like child care, nutrition and health. As it is, the responsibility for educational administration is fragmented in most States, with more than one Education Secretary and several Directors of Education. There is need for greater coordination amongst these multiple agencies and functionaries on the one hand and between Education and other areas of HRD on the other. Appropriate mechanisms should be developed.

Education for Women's Equality is a vital component of the overall strategy of securing equity and social justice in education. Paras 4.2 and 4.3 of the National Policy on Education (NPE), 1986 are very strong and forthright statements on the interventionist and empowering role of education. What comes out clearly from the implementation of NPE, 1986 and its PoA, is the need for institutional mechanisms to ensure that gender sensitivity is reflected in the implementation of all educational programmes across the board. It is being increasingly recognised that the problem of UEE, is in essence, the problem of the girl child. It is imperative that participation of girls is enhanced at all stages of education, particularly in streams like science, vocational, technical and commerce education where girls are grossly under-represented. The education system as a whole should be re-oriented to promote women's equality and education.

Another facet of the overall strategy of securing equity and social justice in education is the concern for the educational needs of SCs/STs, minorities and the physically and mentally handicapped. Here again it is necessary for educational system to be sensitive to the educational needs of these groups; it should be geared up to promote equalisation of educational opportunities.

The formulations on management outlined in this document cover not only structures but also processes. Many of the structures envisaged like the State Advisory Boards of Education (SABEs), District Boards of Education, Village Education Committees (VECs), are participative in nature and facilitate greater coordination between education and support services. The processes envisaged include planning, training, and monitoring and evaluation. Experience since 1987 has established the need for the monitoring arrangement being strengthened and being supplemented by periodic impact studies. The formulations in PoA, 1992 should be implemented with vigour and determination, with adaptation which may be necessary to suit specific situation.

More than ever, there is an increasing awareness about national integration and adherence to certain national values and concerns; observance of secular, scientific and moral values; inculcation of an understanding of our composite culture, with its rich diversity, of our history, the history of freedom struggle and of the achievements of independent India; creation of an awareness of the importance of protection of environment and observance of small family norm; and stress on commitment of youth to manual work and social service. While these aspects have received due attention in the past, further reorganisation of the content and process of education on these lines would be a matter of foremost priority.

Time is of essence, and unless we act now we stand in the danger of once again missing the opportunity of educational reform, so critical not only for the development of our nation but for our very survival.

Recommendations

The PoA's recommendations cover the following areas :

1. Education for Women's Equality
2. Education of SCs and STs and other Backward classes
3. Minorities' Education
4. Education of the Handicapped
5. Adult and Continuing Education
6. Early Childhood Care and Education
7. Elementary Education
8. Secondary Education
9. Navodaya Vidalayas
10. Vocational Education
11. Higher Education
12. Open Education
13. Delinking Degrees from Jobs and Manower Planning
14. Rural Universities and Institutes
15. Technical and Mangement Education
16. Research and Development
17. The Cultural Perspective
18. Development of Languages
19. Media and Educational Technology
20. Sports, Physical Education and Youth
21. Evaluation Process and Examination Reforms
22. Teachers and Their Training
23. Management of Education

Education for Women's Equality

Policy Parameters and Strategies

In pursuance of NPE the main features of the implementation strategy will consist of the following:

(i) to gear the entire education system to play a positive interventionist role in the empowerment of women;
(ii) to encourage educational institutions to take up active programme to enhance women's status and further women's development in all sectors;
(iii) to widen women's access to vocational, technical and professional education at all levels, breaking gender stereotypes; and
(iv) to create a dynamic management structure that will be able to respond to the challenge posed by this mandate.

Plan of Action (PoA)

Strategies outlined below deal primarily with operational details regarding implementation of the PoA:

(i) All the Bureaus of the Department of Education will prepare a concrete action plan addressing gender related concerns in their specific area of work by August 1993. Relevant nodal institutions like the UGC, AICTE, ICSSR, ICHR, CBSE, ICAR, ICMR, IAMR, State Boards, Vocational Education Bureaus etc. will also prepare similar action plans. Part IV, Paras 4.1 to 4.3 of the NPE and Chapter XII of PoA will form the guiding principles for the action plan;
(ii) A monitoring unit will be created in the Planning Division of the Department of Education to ensure integration of gender issues into policies programmes and schemes. This unit will develop indicators for monitoring implementation, ensure effective dissemination of information and coordinate action. This will be done by August 1993;
(iii) Similar monitoring units/bureaus will be set up at the State level;
(iv) Annual reports of all the bureaus and institutions will clearly spell out the steps they have taken to enhance women's and

girls' access to education, ensuring that the content and process of education is sensitive to gender concerns and equal access is assured for science and technical education at all levels.

Empowerment of Women

Education can be an effective tool for women's empowerment, the parameters of which are:

– enhancing self-esteem and self confidence of women;
– building a positive image of women by recognizing their contribution to the society, polity and the economy;
– developing ability to think critically;
– fostering decision-making and action through collective processes;
– enabling women to make informed choices in areas like education, employment and health (especially reproductive health);
– ensuring equal participation in development processes;
– providing information, knowledge and skill for economic independence; and
– enhancing access to legal literacy and information relating to their rights and entitlements in society with a view to enhance their participation on an equal footing in all areas.

The following measures will be taken for achievement of the above parameters and the concerned bureaus and institutions will report on progress as stated in Para 2 of the report:

(i) Every educational institution will take up active programmes of women's development;
(ii) All teachers and instructors will be trained as agents of women's empowerment. Training programmes will be developed by NCERT, NIEPA, DAE, SRCs, DIETs, SCERTs and the University System. Innovative training programmes will be designed with the assistance of concerned organizations and women's groups;
(iii) Gender and poverty sensitization programmes will be developed for teacher educators and administrators. An environment will be created whereby all the sections of the education sector will become alive and sensitive to the role of educa-

tion in eliminating gender disparities; and

(iv) In order to create a greater confidence and to motivate parents to send girls to school, preference will be given to recruitment of women teachers.

Education of Scheduled Castes and Scheduled Tribes and other Backward Sections

Centrally Sponsored Schemes

A number of schemes are for the SCs, STs and other Backward sections. These are (i) Post Matric Scholarship; (ii) Grant-in-aid to voluntary organisations; (iii) Pre-matric scholarships; (iv) Book banks; (v) Boys' and Girls' Hostels; (vi) Coaching and allied schemes. In addition to these, two schemes in the Central sector have also been approved, viz., (i) special educational development programme for girls belonging to SCs of very low literacy levels, and (ii) educational complex in low literacy pockets for development of women's literacy in tribal areas. These programmes are in addition to the special thrust given to the weaker sections in the general programmes for educational devlopment like opening of schools, running of Non-Formal Education (NFE) centres and adult education centres, schemes of Operation Blackboard, upgradation of merit of SC/ST students, reservation in educational institutions, etc.

Elementary Education

Taking into account the experience gained in the implementation of NPE, 1986 and PoA, the following strategies are proposed:

(a) Access and Enrolment

In order to ensure universal access and enrolment of SC children in rural areas, henceforth, in opening primary and upper primary schools priority would be given to the needs of SC habitations and hamlets. As far as possible pre-primary section will be an integral part of such schools.

Every Scheduled Tribe habitation will be provided with a primary school or other suitable institution before the end of the Eighth Five Year Plan in order to ensure universal enrolment and participation.

In tribal areas educational plan will be implemented in an integrated manner. Pre-school education (through Balwadis), Non-Formal Education, elementary education and adult education will be organically linked and integrated to ensure achievement of total literacy of the entire population. This integrated Educational Complex will be responsible for total education within its area serving all children in the age-group 3-14 and adults in the age-group 15 and above.

For SC children access and enrolment will be assured primarily in the formal school. Where SC children are not able to attend the formal school provision for non-formal and distance education centres will be made to ensure universal access and enrolment.

It will be the responsibility of the teachers to organise drives at the beginning of every academic session to enrol all school-age children specially girls belonging to SCs, STs and other backward sections. For this purpose active assistance of voluntary agencies and local communities shall be taken. Traditional and folk media can be very effective in reaching parents and children in remote areas to motivate them.

(b) Participation

Adequate incentives will be provided for the children of SC, ST and other backward sections in the form of scholarships, uniforms, textbooks, stationery and mid-day meals.

All schools, NFE centres and pre-school centres in SC/ST habitations will be equipped with necessary and essential infrastructural facilities in accordance with the norms laid down for Operation Blackboard and for achieving Minimum Levels of Learning (MLL).

Operation Blackboard shall cover within a period of two years all schools in tribal areas and Harijan Bastees irrespective of the date on which the school was set up.

The indigent families among SC/ST will be given incentives to send children, particularly girls, to schools.

(c) Achievement

Children from tribal communities will be taught through the mother tongue in the earlier stages in primary school. Teaching/learning material in the tribal languages will be prepared providing for a transition to the regional language by Class III.

The home language of children of SC/ST may be different from others. Therefore, standard teaching/learning material will be re-written to make them intelligible to the SC/ST children especially in areas where the standard language and the learners' dialect are different.

It will be ensured that MLL already set-up for primary schools will be achieved, that the necessary standards of Rs. 3 are acquired by all children in SC/ST communities. Effective methodologies for measurement of MLL will be implemented.

Adult Education

Adult education programmes will be an integral part of educational micro-planning in all tribal areas.

Under the total literacy campaign SC and ST population will be the major focus for achieving total literacy. Special attention will be paid to adult illiterate women.

Adult education programmes for SCs/STs will essentially be programmes of empowerment. Special and relevant curricula and materials shall be prepared for this purpose as a crash programme.

Post-literacy centres will be set up in SC/ST areas where literacy campaigns have been carried out in order to provide facilities for continued literacy for adult neo-literates, specially women.

Incentives

Under the scheme of pre-matric and post-matric scholarships, the rates will be linked with the increase in the cost of living index.

Scholarships for SC/ST students in upper primary (middle) school and onwards will be distributed through bank/post-office. Scholarships will be payable in advance on the first day of each month. Special provisions will have to be made to allow minor children to operate bank accounts.

Coaching, training and remedial teaching classes will be organised for students of SC/ST and other backward sections in order to enhance the scholastic achievement of these students. Special coaching for entrance examinations for institutions of higher learning, particularly for professional courses to be provided to SC/ST students of Classes X and XII.

Residential facilities will be provided for SC/ST students preparig for competitive examinations.

Additional scholarships will be provided for SC/ST girl students in the secondary and senior secondary classes. Special coaching and remedial courses will be organised for SC/ST girl students.

Merit Scholarship Schemes covering A Grade students will be implemented in all the States.

Books of proven quality including classics from Indian and foreign languages will be abridged, adapted, translated and reproduced and made available at subsidised rates to the children and neo-literates in SC/ST communities.

Reservations

Implementation of reservation will be monitored at all levels and failure to adhere to the same will be made punishable.

Reservation in recruitment of teachers from SC/ST communities will be ensured in all educational institutions.

In Navodaya Vidyalayas, admission for SCs and STs are reserved on the basis of either the national norm of 15 per cent and 7.5 per cent respectively or of the percentage of SC and ST population in the district, whichever is higher. This principle will be considered for adaptation by State Governments in other educational institutions, wherever feasible, the criterion of reservation being the national percentages of 15 and 7-1/2 or the State percentage of SC and ST or the district percentages of SC and ST, whichever is higher.

MINORITIES EDUCATION

Phasing of Targets, Strategies Envisaged and Priority Measures

1. Short-term measures include

(i) Imparting of Technical skills through the 41 Community Polytechnics set up in the areas of pre-dominant minority concentration. There are many areas in which Community Polytechnic programmes have not borne the desired result. Corrective measures need to taken and vigorously implemented. Due publicity and incentives should be provided. (Action : Deptt. of Education – Centre/States);

(ii) University Grant Commission's Scheme of giving assistance to

Universities/Colleges for coaching classes for students belonging to educationally backward minorities to be revamped and expanded to cover more minority concentration areas. Wherever necessary, new coaching centres to be opened including in non-minority concentration areas. (Action : UGC);

(iii) Programme of evaluation of text-books from the stand-point of national integration undertaken by NECRT and State Government to be taken up more systematically for speedy and effective implementation of this programme. (Action : NCERT/SCERTs);

(iv) Orientation programmes for principals/managers and training programmes for teachers of minority educational institutions taken up by NCERT/NIEPA to be intensified (Action : NCERT/NIEPA);

(v) A crash programme of School Improvement consisting of Elementary Education, Non-Formal Education and Adult Education to be implemented on priority basis in minority concentration areas. (Action : Deptt. of Education, M/O HRD);

(vi) The scheme of Resource Centres will be extended for providing training and guidance to minority educational institution situated near these centres. (Action : NCERT, UGC);

(vii) A proper monitoring machinery must be set up at the Centre and States. The Monitoring Committees should be constituted under the chairmanship of eminent public men of the community and well-versed with the problems of minorities. The Committee at the Centre should have all India representation. It should include eminent persons of the community, officers from Education Department and the Ministry of Welfare of the rank of Joint Secretary, Members of Parliament, Vice-Chancellors, representatives of voluntary organisations of repute and a representative from Anjuman Taraqqi-Urdu-i-Hind. The State Committee will submit quarterly reports to the Central Monitoring Committee. Monitoring proforma for the purpose will be carefully designed. State Governments should be requested to form such committees in their respective States on the same pattern with immediate effect. They may also be requested to form District Committees. (Action : Deptt. of Education – Centre and States);

(viii) Arrangement for appointment of regional language teachers in Urdu medium schools in States may be made on priority basis.

(Action : States/UTs);

(ix) There are complaints of standards of education being lowered down in some institutions run by educationally backward minorities. Similarly there are many allegations regarding appointment of teachers and admissions in engineering, medical and other professional colleges. There are also complaints about the general management of institutions at all levels from primary schools to universities;

It is the crying need of the hour that an awakening should be created among the Muslims themselves to run and manage their institutions with academic excellence on the lines of the Institute of Mass Communication, Jamia Millia Islamia. To achieve this, Government of India should extend generous financial grant to such institutions and also provide total protection to Minority Institutions under Article 29 and 30 of the Constitution. The Monitoring Committees at State and Central levels should be charged with the task of ensuring improvement of standards in minority managed institutions. (Action : Deptt. of Education, Ministry of HRD, Ministry of Welfare, States/UTs);

(x) Women's Community Polytechnics should be set up in minority concentration areas on priority basis. (Action : Deptt. of Education – Centre and States/UTs);

(xi) Impelmentation of Guidelines for Recognition of Minority managed educational institutions:

(a) Clear guidelines for recognition and for timely disposal of applications. Each State Government to formulate its recognition policy and giving wide publicity to this. (Action : Deptt. of Education – Central/State Governments);

(b) Effective monitoring arrangement should be made to see the proper implementation of the guidelines. (Action : Deptt. of Education – Central/State Governments);

(c) State Governments should fix a time limit for processing applications for recognition. There should be a maximum period of three months fixed for disposal from the date of receipt of application. (Action : States/UTs); and

(d) The State Government may grant automatic recognition to schools of minorities upto Class V. (Action : States/UTs).

(xii) Special attention should be paid to the minority concentration areas in locating schools so that minority children have access in matters of admission. The Ministry of Welfare will prepare a revised list of minority concentration Blocks/Tehsils (Action : Ministry of Welfare, Deptt. of Education-Centre and States/UTs);

(xiii) Urdu teachers should be appointed in all the Kendriya Vidyalayas and Navodaya Vidyalayas located in minority concentration areas and arrangement for teaching Urdu as a subject should also be made in these schools with immediate effect. (Action : Deptt. of Education, Ministry of HRD);

(xiv) The number of students belonging to educationally backward minority shall determine the appointment of Urdu teachers and teaching of Urdu as a subject and also for establishment of Urdu medium schools. (Action : State Governments); and

(xv) In the schemes of Operation Blackboard, Adult Education and Non-formal Education and other such schemes where Urdu has been neglected so far should be given due importance and Urdu teachers/instructors should be appointed in schools in minority concentration areas and arrangement for Urdu facility should be made with immediate effect. (Action : Deptt. of Education, Ministry of HRD).

2. *Medium-term measures include*

(i) Centrally-sponsored/Central Scheme of Area Intensive Programme for Educationally Backward Minorities in the light of Revised NPE (1986) and PoA and the recommendations of other expert bodies. (Action : Deptt. of Education, Ministry of HRD);

(ii) (a) Centrally-sponsored/Central Scheme of Modernisation of *Madrasa* Education by the introduction of Science, Mathematics and English/Hindi in traditional *Madrasas* and *Maktabs* on voluntary basis. (Action : Deptt. of Education, Ministry of HRD); and

(b) The State Govts. would be encouraged to establish *Madrasa* Boards to look after the education of the minorities. Effective administration of these boards to be ensured through adequate staff support. (Action :

States/UTs).

(iii) Centrally-sponsored/Central Scheme of Appointment of Urdu teachers in the States where Urdu is spoken by a substantial number of people with a view to a more effective implementation of the Three-Language Formula as envisaged in the 1968 Policy, NPE, 1986 and Revised NPE, 1992. (Action : Deptt. of Education, Ministry of HRD);

(iv) A Centrally-sponsored/Central Scheme of Language teachers, funded by the Government of India for more effective implementation of the safeguards guaranteed under the Constitution to linguistic minorities. (Action : Deptt. of Education, Ministry of HRD);

(v) Complaints have been received that NCERT Urdu text-books are not easily available at all or if available are not available on time. A time-bound schedule should be prepared for publication and timely availability of Urdu text-books along with those of Hindi and English. The Bureau for Promotion of Urdu should be directed to publish text-books for primary and secondary classes on priority basis in addition to the text-books being published by NCERT. For this purpose special funds should be provided to BPU. (Action : Deptt. of Education, Ministry of HRD);

(vi) An Urdu Open University may be established with a view to cater to the needs of the Urdu speaking people. (Action : UGC);

(vii) All programmes of Minorities Education should be given wide publicity through Radio, TV and Newspapers in regional and minority languages in order that the programmes launched by the Government really reach the beneficiaries. (Action : Ministry of I & B);

(viii) NCERT should bring out Urdu text-books along with those of Hindi and English. The Bureau for Promotion of Urdu should be directed to publish text-books for primary and secondary classes on top-priority basis. (Action : Deptt. of Education, Ministry of HRD);

(ix) There is a large concentration of minorities in urban slums. A Centrally-sponsored/Central Scheme be devised to cater to their educational, health and nutritional needs. Special infrastructure should be provided for implementing schemes of Operation Blackboard, Adult Education, Non-formal Education etc. (Action : Deptt. of Education, Ministry of HRD; Ministry of

Urban Development);

(x) It should be ensured that the constitutional rights of the minorities in respect of opening and administration of institutions, admissions etc. are fully protected to uphold the cherished ideals of Constitution as defined in Articles 29, 30, and 350-A. (Action : Ministries of HRD, Welfare and Home Affairs, States/UTs);

(xi) Where the situation warrants Urdu medium sections may be opened in the existing secondary schools. Urdu knowing teachers should be appointed in anticipation of students offering Urdu as a medium. This will give the Urdu speaking students an opportunity to mix freely in the schools with students whose mother tongue is not Urdu and will promote national integration. However, new Urdu medium secondary/higher secondary schools should be opened in areas of concentration of educationally backward minorities in special circumstances. In such Urdu medium schools also there should be provision for parallel sections with regional language as a medium. (Action : States/UTs);

(xii) The Centre/State Governments should release grants to minority institutions on a quarterly basis in the interest of work and effeciency. (Action : Central and State Government/UTs);

(xiii) A suitable incentive scheme to be devised to encourage States achieving the targets in respect of Minorities Education. (Action : Deptt. of Education, Ministry of HRD);

(xiv) In areas where there is concentration of the educationally backward minorities, girls hostels to be constructed in schools and colleges on a priority basis. (Deptt. of Education – Centre/States, M/o Welfare and U.G.C.); and

(xv) Voluntary organisations would be encouraged to set up ITIS in minority concentration areas. Where necessary, suitable funding would be provided. (Action : Ministry of Labour, States/UTs).

3. Long-Term Programmes include

(a) Early Childhood Care and Education Centres

Early Childhood Education Centres will be set up in primary schools in areas pre-dominantly inhabited by educationally backward minorities. Socially Useful Productive Work (SUPW) should be introduced in such schools. The Department of Education, Ministry of Human Resource Development should prepare a scheme of assistance to State Governments in this regard. However, the State Governments will be encouraged to start their own programmes in ECCE. (Action : Deptt. of Education, Ministry of HRD).

(b) Primary Education

(i) Institutional system for compilation of statistical information required by Commissioner for Linguistic Minorities regarding educational facilities. (Action : State Govts./UTs);
(ii) Eliminating delay in sanctioning of linguistic minority teachers' posts and appointment of teachers by delegation of powers to District Collectors (Action : State Govts./UTs);
(iii) Survey on availability of text-books in minority languages and setting up of printing facilities in minority languages. (Action : State Govts./UTs);
(iv) Survey on availability of teacher training facilities for teachers in minority languages and measures to enhance such capacity wherever necessary. (Action : State Govts./UTs); and
(v) Efforts will be made to utilise 15 per cent of the curricular time for training in local crafts/trades and to arrange evening classes for children of artisans/agricultural labourers. (Action : State Govts./UTs).

(c) Middle and Higher Secondary Education

(i) A scheme for in-service training from minority institution teachers in Science, Mathematics, Social Sciences, English and Career Guidance, through SCERTs and other resource centres and State career guidance institutions. At present the NCERT has a scheme for such courses. The proposal is to extend this activity through SCERTs and other above-mentioned institutions. (Action : State Govts./UTs);
(ii) A scheme for Orientation Courses for Managers and Principals of minorities institutions in modern educational techniques by SCERT. This is being done by NCERT at present on a small scale. There is a need to increase the coverage. (Action : State Govts./UTs);
(iii) Scheme of appointment of regional language teachers in

minority institutions for national integration and for implementation of the Three Language Formula. (Action : State Govts./UTs);

(iv) A scheme of remedial coaching in minority managed educational institutions. This scheme should also provide for enrichment classes for better students. (Action : State Govts./UTs); and

(v) Minority managed educational institutions will be given fair representation in the scheme for computer literacy in school education (Action : State Govts./UTs).

(d) Higher Education

In the higher education sector, educational trusts, foundations and non-Governmental organisations to be supported and strengthened to cater to the educational needs of educationally backward minorities. (Action : Deptt. of Education – Centre and States/UTs, Ministry of Welfare and State Welfare Departments).

(e) Vocational and Technical Education

Provision of vocational courses in higher secondary schools, specially catering to educationally backward minorities (Action : State Govts./UTs).

Ensuring that in all the programmes on technical and vocational education included in the policy, minority run institutions derive full benefit (Action : State Govts./UTs).

Setting up Crafts Training Institutes in identified minority artisan concentration blocks, with 80 per cent seats for artisans' children. Where these institutions are available, they are to be upgraded on selective basis as Advanced Craft Training Centres. Artisans' children should be given preference in admission to ITI's (Action : Ministries of Labour an Textiles, State Govts./UTs).

(f) Women's Education

(i) As the women literacy and the girls enrolment is lowest among educationally backward minorities, in the schemes of opening of girls schools, appointment of lady teachers, opening of girls' hostels and providing of incentives in the form of mid-day meals, uniforms etc. minorities needs should be fully met. (Action : State Govts./UT's);

(ii) A Production-cum-Training Centre for crafts exclusively for girls preferably with women instructors to the extent possible in each of the identified minority concentration districts. (Action : State Govts./UTs).

(g) Voluntary Efforts in Adult Education and Early Childhood Education

Orientation Courses for professionals from minority communities to motivate voluntary effort; attaching one centre to all minority institutions to create awareness of these schemes and to train supervisors for multiple effect. (Action : State Govts./UTs).

(h) Libraries, Reading Rooms and Extension Work

Scheme for encouraging setting up of libraries, reading rooms etc. in minority areas; projects for educational extension work in a few blocks on an experimental basis (Action : State Govts./UTs)

(i) Scheme for Scholarships

Scheme for scholarships for weaker sections on merit-cum-means basis, with in-built system of placement in good institutions, fee exemption/fee concession for artisans' children and other weaker sections; such help could be routed through Voluntary Agnecies of All India repute. (Action : Deptt. of Education – Centre/States, Ministry of Welfare).

Education of the Disadvantaged

Implementation Strategies

The strategy of area-specific and population-specific micro-planning for UEE is equally relevant for this disadvantaged group. Planning for UEE and adult literacy at all levels – Centre, State, District, Block and Project – should provide for the educational needs of this category of children.

Education of children with disability will be a component in the training of educational planners and administrators as well as preservice and inservice teachers. DIETs, CTEs and IASEs which have been provided facilities for this component will have to pay particular attention to this aspect of teacher training. While drawing up schemes for strengthening SCERTs, cells for education of the handicapped may be considered as envisaged in IEDC.

The material supplied under Operation Blackboard will have to take into consideration special needs of these children. School buildings will have to take note of architectural adjustments needed to ensure access to children with disability, at the construction stage itself so as to avoid expenditure on modifications later on. Special schools need to be opened in the districts which have no speical school facilities. The education of the handicapped should form an essential component in all externally assisted basic education projects being implemented or proposed to be implemented.

Adult and Continuing Education

National Literacy Mission (NLM)

As a result of the evolution of the programmes of literacy, post-literacy and continuing education during the past four years or so under the NLM, a clear and comprehensive conceptualisation of the total programme has already emerged and would be adopted for future work. This will include the following:

(i) Basic literacy for about 200 hours spread over about six months which will basically be a guided learning programme;

(ii) Systematic post-literacy programme for about 50 additional hours spread over two months which will start with guided learning and will culminate into self-learning by making the learner self-reliant; and

(iii) Self-directed continuing education in the perspective of lifelong learning through library service, newspapers for neoliterates, *charcha mandal,* and such other activities. This may also include the skill development programme for personal, social and occupational development.

Process

The process involved in implementation of the mass campaign for total literacy strategy would include the following:

(a) Persuading the State Governments/UT administrations to formulate detailed action plans for the State as a whole as also for each district for achieving total literacy before 1997-98. The imperative of literacy would be built into the educational and development planning process at all levels;
(b) Orientation of political parties, as also representatives of the people (MPs, MLAs, MLCs, Chairmen, Zilla Parishads, Panchayat Samitis, Mandal Panchayats/Panchayats, Municipalities, notified area councils, etc.) to come together, plan together, work together and pledge their unqualified solidarity and support to the campaign experiment despite their ideological and political differences;
(c) Orientation of officers of all departments (of both Central and State Governments) at the State and district levels in the campaign approach so as to secure their co-operation and support to the campaign at all stages of its operationalisation;
(d) Registration of *Saksharata Samitis* in the districts/areas where mass campaigns for total literacy are to be taken up with representation of officials, non-official members, voluntary agencies, educational institutions and opinion leaders in the community/society;
(e) Mass mobilisation of all sections of the society like teachers and students of educational institutions, employers, trade unions, members of disciplined forces, ex-servicemen, banks, co-operatives, educated unemployed youth, voluntary agencies and the volunteers mobilised by them for combating illiteracy. The important role of voluntary agencies in mass-mobilisation will be continued and strengthened;
(f) Peoples' participation in environment building, planning and operationalisation of the campaigns by assigning specific roles to key resource persons, resource persons, master trainers, volunteers, etc. and by serving on various committees at the district, Panchayat Samiti/Mandal Panchayat/Panchayat and Village levels. This should lead to emergence of various grass roots level community institutions, including the Village Education Committees;
(g) Creation of people oriented, well-knit management structures at the district, taluka, block, mandal/panchayat and village levels

consisting of both officials and non-officials to function in a decentralised, debureaucratised and participative mode with a view to ensuring participation and support of people at all levels. For this purpose, services of experienced and committed personnel would be obtained from educational institutions, Central and State Government departments, Central and State public sector undertakings, autonomous bodies, etc. preferably on secondment basis;

(h) Effective involvement of good, committed and reliable voluntary agencies interested in taking up campaigns for total literacy in small and compact areas where total literacy campaigns are not being implemented and bringing them under the umbrella of TLC wherever a TLC is being undertaken with a view to securing their support and services for the campaign;

(i) Mobilising and harnessing all components of the educational system at the university, college/school level for promoting literacy as part of their social obligation;

(j) Elaboration of the present NLM norms into appropriate and specific competencies in literacy and post-literacy for ensuring effective achievement;

(k) Insistence on the preparation of teaching/learning material on the motivation centred technique of Improved Pace and Content of Learning (IPCL) in the campaigns supplemented by readers on host of development messages such as health, family welfare, immunisation, nutrition, maternity protection, child care, protection of environment, small family norm and women's equality, etc.;

(l) Insistence on all institutions/agencies/individuals interested in literacy work to work with understanding, rapport and bonhomie and carry out specific assignment building under the leadership and direction of the concerned *Saksharata Samiti*.

(m) Ensuring implementation of the total literacy campaigns in accordance with the guidelines of the National Literacy Mission Authority (NLMA) combined with such flexibility and freedom as may be necessitated by local conditions; and

(n) The Central/State Governments/UT administrations and Central/State public sector undertakings to make available the personnel at various levels to work for the campaigns as and when requested to do so and to ensure a reasonable continuity in their tenure so as to avoid a dislocation in pace and momentum of the TLC.

Environment Building– A Continued Necessity

Both the literate and the educated will be sensitised to take literacy work with a sense of pride, patriotism and social obligation. The community of learners will be motivated and mobilised for literacy to perceive the need for literacy and internalise this need for their collective well-being. For this purpose, environment building activities would continue to be undertaken through organisation of *Jathas,* street plays and *Nukkad Nataks*, wall writings, literacy campaign, etc.

Early Childhood Care and Education (ECCE)

Integrated Child Development Service (ICDS)

The ICDS is currently the biggest programme of early childhood development with 2.90 lakh *Anganwadis* serving nearly 140 lakh children and about 27 lakh mothers; 91.5 per cent ICDS projects are located in rural and tribal areas and 8.5 per cent in urban slums. Besides the ICDS, by the end of 1991-92 there were 12,470 creches with a coverage of about 3 lakh children below 5 years, 4395 ECE centres in 9 Educationally Backward (EB) States and the Balwadi Nutrition programme serving nearly 2.30 lakh children in the age-group of 3-5 years.

Over the recent years, a number of initiatives have been taken to make the programmes more focused. The measures under ICDS, include emphasis on practical training for *Anganwadi* Workers, and extension work by *Anganwadi* training centres, which are required to adopt 10 *Anganwadis* each for developing them as model *Anganwadis.* To build up resource capabilities in the field, action is afoot to develop CDPO's office into resource centre. Instructional materials for *Anganwadi* Training Centres are also under preparation. Efforts are also being made to distribute education-cum-play materials to *Anganwadis* to improve their pre-school education component. Initiative has also been taken to improve the scheme of creches by reviewing norms for voluntary and community participation. A scheme has been worked out by the Department of Women and Child Development for converging the services under DWCRA, ICDS, pre-school education and related schemes of the Departments of Health, Family Welfare, and Rural Development.

Targets and Phasing

The aim of ECCE is that every child should be assured access to the fulfilment of all basic needs. As such efforts will be made towards universalisation of ICDS by A.D. 2000. By the end of the Eighth Plan, 3.75 lakh *Anganwadi* centres would be established and by A.D. 2000 seven lakh *Anganwadi* centres. *Anganwadis* will be gradually converted into *Anganwadis*-cum-creches. By the end of Eighth Plan, 25 per cent of *Anganwadis* will be converted into Anganwadis-cum-creches. Qualitative improvement of ongoing ECCE programmes would receive high attention. New cost-effective designs of ECCE will also be encouraged and supported.

Strategy of Implementation

The ECCE involves the total development of child, i.e. physical, motor, cognitive, language, emotional, social and moral. The age span under consideration in ECCE is from conception to about 6 years. Even a modest development process during this period includes care of mother during pregnancy (ante-natal health check-up, nutritional support, control of anaemia, immunization for prevention of tetanus following delivery, etc.), hygienic and skilled birth attendance, nutritional care of mother during lactation, correct infant feeding practices, immunization of infant from communicable diseases, mothers' education in the child care, early childhood stimulation and health nutritional support throughout. Thus, ECCE is a complex integral function.

Elementary Education

Four Categories Districts

(i) High literacy districts in which access and enrolment are almost universal and community awareness for education is already high;

(ii) Total literacy campaign districts in which community mobilisation for educational needs has been successfully generated by the National Literacy Mission;

(iii) Low literacy districts in which the provision of education facilities is unsatisfactory and the delivery system functions without any community involvement; and

(iv) Externally assisted project districts with a different management structure and sufficient financial support.

The strategies with regard to access, participation, achievement, environment building, community participation, etc. will be different for the four categories of districts.

District Planning

Under this broad strategy of district planning and based on the experience gained in implementation of NPE, and the RPF, the following strategies are proposed:

(i) Adoption of alternative channels of schooling like voluntary schools and NFE centres for those who cannot avail of conventional full-time schooling;
(ii) Microplanning through involvement of teachers and the community in order to design and implement a family-wise, child-wise plan of action for universal access/enrolment and participation;
(iii) Making parents aware about their responsibility for ensuring the completion of elementary education by their children and for providing at home the facilities and encouragement needed for this purpose;
(iv) Establishment of linkages between programmes of preschool and primary education, and between programmes of literacy and UEE, in total literacy compaign districts;
(v) Improvement of school facilities through revamped Operation Blackboard and connecting it to MLL strategy. It will be extended to upper primary stage;
(vi) Decentralization of educational management for making the schools function so as to ensure universal enrolment, retention and achievement; and
(vii) Introduction of MLLs at primary and upper primary stages including coverage of the non-formal education channel.

Strategies

– Revision of process and content of elementary education to make teaching-learning child centred, activity based and joyful.

- Introduction of continuous and comprehensive evaluation with focus on remedial measures.
- Modification of teacher training programmes in view of changed strategies and programmes.
- Improvement of the monitoring system for UEE.
- Launching a National Mission to achieve the goals envisaged in the revised policy.

District Specific Projects

Further efforts would be made to develop district specific projects, with specific activities, clearly defined responsibilities, definite time-schedule and specific targets. Each district project will be prepared within the major strategy framework and will be tailored to the specific needs and possibilities in the district. Apart from effective UEE, the goals of each project will include the reduction of existing disparities in educational access the provision of alternative systems of comparable standards to the disadvantaged groups, a substantial improvement in the quality of schooling facilities, obtaining a genuine community involvement in the running of schools, and building up local level capacity to ensure effective decentralisation of education planning. That is to say, the overall goal of the project would be reconstruction of primary education as a whole in selected districts instead of a piecemeal implementation of schemes. An integrated approach is more likely to achieve synergies among different programme components.

Provision of Universal Access

Existing schemes will be suitably modified and measures will be taken to incorporate the new policy formulations.

Formal Schooling

New primary schools according to the norms, will be opened in unserved habitations. NFE centres will be opened in smaller habitations and for children who cannot benefit from the school system. In addition, a new scheme of Voluntary Schools will be launched to achieve universal access for children in different areas.

Primary Schools: In 1986, it was estimated that there were approximately 32,000 habitations with a population of 300 or more that required primary schools. Though many new schools have been opened, new habitations have also come into existence and it is estimated that 35,000 new schools will be required. These schools will be opened by the State Governments following the norms specified under Operation Blackboard.

(i) Provision of NFE centres will be based on the Microplanning exercise carried out for UEE. NFE centres will invariably cater to the needs of children, especially girls, who are not able to or who cannot attend the formal school;

(ii) The community will be involved in the setting-up, and supervision of all NFE centres;

(iii) The NFE instructors will be identified with the help of the community. Special efforts will be made to appoint women instructors wherever possible;

(iv) Training of NFE personnel, especially instructors, will be given top priority. Adequate training and re-orientation will be provided;

(v) Training responsibility will be shared by the project, district level institutions like DIETs, DRUs, State level institutions like SCERT, and National institutes like NCERT and NIEPA;

(vi) Project administration will be strengthened for effective decentralisation of management. Necessary administrative and management inputs will be provided at the State and district levels;

(vii) Arrangement will be made for testing of children in the NFE stream with reference to an equivalent stage in the formal system and specific instructions issued to facilitate lateral entry into the formal system for students of the NFE stream;

(viii) Efforts will be made to link non-formal courses with the Open Schools;

(ix) The NFE programme will be linked with the scheme of public libraries, Jana Shiksha Nilayams, etc.;

(x) In total literacy campaign districts follow-up programmes will be taken up for children in the age-group 9-14 to go beyond NLM literacy norms. This wiil form a part of the post literacy and continuing education programme of the district;

(xi) Vocational and technical courses of wide variety will be provided for children and youth who pass out of the Non-formal stream. Shramik Vidyapeeth and Voluntary agencies will be involved in this process; and

(xii) Voluntary agencies will be encouraged to undertake projects of NFE, especially in areas where the formal school system is not able to meet the demands of UEE.

Secondary Education

Broad Parameters of the Strategy

- Progressively bringing in the higher secondary stage (and all its equivalents) as a part of the school system in all States.
- Formulating a National Curriculum Framework for the higher secondary stage as well as development of new curricula and instructional packages based on the semester pattern.
- Reviewing and revising the curricula of secondary education (classes IX and X).
- Implementing a comprehensive scheme of examination reform.
- Improving considerably the physical and infrastructural facilities in secondary and higher secondary schools.
- Providing for diversity of courses in higher secondary schools.
- Reviewing afresh the existing system of pre-service teacher education for the secondary stage and formulating and implementing an improved teacher education system.
- Institutionalising in-service teacher training.
- Transforming the role of the Boards of Secondary Education.
- Strengthening the academic institutions and bodies concerned with research and development in the areas of curriculum, instructional materials and equipment for secondary schools.

Widening Access to Secondary Education

The following step is envisaged:

(i) As a short-term measure, the State Governments would be advised to provide in existing institutions necessary facilities for a diversity of courses, including science, commerce and vocational courses. They would also be advised to immediately initiate services for locating unserved areas and open High (i.e., Secondary) Schools in unserved areas taking the block as a unit so that the ratio of Secondary Schools to Upper Primary schools is not lower than 1:1.86. The distance of the existing schools from the unserved habitations will be duly considered. Special emphasis will be laid on opening schools in backward areas, areas inhabited predominantly by the SCs and the STs.

Navoday Vidayalayas

Review of the Scheme

The scheme was reviewed by the NPERC and by the JRC. While the NPERC was unable to reach any definite conclusion, the JRC recommended continutation of the scheme as originally envisaged subject to the following:

(a) Constant review to keep the scheme as cost-effective as possible;
(b) Ensuring the continued validity and reliability of the admission test by periodic evaluation and appropriate modification of admission procedure; and
(c) More particular attention to the pace-setting role of these institutions.

The Committee also observed the need to think of the future course of the scheme.

Strategies

Keeping in view the considerations outlined by the JRC, the following strategies will now be adopted·

(i) *Coverage:* The objective will be to cover all districts in States accepting the scheme before the completion of the Eighth Plan period and preferably in the next three years. This will mean opening about 50 Navodaya Vidyalayas every year;
(ii) A revised strategy for construction to minimize costs which meshes the long-term reconstruction plans with a need-based short-term plan to enable schools to function till sufficient permanent buildings are available. Given the resource position, the original plan for school campuses can remain only a long-term objective. For the time being, priority would be given to im-

provement of existing structure and to the provision of the essential requirements of a residential school. The permanent construction programme will be revised taking into account cost-effectiveness, re-phasing of the construction schedule, use of local material, merger of the design of the building with the local environment, involvement of the local people in the construction work and feasibility of maintenance, etc. A high level Committee of Architects and Engineers will go into all these aspects and submit its report by June, 1993.

(iii) *Admission Test*

(a) The validity and reliability of the admission tests is the most crucial factor in determining the success of the scheme. A high level committee will be appointed every two years to evaluate the testing process and to suggest modifications of the testing procedure if necessary. This will include consideration of the basic question whether the past approach of having a nation-wide test based on objective type answers is appropriate or whether the test design should not be more local-specific. The first such committee will be appointed immediately; its recommendations will be incorporated in the tests for admission in the academic year 1994-95.

(b) The Navodaya Vidyalaya Samiti will eventually take over the conduct of tests; by mid-1994 a separate cell would be set up for doing so.

(c) The Samiti should also be adequately staffed and equipped for continuous research and evaluation in respect of the admission tests.

(d) All research data thrown up by the testing procedures will be made widely available as an input in broader evaluation of the primary education system.

(iv) *Academic Quality*

Strategies to maintain a high standard of academic achievement will be:

(a) *Recruitment of Teachers:* The Executive Committee of the Samiti will review in March every year the recruitment *vis-a-vis* the manpower requirements. A job-oriented test will form the basis of selection followed by an interview for which about 25 per cent marks should be set and which may include conduct of a demonstration class where feasible. Measures should be devised to attract better talented teachers to Navodaya Vidyalayas.

(b) *Training:* An annual programme of action would be drawn up for this purpose and monitored by the Academic Advisory Committee of the Samiti. Steps would include continued development of in-service training programmes and teaching/learning materials. In addition to in-service courses, short term in-house workshops will be organized for a cluster of Navodaya Vidyalayas and local schools. These workshops will be organized from 1992-93 itself.

(v) *Pace-setting and Networking of Institutions:* The NPE, 1986 expects Navodaya Vidyalayas to become catalysts of a nation-wide programme of school improvement. Navodaya Vidyalayas will be encouraged and given full liberty to play an active role in this area in consultation with the parents, community and local education authority.

Vocational Education

Management of Vocational Education at Various Levels

National Level

(i) A Joint Council of Vocational Education (JCVE) under the chairmanship of Union Education Minister for the planning and coordination of vocational programmes; to provide guidelines for development of vocational programmes at all levels, and to evolve schemes for involvement of public and private sector industry in vocational education;

(ii) The Bureau of Vocational Education in the Department of Education, Ministry of Human Resource Development, would provide secretariat support to the JCVE and oversee the implementation of the programmes; and

(iii) The NCERT through its Department of Vocational Education would function as the apex level Research and Development (R&D) institution giving academic support in the planning and implementation of vocational programmes

Regional Level

(i) Boards of Apprenticeship Training would be augmented to cater to the training needs of vocational students after they complete the vocational courses at the +2 stage; and
(ii) The Regional Colleges of Education (RCE) under NCERT would function as regional vocational teacher training institutions in addition to performing R&D functions.

State Level

(i) The State Council of Vocational Education (SCVE) should be set up as a counterpart of the JCVE;
(ii) The Directorate of Education in the States/UTs should provide the administrative leadership to the vocational education programmes; and
(iii) In the SCERTs, a separate wing would be established to provide R&D support to the programme at the State level.

District Level

A District Vocational Education Committee would be consituted to promote the programme and maintain linkages with the Directorate of Education and other related institutions as well as backward and forward linkages with the community.

School Level

A senior staff member will be incharge of the management and actual implementation of the vocational courses. He will also build up contacts and linkages with the community.

As envisaged by the scheme, the JCVE and its Standing Committee were established at the national level. In view of the magnitude and complexity of the programme and the number of areas requiring close attention it has been decided to set up a Central Institute of Vocational Education (CIVE) under the umbrella of the NCERT, but with considerable functional autonomy. The Institute will be the apex R&D institution in the field of vocational education.

However, at the State level, out of the 24 States and 4 UTs, only 15 States and 2 UTs have set up offices at the Directorate level; only 8

States and one UT have set up organisations at the SCERT level and only 6 States have set up district level organisations for this programme. Many of these States, which have set up offices, have not filled the full contingent of posts required. Only 11 States have established the SCVEs or a similar body as the counterpart of the JCVE at the State level.

The following steps need to be taken:

(i) The State Governments/UTs should set up adequate management structures at all levels as envisaged under the Centrally-sponsored schemes;

(ii) Personnel manning the management structure should be well trained and encouraged to establish linkages with concerned agencies in the Government, voluntary organizations and individuals with specialized training. They should also remain in position for a tenure of atleast three years so as to give continuity to the programme;

(iii) While giving financial assistance preference will be given to States/UTs which have set up adequate management structure;

(iv) The JCVE and SCVE should meet regularly in order to provide the required guidance and co-ordination at the National and State levels respectively; and

(v) The CIVE should be made functionally effective as early as possible.

Higher Education

Strategies of Coordination and Expansion

(i) The establishment of State Councils of Higher Education (SCHE) as statutory bodies in all States during the Eighth Five Year Plan to ensure proper planning and coordination of the development of higher education. In view of the fact that it may not be possible for small States, particularly in the North Eastern region, to establish separate Councils of Higher Education, such States will be encouraged to set up Joint Councils of Higher Education. For the North Eastern region, this responsibility could either be entrusted to the North Eastern Council (NEC) or a Council of Higher Education for all the States.

(ii) Pending the establishment of State Councils of Higher Education, every State Government should, in partnership with UGC, undertake a survey of the existing facilities for higher education in the State and its projected needs up to A.D. 2000. The information collected in the survey should be used to develop, by 1993-94 a computerised Management Information System (MIS) to identify areas of the State which are not properly served by existing universities/colleges, and institutions which are over-crowded and/or deficient in minimum facilities.

(iii) To minimise expenditure on establishment of new colleges and universities it should be ensured that their campuses are compact and that they are established at places where infrastructural facilities like power, communication, road, transport, water, etc. are easily available.

(iv) The optimum utilisation of the existing infrastructure in universities and colleges should be ensured by introduction of extra shifts, especially in metropolitan areas and large cities.

(v) When the need for a college is established, its affiliation to a university is an academic matter and should be given on academic grounds alone, without any other considerations. The final authority for granting affiliation, its continuation, extension or disaffiliation should vest solely with the appropriate university authorities. However, since affiliation may create eligibility for grant-in-aid, the university should consult the State Government concerned before granting affiliation to a private college. States should review the relevant legal provisions to give effect to these recommendations and universities should exercise greater vigour in adhering to UGC guidelines while exercising their powers of affiliation.

(vi) Where the existing colleges fall short of satisfying the conditions of affiliation prescribed by UGC, their requirements should be carefully assessed and brought to the notice of the colleges and the State Government concerned so that they are provided threshold facilities, preferably during the Eighth Five Year Plan. The estalishment of new colleges in States, which have a large number of colleges with sub-standard facilities should be deferred until such time as the existing colleges can be provided with minimum facilities. Efforts should also be made to evolve a consensus among UGC, State Governments and Universities not to continue provisional affiliation of colleges beyond the initial period of five years.

(vii) There is an urgent need to review, revise and update grant-in-aid rules in the light of recent developments in the field of higher education. It is felt that the criteria of 'deficit' as the basis for providing grant-in-aid to colleges should be reviewed and issues such as per capita cost, teacher student ratio, types of courses offered, internal resource generation, performance appraisal of teachers, etc. be taken into account for determining the quantum of grant-in-aid payable to colleges. For this purpose, UGC should formulate model guidelines in this regard.

(viii) The recommendations made by the Gnanam Committee in regard to changes in the management structure of the universities should be implemented by all States as and when approved by CABE.

(ix) The movement towards entrance tests for admission to institutions of higher education will be encouraged and promoted by UGC and State Governments. The services of the National Evaluation Organisation (NEO) should be utilised by the university system for developing, designing and administering entrance tests for admission. During the next three years (i.e., by 1995) all universities should devise Entrance Tests for admission to post-graduate courses and prescribe ceilings for admission to post-graudate and professional courses, keeping in view the availability of teachers, libraries, laboratories, etc. It should be ensured that entrance tests for admission do not militate against students belonging to the weaker sections of society and rural areas who may not be proficient in the use of the English language and lack communication skills.

(x) With escalation in the cost of equipment, books and journals, a system of sharing and pooling of resources within university departments and between neighbouring universities/colleges, particularly in metropolitan areas and large cities, should be worked out within the next year (1993-94) by the UGC in consultation with the State Governments. To ensure better utilisation of equipment costing Rs. 2 lakh or more, their use should be monitored by introducing a system of 'utility audit'.

Rural Universities and Institutes

Central Council of Rural Institutes

The Central Council of Rural Institutes is expected to be set up shortly.

The Central Council of Rural Institutes would:

- promote the concept of rural education on the lines of Mahatma Gandhi's revolutionary ideas on education as envisaged in NPE, 1986; and
- consolidate and develop institutions engaged in programmes of Gandhian Basic Education.

The Central Council of Rural Institutes would, in pursuance of the objectives stated above, undertake measures such as:

(a) Consolidation and reorganisation of existing rural institutes including those launched in the Second Plan;
(b) Encouragement to other educational institutions and voluntary agencies to develop in accordance with Gandhian Philosophy of education;
(c) Recognition and support to elementary, secondary and post-basic institutions based on the concepts of *Nai Talim*;
(d) Strengthening teacher training facilities for Gandhian Basic Education;
(e) Designing a variety of courses at tertiary level around emerging rural occupations;
(f) Strengthening of the content of all these institutions with emphasis on science and technology;
(g) Encouraging field-oriented courses of rural institutes;
(h) Promoting research as a tool for social and rural development; and
(i) Promoting extension services to the community through micro-level planning.

The Central Government would take the initiative of providing resource support both for the development of infrastructure as well as conceptual, methodological and academic inputs in design and structure of programmes, development of teaching and learning materials, evaluation procedures, etc.

Technical and Management Education

Action Plan

All India Council for Technical Education (AICTE)

In order to ensure proper maintenance of norms and standards, accreditation, funding of priority areas, monitoring and evaluation, maintaining parity of certification and awards, and a coordinated and integrated development of technical and management education, the AICTE in its statutory role will be adequately strenthened so as to function in a more decentralised manner with greater effective involvement of State Governments, UT Administrations and technical institutions of good quality. In order to ensure this, the AICTE will take the following steps:

(i) Regulate admissions to all programmes of studies in technical education institutions with reference to manpower requirements and take steps for ensuring that admissions are made as per the approved guidelines;

(ii) Activate the Boards of Studies which have so far not been operationalised and set up more Boards of Studies;

(iii) Regulate effectively the establishment of new technical education institutions and starting of new programmes of studies with reference to the overall needs of the economy;

(iv) Ensure greater involvement of the States in the monitoring and regulation, and coordinated development of technical education;

(v) Activate the accreditation process through the National Accreditation Board (NAB);

(vi) Strengthen the existing Regional Committees and establish additional Regional Committees for effective discharge of the functions assigned to the AICTE;

(vii) Take steps for laying down a realistic fee structure based on actual cost of education and lay down guidelines for its implementation;

(viii) Take steps for introduction of a penal clause in the AICTE Act for effectively curbing malpractices in the technical education system;

(ix) Take suitable steps for enabling institutions to increase internal revenue generation;

(x) Take steps for encouraging and promoting private initiative, support and participation in technical education system;

(xi) Generate revenue for meeting expenditure incurred by the AICTE on services rendered to all technical education institutions;

(xii) Lay down specific guidelines and norms for providing assistance to professional bodies on a selective basis so that they can conduct their activities effectively by way of consultancy, conferences, mission-oriented studies and surveys, conducting seminars and workshops;

(xiii) Introduce a scheme for giving autonomy to selected technical institutions coupled with the concept of accountability so that the institutions can enjoy adequate freedom, flexibility and innovative approaches for meeting the rapidly changing needs of the society; and

(xiv) The AICTE will also lay down norms for granting Deemed University status to the technical institutions under the provisions of the Act on a selective basis.

National Technical Manpower Information System (NTMIS)

A sound data base on technical manpower availability and requirements in the traditional and emerging disciplines is a pre-requisite for regulated and coordinated development of technical education with optimum allocation and utilisation of resources. The AICTE will take over the scheme of National Technical Manpower Information System during 1992-93 and take urgent steps, with the help of Government and non-Governmeent institutions, organisations and professional societies for developing and maintaining a current data-base for the planning and development of technical education in the most effective manner.

The AICTE will also launch schemes for coordination between the Technology Information Forecasting and Assessment Council (TIFAC) and the NTMIS and also prepare a national directory of occupations and job titles and identify the variety of need-based courses and fixing intake level with the help of higher technical institutions, professional bodies and industry. The AICTE will do this in definite time-bound programme.

Technician Education

Technician Education has to play an important role in developing highly skilled middle level technical manpower for the organised as well as the unorganised sectors. Necessary steps will be taken to make technician education flexible, modular and credit-based with provisions for multi-point entry to achieve this goal.

Research and Development

Action Points

1. Research Support

Research support in educational institutions is only through the grants that the faculty members obtain from agencies on a competitive basis. Unfortunately, generally these grants are not associated with institutional overheads. Educational institutions do not have the resources to provide infrastructural support to research projects and this is bringing down the absorptive capacity of these institutions for R&D. Without overheads it will become increasingly difficult for educational institutions to support research even though the faculty members may obtain grants from scientific agencies. It is recommended that at least 20 per cent of the total project grant should be given as overheads to educational institutions. This is of utmost importance.

2. Improvement of Quality of Research

The average quality of research and development has to be improved. Many corrective measures need to be taken both by institutions as well as by funding agencies. It is necessary to be selective in areas of research rather than spreading ourselves thin, specially when the budget situation is so bad. The areas so chosen should be relevant to national needs and to the subject itself. Besides supporting the right areas and providing grants which are commensurate with the area being pursued the promotion of an overall system which nurtures quality is also important. This is the responsibility of the scientists as well as of administrators and planners. Appropriate monitoring and coordinating mechanisms for R&D have to be worked out by universities, UGC, MHRD/AICTE and the scientific agencies.

3. Teaching and Research

Teaching and research should be hand-in-hand in higher educational institutions. It is important therefore, that teachers get an opportunity to involve themselves in research activities. In order to do so, there should be a separate budget-head for research within the budget of educational institutions. At present the recurring grants of educational institutions do not have a research component. Necessary mechanism to provide some support or research in important areas within the budgets of the institutions should be established. It would be desirable to have a Dean or a Board associated with research, within each educational institution. UGC and MHRD/AICTE should earmark a percentage of the grants for R&D.

Linkages

It is essential to have a proper national research funding mechanism in science and engineering. The SERC of the DST is now providing the major funding for big science R&D projects while other organizations provide smaller grants. It may be worth-while to see whether a coordinating mechanism can be established in relation to funding, in addition to increasing the funding for research.

The Cultural Perspective

Action Plan

1. Pre-Primary Stage

(a) Provision of minimum facility for playing space or park for children at this stage.
(b) Training of pre-school teachers in integrating cultural activities with pre-school learning programmes.
(c) Preparation of educational toys and games for preschool students which are indigenous and aesthetic in quality and safe for use by small children.

Primary School Stage

The main objectives at the primary school stage would be:

(a) To impart the child with a basic core of facts about India's cultural heritage by encouraging rural teachers and students to collect folk songs, local history, local folk tribal community and archaeological artefacts;
(b) To integrate and develop students' physical and cognitive skills; and

(c) To create through awareness a feeling of love for India's natural and cultural heritage.

The major activities envisaged for achieving these objectives are the following :

(a) Children School Theatre Movement would be launched with the teacher and children reading/enacting stories, plays and poems in the textbooks in the classroom. Learning of the local folk/tribal community theatre conventions will also be promoted.
(b) Students will be encouraged to participate in creatively meaningful activities. Schools will be advised to invite local craftsmen, artisans etc. for demonstrations of their skills before the impressionable minds of the children.
(c) It shall be ensured that textual materials incorporate a strong and vitalising presence of our heritage, folklore, myths and symbols etc. without making texts either burdensome or obscurantist.
(d) Efforts will be made to incorporate suitable words, idioms proverbs etc. from local dialects in the textbooks.
(e) Too much cultural indoctrination by covering the classroom walls with drawings, stickers, slogans, moral sayings, etc. would be discouraged. Right from childhood a sense of design aesthetics of vacant space and a sense of space would be inculcated.
(f) Teachers' training programmes will be re-oriented to give the teachers capability of imparting instruction in theoretical and demonstrative methodologies in cultural instruction.
(g) Extensive training programmes for in-service teachers in each district will be organised.
(h) School museum corners largely with collections of students themselves in the form of stones, feathers, leaves, etc. will be set up.
(i) Tours will be organised particularly to monuments and places of historical and cultural significance.

Subsequently the above-mentioned activities would be systematised further and the emphasis would be on provision of more developed facilities and specialisation of training for teachers by way of:

(a) preparaton of special books, educational material and audio-visual facilities for primary schools;
(b) institutionalising community interaction in terms of seeking help of local artisans and craftsmen including performing artists like dancers, singers on an organised basis of association, through honorarium, fees, incentives, etc.

Middle/High/Secondary Schools

At the middle/high/secondary school stage the main objectives in cultural instruction will be—

(a) To further strengthen and build up in students love and understanding of India's natural and cultural heritage;
(b) To nurture in students an aesthetic approach based on perception of beauty and a perspective beyond immediate emotional or other passions;
(c) To encourage the schools to be in live contact with local writers, artists, groups to ensure their assistance in guiding young creative talent or group cultural activities;
(d) To impart to the student's personality a broad-based approach that reflects values of secularism, nationalism and consciousness of their constructive role in the larger destiny of India; and
(e) To organise regional or State level competition of school magazines.

The approach would be to enlarge cultural activities mainly through students' own participation community help and building up of certain core facilities. This would include:

(a) Provision of atleast one core/resource teacher for culture in each school.
(b) Reflection of diverse images of natural and cultural, heritage in the school curriculum.
(c) Imparting the curriculum with a distinct outlook, particularly in terms of social studies and history by correcting historical distortions and by giving a value orientation to lessons drawn largely from Indian heritage and great classics.
(d) Organisation of systematic visits to monuments, museums and sanctuaries.

(e) Development of conservation ideas by adoption of monuments by the students and the community and helping to clean and safeguard these monuments.
(f) Inducing among the students an idea of service by motivating them to participate in cleanliness operations, literacy drives, conducting of surveys with particular emphasis on the value of dignity of labour.
(g) Setting up of museum corners with models, illustrations, posters, charts, books and with objects collected by students from their neighbourhood including local crafts, flowers, leaves, feathers etc.
(h) Setting up hobby clubs, book clubs and film clubs in schools.

The cultural exposures would be enlarged in terms of thematic coverage with broadbasing of participation and induction of technology. These aspects would cover the following action:

(a) The network of Navodaya Vidyalayas would be used for development of resource centres in each district to share with other schools in the neighbourhood the facilities of exhibitions, projections through audio-visual technology and models for cultural soft-ware based on the peculiar features of the area.
(b) Extensive cultural meets would be held by the inter-school, inter-district and later at inter-State levels to spot creative talent through a system of awards and scholarships. The idea would be to honour the creatively distinguished, as also the dedicated, through a system of incentives.
(c) Networking of various schools for visits to museums, libraries, galleries and monuments maintained by the States, the Archaeological Survey of India as well as schools which would be identified in various States.
(d) A cultural kit containing an audio-visual and related educational material on Indian culture will be provided to every high school through Central/State sharing scheme.
(e) Special courses would be organised for cultural reorientation of teaching and adminsitrative personnel connected with educational institutions.
(f) Software for satellite programmes on India's natural and cultural property with particular reference to themes of creativity and inculation of values would be developed.

(g) A cultural resurgence would be built up through a system of awards and incentives for honouring teachers and trainers for their expression of cultural creativity and devotion to its promotion.

University Level

At the college and university level, the main emphasis would be on the following aspects:

(a) Broad-basing and diversifying of cultural courses like music, fine arts, performing arts, etc.;
(b) Correction of historical and cultural distortions by reassessing critically the content of existing courses in social sciences, humanities, languages, etc.;
(c) Imparting of cultural instruction to students engaged in highly specialised science or technical courses so as to give their personality an all round development; and
(d) Development of special courses in technical institutions like archaeological engineering, relevance of India's architectural heritage, maintenance of monuments, museology, musical composition etc., apart from performance.

It is proposed to materialise these objectives by adopting the following action plan:

(a) Artists and writers will be invited as Visiting Professors for one or two years under an existing scheme of UGC to energise young talent on campuses of higher education.
(b) Traditional *Gurus* and artists will be given a place/recognition in the teaching system.
(c) Courses in translation and comparative literature will be strengthened.
(d) The NSS is involved in the survey of community arts in the region and in the upkeep, cleaning of local monuments, etc.
(e) Efforts would be undertaken to set up university museums.
(f) Outstanding works of creative writing should be recognised for research degrees.
(g) University education in the fine arts, music, dance, theatre, and literature will be reviewed critically, remodelled and upgraded.

(h) Each University should endeavour to adopt one regional form of culture for special attention regarding teaching, survey, research etc.

(i) University theatre movement will be supported and encouraged.

In the later phases, emphasis would be on enlarging the base as also on sophisticating the courses and technology connected with culture. This would cover the following activities:

(a) Development and networking of specialised courses like archaelogical engineering, traditional Indian architecture and its relevance to contemporary context, use of inexpensive local material for building, etc., in engineering and technical institutions particularly Regional Engineering Colleges, IITs, State Engineering Colleges and Institutions of Architecture.

(b) Capsule courses on these subjects in institutions like Polytechnics and ITIs.

(c) Special fellowships/scholarships/incentives would be given on the basis of State and national competitions for creative and performing arts.

Imperative Requirements of Institutional Infrastructure

It is imperative that the Plan of Action (PoA) should have institutional infrastructure for its implementation and monitoring. This aspect has the following crucial parameters:

(a) strengthening of existing infrastructure;

(b) evolving a system of organised network with institutions in the neighbourhood; and

(c) innovating new institutions to meet the needs of cultural education.

Three Language Formula

The Three Language Formula provides for a study of a Modern Indian Language, preferably one of the Southern languages, apart from Hindi in Hindi-speaking States and of Hindi along with the Regional language and English in the non-Hindi speaking States.

Present Situation

At the time when PoA of 1986 was formulated, it was noted that the implementation of the Three-Language Formula had been less than satisfactory on account of (a) all the languages are not being taught compulsorily at the secondary stage; (b) a classical language has been substituted for a modern Indian language in some States; (c) no concrete provision yet exists (though a scheme is likely to take off very soon) for the teaching of South Indian languages in the Hindi speaking States, (d) duration for compulsory study of three languages varies; and (e) competency levels to be achieved by students of each language have not been precisely specified.

Review of Implementation

The effective implementation of the Three Language Formula would require (a) decision by States, State Boards of Secondary school education, etc., to make the study of three languages compulsory at the secondary stage; (b) prescription of the class from and the duration for which three languages will be taught; (c) specification of objectives of teaching different languages. The State Boards of Secondary Education will be asked to take uniform decisions in line with the recommendations of NCERT and CBSE in these matters; and (d) specification of levels of language proficiency to be reached in respect of each language. Language Institutions under the Ministry like Kendriya Hindi Sansthan (KHS), Central Institute of Indian Languages (CIIL), Central Institute of English and Foreign Languages (CIEFL) in consultation with NCERT, would be asked to prescribe minimum competencies to be achieved.

Strategies of Implementation

The action required would include:

(a) The Central Government should continue to assist the non-Hindi speaking States/UTs for the appointment of Hindi teachers. It may be noted that in accordance with the PoA of NPE 1986, Central Government's assistance for appointment of Hindi teachers in non-Hindi speaking States/UTs has been restored to cent per cent. This scheme should be continued in the

Eighth Plan and beyond;

(b) As suggested in PoA 1986 a scheme for the appointment of MIL teachers in Hindi speaking States has been formulated. Adequate provision subject to availability of resources and effective implementation of the scheme would be ensured with effect from 1993-94;

(c) Apart from establishing teacher training institutions for training of Hindi and MIL teachers in States, facilities for training of language teachers need to be augmented and improved in existing teacher training colleges;

(d) The Ministry's language institutions should continue to undertake programmes facilitating teaching of languages, particularly research in methodology of teaching languages and experimentation in the use of computers and new communication technologies; and

(e) Since one of the constraints in the implementation of the Three Language Formula is non-specification of desirable language competencies as indicated vide (e) in Para 3.2, concerned language institutions under the Department i.e. KHS, CIIL and CIFEL would be advised to complete this exercise within a scheduled time.

Targets

Within a month of approval of PoA, instructions will be issued to the language institutions that a certain level of language competency to be achieved may be determined within a maximum period of one year.

Central assistance will be provided to the States/UTs for appointment of about one thousand Hindi teachers during the Eighth Plan Period.

Monitoring and Evaluation

A Monitoring Cell has been established in KHS for monitoring the scheme of appointment and training of Hindi teachers in non-Hindi speaking States/UTs.

An Inter-Institutional Committee comprising representatives of KHS, CIIL, CIFEL, NCERT and the Department would be constituted to oversee and monitor measures in this regard from time to time. Similar arrangements would have to be made at the State level.

Media and Educational Technology

Strategies and Programmes

(i) The SIETs would be made autonomous. Production facilities in North East will be set up. Subject to availability of resources, creation of programme production facilities in other language zones not covered by SIETs will also be considered.

(ii) In SIETs association of professionals on deputation/contract will be encouraged to professionalise the working environment.

(iii) Professional talent would be associated through commissioned programmes, to supplement the in-house programme production arrangements. The CIET would seek to have 10 per cent of its programmes transmitted on TV produced by professionals outside CIET.

(iv) The EMRCs and AVRCs would be converted into autonomous departments of the university concerned and these institutions would associate professional talent from outside on tenure/contract basis to invigorate the EMRC system. One new AVRC would be set up in each of the remaining larger states in the Eighth Plan.

(v) The UGC would set up adequate master's level courses or post-gradute diplomas in various aspects of educational programme production. To optimise returns on the investments such courses would be started where EMRC/AVRC already exist so that the cost on infrastructure does not have to be repeated. To upgrade the skills of existing technical manpower involved in production of educational TV/Radio programmes, the possibility of introducing Diploma courses in suitable disciplines in certain polytechnics will be examined.

Viewing of the educational programmes during the scheduled transmission time by large number of students poses obvious problems both in terms of management and learner outcome. The problem tends to become unmanageable as the level of students increases. Therefore, individual viewing and viewing in small groups is bound to become more and more important and it is already a fast developing area. To enable more and more students to have access to educational programmes the following measures could be taken:

(i) Provision of receiving sets, Radio-cum-cassette player and TV sets in larger number in Primary Schools/Upper Primary Schools.
(ii) Production of programmes for Upper Primary sector also.
(iii) Special efforts for production of recorded audio-cassettes by CIET/SIETs to ensure optimal utilisation of RCCPs. Special emphasis will be given to production of cassettes dealing with teaching of Hindi and regional languages.
(iv) Augmention of equipments in SIETs/CIET.
(v) Encouragement of educational institutions to raise resources locally to provide electronics hardware, radio, cassette player, TV and VCR for group viewing/listening.
(vi) Marketing of educational cassettes by the IUCEC. The revenues so earned could be used to improve and expand the programme production and viewing facilities in universities/colleges.
(vii) Development of IUCEC as the nodal agency for marketing of educational software of all sectors of education.
(viii) Setting up of training facilities for technical personnel by CIET and IUCEC on regional basis. The facility may be located either in the universities having EMRCs or in the SIETs.
(ix) Development by the IGNOU, of a large range of recorded audio and audio-visual cassettes to support its various distance education courses.
(x) Support by the UGC to the university departments of distance education having enrolment of 5000 or more for supplementing the programme production of the IGNOU. Independent programme production infrastructure would not be created in such departments.

In-service training of teachers would receive more importance through both TV and radio. The arrangements through CIET, once in a week would be made more effective and similar arrangement will be established under UGC transmission.

The programme of continuing education would be given more support through 'Vivek Darpan' and such other programmes and awareness for literacy would continue to be built up through capsules on the TV/Radio.

The working of programme production facilities in the TTTIs would be professionalised and output from these would be optimised. The IITs and Universities would undertake research for developing innovations in Educational Technology and Universities.

The IUCEC and the TTTIs/IITs and other professional agencies would make a sizable beginning for support to professional upgradation programmes for specific professional groups like management, and medicine, etc.

Computers in Education

Present Situation

In the school sector the use of computers has been initiated by the CLASS Project. Though the coverage was modest (2,598 schools) the CLASS project has led to increasing awareness of computer literacy among students, teachers and parents. However, a close scrutiny of the implementation strategy and achievements of the project shows that the project has not met with the desired degree of success, mainly on account of shortcomings in the implementation strategy. The more important among these may be enumerated as under:

- Multiplicity of agencies involved in the implementation of the project and consequent lack of accountability.
- Over emphasis on hardware and one time inputs and neglect of ongoing instructional inputs and softwares.
- Inadequate training and low motivation of teachers.
- Instruction outside school hours.
- Want of curriculum and teaching material.
- Indifferent maintenance.

The existing arrangements for implementation of the project are being reviewed by MHRD to obviate these shortcomings.

A notable initiative, possibly triggered by the CLASS Project, has been the computer literacy programme in fees charging private schools. In most of the schools professional agencies have been contracted for providing the hardware and teaching inputs. In such cases fees are high but the outcomes are good. The CBSE has pioneered the start of Computer Science at higher secondary stage and some State Boards have followed this lead.

In the university sector the UGC is supporting the programme in three parts;

(i) A set of PCs has been given to college for use in educational management and for promoting computer literacy;
(ii) Starting certificate, diploma and degree courses in universities in Computer Science; and
(iii) By giving sizeable computers as central computational facility for research and higher studies purposes universities have been assisted.

Sports, Physical Education and Youth

Sports or Youth Programmes

Specilised programmes for the attainment of excellence in both Sports and Youth Affairs have been proposed which can be implemented within a reasonable period of time.

Studies have shown that there is a positive co-relation between participation of youth in constructive social programmes, or in sports and games, and issues such as better social integration, reduced juvenile delinquency, better general health and fitness, and at a later stage, better productivity and output. Each of these benefits in itself is of considerable significance particularly in the Indian context. In formulating this Programme of Action, therefore, efforts have been made to indicate simple and low cost solutions which are useful and give the maximum return both to the individual and to the society at large.

Due consideration also needs to be given to the broader issue regarding investment in Human Resource Development, particularly in education. Given the significant benefits which accrue to society in terms of the points mentioned above, it is indeed worthwhile investing additional resources in building up an education system which includes activities under Sports and Youth as an integral part of the curriculum.

Sports

Action in following areas will be necessary to implement the policy objectives of the NPE, 1986:

(i) In deciding the curriculum load the need to allocate sufficient time to sports and physical education which the NPE, 1986 holds as an integral part of the learning process should be kept in mind;

(ii) Physical Education and Yoga should be introduced for atleast 45 minutes per day, preferably just after assembly;

(iii) Approved games should be included in the school time table for atleast two periods in a week;

(iv) Special incentives will need to be given to students who perform well in sports and games;

(v) Special incentives may be considered for subject teachers who perform extra duty in conducting classes in Physical Education, Yoga, Sports and Games;

(vi) The basic equipment, such as footballs and volleyballs, may be provided to each school. Similarly, some amount of contingency may be provided to each school;

(vii) A scheme for the creation and improvement of play-grounds should be taken up on a phased basis under JRY and NRY;

(viii) An intensive and extensive programme of teachers training to equip all subject teachers with the necessary skills to impart training in Physical Education, Games and Yoga will be necessary;

(ix) The present programme to train and recruit Physical Education Teachers for high schools should be expanded;

(x) New schools may be established/recognised only if playgrounds are available;

(xi) A comprehensive system of Inter-school tournaments and championships in select disciplines should be introduced over a period of time. This system should culminate in a National School Championship; and

(xii) Special cash awards to winning schools and a special system of incentive for successful athletes also needs to be introduced.

As the coordination and cooperation of all State Governments and UTs will be necessary to implement the above suggestions, it is recommended that this issue may be taken up and discussed as a special agenda item in a special meeting of CABE. To provide the CABE necessary background material, a CABE Committee would be constituted to consider all aspects of Sports and Physical Education as envisaged in the NPE, 1986.

For the promotion of Sports and Games at the University level, the following measures may be considered for implementation:

(i) Special incentives for athletes and sports persons in select disciplines to enable them to continue their studies;

(ii) A phased programme to develop infrastructure facilities for sports and games, including sports science and sports medicine support, may be undertaken;

(iii) Appointment of Physical Education teachers and coaches in select disciplines in Universities equipped with adequate infrastructure should be taken up on a phased basis; and

(iv) A comprehensive system for Inter-college and Inter-university tournaments and championships should be introduced in a phased manner. Necessary financial incentives to hold these tournaments should also be provided.

Evaluation Process and Examination Process

Strategies of Reform

(a) Elementary Stage

- The minimum levels of learning (MLLs) in language (mother tongue), mathematics and environmental studies for Classes I-V have been developed by MHRD at the national level. Similar exercise to develop these in the remaining areas and classes of elementary curriculum will be carried out.
- These MLLs will be adapted/adopted by the concerned agency in each State and district to suit the local conditions.
- Since no detention policy is envisaged at the primary stage, the main function of evaluation will be diagnostic in nature so as to provide remedial help to the pupils.
- The concerned agency in each state will prepare a flexible scheme of Continuous Comprehensive Evaluation (CCE) at the elementary stage so as to make the evaluation process an integral part of teaching and learning at this stage. The CCE will cover cognitive, affective and psychomotor areas of pupils' growth and will employ a variety of tools and techniques of evaluation for collecting evidence on different dimensions of pupils' growth. These evaluations will be reported in the form of grades on a comprehensive proforma. Appropriate procedures for ensuring reliability, validity, objectivity and transparency of the evaluations will be suggested by the concerned agency in each state.

(b) Secondary Stage

- Each State Board will lay down expected levels of attainments at Classes IX to XII and prescribe appropriate courses of studies to accomplish these levels in terms of knowledge and/or comprehension, communication skills, understanding, application, analysis, synthesis, judgements, etc.
- In each State the concerned agency will prepare a flexible scheme of CCE for the secondary/senior secondary stage to suit a variety of specific situations obtaining in different regions and types of schools. Certain models have been developed by NCERT and other agencies which could be looked into for guidance.

(c) Higher Education Stage

- Selection tests for admissions to all professional and technical courses will be conducted on an all India basis.
- Each University will prepare broad guidelines for grading to be followed by individual colleges, institutions and departments under its jurisdiction. Orientation programmes may be organised to familiarize the teachers with the grading system.
- The movement towards entrance tests for admission to institutions of higher education will be encouraged and promoted by UGC and State Governments. The services of the National Evaluation Organisation (NEO) should be utilized by the university system for developing, designing and administering entrance tests for admission.

(d) Strategies Common for all Stages

- The emphasis will be laid on testing of expected levels of achievement of a variety of learning objectives in order to ensure due importance to higher abilities of understanding, application, analysis, synthesis, judgement and parallel parameters and not only to memory.
- The semester system when introduced at the secondary stage and onwards should, interalia, provide for:

(a) flexibility in the combination of courses; and

(b) accumulation of credits to enable the pupils to proceed at their own pace resulting in upward and horizontal mobility of the students across the country.

- Appropriate courses in examination reform will be developed by Indira Gandhi National Open University through distance education mode in collaboration with NCERT for the large scale training of different kinds and levels of personnel.
- An Examination Reform Centre will be established at the UGC for coordination, documentation and dissemination of information on examination reforms in higher education. Similarly, NCERT would perform this function at school stage.

(e) External Examinations: Nature and Conduct

The possibility of introducing legislation to define various malpractices connected with examination and to treat them as cognizable and unavailable offences will be considered.

(f) National Evaluation Organisation (NEO)

It will be devoloped as a quality control mechanism.

Teachers and Their Training

Action Plan

Centrally-sponsored Scheme of Teacher Education

While attempts will be made to provide maximum coverage through DIETs/CTEs/IASEs, special orientation programmes for teachers will also be launched and Teachers' Centres and School Complexes will be tried out on pilot basis. The emphasis under the training programmes will be on training in the use of Operation Blackboard materials and orienting the teachers towards Minimum Levels of Learning (MLLs) strategy with a focus on teaching of language, Mathematics and environmental studies.

Under the DIETs, all the districts in the country will be covered by the end of the Eighth Five Year Plan; about 250 CTEs/IASEs will be set up by that period. Efforts will also be made to provide programme support to other STEIS and also to develop training institutions not covered under the DIETs/CTEs/IASEs scheme. The SCERTs will be made independent and autonomous, overseeing the functioning of DIETs, DRUs, etc. and the NCTE will be conferred autonomous and statutory status and State Boards of Teacher Education will be set up for effective role in maintaining the standards of teacher training institutions and other related functions.

The norms of Central assistance under the scheme will be reviewed and revised suitably:

(i) Keeping in view the increased costs and other norm-based requirements; and

(ii) Formulation by the States of an effective personnel policy and of suitable implementation strategy will be made a pre-condition for Central assistance. Delegation of powers to the Principals and release of money in time will also be made pre-conditions. The possibility of releasing funds through autonomous SCERTs will also be explored and encouraged. Encouragement will be given to non-governmental teacher education institutions for upgradation; the possibility of releasing funds either directly or through SCERTs or through other agencies will be explored.

Efforts will also be made to provide training for preschool education.

In the area of secondary teacher education, some of the better existing institutions will be provided programme support so that benefit of in-service training could be provided to larger number of secondary teachers. This will be in addition to the existing scheme of CTEs/IASEs.

A special programme will be launched for preparation and production of teaching-learning materials for teacher education in different languages.

Teacher Educators

The existing programme for teacher educators will be suitably modified taking into account the present day training needs.

Management of Education

In view of the constraint of resources, cost effectiveness has to be promoted in educational planning and administration at all levels. Location and establishment of institutions should be planned rationally with due regard to the catchment areas of existing institutions, identification of unserved and underserved areas, and the possibility of expanding facilities in existing institutions. As far as possible facilities should be shared among institutions and extra shifts resorted to in urban areas to provide better utilisation of resources. The chapters on Higher Education and Technical Education have spelt out some measures in this regard.

All procedures and processes which hamper the functioning of institutions and hold up programme implementation must be reviewed and simplified. For example, migration, conduct and identification certificates and similar other plethora of outmoded practices only hinder programmes of education. Simplified manual of instructions and codes must be evolved to facilitate the proposed reforms in education. Modernization of education offices will enchance their efficiency.

Strengthening of Educational Planning and Administration

(a) School and Educational Complexes

School complexes will be promoted as a network of institutions on a flexible pattern to provide synergic alliances to encourage professionalism among teachers, to ensure observance of norms and conduct and to enable the sharing of experiences and facilities. The school complex will serve as the lowest viable unit of area planning and will form a cluster of 8-10 institutions in which different institutions can reinforce each other by exchanging resources, personnel, materials, teaching aids, etc. and using them on a sharing basis.

It is expected that in course of time, school complexes when fully developed, will take over much of the inspection functions including educational mapping, grading of institutions and identifying strength and weakness of individual schools. Inspection to be conducted will invoke a culture of participation and providing correctives rather than the existing practice of finding faults. These inspections will be in addition to the normal routine inspection functions of district/block level inspecting authorities.

Guidelines for functioning of school complexes have been prepared and communicated to the State Governments. Although a number of States have experimented with the scheme of school complexes, the programme is yet to emerge as a comprehensive and systematically administered one. As the institutional resource endowment varies from place to place, there can be no single model for creation of school complexes. Every state has to evolve its own operational model based on its experiences or by drawing upon experiences of other States. The States may prescribe necessary guidelines for creation and functioning of school complexes and define the nature, mode, type of planning and inspection work to be performed by them. Considering that some of the schools forming part of the complex will be non-government institutions the State Governments may give them necessary assistance to facilitate their participation. It would be desirable that the recommendations regarding the school complex programme are implemented on a State-wise basis during the Eighth Plan period.

At the same time it is desirable to attempt larger networking of institutions in a district in the shape of educational complexes on an experimental basis during the Eighth Plan period. In the educational complex, the networking could be done from the primary to college and university level. The Central Government may develop in the next two years guidelines for organising this on an experimental basis in situations where the atmosphere is congenial for launching such complexes. While developing the educational complexes, support from institutions like DIET, Teacher Education Colleges, ITIs, Polytechnics, particularly community polytechnics may also be sought.

(b) Block Level Administration

It is observed that the block-level set up of educational administration is very weak almost all over the country. The supervisors often have little contact with the schools. The routine administrative duties such as collecting statistics, disbursement of salaries, posting and transfers of the staff take up most of their time. The following steps may be taken to improve the functioning of block-level education set up:

(i) Norms, not only on the basis of number of schools but also number of teachers should be evolved through systematic studies so that the block-level education officer may effectively cope with his administrative responsibilities and supervisory functions; and

(ii) Most of the time of block-level education officers is spent on routine administrative work. Their duties may be laid down in detail so that their support for the academic programmes gets due importance.

(c) District Educational Administration

The jurisdiction of a district for the educational purpose may be coterminus with its revenue jurisdiction. The big districts could be divided into sub-educational districts but these will be coordinated and controlled by a Chief Education Officer (CEO) for the whole district. He will look after all levels of education – primary, middle, secondary and higer secondary, non-formal and adult education. The Planning and Statistics branch of CEO will be provided with computer facilities for Educational Management Information System (EMIS).

For purposes of academic inspections, district supervisors of education may be provided on the basis of number of schools to be looked after for academic supervision. In discharge of these functions, the supervisors will also be suitably strengthened to discharge their functions.

PART II

EDUCATIONAL STATISTICS

7

EDUCATIONAL STATISTICS

Introduction

Treatment of acute as well as normal cases demand that the 'Case History' of the patient be prepared in some detail to enable the experts to come to concurrent conclusions with regard to the nature of the malady and the line of its treatment. The educational statistics which serve as the 'Case History' of Indian education are facing a serious crisis. Following statements on diverse issues, serve as background.

1. Expansion of Literacy Educational Facilities

Statement No. 7.1
Literacy Rate – India : 1951-1991

Year	Persons	Males	Females
1951	18.33	27.16	8.86
1961	28.31	40.40	15.34
1971	34.45	45.95	21.97
1981	43.56	56.37	29.75
	(41.42)	(53.45)	(28.46)
1991	52.11	63.86	39.42

Note: 1. Literacy rate for 1951, 1961 and 1971 related to population aged five years and above. The rates for the years 1981 and 1991 relate to the population aged seven years and above. The literacy rates for the population aged five years and above in 1981 have been shown in brackets.

2. The 1981 rates exclude Assam where the 1981 Census could not be conducted. The 1991 Census rates exclude Jammu and Kashmir where the 1991 Census could not be conducted.

Statement No. 7.2
Number of Literates and Illiterates among Population:
Population Aged Seven Years and Above – India
1981-1991

Year	Persons	Males	Females
(1)	(2)	(3)	(4)
Literates			
1981	233,947	156,953	76,994
1991	352,082	224,288	127,794
Increase in 1991 over 1981	118,315	67,335	50,800
Illiterates			
1981	301,933	120,902	181,031
1991	324,030	126,694	197,336
Increase in 1991 over 1981	22,097	5,792	16,305

Note: 1. The figure excludes Assam and Jammu and Kashmir. For Assam, the 1981 figures are not available as the 1981 Census could not be held there, while for Jammu and Kashmir, the 1991 figures are not available as the 1991 Census was not conducted there.

2. Figures of literate population for 1991 are as per the provisional results of the 1991 Census. The figures of illiterate population aged seven years and above are estimated figures based on certain assumptions on population age structure and are likely to undergo change.

Statement No. 7.3
Percentage of Literates to Estimated Population Aged 7 Years and Above

State/UT	1981			1991		
	Persons	Males	Females	Persons	Males	Females
India	**43.56**	**56.37**	**29.75**	**52.11**	**63.86**	**39.42**
1. Andhra Pradesh	35.66	46.83	24.16	45.11	56.24	33.71
2. Arunachal Pradesh	25.54	35.11	14.01	41.22	51.10	29.37
3. Assam	NA	NA	NA	53.42	62.34	43.70
4. Bihar	32.03	46.58	16.51	38.54	52.63	23.10
5. Goa	65.71	76.01	55.17	76.96	85.48	68.20
6. Gujarat	52.21	65.14	38.46	60.91	72.54	48.50
7. Haryana	43.85	58.49	26.89	55.33	67.85	40.94
8. Himachal Pradesh	51.17	64.27	37.72	63.54	74.57	52.46
9. Jammu and Kashmir	32.68	44.18	19.55	NA	NA	NA
10. Karnataka	46.20	58.72	33.16	55.98	67.25	44.34
11. Kerala	81.56	87.74	75.65	90.59	94.45	86.93
12. Madhya Pradesh	34.22	48.41	18.99	43.45	57.43	28.39
13. Maharashtra	55.83	69.66	41.01	63.05	74.84	50.51
14. Manipur	49.61	64.12	34.61	60.96	72.98	48.64
15. Meghalaya	42.02	46.62	37.15	48.26	51.57	44.78
16. Mizoram	74.26	79.37	68.60	81.23	84.06	78.09
17. Nagaland	50.20	58.52	40.28	61.30	66.09	55.72
18. Orissa	40.96	56.45	25.14	48.55	62.37	34.40
19. Punjab	48.12	55.52	39.64	57.14	63.68	49.72
20. Rajasthan	30.09	44.76	13.99	38.81	55.07	20.84
21. Sikkim	41.57	52.98	27.35	56.53	64.34	47.23
22. Tamil Nadu	54.38	68.05	40.43	63.72	74.88	52.29
23. Tripura	50.10	61.49	38.01	60.39	70.08	50.01
24. Uttar Pradesh	33.33	47.43	17.18	41.71	55.35	26.02
25. West Bengal	48.64	59.93	36.07	57.72	67.24	47.15
26. A and N islands	63.16	70.28	53.15	73.74	79.68	66.22
27. Chandigarh	74.81	78.89	69.31	78.73	82.67	73.61
28. Dadra and Nagar Haveli	32.70	44.69	20.38	39.45	52.07	26.10
29. Daman and Diu	59.91	74.45	46.51	73.58	85.67	61.38
30. Delhi	71.93	79.28	62.57	76.09	82.63	68.01
31. Lakshadweep	68.42	81.24	55.32	79.23	87.06	70.88
32. Pondicherry	65.14	77.09	53.03	74.91	83.91	65.79

NA = stands for not available.

Note: Literacy rates for 1981 excludes Assam where the 1991 census could not be held and the literacy rates for 1991 exclude Jammu and Kashmir where the 1991 census could not be conducted. The literacy rates for India for 1981 and 1991 excluding Assam and Jammu and Kashmir work out as under:

	Persons	*Males*	*Females*
1981	43.66	56.49	29.84
1991	52.07	63.90	39.31

Statement No. 7.4

States and Union Territories arranged in Descending Order of Literacy Rate among Persons, Males and Females : 1991

	Persons		Males		Females	
Rank	State/ Union Territory	Rate	Literacy State/ Union Territory	Literacy Rate	State/ Union Territory	Literacy Rate
1.	Kerala	90.59	Kerala	94.45	Kerala	86.93
2.	Mizoram	81.23	Lakshadweep	87.06	Mizoram	78.09
3.	Lakshadweep	79.23	Daman and Diu	85.67	Chandigarh	73.61
4.	Chandigarh	78.73	Goa	85.48	Lakshadweep	70.88
5.	Goa	76.96	Mizoram	84.06	Goa	68.20
6.	Delhi	76.09	Pondicherry	83.91	Delhi	68.01
7.	Pondicherry	74.91	Chandigarh	82.67	A and N Islands	66.22
8.	A and N Islands	73.74	Delhi	82.63	Pondicherry	65.79
9.	Daman and Diu	73.58	A and N Islands	79.68	Daman and Diu	61.38
10.	Tamil Nadu	63.72	Tamil Nadu	74.88	Nagaland	55.72
11.	Himachal Pradesh	63.54	Maharashtra	74.84	Himachal Pradesh	52.46
12.	Maharashtra	63.05	Himachal Pradesh	74.57	Tamil Nadu	52.29
13.	Nagaland	61.30	Manipur	72.98	Maharashtra	50.51
14.	Manipur	60.96	Gujarat	72.54	Tripura	50.01
15.	Gujarat	60.91	Tripura	70.08	Punjab	49.72
16.	Tripura	60.39	Haryana	67.85	Manipur	48.64
17.	West Bengal	57.72	Karnataka	67.25	Gujarat	48.50
18.	Punjab	57.14	West Bengal	67.24	Sikkim	47.23
19.	Sikkim	56.53	Nagaland	66.09	West Bengal	47.15
20.	Karnataka	55.98	Sikkim	64.34	Meghalaya	44.78
21.	Haryana	55.33	India	63.86	Karnataka	44.34
22.	Assam	53.42	Punjab	63.68	Assam	43.70
	India	52.11	Orissa	62.37	Haryana	40.94
23.	Orissa	48.55	Assam	62.34	India	39.42
24.	Meghalaya	48.26	Madhya Pradesh	57.43	Orissa	34.40
25.	Andhra Pradesh	45.11	Andhra Pradesh	56.24	Andhra Pradesh	33.71
26.	Madhya Pradesh	43.45	Uttar Pradesh	55.35	Arunachal Pradesh	29.37
27.	Uttar Pradesh	41.71	Rajasthan	55.07	Madhya Pradesh	28.39
28.	Arunachal Pradesh	41.22	Bihar	52.63	Dadra and Nagar Haveli	26.10
29.	Dadra and Nagar Haveli	39.45	Dadra and Nagar Haveli	52.07	Uttar Pradesh	26.02
30.	Rajasthan	38.81	Meghalaya	51.57	Bihar	23.10
31.	Bihar	38.54	Arunachal Pradesh	51.10	Rajasthan	20.84

Note: Excludes Jammu and Kashmir where the 1991 Census was not held.

Statement No. 7.5
Growth of Recognised Educational Institutions Since 1951

Year	Primary	Upper Primary	High/Hr. Sec. Schools Inter./ Pre-Degree Jr. Colleges	Colleges for Genl. Edn	Colleges for Prof. Edn	Univer-sities
1950-51	209671	13596	7416	370	208	27
1960-61	330399	49663	17329	967	852	45.
1970-71	408378	90621	37051	2285	992	82
1980-81	494503	118335	51624	3421	1156	110
1990-91	558392	146636	78619	4862	886	146

Statement No. 7.6
Sex-wise Enrolment by Stages/Classes Since 1951
School Level

(In lakhs)

Year	Primary			Upper Primary			High/Hr. Secondary		
	Boys	Girls	Total	Boys	Girls	Total	Boys	Girls	Total
1950-51	138	54	192	26	5	31	13	2	15
1960-61	236	114	350	51	16	67	27	7	34
1970-71	357	213	570	94	39	133	57	19	76
1980-81	453	285	738	139	68	207	84	35	119
1990-91	581	410	991	209	124	333	140	69	209

Statement No. 7.7
Distribution of Teachers by Type of Schools Since 1951

(In 000's)

Year	Primary			Upper Primary			High/Hr. Secondary		
	Boys	Girls	Total	Boys	Girls	Total	Boys	Girls	Total
1950-51	456	82	538	73	13	86	107	20	127
1960-61	615	127	742	262	83	345	234	62	296
1970-71	835	225	1060	463	175	638	474	155	629
1980-81	1020	343	1363	598	253	851	658	254	912
1990-91	1167	470	1637	706	353	1059	857	416	1273

Statement No. 7.8
Educational Institutions (1990-91)
(As on 30th September 1990)

Sl. No.	State/ U.Ts.	Primary	Middle	High-school/ Hr. Sec./ Interme-diate Pre-Degree/ Jr. Colleges	Colleges for General Education	Colleges for Prof. @ Education	Colleges for Univer-sities*
1.	Andhra Pradesh	48731	6118	6695	403	82	17
2.	Arunachal Pradesh	1122	254	113	4	0	1
3.	Assam	28876	5703	3443	213	15	3
4.	Bihar	53252	13170	4097	557	31	11
5.	Goa	1014	112	372	15	4	1
6.	Gujarat	13174	17084	5075	230	59	10
7.	Haryana	4922	1321	2266	119	22	4
8.	Himachal Pradesh	7522	1101	1037	39	4	3
9.	Jammu and Kashmir	8712	2320	1097	27	9	3
10.	Karnataka	23539	16318	5110	403	132	9
11.	Kerala	6772	2911	2568	133	31	6
12.	Madhya Pradesh	66849	13977	3973	448	37	12
13.	Maharashtra	39121	18849	10374	582	195	18
14.	Manipur	3226	693	440	31	4	1
15.	Meghalaya	4163	693	303	23	1	1
16.	Mizoram	1109	544	205	13	1	0
17.	Nagaland	1287	341	148	15	1	0
18.	Orissa	40033	9405	4926	244	20	5
19.	Punjab	12372	1425	2743	171	26	4
20.	Rajasthan	30231	8629	3733	159	41	9
21.	Sikkim	510	122	75	1	0	0
22.	Tamil Nadu	29979	5624	5158	214	71	15
23.	Tripura	2083	436	454	13	2	1
24.	Uttar Pradesh	76545	14582	5999	418	24	25
25.	West Bengal	50827	4179	6804	302	62	11
26.	A and N Islands	186	41	66	2	1	0
27.	Chandigarh	54	27	68	12	2	2
28.	Dadra and Nagar Haveli	120	41	11	0	0	0
29.	Daman and Diu	46	20	19	1	0	0
30.	Delhi	1655	485	1130	63	6	11
31.	Lakshadweep	19	4	11	0	0	0
32.	Pondicherry	341	107	106	7	3	1
	India	558392	146636	78619	4862	886	184

* Includes Deemed Universities and Institutions of National Importance.

@ Includes only Colleges of Engineering, Technology, Medical and Teacher Training.

Source: *Selected Educational Statistics*, 1990-91.

Statement No. 7.9
Enrolment by Stages (1990-91)

(As on 30-9-1990)

Sl. No.	State/ U.Ts.	Primary			Middle			Sec./Hr.Sec.			Hr. Education*		
		Boys	Girls	Total	Boys	Girls	Total	Boys	Girls	Total	Boys	Girls	Total
1.	Andhra Pradesh	4301744	3234834	7536578	1343686	780407	2124093	915175	466376	1381551	187723	77444	265167
2.	Arunachal Pradesh	65043	47154	112197	15956	10133	26089	10688	5008	15696	1293	312	1605
3.	Assam	1893197	1656888	3550085	640427	435770	1076197	341313	235458	576771	78246	33212	111458
4.	Bihar	5723453	2841810	8565263	1559587	560989	2120576	1043970	252742	1296712	401154	94041	495195
5.	Goa	71483	64373	135856	43464	37449	80913	32234	26811	59045	5735	5815	11550
6.	Gujarat	3222000	2458000	5680000	1138000	750000	1888000	701000	428000	1129000	158325	113975	272300
7.	Haryana	954490	734917	1689407	439601	251214	690815	283906	126104	410010	44943	29204	74147
8.	Himachal Pradesh	371102	319123	690225	188667	146131	334798	171205	105178	276383	7269	3357	10626
9.	Jammu and Kashmir	450374	288386	738760	190878	100860	291738	122903	58410	181313	16395	10958	27353
10.	Karnataka	3064914	2617318	5682232	1015914	697952	1713866	738367	377862	1116229	178459	76858	255317
11.	Kerala	1623059	1532817	3155876	961533	908127	1869660	573061	589066	1162127	77285	88771	166056
12.	Madhya Pradesh	4863414	3131075	7994489	1764639	889261	2653900	758169	248660	1006829	164317	71032	235349
13.	Maharashtra	5397629	4624412	10022041	2292177	1602467	3894644	1968072	1051583	3019655	399508	243778	643286
14.	Manipur	143515	121074	264589	42340	36360	78700	39543	29037	68580	12642	8319	20961
15.	Meghalaya	124393	118177	242570	36909	32451	69360	31437	27167	58604	4339	2859	7198
16.	Mizoram	63183	57117	120300	19568	19509	39077	11440	10167	21607	1281	918	2199

(Contd.

Statement No. 9 (*Contd.*)

Sl. No.	State/ U.Ts.	Primary			Middle			Sec./Hr.Sec.			Hr. Education*		
		Boys	Girls	Total	Boys	Girls	Total	Boys	Girls	Total	Boys	Girls	Total
17.	Nagaland	78810	66600	145410	28617	26904	55521	13641	10974	24615	2072	1007	3079
18.	Orissa	2174000	1446000	3620000	548500	427300	975800	614986	313215	928201	50228	17423	67651
19.	Punjab	1108729	947026	2055755	487970	364470	852440	362704	251615	614319	42235	38492	80727
20.	Rajasthan	3141437	1371810	4513247	1033336	825398	1318734	642283	152889	795172	74256	24958	99214
21.	Sikkim	38873	33625	72498	7776	7038	14814	5124	3588	8712	0	0	0
22.	Tamil Nadu	4182459	3581414	7763873	1814266	1344281	3158547	988149	648138	1636287	149787	89977	239764
23.	Tripura	221084	181220	402304	68964	52502	,121466	39797	26023	65820	7330	3505	10835
24.	Uttar Pradesh	8889785	5050215	13940000	3240428	1229582	4470010	2268912	698903	2967815	359801	115796	475597
25.	West Bengal	5313432	3960689	9274121	1578095	1164672	2742767	1058516	540100	1598616	196157	134837	330994
26.	A. and N. Islands	21042	18770	39812	9886	8022	17908	6631	5583	12214	962	778	1740
27.	Chandigarh	26382	23248	49630	13584	12362	25946	23132	18024	41156	7099	6865	13964
28.	Dadra and Nagar Haveli	9821	6791	16612	2820	1598	4418	1526	905	2431	0	0	0
29.	Daman and Diu	4992	4787	9779	4063	3438	7501	3791	2504	6295	202	168	370
30.	Delhi	490965	429868	920833	280346	225354	505700	215397	170405	385802	74349	54634	128983
31.	Lakshadweep	4518	3830	8348	1743	1409	3152	1081	653	1734	0	0	0
32.	Pondicherry	55394	50236	105630	30551	25298	55849	15418	12683	28101	2964	2321	5285
	India	58094716	41023604	99118320	20844291	12438708	3328999	14003571	6893831	20897402	2706356	135614	4057970

* Excludes enrolment in Ph.D/M.Phil and all professional courses except Engineering (B.E./B. Tach/B. Arc.), Medicine (MBBS) and Teacher Training (B.Ed./B.T.).

Source: *Selected Educational Statistics*, 1990-91.

Statement No. 7.10
Enrolment by Stages (Scheduled Castes) 1990-91

(As on 30-9-1990)

Sl. No.	State/ U.Ts.	Primary			Middle			Sec./Hr.Sec.			Hr. Education*		
		Boys	Girls	Total	Boys	Girls	Total	Boys	Girls	Total	Boys	Girls	Total
1.	Andhra Pradesh	855619	630067	1485686	226832	123318	350150	135960	61229	197189	23233	7431	30664
2.	Arunachal Pradesh	63	37	100	9	6	15	7	5	12	0	0	0
3.	Assam	193290	176980	370270	63160	45912	109072	36692	23692	60384	6160	2257	8417
4.	Bihar	789358	294802	1084160	160231	40776	201007	67354	11107	78461	0	0	0
5.	Goa	1679	1450	3129	596	417	1013	287	211	498	67	38	105
6.	Gujarat	311000	235000	546000	114700	64000	178700	72200	31900	104100	14270	5790	20060
7.	Haryana	211603	166541	378144	69753	31549	101302	33879	7924	41803	3689	625	4314
8.	Himachal Pradesh	92265	75450	167715	39397	24570	63967	23428	9855	33283	681	137	818
9.	Jammu and Kashmir	36200	23800	60000	15700	8430	24130	6420	2340	8760	0	0	0
10.	Karnataka	489228	398934	888162	144875	92720	237595	97834	40406	138240	19105	4869	23974
11.	Kerala	188287	176914	365201	104829	98190	203019	58118	62374	120492	5286	5732	11018
12.	Madhya Pradesh	776251	376471	115722	219579	108008	327587	88687	19089	107776	15438	2866	18304
13.	Maharashtra	803284	655676	1458960	315224	197792	513016	230903	105428	336331	44255	9151	53406
14.	Manipur	1968	1995	3963	540	502	1042	627	568	1195	270	214	484
15.	Meghalaya	1314	1280	2594	535	385	920	875	442	1317	153	112	265

(Contd.)

Statement No. 10 (*Contd.*)

Sl. No.	State/ U.Ts.	Primary			Middle			Sec./Hr.Sec.			Hr. Education*		
		Boys	Girls	Total	Boys	Girls	Total	Boys	Girls	Total	Boys	Girls	Total
16.	Mizoram	@	@	@	@	@	@	@	@	@	@	@	@
17.	Nagaland	@	@	@	@	@	@	@	@	@	@	@	@
18.	Orissa	420000	268000	688000	105100	41100	146200	55915	17074	72989	3698	768	4466
19.	Punjab	393526	309068	702594	116390	76109	192499	66689	36665	103354	6838	2859	9697
20.	Rajasthan	524720	170993	695713	155320	20001	175321	84929	6190	91119	6453	333	6796
21.	Sikkim	2271	1995	4266	343	326	669	191	153	344	0	0	0
22.	Tamil Nadu	838389	691023	159412	324308	226534	550842	159999	79458	239457	22682	9445	32127
23.	Tripura	40114	33387	73501	11628	8139	19767	5926	3332	9258	916	335	1251
24.	Uttar Pradesh	1753066	676224	2429290	337523	82523	420046	320046	47848	367894	53564	4031	57595
25.	West Bengal	875964	583280	1459244	165098	84470	249568	120254	50844	171098	17364	7753	25117
26.	A. and N. Islands	@	@	@	@	@	@	@	@	@	@	@	@
27.	Chandigarh	7437	6352	13789	2937	2344	5281	1850	1866	3716	470	164	634
28.	Dadra and Nagar Haveli	163	151	314	109	75	184	85	58	143	0	0	0
29.	Daman and Diu	194	168	362	122	138	260	193	111	304	12	3	15
30.	Delhi	119137	90739	209876	47361	30631	77992	31867	13722	45589	4968	2717	7685
31.	Lakshadweep	10	7	17	7	6	13	7	5	12	0	0	0
32.	Pondicherry	10524	10719	21243	4894	4445	9339	1601	1118	2719	332	140	472
	India	9736924	6057503	15794427	2747100	1413416	4160516	1702823	635014	2337837	249904	67770	317684

* Excludes enrolment in Ph.D./M. Phil and all professional courses except Engineering (B.E./B.Tech/B. Arc.), Medicine (MBBS) and Teacher Training (B.Ed./B.T.).

@ No castes were scheduled by the President of India for Nagaland, A and N Islands and Lakshadweep.

Source: *Selected Educational Statistics*, 1990-91

Statement No. 7.11
Enrolment by Stages (Scheduled Tribes) 1990-91

(As on 30-9-1990)

Sl. No.	State/ U.Ts.	Primary			Middle			Sec./Hr.Sec.			Hr. Education*		
		Boys	Girls	Total	Boys	Girls	Total	Boys	Girls	Total	Boys	Girls	Total
1.	Andhra Pradesh	323476	199536	523012	58966	24287	83253	29441	10102	39543	3274	830	4104
2.	Arunachal Pradesh	48200	33962	82162	10884	6468	17352	7672	2859	10531	997	207	1204
3.	Assam	322216	271020	593236	74245	49960	124205	49559	31392	80951	6747	2552	9299
4.	Bihar	471823	247489	719312	99885	40445	140330	42816	15432	58248	0	0	0
5.	Goa	198	123	321	35	12	47	3	0	3	0	0	0
6.	Gujarat	514000	366000	880000	124000	69000	193000	61300	31600	92900	13400	7135	20535
7.	Haryana	@	@	@	@	@	@	@	@	@	@	@	@
8.	Himachal Pradesh	15642	12146	27788	6793	3319	10112	4244	1689	5933	255	56	311
9.	Jammu and Kashmir	@	@	@	@	@	@	@	@	@	@	@	@
10.	Karnataka	122261	100988	223249	35223	23860	59083	19854	10182	30036	4318	832	5150
11.	Kerala	22000	20012	42012	8142	7783	15925	3889	3652	7541	315	258	573
12.	Madhya Pradesh	940731	393331	1334062	215472	111288	326760	86091	16553	102644	10058	2037	12095
13.	Maharashtra	509215	387919	897134	145486	78313	223799	78299	31530	109829	8765	2157	10922
14.	Manipur	50666	42074	92740	9188	7282	16470	7036	5179	12215	1574	892	2466
15.	Meghalaya	104420	98926	203346	30401	28470	58871	25293	22002	47295	2617	1913	4530
16.	Mizoram	62666	56336	119002	19368	19298	38666	10847	9699	20546	212	110	322

(Contd.)

Statement No. 7.11 (*Contd.*)

Sl. No.	State/ U.T.	Primary			Middle			Sec./Hr.Sec.			Hr. Education*		
		Boys	Girls	Total	Boys	Girls	Total	Boys	Girls	Total	Boys	Girls	Total
17.	Nagaland	77039	71301	148340	21227	18039	39266	9516	7687	17203	1696	871	2567
18.	Orissa	522000	246000	768000	93100	38100	131200	34048	13172	47220	2842	612	3454
19.	Punjab	@	@	@	@	@	@	@	@	@	@	@	@
20.	Rajasthan	373292	111834	485126	95273	10410	105683	53498	3088	56586	5070	143	5213
21.	Sikkim	8250	7218	15468	1728	1657	3385	1038	892	1930	0	0	0
22.	Tamil Nadu	39003	29552	68555	11823	7183	19006	5594	3506	9100	473	158	631
23.	Tripura	76830	55577	132407	16169	10036	26205	6951	3194	10145	364	100	464
24.	Uttar Pradesh	21584	12625	34209	5353	1634	6987	5933	1522	7455	1228	502	1730
25.	West Bengal	316631	134878	451509	43094	14830	57924	20092	10560	30652	775	284	1059
26.	A. and N. Islands	1763	1621	3384	1038	894	1932	1403	1282	2685	18	8	26
27.	Chandigarh	0	0	0	0	0	0	68	32	100	95	27	122
28.	Dadra and Nagar Haveli	8345	5527	13872	2067	974	3041	853	390	1243	0	0	0
29.	Daman and Diu	669	578	1247	499	492	991	259	142	401	75	32	107
30.	Delhi	298	274	572	247	148	395	225	158	383	397	238	635
31.	Lakshadweep	4393	3729	8122	1682	1336	3018	976	565	1541	0	0	0
32.	Pondicherry	@	@	@	@	@	@	@	@	@	@	@	@
	India	4957611	2910576	7868187	1131388	575518	1706906	566798	238061	804859	65565	21954	87519

* Excludes enrolment in Ph.D./M. Phil. and all professional courses except Engineering (B.E./B.Tech/B.Arc.) Medicine (MBBS) and Teacher training (B.Ed./B.T.).

@ No. tribes were scheduled by the President of India in Haryana, Jammu and Kashmir, Punjab, Chandigarh, Delhi and Pondicherry.

Source: *Selected Educational Statistics*, 1990-91.

Statement No. 7.12
Enrolment Per Lakh Population (1990-91)

Sl. No.	State/U.Ts.	Total		Scheduled Castes		Scheduled Tribes	
		Primary	Middle	Primary	Middle	Primary	Middle
1.	Andhra Pradesh	11367	3204	15069	3551	13302	2117
2.	Arunachal Pradesh	13070	3039	2381	357	13723	2898
3.	Assam	15924	4827	26619	7841	24212	5069
4.	Bihar	9921	2456	8656	1605	10026	1956
5.	Goa	11626	6924	12319	3988	2841	416
6.	Gujarat	13795	4585	18541	6068	15030	3296
7.	Haryana	10353	4234	12152	3255	—	—
8.	Himachal Pradesh	13504	6550	13333	5085	11770	4283
9.	Jammu and Kashmir	9571	3780	9357	3763	—	—
10.	Karnataka	12679	3824	13154	3519	10125	2680
11.	Kerala	10878	6445	12569	6987	14060	5330
12.	Madhya Pradesh	12088	4013	12361	3513	8782	2151
13.	Maharashtra	12733	4948	25976	9134	12403	3094
14.	Manipur	14485	4308	17382	4570	18596	3303
15.	Meghalaya	13778	3940	35534	12603	14335	4150
16.	Mizoram	17531	5695	—	—	18527	6020
17.	Nagaland	11962	4567	—	—	14533	3847
18.	Orissa	11488	3097	14895	3165	10866	1856
19.	Punjab	10182	4222	12950	3548	—	—
20.	Rajasthan	10285	3005	9303	2344	9055	1973
21.	Sikkim	17963	3670	18468	2896	16543	3620
22.	Tamil Nadu	13954	5677	14982	5396	11516	3193
23.	Tripura	14657	4425	17737	4770	16949	3354
24.	Uttar Pradesh	10046	3221	8275	1431	11740	2398
25.	West Bengal	13642	4035	9763	1670	11680	1498
26.	A and N Islands	14321	6442	—	—	10132	5784
27.	Chandigarh	7746	4050	15253	5842	—	—
28.	Dadra and Nagar Haveli	11994	3190	9813	5750	12645	2772
29.	Daman and Diu	*	*	*	*	*	*
30.	Delhi	9827	5397	12418	4615	—	—
31.	Lakshadweep	16147	6097	—	—	16816	6248
32.	Pondicherry	13381	7075	16886	7424	—	—
	India	11745	3944	12078	3181	11741	2547

* Included in Goa.

Statement No. 7.13
Drop-Out Rates 1987-88

(Rs. in lakhs)

Sl. No.	State/U.Ts.	Class I-V			Class I-VIII		
		Boys	Girls	Total	Boys	Girls	Total
1.	Andhra Pradesh	52.42	58.52	55.03	67.77	77.01	71.68
2.	Arunachal Pradesh	58.75	58.43	58.63	75.20	75.91	75.44
3.	Assam	51.59	59.47	55.01	70.91	74.45	72.44
4.	Bihar	63.88	68.93	65.63	76.77	84.19	79.08
5.	Goa	2.19	8.78	5.33	20.69	27.63	23.95
6.	Gujarat	38.06	46.87	41.92	56.30	67.69	61.67
7.	Haryana	24.35	31.61	27.32	33.01	48.22	38.62
8.	Himachal Pradesh	28.06	29.32	28.63	16.92	34.42	24.68
9.	Jammu and Kashmir	28.08	41.45	33.44	46.63	58.51	51.25
10.	Karnataka	43.28	57.36	50.16	61.04	72.07	66.10
11.	Kerala	–5.12	–3.62	–4.39	15.97	15.00	15.49
12.	Madhya Pradesh	36.64	48.04	41.04	49.88	66.65	55.78
13.	Maharashtra	34.69	45.71	39.82	53.07	68.01	59.87
14.	Meghalaya	31.43	33.40	32.35	66.42	61.61	64.22
15.	Mizoram	37.28	38.72	37.98	45.35	42.49	43.98
16.	Nagaland	37.22	33.43	35.45	58.15	55.13	56.90
17.	Orissa	40.05	37.32	38.97	60.28	71.25	64.86
18.	Punjab	36.81	37.81	37.27	59.69	67.26	63.23
19.	Rajasthan	53.12	60.75	52.25	62.81	76.82	66.35
20.	Sikkim	60.19	58.50	59.86	63.83	60.11	62.51
21.	Tamil Nadu	19.44	24.46	21.78	44.08	53.14	48.22
22.	Tripura	59.14	58.02	58.65	73.95	75.96	74.83
23.	Uttar Pradesh	47.84	47.24	47.65	49.88	63.34	54.20
24.	West Bengal	62.35	65.76	63.81	74.32	76.91	75.41
25.	A and N Islands	18.60	22.74	20.54	38.35	39.59	36.31
26.	Chandigarh	–21.00	24.41	4.78	5.54	13.01	8.94
27.	Dadra and Nagar Haveli	29.37	45.58	36.14	63.98	70.52	66.81
28.	Daman and Diu	2.24	8.82	5.34	21.03	27.97	23.95
29.	Delhi	14.40	25.40	19.76	9.64	24.20	16.73
30.	Lakshadweep	–2.96	11.38	4.02	40.96	56.82	48.45
31.	Pondicherry	11.55	0.83	–5.59	3.11	31.52	16.29
32.	Manipur	71.35	72.04	71.67	76.58	87.86	77.90
	Total	43.35	49.42	46.97	58.80	67.55	62.29

Drop-out rate: calculated as follow :

Drop-out rate from class I to V for the year 1987

$$\frac{\text{(No. of students enrolled in Class I in 1983-84)} - \text{(No. of students enrolled in Class V in 1987-88)}}{\text{No. of students enrolled in class I in 1983-84}} \times 100$$

Drop-out rate from class I to VIII for the year 1987-88

$$\frac{\text{(No. of students enrolled in Class I in 1980-81)} - \text{(No. of students enrolled in Class VIII in 1987-88)}}{\text{No. of students entrolled in Class I in 1980-81}} \times 100$$

This ratio does not take into account :

(i) Repeaters, and (ii) Children who enter the system after Class I.

Statement No. 7.14
Drop-Out Rates SC and ST 1987-88

Sl. No.	State/U Ts.	Class I to V SC	Class I to V ST	Class I to VIII SC	Class I to VIII ST
1.	Andhra Pradesh	64.10	68.84	82.01	88.04
2.	Assam	55.48	64.47	63.24	77.27
3.	Bihar	69.65	72.33	84.07	86.60
4.	Gujarat	44.23	63.72	61.04	78.84
5.	Haryana	36.94	—	57.27	—
6.	Himachal Pradesh	34.71	36.81	39.79	39.99
7.	Jammu and Kashmir	N.A.	—	N.A.	—
8.	Karnataka	66.38	43.83	73.96	66.90
9.	Kerala	N.A.	18.69	24.99	46.48
10.	Madhya Pradesh	42.93	55.93	57.43	71.39
11.	Maharashtra	47.24	63.24	64.10	78.93
12.	Manipur	35.04	77.57	86.27	85.35
13.	Meghalaya	56.99	77.82	78.46	90.42
14.	Nagaland	—	36.11	—	61.22
15.	Orissa	52.26	74.26	74.16	86.59
16.	Punjab	45.46	—	78.29	—
17.	Rajasthan	62.96	75.40	73.28	76.61
18.	Sikkim	72.45	60.25	78.26	56.95
19.	Tamil Nadu	24.48	37.91	54.54	39.21
20.	Tripura	63.15	77.40	81.10	83.93
21.	Uttar Pradesh	48.43	54.73	58.01	59.92
22.	West Bengal	58.17	64.56	80.96	85.09
23.	A and N Islands	—	4.07	—	40.12
24.	Arunachal Pradesh	13.00	64.61	67.09	77.89
25.	Chandigarh	N.A.	—	N.A.	—
26.	Dadra and Nagar Haveli	N.A.	43.89	36.67	76.80
27.	Delhi	28.78	—	55.39	—
28.	Goa, Daman and Diu	38.60	21.74	57.85	57.02
29.	Lakshadweep	—	N.A.	—	50.22
30.	Mizoram	N.A.	30.19	N.A.	51.43
31.	Pondicherry	N.A.	—	29.45	—
	Total	48.84	62.37	67.73	78.51

Census was not conducted in Assam.

Source: (i) *Fifth All-India Educational Survey.*
(ii) Annual Statistics of the Department of Education.

Note: No castes were scheduled by the President of India for Nagaland, A and N Islands and Lakshadweep and no tribes were scheduled in Haryana, Jammu and Kashmir, Punjab, Chandigarh, Delhi and Pondicherry.

2. Teachers : Statewise and Stagewise and Total

Statement No. 7.15
Number of Teachers: 1990-91

Sl. No.	State/ U.Ts.	Primary Schools			Middle Schools			Sec./Hr. Secondary Schools		
		Male	Female	Total	Male	Female	Total	Male	Female	Total
1.	Andhra Pradesh	79219	31638	110857	28270	13567	41837	56993	25856	82849
2.	Arunachal Pradesh	1896	470	2366	1355	316	1671	1788	385	2173
3.	Assam	57738	14586	72318	31742	6304	38046	33301	9150	42451
4.	Bihar	95355	22286	117641	78917	19447	98364	40623	6521	47144
5.	Goa	1123	1789	2912	364	476	840	3291	3832	7123
6.	Gujarat	22500	13800	36300	73500	61750	135250	43808	13983	57791
7.	Haryana	9012	6449	15461	7167	4648	11815	28047	19168	47215
8.	Himachal Pradesh	10980	6020	17000	5700	1300	7000	9100	3800	12900
9.	Jammu and Kashmir	8159	5565	13724	11822	5807	17629	12987	6015	19002
10.	Karnataka	29903	11599	41502	56112	35620	91732	40365	12188	52553
11.	Kerala	18231	31542	49773	19875	31755	51630	36125	56972	93097
12.	Madhya Pradesh	136161	40043	176204	60932	19956	80888	39282	11473	50755
13.	Maharashtra	72626	48485	121111	93365	55555	148920	135277	58681	193958
14.	Manipur	8187	2397	10584	4187	1168	5355	5130	2184	7314
15.	Meghalaya	4243	2486	6729	1895	1114	3009	1495	1446	2941

(*Contd*

Statement No. 7.15 (*Contd.*)

Sl. No.	State/ U.Ts.	Primary Schools			Middle Schools			Sec./Hr. Secondary Schools		
		Male	Female	Total	Male	Female	Total	Male	Female	Total
16.	Mizoram	2058	1689	3747	2626	636	3262	1244	242	1486
17.	Nagaland	4531	1701	6232	2807	791	3598	2161	1031	3192
18.	Orissa	78155	26265	104420	31026	6375	37401	33797	7805	41602
19.	Punjab	22139	25702	47841	5267	4205	9472	27771	21956	49727
20.	Rajasthan	55440	18768	74208	52897	17456	70353	48401	13721	62122
21.	Sikkim	1608	637	2245	1078	487	1565	1243	838	2081
22.	Tamil Nadu	70452	49921	120373	33608	31928	65536	67660	49157	116817
23.	Tripura	6847	1755	8602	3286	840	4126	7118	2868	9986
24.	Uttar Pradesh	215553	48176	263729	76442	18837	95279	80256	16439	96695
25.	West Bengal	144112	40636	184748	18092	7139	25231	78326	41691	120017
26.	A. and N. Islands	473	251	724	351	349	700	1179	931	2110
27.	Chandigarh	78	686	764	85	506	591	886	2233	3119
28.	Dadra and Nagar Haveli	110	50	160	169	215	384	114	44	158
29.	Daman and Diu	119	159	278	139	91	230	166	57	223
30.	Delhi	8243	13943	22186	2269	3396	5665	17080	23581	40661
31.	Lakshadweep	153	71	224	75	49	124	268	67	335
32.	Pondicherry	1086	849	1935	1063	729	1792	1717	1188	2905
	India	1166484	470414	1636898	706483	352812	1059295	856999	415503	1272502

Source: *Selected Educational Statistics, 1989-90.*

3. Budget

Statement No. 7.16
Budget of Education Departments of States/UTs for the Year 1990-91
Ranked in Order of Percentage of Education Budget to Total State Budget

(Rs. in lakhs)

Sl. No.	State/U.Ts.	Budget of Education Department			% of Edu. Budget to Total State Budget
		Plan	Non-Plan	Total	
1	2	3	4	5	6
1.	West Bengal	12363	145051	157414	28.0
2.	Kerala	3307	64978	68285	26.3
3.	Delhi	2606	24323	26929	26.2
4.	Bihar	7447	111807	119254	25.7
5.	Chandigarh	372	3747	4119	24.3
6.	Manipur	789	5638	6427	23.5
7.	Assam	9598	30814	40412	22.0
8.	Daman and Diu	107	308	415	21.9
9.	Goa	1189	5236	6425	21.8
10.	Rajasthan	7664	67989	75653	21.8
11.	Karnataka	8895	76481	85376	21.3
12.	Himachal Pradesh	3327	14694	18021	21.1
13.	Gujarat	1731	84149	85880	20.7
14.	Andhra Pradesh	10740	97463	108203	20.6
15.	Tripura	1849	8898	10747	20.3
16.	Tamil Nadu	3997	92375	96372	20.0
17.	Orissa	15722	34770	50492	19.8
18.	Punjab	541	47181	47722	18.8
19.	Pondicherry	872	2654	3526	18.1
20.	Sikkim	764	1518	2282	17.8
21.	Maharashtra	2445	144734	147179	17.6
22.	Meghalaya	1288	4503	5791	17.3
23.	Uttar Pradesh	15896	144572	160468	16.6
24.	Madhya Pradesh	12112	67466	79578	15.6
25.	Haryana	3451	26324	29775	15.5
26.	Mizoram	741	3131	3872	14.8
27.	Jammu and Kashmir	2395	11415	13810	14.4
28.	Arunachal Pradesh	983	2077	3060	13.4
29.	A and N Islands	306	1463	1769	12.3
30.	Nagaland	685	3491	4176	11.7
31.	Lakshadweep	55	328	383	10.2
32.	Dadra and Nagar Haveli	48	263	311	10.1
	All States/UTs.	131893	1318424	1450317	20.0

Statement No. 7.17
Sectorwise Plan + Non-plan Expenditure on Education
During the Seventh Plan Period (1985-90)

(Rs. in Lakhs)

Sl. No.	State/U.Ts.	Elementary Education	Secondary Education	Special Education Including Adult Education	U and H Education	Technical Education	Others	Total
1	2	3	4	5	6	7	8	9
1.	Andhra Pradesh	161479	102131	3804	72479	10215	2778	352886
2.	Arunachal Pradesh	8045	4386	176	741	—	1188	14536
3.	Assam	86408	36979	2474	15194	3529	5455	150039
4.	Bihar	239233	55769	13301	48313	4262	2517	363395
5.	Goa	5633	10229	188	2854	1042	233	20179
6.	Gujarat	151323	92352	1958	28243	8239	4157	286272
7.	Haryana	44776	42945	2464	16037	2449	906	109577
8.	Himachal Pradesh	30719	18903	665	5306	620	1411	57624
9.	Jammu and Kashmir	25978	20756	950	7468	1847	840	57839
10.	Karnataka	143150	76251	3794	36917	6974	1739	268825
11.	Kerala	137849	75196	1830	35855	11003	2013	263746
12.	Madhya Pradesh	130381	54995	3129	31139	9361	1112	230117
13.	Maharashtra	253552	207899	3976	55515	21298	12584	554824
14.	Manipur	10669	7051	447	4602	240	311	23320
15.	Meghalaya	7496	5647	428	1485	172	448	15676
16.	Mizoram	6943	3350	824	1148	220	493	12978
17.	Nagaland	10593	4011	806	1160	282	89	16941
18.	Orissa	82968	38518	2307	22159	2915	857	149724
19.	Punjab	57001	82237	1300	24292	2123	1123	168076
20.	Rajasthan	124250	80897	4062	24948	3327	1807	239291
21.	Sikkim	2611	4714	260	194	—	215	7994
22.	Tamil Nadu	167814	111095	3805	44682	12672	1501	341569
23.	Tripura	9906	14330	1630	2174	480	214	28734
24.	Uttar Pradesh	304976	195732	9380	47534	16243	1696	575561
25.	West Bengal	142032	153174	3942	46885	7481	14742	368256
26.	A and N Islands	3590	1589	40	284	107	218	5828
27.	Chandigarh	2593	1777	82	6315	1687	107	12561
28.	Dadra and Nagar Haveli	693	203	12	—	2	98	1008
29.	Daman and Diu	606	342	7	92	93	69	1209
30.	Delhi	19285	64441	433	735	4227	2255	91376
31.	Lakshadweep	759	466	18	235	—	55	1533
32.	Pondicherry	4858	3013	115	1523	1694	294	11497
	All States/UTs	2378169	1571378	68608	586510	134803	63525	4802993

Source : *Budget Documents of States/UTs.*

Note : The Above Figures correspond to actuals for 1985-89 and R.E. for 1989-90.

Statement No. 7.18

Percentage of Sectorwise Expenditure (Plan + Non-Plan) to Total Expenditure on Education During Seventh Plan Period

Sl. No.	State/U.Ts.	Elementary Education	Secondary Education	Special Education	U and H Education	Technical Education	Others
1.	Andhra Pradesh	45.8	28.9	1.1	20.5	2.9	0.8
2.	Arunachal Pradesh	55.3	30.2	1.2	5.1	—	8.2
3.	Assam	57.6	24.6	1.6	10.1	2.4	3.6
4.	Bihar	65.8	15.3	3.7	13.3	1.2	0.7
5.	Goa	27.9	50.7	0.9	14.1	5.2	1.2
6.	Gujarat	52.9	32.3	0.7	9.9	2.9	1.5
7.	Haryana	40.9	39.2	2.2	14.6	2.2	0.8
8.	Himachal Pradesh	53.3	32.8	1.2	9.2	1.1	2.4
9.	Jammu and Kashmir	44.9	35.9	1.6	12.9	3.2	1.5
10.	Karnataka	53.3	28.4	1.4	13.7	2.6	0.6
11.	Kerala	52.3	28.5	0.7	13.6	4.2	0.8
12.	Madhya Pradesh	56.7	23.9	1.4	13.5	4.1	0.5
13.	Maharashtra	45.7	37.5	0.7	10.0	3.8	2.3
14.	Manipur	45.8	30.2	1.9	19.7	1.0	1.3
15.	Meghalaya	47.8	36.0	2.7	9.5	1.1	2.9
16.	Mizoram	53.5	25.8	6.3	8.8	1.7	3.8
17.	Nagaland	62.5	23.7	4.8	6.8	1.7	0.5
18.	Orissa	55.4	25.7	1.5	14.8	2.0	0.6
19.	Punjab	33.9	48.9	0.8	14.5	1.3	0.7
20.	Rajasthan	51.9	33.8	1.7	10.4	1.4	0.8
21.	Sikkim	32.7	59.0	3.3	2.4	—	2.7
22.	Tamil Nadu	49.1	32.5	1.1	13.1	3.7	0.4
23.	Tripura	34.5	49.9	5.7	7.6	1.7	0.7
24.	Uttar Pradesh	53.0	34.0	1.6	8.3	2.8	0.3
25.	West Bengal	38.6	41.6	1.1	12.7	2.0	4.0
26.	A and N Islands	61.6	27.3	0.7	4.9	1.8	3.7
27.	Chandigarh	20.6	14.1	0.7	50.3	13.4	0.9
28.	Dadra and Nagar Haveli	68.8	20.1	1.2	—	0.2	9.7
29.	Daman and Diu	50.1	28.3	0.6	7.6	7.7	5.7
30.	Delhi	21.1	70.5	0.5	0.8	4.6	2.5
31.	Lakshadweep	49.5	30.4	1.2	15.3	—	3.6
32.	Pondicherry	42.3	26.2	1.0	13.2	14.7	2.6
	All States/UTs	49.5	32.7	1.4	12.2	2.8	1.3

Statement No. 7.19
Sectorwise Approved Plan Outlay for 1991-92

(Rs. in Lakhs)

Sl. No.	State/U.Ts.	Elementary Education	Adult Education	General Education	Technical Education	Total (Col. 5+ Col. 6)
1	2	3	4	5	6	7
1.	Andhra Pradesh	2000	195	3451	390	3841
2.	Arunachal Pradesh	2065	88	2950	—	2950
3.	Assam	5740	300	7176	703	7879
4.	Bihar	8800	1200	11000	2500	13500
5.	Goa	392	40	1120	300	1420
6.	Gujarat	1604	300	2724	2295	5019
7.	Haryana	1740	100	3630	1600	5230
8.	Himachal Pradesh	2000	50	3600	544	4144
9.	Jammu and Kashmir	2000	111	5174	139	5313
10.	Karnataka	3084	332	6236	814	7050
11.	Kerala	164	25	1062	1900	2962
12.	Madhya Pradesh	7759	550	16412	2811	19223
13.	Maharashtra	2553	297	5300	3000	8300
14.	Manipur	543	65	1086	83	1169
15.	Meghalaya	1418	89	2025	25	2050
16.	Mizoram	445	15	817	70	887
17.	Nagaland	500	27	907	134	1041
18.	Orissa	2770	310	3832	1032	4884
19.	Punjab	1539	101	2300	3720	6020
20.	Rajasthan	4174	115	8825	1455	10280
21.	Sikkim	615	6	1000	75	1075
22.	TamilNadu	5300	345	6370	450	6820
23.	Tripura	1182	58	2233	25	2258
24.	Uttar Pradesh	6041	340	13288	5134	18422
25.	West Bengal	2900	450	7564	1489	9053
26.	A and N Islands	355	5	778	195	973
27.	Chandigarh	165	5	577	200	777
28.	Dadra and Nagar Haveli	119	3	178	20	198
29.	Daman and Diu	60	2	104	109	213
30.	Delhi	4450	40	6700	1800	8500
31.	Lakshadweep	17	3	125	—	125
32.	Pondicherry	400	8	849	326	1175
	All State/UTs	72874	5575	129393	33338	162731

Source: Analysis of Annual Plan 1991-92, by Planning Commission.

Statment No. 7.20
Percentage of Sectorwise Approved Plan Outlay 1991-92

Sl. No.	State/U.Ts.	Elementary Education	Adult Education	General Education	Technical Education
1	2	3	4	5	6
1.	Andhra Pradesh	52.1	5.1	89.8	10.2
2.	Arunachal Pradesh	70.0	3.0	100.0	Nil
3.	Assam	72.9	3.8	91.1	8.9
4.	Bihar	65.2	8.9	81.5	18.5
5.	Goa	27.6	2.8	78.9	21.1
6.	Gujarat	32.0	6.0	54.3	45.7
7.	Haryana	33.3	1.9	69.4	30.6
8.	Himachal Pradesh	48.3	1.2	86.9	13.1
9.	Jammu and Kashmir	37.6	2.1	97.4	2.6
10.	Karnataka	43.7	4.7	88.5	11.5
11.	Kerala	5.5	0.8	35.9	64.1
12.	Madhya Pradesh	40.4	2.9	85.4	14.6
13.	Maharashtra	30.5	3.6	63.9	36.1
14.	Manipur	46.4	5.6	92.9	7.1
15.	Meghalaya	69.2	4.3	98.8	1.2
16.	Mizoram	50.2	1.7	92.1	7.9
17.	Nagaland	48.0	2.6	87.1	12.9
18.	Orissa	56.9	6.4	78.8	21.2
19.	Punjab	25.6	1.7	38.2	61.8
20.	Rajasthan	40.6	1.1	85.8	14.2
21.	Sikkim	57.2	0.6	93.0	7.0
22.	TamilNadu	77.7	5.1	93.4	6.6
23.	Tripura	52.3	2.6	98.9	1.1
24.	Uttar Pradesh	32.8	1.8	72.1	27.9
25.	West Bengal	32.0	5.0	83.6	16.4
26.	A and N Islands	36.5	0.5	80.0	20.0
27.	Chandigarh	21.2	0.6	74.3	25.7
28.	Dadra and Nagar Haveli	60.1	1.5	89.9	10.1
29.	Daman and Diu	28.2	0.9	48.8	51.2
30.	Delhi	52.4	0.5	78.8	21.2
31.	Lakshadweep	13.6	2.4	100.0	Nil
32.	Pondicherry	34.0	0.7	72.3	27.7
	All States/UTs	44.8	3.4	79.5	20.5

Statement No. 7.21
Budget Provision of Education Departments of States/UTs as Percentage of State Net Domestic Product, 1988-89

Sl. No.	State/U.Ts.	% of Budget of Education Deptt. To State N.D.P.
1.	Andhra Pradesh	4.0
2.	Arunachal Pradesh	10.0
3.	Assam	4.8
4.	Bihar	3.3
5.	Goa	5.3
6.	Gujarat	3.4
7.	Haryana	2.6
8.	Himachal Pradesh	6.8
9.	Jammu and Kashmir	N.A.
10.	Karnataka	3.9
11.	Kerala	6.1
12.	Madhya Pradesh	3.3
13.	Maharashtra	2.8
14.	Manipur	9.5
15.	Meghalaya	N.A.
16.	Mizoram	N.A.
17.	Nagaland	10.3
18.	Orissa	4.3
19.	Punjab	2.8
20.	Rajasthan	4.2
21.	Sikkim	N.A.
22.	TamilNadu	3.4
23.	Tripura	N.A.
24.	Uttar Pradesh	3.0
25.	West Bengal	3.7
26.	A and N Islands	9.6
27.	Chandigarh	N.A.
28.	Dadra and Nagar Haveli	N.A.
29.	Goa Daman and Diu	N.A.
30.	Delhi	3.2
31.	Lakshadweep	N.A.
32.	Pondicherrry	5.7

Note : The figures are based on the figures of State Net Domestic Product as mentioned in the Economic Survey 1990-91.
N.A. = Not Available.

4. Centrally Sponsored Schemes

Statement No. 7.22
Assistance to States/UTs for Operation Blackboard Scheme

(Rupees in lakh)

Sl. No.	State/Union Territory	Amount released				
		1987-88	1988-89	1989-90	1990-91	1991-92 (Anticipated)
1.	Andhra Pradesh	621.62	1590.77	1209.29	2095.00	3803.77
2.	Arunachal Pradesh	63.17	71.81	46.76	82.16	82.16
3.	Assam	826.69	0.00	692.41	–	420.48
4.	Bihar	1868.41	2151.64	1407.66	1684.02	–
5.	Goa	12.03	23.62	37.32	47.47	24.77
6.	Gujarat	466.43	0.00	727.44	503.10	619.70
7.	Haryana	62.93	117.33	111.39	–	292.17
8.	Himachal Pradesh	148.75	280.94	458.09	297.03	456.10
9.	Jammu and Kashmir	156.90	347.04	0.00	–	678.37
10.	Karnataka	168.67	853.09	537.08	717.54	1816.49
11.	Kerala	151.11	223.44	0.00	156.12	82.90
12.	Madhya Pradesh	1194.10	1981.26	0.00	1344.78	846.91
13.	Maharashtra	545.03	0.00	788.33	612.22	2795.46
14.	Manipur	38.03	98.78	0.00	47.88	90.10
15.	Meghalaya	78.37	0.00	0.00	100.49	177.09
16.	Mizoram	11.80	22.88	8.74	8.87	66.80
17.	Nagaland	25.66	24.67	42.98	5.85	5.85
18.	Orissa	753.00	1105.45	864.25	1818.32	800.00
19.	Punjab	334.11	384.25	115.69	219.29	502.59
20.	Rajasthan	1175.25	1123.68	1568.63	3456.83	2202.14
21.	Sikkim	41.57	9.06	0.00	15.36	9.57
22.	Tamil Nadu	480.80	856.92	1213.02	510.24	449.96
23.	Tripura	42.12	0.00	49.59	7.70	64.41
24.	Uttar Pradesh	1759.43	1893.44	2757.26	860.94	412.37
25.	West Bengal	0.00	384.34	0.00	349.46	140.02
26.	A and N Islands	0.00	0.00	8.27	–	3.82
27.	Chandigarh	0.00	0.00	1.17	–	–
28.	Dadra and Nagar Haveli	1.99	0.00	0.00	4.14	–
29.	Daman and Diu	0.00	1.19	0.00	–	–
30.	Delhi	32.49	0.00	32.39	53.59	–
31.	Lakshadweep	0.48	0.00	0.00	–	–
32.	Pondicherry	0.00	27.20	20.32	10.72	–
	Total	11061.24	13572.80	12698.08	15009.12	16844.00

Statement No. 7.23
Assistance to States/UTs for Non-Formal Education Scheme

(Rupees in lakh)

Sl. No.	State/Union Territory	Amount released				
		1987-88	1988-89	1989-90	1990-91	1991-92 (Anticipated)
1.	Andhra Pradesh	318.14	498.00	650.55	581.78	616.36
2.	Assam	182.01	203.23	264.96	159.40	181.88
3.	Bihar	1030.76	466.25	88.02	667.72	233.55
4.	Haryana	11.46	—	—	—	—
5.	Jammu and Kashmir	—	64.68	—	—	—
6.	Karnataka	23.80	57.03	—	—	—
7.	Madhya Pradesh	340.60	605.64	628.32	781.95	695.86
8.	Mizoram	2.19	2.07	2.22	2.06	2.44
9.	Orissa	100.11	341.33	259.85	109.84	241.56
10.	Rajasthan	183.36	164.69	165.89	236.61	361.36
11.	Tamil Nadu	7.02	6.39	—	—	—
12.	Uttar Pradesh	1082.33	544.31	485.30	925.47	1616.35
13.	West Bengal	267.18	100.00	41.49	—	—
14.	A and N Islands	0.18	—	—	—	—
15.	Chandigarh	1.29	1.42	0.85	2.82	2.25
16.	Dadra and Nagar Haveli	2.06	—	—	—	—
17.	Manipur	—	10.27	—	24.59	62.42
18.	Gujarat	—	—	40.74	—	—
	Total	3552.49	3065.31	2628.19	3492.24	4014.03

Statement No. 7.24
Assistance to States/UTs for Teacher Training Programme

(Rupees in lakh)

Sl. No.	State/Union Territory	Amount released				
		1987-88	1988-89	1989-90	1990-91	1991-92 (As on 15-1-92)
1.	Andhra Pradesh	267.76	276.85	416.39	106.00	365.25
2.	Arunachal Pradesh	35.70	3.00	0.00	—	—
3.	Assam	182.75	264.90	182.45	35.00	88.30
4.	Goa	0.00	0.00	28.30	2.00	5.50
5.	Gujarat	281.29	183.23	0.00	—	—
6.	Haryana	66.50	178.40	10.00	52.82	78.23
7.	Himachal Pradesh	0.00	129.30	0.00	—	—
8.	Jammu and Kashmir	150.35	156.15	174.70	—	168.20
9.	Kerala	60.74	100.40	280.00	94.81	49.70
10.	Madhya Pradesh	448.42	490.60	439.20	386.28	—
11.	Maharashtra	0.00	380.80	0.00	—	—
12.	Manipur	0.00	33.70	0.00	1.00	—
13.	Mizoram	31.50	3.00	0.00	31.85	23.50
14.	Nagaland	0.00	32.00	0.00	28.00	—
15.	Orissa	274.05	211.95	198.77	33.00	140.67
16.	Punjab	179.00	86.00	152.30	108.40	—
17.	Rajasthan	335.40	349.85	547.04	438.15	149.56
18.	Sikkim	0.00	35.50	0.00	—	36.88
19.	Tamil Nadu	208.70	342.50	798.52	105.00	319.00
20.	Tripura	0.00	0.00	26.60	—	—
21.	Uttar Pradesh	536.46	363.87	250.63	363.59	—
22.	West Bengal	132.69	15.00	0.00	—147.69@	—
23.	Delhi	56.20	14.90	63.97	40.05	74.57
24.	Pondicherry		—	—	—	30.00
	Total	3247.51	3651.90	3568.87	1678.26	1529.36

@ Due to non-implementation of the Projects, Sanctions issued in 1987-88 and 1988-89 were revoked in March, 1991.

Statement No. 7.25

Assistance to States/UTs for Vocationalisation Scheme

(Rupees in lakh)

Sl. No.	State/Union Territory	Amount released				
		1987-88	1988-89	1989-90	1990-91	1991-92 (As on 12/91)
1.	Andhra Pradesh	562.63	730.32	177.06	886.85	225.54
2.	Arunachal Pradesh	—	—	—	—	—
3.	Assam	30.10	82.61	—	42.62	140.28
4.	Bihar	136.09	—	7.41	558.61	—
5.	Goa	68.53	28.47	64.59	80.63	49.50
6.	Gujarat	—	236.64	1173.31	778.031	455.25
7.	Haryana	276.12	353.03	129.87	184.83	130.00
8.	Himachal Pradesh	30.90	1.86	98.06	177.475	52.50
9.	Jammu and Kashmir	—	—	—	16.50	—
10.	Karnataka	93.00	244.70	49.21	156.80	—
11.	Kerala	—	226.42	223.44	353.23	—
12.	Madhya Pradesh	57.16	745.00	1121.48	1221.42	—
13.	Maharashtra	495.90	469.66	509.38	267.21	400.00
14.	Manipur	—	11.68	—	—	—
15.	Meghalaya	—	—	—	20.75	—
16.	Mizoram	21.42	7.12	—	16.68	—
17.	Nagaland	8.00	—	—	14.84	—
18.	Orissa	156.19	600.00	83.72	510.40	—
19.	Punjab	211.59		50.25	371.71	—
20.	Rajasthan	58.34	159.22	72.35	561.543	59.93
21.	Sikkim	—	—	—	5.325	—
22.	Tamil Nadu	112.56	225.00	358.11	279.558	—
23.	Tripura	—	—	—	—	—
24.	Uttar Pradesh	829.88	800.00	203.69	707.25	97.35
25.	West Bengal	40.69	—	—	—	—
26.	A and N Islands	—	—	3.24	3.238	—
27.	Chandigarh	—	42.70*	42.70	12.34	12.15
28.	Dadra and Nagar Haveli	—	—	—	—	—
29.	Daman and Diu	—	—	—	—	—
30.	Delhi	36.52		4.18	42.86	—
31.	Lakshadweep	—	—	—	—	—
32.	Pondicherry	—	—	—	16.63	—
	Total	3225.62	4964.43	4372.05	7287.33	1622.50

* Rs. 42.70 lakhs shown against Chandigarh in 1988-89 could not be claimed by Chandigarh Admn. during 1988-89.

Statement No. 7.26
Assistance to States/UTs for Science Education Scheme

(Rupees in lakh)

Sl. No.	State/Union Territory	Amount released				
		1987-88	1988-89	1989-90	1990-91	1991-92 (As on 12/91)
1.	Andhra Pradesh	99.25	107.15	400.37	132.25	—
2.	Arunachal Pradesh		3.72			—
3.	Assam		295.32	90.25	141.66	—
4.	Bihar		365.44	11.24		—
5.	Goa	35.99		36.03	56.76	—
6.	Gujarat			142.31		—
7.	Haryana		279.66			—
8.	Himachal Pradesh	99.55	216.13		139.84	—
9.	Jammu and Kashmir	30.67		97.95	167.10	—
10.	Karnataka	417.70	95.69	45.75	167.88	—
11.	Kerala	200.92		199.43	152.72	—
12.	Madhya Pradesh	113.55	300.00	244.56	7.28	—
13.	Maharashtra	626.10			5.42	—
14.	Manipur		108.00		87.05	—
15.	Meghalaya				35.20	—
16.	Mizoram	13.78		87.76	84.42	—
17.	Nagaland	11.55		8.40		—
18.	Orissa	200.00		268.82		—
19.	Punjab	130.06		1.37	349.97	171.14
20.	Rajasthan	349.52			139.84	—
21.	Sikkim			12.41	20.14	—
22.	Tamil Nadu	217.69	194.41	251.13	93.37	—
23.	Tripura		27.45		0.74	—
24.	Uttar Pradesh	313.47	300.00	98.10	13.45	—
25.	West Bengal		514.37		147.18	—
26.	A and N Islands	7.34		21.52	5.84	—
27.	Chandigarh	5.82			20.18	—
28.	Dadra and Nagar Haveli				5.22	—
29.	Delhi	53.47	73.42	102.59	55.60	—
30.	Daman and Diu			4.56		—
31.	Ladshadweep	0.23		1.28		—
32.	Pondicherry		20.82	7.03	4.32	—
	Total	2926.66	2901.58	2132.86	2033.43	171.14

Statement No. 7.27
Assistance to States/UTs for Education Technology Scheme

(Rupees in lakh)

Sl. No.	State/Union Territory	Amount released				
		1987-88	1988-89	1989-90	1990-91	1991-92 (As on 15-1-92)
1.	Andhra Pradesh	247.00	278.11	113.00	227.90	37.74
2.	Arunachal Pradesh	—	1.72	1.14		
3.	Assam	—	20.92	42.20	73.53	
4.	Bihar	—	23.54	8.33		6.49
5.	Goa	3.24	3.31	1.76	5.29	
6.	Gujarat	273.75	—	173.65	96.19	
7.	Haryana	—	7.04	39.90	50.50	
8.	Himachal Pradesh	9.62	10.72	45.80		
9.	Jammu and Kashmir	—	9.00	17.82	102.99	
10.	Karnataka	22.52	60.38	66.37	15.81	
11.	Kerala	7.16	13.46	27.87		12.17
12.	Madhya Pradesh	—	193.80	30.46	29.16	
13.	Maharashtra	—	72.00	93.00	126.20	
14.	Manipur	—	1.82	1.21	10.08	16.19
15.	Meghalaya	—	0.90	4.23	5.00	5.08
16.	Mizoram	2.18	6.03	9.13		0.11
17.	Nagaland	2.82	—	7.72		
18.	Orissa	45.84	78.03	128.80	258.25	
19.	Punjab	—	19.84	48.23	60.00	
20.	Rajasthan	—	113.62	91.92		
21.	Sikkim	—	2.82	1.88	3.50	
22.	Tamil Nadu	—	30.00	70.00	100.00	
23.	Tripura	—	0.26	0.17	0.06	
24.	Uttar Pradesh	72.00	112.26	20.84		
25.	West Bengal	—	19.46	12.97		
26.	A and N Islands	—	0.48	0.32	0.50	
27.	Chandigarh	—	1.37	0.48	1.11	
28.	Delhi	28.64	36.11			
29.	Daman and Diu	—	0.18	0.12		
30.	Dadra and Nagar Haveli	0.33	—	0.22		0.36
31.	Lakshadweep	0.16	0.03	0.13		
32.	Pondicherry	—	1.84	1.23		
	Total	715.26	1119.05	1060.90	1165.57	78.14

Statement No. 7.28
Assistance to States/UTs for Environment Education Scheme

(Rupees in lakh)

Sl. No.	State/Union Territory	Amount released				
		1987-88	1988-89	1989-90	1990-91	1991-92 (As on Dec. 91)
1.	Andhra Pradesh	22.37		20.16		
2.	Arunachal Pradesh	4.81				
3.	Assam	4.20			12.85	
4.	Bihar	20.17				
5.	Goa			8.45		
6.	Gujarat		4.82			
7.	Haryana		0.66			
8.	Himachal Pradesh	9.15				
9.	Karnataka	8.04	24.11	58.90		
10.	Kerala		2.07			
11.	Madhya Pradesh	9.60	28.80			
12.	Maharashtra		9.73			
13.	Mizoram	1.82	1.97			
14.	Orissa	18.47				
15.	Rajasthan	37.52		16.56		
16.	Tamil Nadu	17.73	16.55	33.86		
17.	Tripura	3.04		9.12		
18.	Uttar Pradesh		13.85			
19.	A and N Islands	2.48				
20.	Delhi		7.73	9.71		
21.	Pondicherry	0.94		2.16		
	Total	160.34	110.29	158.92	12.85	

Statement No. 7.29

Assistance to States/UTs for Integrated Education for Disabled Children

(Rupees in lakh)

Sl. No.	State/Union Territory	Amount released				
		1987-88	1988-89	1989-90	1990-91	1991-92 (As on 31-12-91)
1.	Andhra Pradesh		14.71		12.80	
2.	Bihar	10.10	1.70	2.62	7.67	
3.	Gujarat	4.24		8.57	5.87	21.03
4.	Haryana			20.55	19.77	
5.	Himachal Pradesh		8.24	5.63	7.40	7.21
6.	Jammu and Kashmir				19.98	
7.	Karnataka	16.29	28.78	10.86		12.26
8.	Kerala	61.08	55.00	60.00	100.47	0.20
9.	Madhya Pradesh		0.63	1.16	17.40	
10.	Manipur				3.97	
11.	Maharashtra	16.40	19.42	14.27		
12.	Mizoram	10.00	10.00	16.79	24.79	31.72
13.	Nagaland	5.55	10.76	10.74	9.36	10.79
14.	Orissa	18.47	13.99	15.03	23.87	22.47
15.	Punjab	4.17	4.58			12.00
16.	Rajasthan	48.26		33.23	33.44	3.61
17.	Tamil Nadu				5.76	
18.	Uttar Pradesh	9.55		11.95	16.97	
19.	A and N Islands	11.41	14.28	15.65	13.90	16.08
20.	Delhi	10.58	11.77	12.17	18.92	
21.	Goa			0.09	0.45	
22.	Daman and Diu				0.49	0.53
	Total	226.1	193.86	239.31	343.28	137.90

Statement No. 7.30
Statewise Expenditure on Running Navodaya Vidyalayas

(Rupees in Lakh)

Sl. No.	State/Union Territory	Amount released						
		1987-88	1988-89	1989-90	1990-91		1991-92 (Anticipated)	
					N. Plan	Plan	N. Plan	Plan
1.	Andhra Pradesh	115.80	227.90	270.92	287.25	67.82	273.15	159.30
2.	Arunachal Pradesh	19.12	42.48	61.59	44.85	6.58	43.30	27.10
3.	Bihar	159.94	296.13	372.11	375.94	104.79	344.45	190.85
4.	Goa	10.61	17.99	20.12	25.81	4.32	21.30	11.75
5.	Gujarat	32.72	73.27	85.24	86.89	25.44	82.40	57.90
6.	Haryana	50.87	94.18	124.73	110.51	47.29	121.45	74.80
7.	Himachal Pradesh	71.16	109.65	128.34	140.70	31.79	123.35	60.90
8.	Jammu and Kashmir	88.13	125.46	143.66	148.62	30.57	154.20	100.20
9.	Karnataka	110.23	223.88	247.72	259.37	57.06	252.50	140.20
10.	Kerala	75.09	140.47	142.85	183.92	39.86	150.90	83.90
11.	Madhya Pradesh	161.18	285.10	323.43	317.15	96.87	322.15	206.80
12.	Maharashtra	128.35	211.99	261.49	272.70	71.53	269.25	150.05
13.	Manipur	17.29	67.88	77.30	88.01	25.24	72.90	54.95
14.	Meghalaya	28.66	29.20	36.17	35.02	3.13	29.25	16.25
15.	Mizoram	11.73	18.85	17.63	19.16	3.68	13.35	11.60
16.	Nagaland	1.31	13.34	12.16	11.83	2.22	9.35	4.60
17.	Orissa	97.06	155.21	171.21	162.32	43.30	164.60	92.85
18.	Punjab	45.71	67.56	99.44	96.38	30.36	98.35	62.05
19.	Rajasthan	86.08	201.19	254.58	243.33	93.88	248.85	159.15
20.	Sikkim	7.99	7.04	9.24	13.18	1.01	9.60	4.80
21.	Tripura	—	4.08	13.39	10.35	4.31	12.25	8.50
22.	Uttar Pradesh	171.72	307.60	402.42	407.17	119.76	366.95	250.75
23.	A and N Islands	12.83	18.30	28.85	32.50	3.98	24.40	11.75
24.	Chandigarh	4.04	5.77	9.79	11.02	7.15	10.85	8.20
25.	Delhi	—	8.79	10.24	9.34	3.32	10.00	8.75
26.	Daman and Diu	4.35	10.46	12.38	12.48	4.20	11.45	12.25
27.	Dadra and Nagar Haveli	15.27	11.25	14.35	14.53	0.30	11.30	5.15
28.	Lakshadweep	—	16.34	8.13	15.24	2.97	7.90	6.00
29.	Pondicherry	28.21	45.26	54.56	55.36	10.01	54.95	26.80
	Total	1555.45	2836.62	3414.04	3490.93	942.74	3314.70	2008.15

5. Financial Allocations for Important Programmes (1991-1992 and 1992-93)
Statement No. 7.31

(Rupees in Lakhs)

Sl. No.	Items	Plan/ Non-Plan	Budget Estimates 1991-92 Original	Budget Estimates 1991-92 Revised	Budget Estimates 1992-93
1	2	3	4	5	6
I. Elementary Education					
1.	Operation Blackboard	Plan	10000.00	17000.00	9914.00
2.	(i) Non-formal Education Centres (composite) for 9-14 age group	Plan	4500.00	2400.00	4085.00
	(ii) Non-formal Education Centres for girls	Plan	3000.00	1600.00	2725.00
	(iii) Grants to Voluntary Agencies	Plan	3000.00	1000.00	2200.00
		Non-Plan	15.00	Nil	Nil
	(iv) Shiksha Karmi Project in Rajasthan undertaken with financial assistance from S.I.D.A.	Plan	230.00	230.00	470.00
	(v) Bihar Education Project	Plan	600.00	600.00	1200.00
	(vi) NCTE	Plan	100.00	30.00	50.00
	(vii) Monitoring of UEE		–	–	86.00
	(viii) Operationalising Microplanning		–	–	300.00
	(ix) Improvement of Learners' Achievement		–	–	200.00
	(x) Lok Jumbish		–	10.00	200.00
	(xi) World Bank assisted U.P. Project		–	–	10.00
	(xii) South Orissa Project		–	–	10.00

(Contd.)

(Contd.)

1 2	3	4	5	6
3. Teacher Education (i) Mass Orientation Programme for School Teachers (ii) District Institutes of Education and Training (DIETs) (iii) College of Teacher Education and Institute of Advanced Study in Education (iv) State Councils of Educational Research and Training (SCERTs)	Plan	6424.00	4000.00	6450.00
II. Secondary Education				
1. Vocationalisation of Education	Plan	8900.00	6500.00	7900.00
2. Integrated Education of Disabled Children	Plan	400.00	400.00	350.00
3. Yoga	Plan	80.00	80.00	60.00
	Non-Plan	30.00	30.00	30.00
4. National Open School	Plan	100.00	100.00	150.00
	Non-Plan	46.00	46.00	46.00
5. Grants to NCERT	Plan	350.00	203.72	300.00
	Non-Plan	2282.00	2012.78	2220.00
6. Population Education	Plan	100.00	100.00	100.00
7. Science Education	Plan	2397.00	1898.00	2198.00
8. Environmental Education	Plan	300.00	200.00	290.00
9. Educational Technology	Plan	1700.00	1400.00	1400.00
	Non-Plan	142.00	Nil	Nil
10. CLASS	Plan	600.00	600.00	600.00
11. Kendriya Vidyalaya Sangathan	Non-Plan	16301.00	16301.00	16301.00
12. Central Tibetan Schools Administration	Non-Plan	421.00	421.00	421.00
13. Navodaya Vidyalaya Samiti	Plan	6000.00	7660.00	7500.00
	Non-Plan	4450.00	4450.00	4450.00
III. Higher Education and Research				
1. University Grants Commission	Plan	12800.00	14168.00	12400.00
	Non-Plan	23820.00	26003.00	24709.00
2. Indian Institutes of Advanced Study, Shimla	Plan	35.00	35.00	35.00
	Non-Plan	110.50	109.00	110.50

(Contd.)

(Contd.)

1	2	3	4	5	6
3.	Indian Council of Philosophical Research	Plan	45.00	45.00	40.00
		Non-Plan	65.00	55.00	65.00
4.	Indian Council of Historical Research	Plan	35.00	32.00	35.00
		Non-Plan	130.00	130.00	130.00
5.	All India Insitute of Higher Learning	Plan	20.00	34.75	38.00
		Non-Plan	17.85	17.85	19.00
6.	Indian Council of Social Science Research	Plan	275.00	324.00	250.00
		Non-Plan	424.25	424.25	424.25
7.	Shastri Indo-Canadian Institute	Plan	—	—	—
		Non-Plan	61.25	61.25	65.00
8.	Revision of salary scales of teachers in University and Colleges	Plan	—	—	—
		Non-Plan	7000.00	6000.00	6000.00
9.	National Research Professors	Plan	—	—	—
		Non-Plan	6.00	6.00	6.00
10.	Loan to Panjab University	Plan	50.00	50.00	50.00
		Non-Plan	—	—	—
11.	Dr. Zakir Husain Memorial College Trust	Plan	20.00	20.00	25.00
		Non-Plan	6.30	6.30	6.30
12.	Association of Indian Universities	Plan	10.00	10.00	12.00
		Non-Plan	12.15	22.15	12.15
13.	Indira Gandhi National Open University	Plan	900.00	657.00	1000.00
		Non-Plan	776.00	500.00	753.00
14.	Strengthening of Administrative Machinery	Plan	5.00	5.00	5.00
		Non-Plan	—	—	—
15.	National Council of Higher Education	Plan	1.00	1.00	5.00
		Non-Plan	—	—	—
16.	National Testing Service	Plan	40.00	10.00	25.00
IV. International Cooperation					
1.	C. 6 (5) (5) Reorganisation of INC Library into a full-fledged Documentation and Reference Centre for Unesco Publications in India.	Plan	100.00	100.00	150.00
2.	C. 6 (5) (6) Holding of Meeting of Committees/ Conferences in furtherance of Unesco aims and objectives	Plan	400.00	300.00	350.00
3.	C. 6 (5) (7) Strengthening of Voluntary Organisatons engaged in Unesco programme and activities	Plan	200.00	150.00	200.00

(Contd.)

(Contd.)

1	2	3	4	5	6
4.	C. 6(1) (2) Auroville Management	Plan	1000.00	1000.00	1000.00
5.	Strengthening of External Academic Relations	Plan	300.00	300.00	300.00
6.	C. 6(4) (2) Expenditure on Publication of Hindi and Tamil Editions of Unesco Courier	Non-Plan	1800.00	1800.00	1800.00
7.	C. 6(4) (9) Other Items-Grant to Non-Governmental organisations for programme of INC	Non-Plan	30.00	25.00	25.00
8.	C. 6(4) (9) Other Items-Indian National Commission of Cooperation with Unesco	Non-Plan	65.00	60.00	60.00
9.	C. 6(4) (9) Other Items-Hospitality and Entertainment	Non-Plan	5.00	5.00	5.00
10.	C. 6 (4) (1) Contribution to Unesco	Non-Plan	23500.00	29000.00	29700.00
11.	C. 6(4) (5) Visit of Foreign Delegation to India	Non-Plan	500.00	500.00	500.00
12.	C. 6(4) (6) Deputation and Delegation abroad	Non-Plan	500.00	500.00	500.00
13.	C. 6(1) (2) Auroville Management	Non-Plan	600.00	1600.00	1600.00
V. Book Promotion and Copy Right					
1.	Regional Offices/Book Centres	Plan	25.00	23.25	25.00
2.	Nehru Bal Pustakalaya	Plan	50.00	42.15	50.00
3.	Aadan-Pradan	Plan	10.00	4.65	9.00
4.	Subsidy Scheme	Plan	20.00	11.65	20.00
5.	Reproduction of Books in Punjabi	Plan	6.00	5.54	5.00
6.	Normal Promotional Activities	Plan	25.00	24.05	30.00
7.	Nehru Bhavan	Plan	5.00	5.00	5.00
8.	Publication for Post-Literacy Education	Plan	15.00	12.75	10.00
9.	Publication for School-Library Programme	Plan	8.00	2.80	4.00
10.	Publication of Classic-Literature	Plan	3.00	1.90	2.00
11.	I.S.B.N. (NERC)	Plan	1.00	0.01	Nil

(Contd.)

(Contd.)

1	2	3	4	5	6
12.	Collaboration Programme for Republication of Foreign University Text Books	Plan	2.00	2.00	2.00
13.	Book Export Promotional Activities	Plan	12.00	10.00	12.00
14.	Setting up National Authors Society	Plan	1.00	1.00	2.00
15.	New Sale Promotion Measures	Plan	6.00	11.00	2.00
16.	Core-Books Project	Plan	2.00	1.25	3.00
17.	Book-Promotional Activities and Financial Assistance to Voluntary Organisations	Plan	6.00	6.00	5.00
18.	National Book Development Council	Plan	2.00	2.00	2.00
19.	Maintenance, Establishment and Publishing	Non-Plan	168.00	153.55	168.00
20.	Normal Promotional Activities	Non-Plan	42.00	30.95	42.00
21.	India's contribution to WIPO	Non-Plan	20.00	21.00	25.00
22.	International Copyright Union (CEP)	Non-Plan	2.00	2.00	2.00
23.	World Book Fair	Non-Plan	50.00	50.00	5.00
VI. Scholarships					
1.	National Scholarships Scheme	Plan	110.00	90.00	100.00
2.	National Loan Scholarships Scheme	Non-Plan	285.00	285.00	285.00
3.	National Loan Scholarships Scheme Write-off etc.	Non-Plan	14.20	14.20	14.20
4.	50% share of the State Govts. in respect of recoveries under National Loan Scholarships Scheme	Non-Plan	22.00	22.00	22.00
5.	Scheme for upgradation of Merit of SC/ST	Plan	55.00	25.00	55.00
6.	Scholarships at Secondary stage for Talented children from Rural Areas	Plan	85.00	35.00	60.00
7.	Scholarships in approved residential secondary Schools	Non-Plan	220.00	120.00	205.00

(Contd.)

(Contd.)

1	2	3	4	5	6
8.	Grant-in-aid scheme of scholarships to students from non-Hindi speaking States for Post-Matric Studies in Hindi	Non-Plan	34.10	34.10	34.10
VII. Promotion of Languages					
Hindi					
1.	Central Hindi Directorate	Plan	65.00	63.00	63.00
		Non-Plan	121.50	123.50	127.03
2.	Commission for Scientific and Technical Terminology	Plan	16.00	18.00	18.00
		Non-Plan	50.00	51.00	52.20
3.	Kendriya Hindi Sansthan, Agra	Plan	55.00	52.00	52.00
		Non-Plan	177.00	177.00	177.00
4.	Appointment of Hindi teachers and their training	Plan	260.00	185.00	185.00
5.	Assistance to Non-Govt. organisations-Dakshin Bharat Hindi Prachar Sabha and other NGCS including publication in Hindi	Plan	180.00	180.00	180.00
		Non-Plan	102.50	102.50	102.50
6.	Propagation of Hindi abroad	Plan	20.00	20.00	20.00
		Non-Plan	11.00	11.00	11.00
7.	Hindi University	Plan	5.00	1.00	1.00
Modern Indian Languages					
8.	Central Institute of Indian Languages and its Regional Language Centres including Tribal Languages Development	Plan	85.00	88.00	88.00
		Non-Plan	214.00	220.00	224.00
9.	Tarragi-e-Urdu Board including Gujaral Committee	Plan	70.00	70.00	70.00
		Non-Plan	42.00	43.00	43.37
10.	Financial Assistance to NGOs (other than Sindhi, Urdu and Hindi) Plus ULB	Plan	30.00	26.00	26.00
		Non-Plan	10.00	10.00	10.00
11.	Financial Assistance to NGOs for Sindhi including Sindhi Vikas Board, Financing of book production in Sindhi	Plan	10.00	10.00	10.00
12.	Modern Indian Language Teachers	Plan	100.00	41.00	41.00

(Contd.)

(Contd.)

1	2	3	4	5	6
English					
13.	English teaching and District Centres, RIE and ELTIS, strengthening of these Institutes and use of Electronic Media etc. financial assistance for publication.	Plan	85.00	72.00	72.00
Sanskrit					
1.	Grants to Vol. Skt. Organisation Adarsh Sanskrit Mahavidyalayas/ Shodh Sansthan	Plan Non-Plan	75.00 95.00	105.00 120.00	80.00 95.00
2.	Shri Lal Bahadur Shastri Rashtriya Sanskrit Vidyapeeth, New Delhi	Plan Non-Plan	10.00 93.00	10.00 80.50	10.00 93.00
3.	Grants to Rashtriya Sanskrit Vidyapeeth, Tirupati	Plan Non-Plan	10.00 70.00	10.00 53.65	10.00 70.00
4.	Grants to Rashtriya Sanskrit Sansthan, New Delhi	Plan Non-Plan	151.00 315.00	110.00 258.85	151.00 315.00
5.	Development of Sanskrit Education in States/UTs	Plan	56.00	56.00	56.00
6.	Grants to Rashtriya Veda Vidya Pratishthan	Plan	45.00	45.00	45.00
7.	Preservation of Oral Tradition of Vedic recitation and All India Education contest	Plan	7.00	7.00	7.00
8.	Grants/Scholarships for Classical Languages (Arabic and Persian)	Plan	14.00	14.00	15.00
VIII. Adult Education					
1.	Rural Functional Literacy	Plan	2500.00	1500.00	1500.00
2.	Nehru Yuva Kendra Sangathan	Plan	125.00	125.00	150.00
3.	Post Literacy and Continuing Education	Plan	1000.00	1000.00	1000.00
4.	Strengthening of Administrative Structure	Plan	500.00	595.00	700.00
5.	Mass Programme of Functional Literacy	Plan	500.00	400.00	375.00
6.	Technology Demonstration	Plan	100.00	55.00	50.00
7.	Voluntary Agencies	Plan	1500.00	1200.00	1800.00
8.	Shramik Vidyapeeths	Plan	100.00	119.00	130.00

(Contd.)

(Contd.)

1	2	3	4	5	6
9.	Directorate of Adult Education	Plan	110.00	144.00	110.00
10.	National Literacy Mission	Plan	10.00	10.00	25.00
11.	Cultural Exchange Programme	Plan	5.00	2.00	5.00
12.	Special Project	Plan	5375.00	5150.00	5865.00
13.	National Institute of Adult Education	Plan	175.00	100.00	150.00
1.	Rural Functional Literacy Project	Non Plan	270.00	294.00	270.00
2.	Literacy House, Lucknow	Non Plan	17.20	16.84	17.08
3.	Shramik Vidyapeeth	Non Plan	113.30	113.30	114.54
4.	Directorate of Adult Education	Non Plan	124.00	128.00	133.00
5.	Printing Press	Non Plan	3.50	2.86	3.38
6.	Post Literacy	Non Plan	30.00	—	30.00
IX	**Technical Education**				
I.	Direction and Administration				
1.	National Technical Man-Power Information System (NTMIS) D. 7 (2)	Plan	100.00	50.00	100.00
		N. Plan	50.00	57.00	50.00
2.	Re-Organisation, Restructuring and Strengthening of AICTE, its Committees/ Boards D. 1(3)	Plan	100.00	10.00	180.00
		Non Plan	—	—	—
3.	Strengthening of existing institutions and establishing new institutions for non-corporate and unorganised sectors D. 1(2)	Plan	10.00	10.00	—
		Non Plan	—	—	—
	Training				
4.	Regional Engineering Colleges (RECs D. 6(2)	Plan	2400.00	1890.90	2400.00
		Non Plan	2186.00	2072.00	2186.00
5.	Apprenticeship Training D. 2(5) and D. 2 (6)	Plan	250.00	233.00	250.00
		Non Plan	508.00	495.00	508.00
6.	Central Institutions :				
	— Technical Teachers' Training Institutes (TTTIs) D. 2(1)	Plan	500.00	330.00	600.00
		Non Plan	490.70	372.00	501.90

(Contd.)

(Contd.)

1	2	3	4	5	6
	— National Institute for Training in Industrial Engg. (NITTIE) D. 2 (2)	Plan Non Plan	150.00 266.20	150.00 268.20	150.00 266.20
	— National Institute of Foundary and Forge Technology (NIFFT) D. 2 (3)	Plan Non Plan	100.00 117.60	100.00 117.60	100.00 117.60
	— School of Planning and Architecture (SPA) D. 2 (4)	Plan Non Plan	250.00 180.00	250.00 170.00	250.00 180.00
Research					
7.	Indian Institutes of Technology (IITs) D. 6(1) to D. 6(1) (5)	Plan Non Plan	1500.00 9388.30	1640.00 9480.80	1600.00 9481.10
8.	Indian Institutes of Management (IIMs) D. 6(4) (1) to D. 6(4) (4)	Plan Non Plan	900.00 959.20	800.00 959.00	800.00 959.20
9.	Development of P.G. Courses	Plan Non Plan	110.00 400.00	50.00 400.00	100.00 400.00
10.	Development of Management Education Courses at Non University Centres D. 6(3)	Plan Non Plan	30.00 9.85	1.00 —	40.00 10.35
11.	Institutional Network Scheme D. 7 (1) (1)	Plan Non Plan	100.00 —	100.00 —	— —
12.	International Centre for Science and Technology Education (ICSTE) D. 3(2)	Plan Non Plan	1.00 —	10.00 —	10.00 —
13.	Research and Development (R&D) in selected higher technical institutions D. 3(4)	Plan Non Plan	350.00 —	350.00 —	250.00 —
14.	Community Polytechnics D. 5 (1)	Plan Non Plan	200.00 165.00	200.00 175.00	300.00 184.90
15.	Modernisation and removal of obsolescence D. 6 (5) (3)	Plan Non Plan	3300.00 —	3000.00 —	3000.00 —
16.	Thrust areas of Technical Edn. (i) Strengthening of facilities in crucial areas of technology where weakness exists D. 6(5) (1)	Plan Non Plan	800.00 —	731.00 —	750.00 —

(Contd.)

(Contd.)

1	2	3	4	5	6
	(ii) Creation of infra-structure in areas of emerging technology D. 6 (5) (2)	Plan Non Plan	900.00 220.00	900.00 220.00	900.00 220.00
	(iii) Programmes of new and improved technologies offering courses in Specialised fields D. 2 (8)	Plan Non Plan	800.00 —	800.00 —	750.00 —
17.	Institution-Industry interaction D. 6 (6)	Plan Non Plan	100.00 —	80.00 —	80.00 —
18.	Continuing education D.6(7)	Plan Non Plan	149.00 —	65.00 —	100.00 —
19.	Indian Institute of Technology, Assam D. 6(1) (6) and F. 3(15) (1)	Plan Non Plan	300.00 —	340.00 —	800.00 —
20.	Longowal Institute of Engineering and Technology D. 7 (6)	Plan Non Plan	500.00 —	800.00 —	500.00 —
21.	University Grants Commission Schemes D. 4 (1)	Plan Non Plan	2200.00 —	2230.00 —	2200.00 —
22.	Educational Consultants India Ltd. (Ed. CIL) and A A1 (1)	Plan Non Plan	10.00 —	10.00 —	— —
23.	Super Computer IISc., Bangalore D. 4(2)	Plan	2200.00	732.00	600.00
24.	National Accreditation Board D. 1 (4)	Plan Non Plan	15.00 —	1.00 —	20.00 —
25.	Staff Development and Training D. 2 (9)	Plan Non Plan	5.00 —	1.00 —	18.00 —
26.	Technology Forecasting D3 (5)	Plan Non Plan	5.00 —	1.00 —	20.00 —
27.	Assistance to Professional Bodies D. 7 (7)	Plan Non Plan	5.00 —	1.00 —	20.00 —
28.	World Bank Project Support to Technician Education D5 (3) (1)	Plan Non Plan	60.00 —	25.00 —	80.00 —
29.	Regional Offices D. 1 (1) D1 (3)	Non Plan	46.40	46.40	50.00
30.	Quality Improvement Programmes D. 2 (7)	Non Plan	190.00	290.00	290.00

(Contd.)

(Contd.)

1	2	3	4	5	6
31.	Partial Financial Assitance (PFA) to Indian Scientists going Abroad D. 3 (3)	Non Plan	2.00	1.00	2.00
32.	Indian Society for Technical Education (ISTE) D. 7 (3)	Non Plan	0.60	0.50	0.60
33.	A.I.T., Bangkok, D. 7 (4)	Non Plan	12.15	12.00	12.15
34.	Delegation under Cultural Exchange Programmes D. 7(5)	Non Plan	1.00	0.50	1.00
35.	Revision of Salary Scales of teachers of technical institutions/assistance/ to State/Institutions Colleges. F. 1 (8) (1)	Non Plan	850.00	850.00	800.00

PART III

OTHER FACETS OF EDUCATION

8

REPORT OF UGC COMMITTEE ON ACADEMIC CALENDAR IN INDIAN UNIVERSITIES (1990)*

PART I

Introduction

In recent years, Indian Universities have lost a great deal of credibility and have attracted severe criticism for their failure to discharge their basic functions of completion of teaching and awarding of degrees in the prescribed time schedule. Consequently, the career prospects of a large number of students have been adversely affected disruption of the academic session limits the mobility of students by depriving them of admission in prestigious institutions of higher education outside their State. The non-completion of courses in time increases the financial burden of the State and parents/guardians of students.

Generally, the Academic Session in Indian Universities starts between June and August every year and ends between March and May. However, during the past few years a number of Universities in the country particularly those with the large number of affiliated colleges, have not been able to maintain the academic calendar for a number of years.

The National Policy of Education (1986) and its Programme of Action emphasized the need to ensure the efficiency and effectiveness in the functioning of our Universities. Practical measures to give shape to this concern were discussed by the Central Advisory Board of Education at its meeting held in March 1988. The Board made the following recommendations:

---

* UGC, New Delhi, 1990

"Urgent steps are called for to ensure the effectiveness and efficiency of the existing system and its functioning. Adherence to a predetermind academic calendar is essential to achieve this objective. Within each State an academic calendar indicating the date of admission, date of commencement of the session, vacation, dates of examinations and announcement of results should be framed which should be strictly adhered to by the universities and colleges. In course of time, the possibility of developing a national calendar should be explored."

The Conference of Education Secretaries of all the State Governments held on June 17-18, 1988 reviewed the action taken on this direction whereas many other State Governments have to move accordingly.

In view of above, the University Grants Commission constituted a committee under the Chairmanship of Professor G.J.V.J. Raju, Chairman, State Council for Higher Education, Andhra Pradesh to make recommendations regarding formulation and implementation of academic calendar in Indian Universities. The other members of the Committee were:

1. Prof. K.V. Ramana
   Vice-Chancellor,
   Andhra University,
   Waltair.

2. Prof. S.M. Dasgupta
   Vice-Chancellor,
   Bhopal University, Bhopal.

3. Prof. V.D. Gupta
   Vice-Chancellor,
   Gorakhpur University
   Gorakhpur.

4. Dr. M.L. Lakhanpal
   Vice-Chancellor,
   Jammu University,
   Jammu.

5. Dr. D.M. Nanjundappa
   Vice-Chancellor,
   Bangalore University,
   Bangalore.

6. Dr. B.M.L. Tiwari
   Director of Higher Education,
   Govt. of U.P.
   Allahabad.

7. Dr. M.L. Mehta
   Additional Secretary,
   U.G.C.

The Committee met on 3rd April and 15th June, 1989 in the office of the University Grants Commission at New Delhi.

Observations and Recommendations of the Committee

We have deliberated in depth about the various aspects of the issue and we make the following observations/recommendations for implementation of an academic calendar in Universities/States:

1. The inability of universities to enforce the academic calendar could be attributed to the unprecedented increase in the number of students and the number of examinations, strikes and agitations by students; teachers and non-teaching staff; indiscipline; inadequacy of infrastructural facilities and participation of students in politics, etc. Most of these factors are closely interrelated, e.g., delay in holding examinations, leads to delay in announcement of results. Consequently, the commencemeent of the next academic session gets delayed. Cumulative delays cause disruption of the academic session. In a few universities entire academic sessions have been lost resulting in zero year.
2. It would be ideal if there could be a National Academic Calendar for all the universities in the country. However, to begin with, each State should have an academic calendar to be followed by all the universities in the State for the regular students in all the faculties and for all the courses. The UGC guidelines on teaching days etc., be followed while formulating the calendar, i.e., every university shall ensure that the number of actual teaching days for the first degree course does not go below 180 days in an academic year.
3. The academic calendar should, *inter alia*, at least provide for the following:

   - Date from which the University/Colleges open for the academic session;
   - Schedule for admissions to undergraduate, postgraduate, M.Phil, and Ph.D. courses etc., indicating clearly dates on which the admissions start and end;
   - Dates by which transfer from other universities/colleges to be finalised;
   - Schedule of terms, holidays and vacations;

– Schedule for examinations and declaration of results; and
– Schedule for admission to university/college hostels.

4. We have given considerable thought to the formulation of the academic calendar by the universities and we are of the view that the UGC should give only broad guidelines which should enable the universities to formulate the academic calendar.

The following could be considered as a model academic calendar for the first degree students for suitable adoption by the universities in a State:

1st Monday of July	.....	Beginning of academic session for the second and third year students.
3rd Monday of July	.....	Beginning of the academic session for the first year students.
14th August	.....	Last date for admissions.
15th May (Next year)	.....	All examinations are completed.
30th June (Next year)	.....	Declaration of all results.

Similar model may also be developed for postgraduate and research students.

5. It would be helpful to implement the academic calendar if:

(a) The number of holidays is regulated and that besides the national holidays, the number of regional/State/local holidays do not exceed 7days in a year;
(b) The period of examination does not exceed beyond six weeks and that the number of examination days are cut down by suitable grouping of the subjects;
(c) The total period of vacations does not exceed eight weeks in a year to be availed in one or two spells;
(d) The period of preparatory leave for examination etc. is of about two weeks duration; and
(e) The nember of specialisation in a subject/optionals should be suitably grouped; so that at the undergraduate level the number of papers in specialisations/optional papers at the undergraduate level is minimum.

6. There has been a drastic reduction in the number of teaching days in an academic year due to various reasons. A substantial part of the academic session is used for conduct of examinations, evaluation of answer books and declaration of results. If to these is added the number of days used by the students for preparation, the resultant loss of days will be considerable. We have, therefore, suggested the compression of number of examinations days, required for evaluation and declaration of results. This compression is absolutely essential if the number of teaching days is to be kept to the bare minimum of 180 days. This will be possible only if separate examinations are conducted for students of different streams like university teaching departments, the students from affiliated colleges and students coming through correspondence courses and private appearance.

The Committee recommends that:

1. There should be separate examinations for the students of correspondence/external/privare students *vis-a-vis* the students from the formal streams; and
2. There may be separate examinations for the students enrolled in the affiliated colleges *vis-a-vis* the students in the university departments.

To ensure this, it will be necessary to have independent examination cells which will be responsible for setting up papers, conduct of examinations, and declaration of results for these three different streams in a time-bound manner under the overall supervision of the Registrar/Controller of Examination of the University.

7. It becomes imperative that the postgraduate departments should hold entrance test, since students coming from different streams would be seeking admission to the postgraduate classes.
8. There should be no supplementary examinations at the postgraduate level. However, there could be a provision for carry over at the undergraduate level in one paper or compartmental to be conducted in the month of August in the same year.

9. In all the States the payment of postmatric scholarships is linked up with the students staying in the university attached hostels. This condition in the award of scholarships must be deleted. The students should be allowed to stay in the hostels; while the academic activities of the university are on. Students should vacate the hostels as soon as the Annual Examinations are over. With the commencement of summer holidays the students should vacate the hostels for handing over to the authorities for annual-repairs and other maintenance work etc. and to enable the University to be ready to receive students in the next academic session. This method will also ensure that the students staying in the hostels may not unnecessarily try to extend the academic sessions and thereby disrupting the proposed academic calendar.
10. In order to ensure that the academic calendar is successfully implemented the teachers must cooperate in the invigilation and evaluation work which normally falls during the vacations thereby creating difficulties for the university authorities to command sufficient teachers for this purpose. To circumvent these difficulties, some States have already made examination work mandatory for all teachers. It is, therefore, recommended that the teachers involved in the examination work in various ways during vacations may be given earned leave in lieu of vacations and if possible the privilege of encashing the same as is done for other officers. Further all work associated with examination should be considered as a part of the duty of the teachers as is being done in many States.
11. The conduct of examination and the declaration of results of large number of students every year in an increasing number of courses with whatever permutations and combinations has become too intricate and complex task to be handled manually. Several universities have achieved success in this task by introducing computerisation. It would be desirable to have computerisation of examination results on a priority basis.
12. All activities which may hinder timely holding of the examinations will need to be reviewed continuously and proper solutions are found for their resolution. It would be helpful if the element of election is replaced by that of nomination in the students unions etc. The nomination should be based on the criteria of excellence in academic, curricular and co-curricular matters.

13. A beginning be made by implementing an academic calendar in all the States by the academic session of 1990-91 and a national calendar thereafter and towards this end appropriate Statutes/Ordinances are finalised in time incorporating the provisions of the statutory academic calendar. The status may also provide for the following:

    - A minimum of 180 teaching days in the universities and colleges every year.
    - Last date for admission.
    - Last date for the completion of the examination.
    - Last date for the declaration of results.

14. Each University should prepare an academic calendar for the next academic session during the summer vacations in consultation with the Principals of Colleges, University teachers and students etc. Timely formulation of the calendar and its wide circulation to the teachers and students is important. Provision of essential students services for ensuring timely availability of information, necessary forms etc. would also help in the implementation of the academic calendar.
15. The implementation of the calendar in a University be monitored by a committee under the Chairmanship of the Vice-Chancellor of the University and including some college principals. University teachers and students with Controller of Examinations as the Member-Secretary. The Committee would be responsible to monitor the implementation of the calendar and to suggest measures for its effective implementation from time to time. It meet periodically but less than once in three months. A sub-committee of the main committee consisting of a senior professor, a principal, controller of examinations, etc., monitors the implementation of the calendar once in a month.

    At the State level, the implementation of the calendar in the State is monitored by the State Council for Higher Education or by the Committee of the Vice-Chancellors of the State. Normally, the Education Secretaries of the State participate in these meetings and as such it would be possible to thrash out the problems being faced by the Universities for the implementation of the academic calendar.
16. We strongly recommend that a one time grant may be given by

the UGC to the universities for introducing academic calendar.

The Non-recurring grant which may be up to Rs. 5.00 lakhs for a university may be used for augmenting computer facilities for the purpose of examination and for other measures to implement the academic calendar. The recurring assistance may vary from Rs. 30,000 to Rs. 50,000 p.a. for unitary universities and Rs. 50,000 to Rs. 1.00 lakh for affiliating universities. UGC assistance may be made available for a period of three years.

The Scheme of a common academic calendar in a State be introduced in all the States on a priority basis and towards this end UGC assistance be also provided early.

17. We conclude that each university should have its academic calendar with immediate effect and that a State level Calendar should emerge by 15th June, 1990 so that the State level academic calendar may be implemented from the academic session 1990-91. The academic calendar should be provided in the Statutes of the Universities and that the UGC assistance on 100% basis is provided to the universities immediately. The implementation of the academic calendar in the universities/States is monitored at the National level by the UGC appropriately and its progress is considered by the Commission at least once in a year. UGC must as a first step insist on receiving the academic calendars of the various universities each year before 1st April.

PART II

REPORT OF THE UGC COMMITTEE ON ACADEMIC CALENDAR

I. Introduction

1.1 The UGC had appointed a Committee to make recommendations about the implementation of the Academic Calendar in the universities. The recommendations made by the Committee were accepted by the Commission and circulated to the States/universities for implementation.

1.2 These recommendations were also considered by the Central Advisory Board on Education in their meeting held on 6-7th July, 1989 when the following observations were made:

> "The Group welcomed the model calendar which has been prepared by the UGC Committee and circulated to all the States/universities. The Group was in agreement with the suggestions of the Committee that all the States should try to adhere to the prescribed 180 days of teaching. It was also agreed that though the States may make adjustments, thay should keep to the prescribed 180 days and have schedule of admission/teaching days, examinations and announcement of results so that there is facility for mobility of students from one State to the other.
>
> It was also suggested that the implementation of the Academic Calendar should be regularly monitored by a Committee presided over by the Vice-Chancellors at the University level, by the State Councils of Higher Education at the State level and the UGC/Central Government at the national level."

1.3 The matter was also considered by the Commission in its meetings held on 3rd April, 1989 and 7th October, 1989 when the Commission while considering one-time grant desired that an appropriate mechanism for monitoring the implementation of the academic calendar and a suitable scheme of awards to the universities in this regard be worked out and that the matter be brought before the Commission again in its meeting to be held on 27th November, 1989.

1.4 The Committee met on 8th November, 1989 and considered further the matter in the light of the decision of the Commission. Professor Dasgupta and Professor Najundappa could not attend the meeting.

II. Observations and Recommentations of the Committee

2.1 *Monitoring Mechanism*

1. *Approach*

The Committee in this regard was guided by the recommendations made by the CABE in their meeting held on 6-7th July, 1989 as under:

> "Implementation of the Academic Calendar should be regularly monitored by:

– a committee presided over by the Vice-Chancellors at the University Level;
– State Council for Higher Education at the State Level;
– UGC/Central Government at the Central Level.

2. *University Level*

(1) Each university should constitute a Committee preferably not more than 15 members under the Chairmanship of the Vice-Chancellor and including a few university Deans, Heads of Departments, few College Principals, a representative of the State Government/State Council for Higher Education, Dean of College Development Council, Controller of Examination and Registrar as Member Secretary.

(2) The Committee meets normally three times in an Academic Session preferably in September/January (next year) and July (next year) to monitor the implemention of the Academic Calendar.

(3) The first meeting (September) relates to the monitoring of the beginning of the Academic Session and admissions, the second in January (next year) relates to the monitoring of the progress of implementation of teaching days and the third meeting in July (next year) relates to the completion of the conduct of the examinations and declaration of results.

(4) There will be a special meeting once in an Academic year preferably in April-May where the university (a) reviews the implementation of the Academic Calendar in the previous Academic year; (b) formulates the Academic Calendar for the next Academic Session, and (c) suggests corrective measures for the implementation of at least 180 teaching days and schedule of academic calendar.

The schedule of meeting could be suitably fixed keeping in view the Academic Calendar prescribed by the universities.

(5) The university may obtain the feed back about the implementation of Academic Calendar from the colleges in a prescribed form in this regard and the colleges be advised to send the monitoring report in time for consideration of the university level Committee.

(6) The university should compile the data about the implementation of the Academic Calendar in the university departments/

colleges and forward the same to the UGC, State Council for Higher Education and the State Goverment in a prescribed form.

3. *State Level*

(1) The implementation of the Academic Calendar by the universities in the States be monitored by the State Council for Higher Education and in the State where such Councils are yet to be established, this should be done by the State Government.

(2) The State Government/State Council of Higher Education may monitor the implementation of the Calendar in the universities by collecting the essential information and also by discussing the same in the meeting of the Vice-Chancellors of the State universities perferably twice every year. While doing this, UGC representative be also invited.

(3) The State Council for Higher Education/State Government may send the status of implementation of the Academic Calendar to the UGC/Government of India in the form prescribed.

4. *National Level*

At the national level, the monitoring of the implementation of the Calendar be done by the UGC at least once a year through a National Level Committee which may include few Vice-Chancellors, few Principals, Deans of College Development Councils, State-Council for Higher Education/State Governments etc. The Committee will oversee the implementation of the programme and suggest corrective measures to the Commission. The information received from the State be compiled and placed before the Commission. Simultaneously, it should also be discussed in the conference of the Vice-Chancellors and corrective measures formulated for consideration of the UGC. At this stage efforts be also made to develop a National Calendar to be followed by all the States in order to promote the mobility of the students from one state to the other.

III. **Awards to Universities**

It would encourage the universities to implement the academic calendar if the scheme of awards is introduced by the UGC in this regard with the following broad guidelines:

1. The UGC identifies four universities under the category of affiliating universities and one under the category of unitary/deemed universities as per criteria to be prescribed each year from all over the country to be given awards under these categories:

   A. Affiliating Universities:

Cat. 'A'	Rs. 15.00 lakhs
Cat. 'B'	Rs. 10.00 lakhs
Cat. 'C'	Rs. 7.50 lakhs
Cat. 'D'	Rs. 5.00 lakhs

   B. Unitary/Deemed Universities: Rs. 10 lakhs.

   The categorisation of the affiliating universities will, *inter alia*, be based on number of departments, colleges, number of students taking the examinations in different subjects and number of subjects in which examinations offered etc., the details of which to be worked out separately.
2. The awards may be utilised by the universities for promoting implementation of the academic calendar in universities/colleges as also for other purposes including students/teachers amenities. The awards should be utilised for developing infrastructural facilities.
3. One university under each category will be recommended giving full justification to the UGC by the State-level committee as recommended earlier.
4. UGC may suggest grading criteria to the States in this regard.
5. The National Committee of the UGC will finally recommend the names of the universities in this regard to the Commission.

Other Measures

1. The report of the Committee on Academic Calendar, its monitoring mechanism and awards be sent to all Chancellors, Visitors of Central Universities, State Governments, SCHE, Vice-Chancellors and if possible to all colleges.
2. The implementation of the Academic Calendar be reviewed regularly by the National Committee of the UGC.
3. The UGC may request the Chancellors/Visitors to kindly help in expediting the approval of statutes in this regard.

9

REPORT OF THE CURRICULUM DEVELOPMENT CENTRE IN EDUCATION: B. ED. COURSES (1990)*

Introduction

Curriculum is the pivot of contact between the intentions which initiate educational reforms and the reality of teaching-learning encounter, which ultimately determine the success of the changes attempted. A well developed curriculum has been accepted as the most patent instrument of educational reconstruction which can justify and contribute to the meaning and possibilities of the total system. Against this description, planning a curriculum in any discipline becomes a complex and highly professional activity.

The establishment of Curriculum Development Centres in various subjects by the UGC for preparation of model curriculum in each subject and the guidelines formulated have provided a facilitating situation.

The University of Kerala accepted the invitation from the UGC and set up the UGC Curriculum Development Centre in Education at the Department of Education, University of Kerala, Trivandrum. Dr. Vasantha Ramkumar Professor and Head, Department of Education, and Dean, Faculty of Education, University of Kerala was nominated as National Coordinator with effect from September 22, 1986.

4.3 Terms of Reference of the Committee: U.G.C. Guidelines

1. The Committee will examine the existing curriculum in the

* Broughtout by University Grants Commission, New Delhi.

Note : Para numbers refer to para numbers of the Report.

respective subjects of different universities in the country i terms of quality as well as workload.

2. The Committee will examine how the new curriculum wou promote human resource development and identify areas whi are crucial to make education meaningful in the task of nation development.
3. The Committee will devise a model curriculum which will relevant to the requirements of the country.
4. The Committee will suggest textual materials which would required to follow the new curriculum.
5. The Committee will suggest ways and means for prepari text-books, teaching aids, library as well as laboratory equi ments in implementing the proposed curriculum.
6. It should also indicate how the teachers are to be trained in der to impart education according to the revised curriculum.

4.4 Constitution of Committee for Under-graduate Level

Eleven specialists in the discipline from different Universities were vited to be members of the committee on the basis of their long perience and expertise in the field of education. Two members w co-opted from the Curriculum Development Centre.

4.5 Curriculum Development Committee: Under-graduate Level

1. Prof. H.Visweswaran, Professor Emeritus, Sri Ramakrishna Mission Vidyalaya P.O., Coimbatore - 641 020, Tamil Nadu.
2. Prof. S.Rajagopalan, Professor and Head, Deptt. of Educatio Annamalai University, Annamalainagar-608 002
3. Prof. Snehalata Shukla, Head, Deptt. of Teacher Education, NCERT, New Delhi - 110016.
4. Prof. S.P. Kulshresta, Professor, Deptt. of Teacher Education D.A.V. College, Dehra-Dun-248 001 (UP).
5. Prof. Suresh Shukla, Professor and Head, Deptt. of Educat Central Institute of Education, University of Delhi, 33, Ch Marg, Delhi-110007.
6. Prof. Balasubramanian, Reader-in-charge, Deptt. of Educat University of Madras, Madras-5.
7. Prof. M. Khajapeer, Professor and Head, Deptt. of Educat

Bangalore-560 056.
8. Prof. P.S. Vijaya Raghavan, Professor, S.N. Training College, Nedumganda, Kerala.
9. Prof. M.S. Sonar, Professor and Head, Deptt. of Education, Shivaji University, Vidyanagar, Kolhapur-416 004.
10. Prof. U.N. Dixit, Professor, Udaipur Vidyabhavan Teachers College, Udaipur-313 001, Rajasthan.
11. Prof. C.L. Anand, Professor of Education, Deptt. of Education, North Eastern Hill University, Shillong-793 001.
12. Prof. K.R. Sivadasan, Professor, Deptt. of Education, University of Kerala, Thycaud, Trivandrum-14.
13. Dr. K.N. Lalithamma, Reader, Deptt. of Education, University of Kerala, Thycaud, Trivandrum-14.
14. Prof. Vasantha Ramkumar, Professor and Head, Deptt. of Education, National Co-ordinator, Curriculum Development Centre, University of Kerala, Thycaud, Trivandrum-14.

4.6 **Committee Meetings**

The Committee met on five occasions on the dates indicated below in the Deptt. of Education, University of Kerala and deliberated in the various issues related to the development of Curriculum for the Undergraduate course in Education and by consensus designed and developed a Curriculum. The second meeting was a combined sitting with the post-graduate course – Committee at which various aspects of the articulation of the undergraduate course with the post-graduate course were discussed:

First Meeting	:	9th to 12th Dec., 1986
Second Meeting	:	5th to 8th Feb., 1987
Third Meeting	:	3rd to 6th March, 1987
Fourth Meeting	:	27th June to 2nd July, 1987
Fifth Meeting	:	28th to 31st Jan., 1988.

In-between the meeting the members were requested to prepare draft materials and these materials were circulated among Committee members and experts in the field for comments. On the subsequent meetings the comments received were reviewed and the final revision of the draft materials arrived at.

4.7 **Experts Consulted**

Dr. Krishna Swamy, CIE and FL., Hyderabad; Dr. R. Sudarsana, Tamil Nadu Agriculture Uty., Prof. Koothanainar, Special Officer of English School Education, Madras; Prof. K.C. John, Govt. Training College, Trivandrum; Prof. S. Arputham, Madurai Kamaraj University; Prof. R. Venkatasubramanian, Sri Ramakrishna Mission Vidyalaya, Coimbatore; Dr. S. Sundararajan, Annamalai University; Dr. S. Purushothaman, Ramakrishna Mission Vidyalaya College of Education; Dr. Rosaiah, Master College of Education, Madras; Prof. Andal Raghavan, NKT College of Education, Madras; Prof. J. Ramachandran, Annamalai University; Dr. A. Panniselvan, Teachers College Madras; Prof. Nalini Raman, Besant Nagar, Madras; Prof. P.S. Chandra, Lady Wellingdon College of Education, Madras.

4.8 **Participation of the Faculty of Deptt. of Education, University of Kerala**

The Syllabi of all the Universities were analysed and exhaustive draft syllabi for the core papers were prepared by the Faculty Members of the Department of Education, University of Kerala.

7.0 **Suggested Model for Bachelor's Course in Teacher Education**

The Committee has suggested an alternative model for the undergraduate level of teacher education. The Committee also considered the opinions of educationists through a questionnaire sent out by the Centre for the purpose.

It has three parts, namely: Part A - THEORY, Part B - PRACTICE and Part C - INTERNSHIP. The structure of the course is given below:

Duration: 2 Years - 1-1/2 years of instruction and 6 months' internship.

The undergraduate level of Teacher Education is to cover primary education as well.

PART A - THEORY

Core Subjects

Paper 1 - The Learner - Nature and Development
Paper 2 - Teacher and Education in Indian Society
Paper 3 - Teaching-Learning Process
Paper 4 - Section A - School Management
Section B - Electives

Electives

1. Guidance and Counselling
2. Adult and Continuing Education
3. Early Childhood Education
4. School Library Service
5. Work Experience
6. Health and Physical Education
7. Co-curricular Activities
8. Computer Education
9. Population Education

Optional Subjects

First Optional - Paper V - Methods of Teaching
Paper VI - Pedagogical Analysis
Second Optional - Paper VII - Methods of Teaching
Paper VIII - Pedagogical Analysis

Provision to be made for methods of teaching and pedagogical analysis of subjects at Higher Secondary and Secondary Levels.

PART B - PRACTICE

1. Practice Teaching
2. Practical work
3. Camp
4. Work Experience
5. Participation in Co-curricular Activities

PART C - INTERNSHIP

Phase 1 : Orienting to internshop programme
Phase 2 : Observing schools and school systems and assisting subject teacher.
Phase 3 : Working as a regular teacher

Alternative Papers for elementary level

Paper 7 : Child Psychology
Paper 8 : Content and Methodology of Teaching
(1) Language,
(2) Arithmetic, and
(3) Environmental Science

SCHEME OF EVALUATION

Papers/Activity	Mode of Evaluation	Marks
PART A THEORY		
Papers I to VIII	External (8 × 100)	800
PART B - PRACTICE		
1. Practice Teaching	Internal	200
2. Practical work (related to theory papers)	Inernal (8 ×50)	400
3. Camp	Internal	50
4. Work Experience	Internal	100
5. Participation in co-curricular Activities	Internal	50
	Total	1600

PART C - INTERNSHIP

Certification will be done on the successful completion and the assessment of internship

7.0.1 *Rationale for Suggested Model*

B.Ed. at present is one-year degree course in most universities. The exceptions are (i) Doctor Hari Singh Gour Viswavidyalaya, Saugar and (ii) Jadavpur University where the duration of the B.Ed. Programme is 1-1/2 years. In Regional Colleges of Education, a four-year integrated course of B.A./B.Sc. and B.Ed. called B.Ed./B.Sc.Ed. is offered. In some Universities like Berhampur University a plus three B.A. in Education has been started in 1985. The Particulars of the course are not available to the Committee.

The duration of one year was fixed the for L.T. Course in India many years ago, when the teacher education was in its infant stage. Today this field has so developed that it is not easy to attain the professional skills required of teachers within the short duration of one year. The research in teacher education, the new learning theories, instructional strategies, the development of allied subjects like psychology and sociology and the growth of educational technology have enlarged the scope of the teacher education curriculum which will require a longer duration of the course. One year education is inadequate for a profession like teaching. The M.Ed. programme has its own specific objectives and cannot be designed as a sequential programme for continuing the skill development. Teaching skills are to be developed at the B.Ed. level and the study of education with a strong emphasis on theoretical foundation is to be taken up at the M.Ed. level.

The Committee is of the opinion that at present full justice is not done to practice teaching at the B.Ed. level for want of time and a comprehensive programme. A teacher with little practice is more dangerous than a 'raw' teacher. In the existing practice, a student teacher is supposed to teach only 15-20 lessons under practice teaching. This is inadequate for a person to be initiated into the profession of teaching. The new techniques of training like microteaching and the teaching experience in the form of internship, if introduced require lengthening of the course.

In view of the eight papers to be introduced under theory and more intensified practice teaching, the teacher education programme of two years duration is justified.

The Saugar experiment is the only exception in India. The Doctor Hari Singh Gour Vishwavidyalaya, Saugar has the B.Ed. programme of 1-1/2 years' duration out of which the last five months have been set apart for Internship; Phase II for "acclimatising" the student teacher with the realistic school structure, its functioning and constituents of teaching-learning process and then to prepare him for teaching in guided and self-managed situations."

A longer duration is not a new concept. In the suggested model, the proposed duration is two years. In order to cover the rich and varied content in teacher education and provide adequate practice teaching and six months internship, a period of two years is essential.

Eligibility for Admission

The admission to the course will be open to graduate of recognised universities. A certain number of seats may be set apart for postgraduates. The committee suggests the criteria for admission to be minimum of 50 per cent marks in the performance in an entrance examination followed by an interview.

The course

Part A - Theory

The four papers in this part are the outcome of the review of all theory papers prescribed in different universities in India. Most common papers now offered in the universities are given below:

Paper 1: Teacher Education in the Emerging Indian Society, Education in Indian Society.

Paper 2:

Educational Psychology
Psychological Foundations of Education
Psychology of Growth and Learning
Psychology in Education
Foundations of Education - Psychological
Psycho-Pedagogy

Paper 3:

Basic Principles and Methods of Teaching and School Organisation
Evaluation, Mental Measurement and Statistics
School Organisation and Modern School Practices
School Organisation and Educational Technology
School Organisation and Administration

Electives: A large number of subjects have been included under this section. They are:

1. Education in Contemporary India
2. School Organization
3. Educational Technology
4. School and Educational Management and Special Fields of Education
5. Theory of Education
6. Principles of Education
7. Education and society
8. Education in Modern India
9. Teaching of School Subject-I
10. Principles and Techniques of Education
11. Problems of Indian Education
12. Comparative Education
13. Population Education
14. Guidance and Counselling
15. Educational Evaluation
16. Education of the Socially Disadvantaged
17. Education of the Gifted
18. Mental Hygiene
19. Adult Education
20. Non-formal Education
21. Physical Education
22. Library Education
23. SUPW
24. Action Research
25. Infant Education
26. Educational Administration and Supervision
27. Contributions of Great Educators
28. Curriculum Development
29. Models of Teaching
30. Environmental Studies
31. Programmed Learning
32. Teacher Education
33. Health Education
34. Higher Secondary Education
35. Rural Education
36. Economics of Education

37. Moral Education
38. Measurement and Evaluation
39. School Administration
40. Experimental Education
41. Speech Skill
42. Reading Skill
43. Elementary Education
44. Institutional Planning and Administration
45. Diagnostic and Remedial Teaching
46. Philosophical and Sociological Foundations of Education
47. Scientific bases of Educational Practices including School Organization, Methodology of Teaching
48. Mental and Health Education and Educational Measurement

The theory papers in the existing curriculum have been subsumed under four papers and these papers are further enriched with modern concepts and principles in education under Part A – Theory of the suggested model.

While the focus of Paper I is on the child who is the learner, Paper II lays emphasis on Sociological and Philosophical implications for education in the context of Indian Society. Paper III deals with the instructional strategies and evaluation in the context of educational technology. Paper IV is an additional compulsory core paper covering school management under Section A and subject concerning a major issue in Indian Education under Section B. Elective.

Optional Subjects

In most universities two-optional system is followed. In a very few universities single optimal system is prevalent. In the suggested course the former system is adopted. In many parts of India, schools have only one or two sections in a standard at high school level. If teachers are trained in only one subject, they cannot be given sufficient teaching work in such schools. The single optional system in a one year programme may be more appropriate for post-graduates who are later appointed in higher secondary schools. But all post-graduates may not get themselves employed in higher secondary schools soon after their completing the B.Ed. course and very many of them may have to seek employment in high schools in rural areas in which case they are likely to teach two different subjects.

Each optional subject has two papers – one covering methods of teaching and the other pedagogical analysis of the content of school subject. The pedagogical analysis is a promising exercise for teacher trainees. It was introduced in some universities only. In the beginning there was only the study of certain select areas in the optional subject prescribed for the B.A./B.Sc. course. Later the content study has taken the shape of pedagogical analysis of the content of the B.A./B.Sc. degree. Since universities like Gandhiji University felt that the pedagogical analysis of the B.A./B.Sc. level syllabus of the subject was too much for a graduate or even a postgraduate who is not given to teach the subject at the B.A./B.Sc. level, the pedagogical analysis was limited to the content prescribed for high school classes. The Committee is of the opinion that pedagogical analysis of the subject is essential for a better understanding of the teaching-learning process. The Committee recommends to include under Paper IV and Paper VIII the pedagogical analysis of the content of optional subjects prescribed for the high schools/higher secondary schools. (The guidelines for the analysis and models for languages, sciences and social sciences must be prepared in a national workshop of eminent teacher educators in India, if possible from abroad).

Teaching at Higher Secondary School

The minimum professional qualification for higher secondary school teaching is B.Ed. degree. But the B.Ed. degree programme does not envisage the professional training of higher secondary school teachers. At this level the method of teaching must be different from that at secondary level. It must be oriented to problem-solving, seminar, discussion and the like. Several methods of teaching at higher stages of education are being developed. Nevertheless, a separate teacher education programme for this comparatively small group of teachers for higher secondary schools is not advisable at present. But provision is made in the suggested model for methods of teaching and pedagogical analysis of subjects at higher secondary level. If this is introduced, a small percentage of seats must be set apart for postgraduates who aspire to become teachers in higher secondary schools.

Teaching at Elementary Level

More and more trained graduates are employed in elementary schools.

An elementary school teacher is expected to teach all school subjects. The trained graduates are competent to teach either one or two subjects. The new model gives provision for training to teach all subjects at elementary schools by Paper VI - Child Psychology and Paper VIII - Content and Methodology of Teaching (i) Language, (ii) Arithmetic and (iii) Environmental Sciences.

PART B - PRACTICE

The highlight of the proposed model is that theory and practice have been given equal status in the teacher education programme by including two strong components viz., Part B Practice and part C Internship.

Part B Practice consists of four distinct parts like practice teaching, practical work, camp, work experience and participation in co-curricular activities. The practical work is related to the eight papers under Part A theory.

PART C - INTERNSHIP

After the student teacher has completed the course and appeared for the examination he/she is exposed to the school in its natural setting. The student teacher will be oriented to internship under Phase I of the programme. The major purpose of Phase II of the internship is to "acclimatize the student teacher with the realistic school structure and its functioning." Phase III is intended for student teacher to experience the teaching-learning process in real situation and to undertake teaching as done by experienced teacher. The proposed internship is comparable with that of any professional course. The duration of the internship is proposed to be six months from November to March in the second academic year (4th Semester). The certification is done after the successful completion of internship.

Name of the Course

The suggested course is more intensive and qualitatively at a higher level than the current B.Ed./B.T. courses and as such the degree or title awarded to candidates who undergo and successfully complete this course should be different from the B.Ed./B.T. It is hoped that the NCTE will soon become a statutory body and secure "accreditation authority". When the courses offered at various universities are accredited by the NCTE, a common nomenclature for the degree or title may be acceptable for all. It is suggested that the candidates who successfully complete the course (2 years duration with all the components suggested in this curriculum) be given the title Fellow of Education Faculty (FEF) irrespective of the various types of degrees (Bachelor, Master, Honours, Science, Arts, Education) that the various universities offer to conform to the general practice they observe in the award of degrees to various faculties. The universities may be given the option to have their own nomenclature to the degree they award but would be required to get the degrees accredited by the NCTE and NCTE would offer the title FEF to the candidates who pass out by the accredited degree courses and this title awarded by a National body will have its prestige and acceptance all over the country. The responsibility for maintaining a national standard will then devolve on the NCTE.

Scheme of Evaluation

Theory and Practice have been given equal weightage, 800 marks have been allocated for each part, the total marks coming to 1600. Both the internal evaluation and external evaluation are proposed. In addition, there is an intensive assessment of internship. Only theory papers under Part A will be subjected to external evaluation. The system of continuous evaluation is recommended.

11.0 **Recommendations**

Curriculum change is a complex process which involves the interaction of objectives, methods, materials and personnel. Its effectiveness is characterised by movement from one position to another, for each of these components singly and as an intergrated whole. A conscious effort at change has to follow the preparation of the new curriculum, to prevent the stagnation which is often seen in the implementation process, the misplaced emphasis on a few activities that results in gaps, the gradual dilution of standards when the curriculum is handled by a large body of personnel with varying interests, capabilities and expertise and who are not direct participants in the process of curriculum development and the unpredicability of institutional conditions for implementation.

The recommendations for the implementation of the curriculum are intended to:

1. *enable the implementation process to be initiated and carried out smoothly, with adequate support and close monitoring at the State, Regional and National levels.*
2. *provide a stable framework for Curriculum Development as an ongoing process, incorporating preparation, implementation and evaluation as continuing activities.*
3. *raise the standard of under-graduate teaching in education for which Curriculum Development is a critical but not the only requirement, with curriculum development as the starting point for action.*
4. *develop curriculum development as an important area of inquiry within the discipline of education.*
5. *initiate discussion and debate at the National, Regional and State levels on the curriculum.*

Categorisation of Recommendations

The recommendations are presented as:

A. Steps to be taken to finalise the curriculum and recommendations for effecting them.
B. Actions to be initiated to implement the curriculum and recommendations for carrying them out.
C. Details of structure required to intitiate, co-ordinate and evaluate the implementation of the curriculum and to do further studies in the area and recommendations concerning agencies, institutions and bodies needed.

A. *Finalisation of the Curriculum*

A. 1. *Steps to be taken to finalise the Curriculum*

The following tasks remain to be completed before a final curriculum can emerge:

1. The modules of the core papers need to be refined.
2. The basic and further readings have to be categorised modulewise, from the total bibliography
3. Elective papers have to be prepared.
4. Bibliography for elective papers need to be compiled.
5. Basic books for core papers require to be written.

6. The content of specific teacher training programmes needs to be further detailed.
7. The reacting of teacher educators to the curriculum have to be obtained and the curriculum modified on this basis.

A. 2 *Recommendations for finalisation of the Curriculum*

To complete the above-mentioned tasks for finalisation of the curriculum it is recommended that:

1. The U.G.C. Curriculum Development Centre at the Department of Education, University of Kerala, be requested to continue functioning for another one year with a fresh budget allocation and change in manner of functioning.
2. The present national committes be permitted to continue and to meet at least four times to complete the curriculum for the different specialisation papers.
3. Six workshops to be organised of ten days duration to translate the curriculum for the specialisation papers into modules, with experts identified in terms of the particular expertise required.
4. The curriculum prepared by the Curriculum Development Centre to be discussed and modifications made before it is accepted and implemented. To enable focused discussion on the curriculum the following suggestions are made :

(a) *National Meeting*

The draft curriculum should be discussed at a National Meeting of U.G.C. officials, the Curriculum Committee members and thirty invited teacher educators (Deans and Professors of Education, Principals of Teacher Training Colleges) from all over the country.

(b) *Regional Seminars*

Six regional seminars, organised by U.G.C. in collaboration with six departments of Education at which teacher educators and administrators, at the under-graduate level, research workers and other personnel in the field of teacher education, including those involved with the graduate programme, are to be given the opportunity to discuss and react to the draft curriculum.

(c) *State level Seminars*

State level Seminars organised by the U.G.C. and the University Departments of Education at which concerned teaching faculty of Bachelors course in education discuss and give their reactions to the curriculum.

(b) *Action to be initiated to implement the Curriculum*

B. 1. *Understanding the context for implementation*

To implement the new curriculum certain background information is required. The Curriculum Committee has provided a status survey of the existing curriculum in terms of structure, papers, and scheme of evaluation, but has not provided information on facilities in institutions and particular competencies required for teacher orientation, as it lay beyond its scope.

To obtain this information it is recommended:

1. A National Survey on existing conditions in under-graduate teacher training institutions to be conducted and a report prepared.
2. A National Committee to be entrusted with this task, with the necessary sponsorship facilities and finances provided by UGC.
3. National Regional and State agencies to be represented through

   (a) membership in committees; and
   (b) participation in the survey

B. 2. *Dissemination of Information on the Curriculum*

The curriculum requires a large number of personnel for its actual implementation and the involvement of both active and passive members of a wider community for its acceptance and use. The rationale for the changes have to be spelt out and debated to establish the relevance for the changes. The curriculum has to be understood before it is translated and one of the important tasks for effective implementation is discussion of the ideas and materials of the curriculum. The rationale, objectives, structure and other elements have to be clearly explained particularly when the changes have been very significant. The present curiculum has given a changed structure of the course and the duration of the course has been lengthened. The full implications of these changes need to be analysed and communicated. The curriculum has also been presented through modules. The use of modules is not widespread as yet, particularly in certain disciplines of which education is one. An understanding of the principles and procedures involved in the modular approach, and of the requirements for implementation have to be built-up.

The following recommendations are made for exposure of the curriculum.

1. Publication of a Curriculum Bulletin which would provide the required information on the characteristics of the curriculum and its widerspred circulation through a network of State, Regional and National agencies.
2. Organisation of local based small group discussions/Seminars with national resource persons for clearing doubts and identifying particular hindering factors.
3. Arrangement of National level lectures on the curriculum to place the curriculum in a wider perspective.
4. Publication of articles in the media by eminent educationists on the existing conditions, indicating the need for change and presenting the possibilities of the new curriculum.
5. Specific literature to be prepared and seminars to be organised on the modalities for use of modules in teaching to orient teachers with the requirements for effective teaching through modules.

B. 3. *Development of materials to support the curriculum*

The materials required have been spelt out earlier. They include:

1. Comprehensive and annotated bibliographies.
2. Different papers of the prescribed curriculum
3. Reports of curriculum analysis of papers which would serve as Handbooks.
4. Basic texts and translations.
5. Supportive audio-visual materials.
6. Educational technology hardware and software

7. Test materials
8. Comprehensive Question Bank.

To provide these materials the following actions are suggested:

1. Compiling and collating tasks are to be completed at the existing curriculum development centre as part of finalisation of the curriculum.
2. Materials required are to be prepared at creative workshops with specially invited participants.
3. Systematic curriculum analysis to be initiated at the identified national centre.

To initiate and complete these actions the following recommendations are made.

1. Agencies, institutions and bodies at the State, Regional and National levels are to be set up for the tasks.
2. Teacher Training Colleges have to be provided the capability to utilise the materials prepared through ad hoc grants for the purpose from the UGC.

B. 4. *Development of Curriculum as an Area of Inquiry*

Curriculum Development has grown as an area of inquiry and it now requires focused attention both in terms of theory and practical applications. To reflect this development and to enable the departments of education to provide leadership in the area of curriculum development in other disciplines as well the following recommendations are made:

1. Systematic curriculum analysis has to be undertaken, and the results to be reported by National and Regional Curriculum Development Centres established for the purpose.
2. Research in curriculum related areas has to become the focus of concern of research scholars and the teaching faculty.

To enable a large number of research workers to be engaged in the work it is recommended that:

(a) U.G.C. allot research scholarships specifically for research in curriculum at the doctoral and post-doctoral levels;

(b) Curriculum research to be included in the Research agenda of National agencies; and

(c) Experts in curriculum studies from foreign universities be invited as Visiting Professors in Departments of Education, which should serve as nodal agencies for teacher training colleges in the different areas.

B. 5. *Strengthening of Teacher Training Colleges in terms of physical facilities, teaching personnel and scope of functioning*

Strengthening of Teacher Training Colleges

To implement the curriculum meaningfully certain vital requirements need to be provided. They include:

(i) Adequate library;
(ii) Reprographic facilities;
(iii) Computer and video units;
(iv) Testing materials; and
(v) Adequate staff structure.

Based on the status survey findings as suggested earlier, the requirements for each training colleges need to be worked out.

To enable this task to be completed it is recommended that UGC Committees for different regions be set up with six members to inspect each institution in the identified area and analyse its requirements and report to the UGC.

C. *Agencies, Institutions and Bodies for Implementation of the Curriculum*

A systematic structure for implementation of the curriculum is required if the initiative taken in curriculum development is to have the follow through. The agencies, institutions and bodies of the strucuture could (1) disseminate information on the rationale of the curriculum developed, on the capabilities and resources required on the part of the education system, and on the new approaches needed in inservice training, (2) provide the support system required in terms of direction, materials and personnel, (3) engage in field-data collection which would serve as a framework for assessing effectiveness; and (4) sponsor all the actions recommended in an integrated manner. Careful continuous monitoring of the implemntation of the curriculum requires a process of constant commincation and feedback. The suggested structure is outlined here:

C.1. *A National Curriculum Development Centre to be Established by U.G.C.*

This Centre will :

(a) integrate the different activities for finalising the development and implementation of the curriculum.
(b) disseminate information on the descriptive characteristics of the new curriculum through its various publications.
(c) publish the results of research in Curriculum Development through the Journal of Curriculum Studies.
(d) arrange guest lectures at the National level on Curriculum related areas.
(e) identify experts in the area of Curriculum Development and provide resource personnel.
(f) organize National seminars on the different issues in Curriculum Development and Implementation.
(g) prepare resource materials, including textbooks through group and individual efforts to support the new curriculum.
(h) develop programmes for teacher training in collaboration with regional centres and teacher training institutions.
(i) develop tools and materials for evaluation of curricular outcomes.
(j) organise a curriculum materials library to serve as the nodal centre for curriculum research and studies.
(k) carry out research studies in the area of curriculum.
(l) edit and publish the Journal of Curriculum Studies.

Note : The present UGC Curriculum Development Centre at the Department of Education, University of Kerala which has also been identified for Special Assistance by the University Grants Commission with Curriculum Development as an important thrust area has the potential to be organised into the National Curriculum Development Centre.

C.2. *Six Regional Curriculum Development Centres* to be identified by UGC with networking arrangements with the National Centre to provide leadership in Curriculum Development in defined areas. Six

Departments of Education in Universities could be identified by the UGC for this purpose.

Regional Centres will:

(a) co-operate with the national centre in all its activities;
(b) publish and distribute curriculum bulletins to teacher education institutions in the region;
(c) organize regional seminars;
(d) disseminate information on the curriculum;
(e) provide leadership for teacher training activities in the area;
(f) carry out research studies in the area of curriculum;
(g) organise libraries in identified areas of specialisation within Curriculum Development; and
(h) arrange lectures on curriculum related areas.

C.3. *Ten Teacher Training Institutions to be established* in ten Universities by the U.G.C. which would work in close collaboration with Regional and National Centres.

Teacher Training Institutions will:

(a) organise different types of inservice programmes for teachers of under-graduate Courses in the area;
(b) distribute curriculum bulletins to the teachers;
(c) obtain feedback from teachers and communicate to Regional and National Centres;
(d) co-operate with Regional and National Centres in all their activities; and
(e) carry out action research studies.

C.4. *Curriculum Implementation Cells* to be established in atleast one University Department of Education in each of the States not covered by the National and Regional Curriculum Development Centres.

Curriculum Implementation Cells will :

(a) monitor the implementation of the curricula at the State level; and

(b) provide feedback information to teacher training institutions, regional centres and national centres.

C.5. *Curriculum Materials Units* to be an integral part of the National and Regional Currculum Development Centres for the preparation of resource materials for development and implementation of the new curriculum.

Curriculum Materials Units will:

(a) collect curriculum materials and resource materials from different institutions for study;
(b) prepare materials according to local requirements;
(c) disseminate information on materials available; and
(d) prepare new materials

C.6. *Department of Curriculum Studies*

Certain Departments of Education which have the interest and the capability are to be identified and assisted for teaching and research in specialisations within the area of Curriculum, through the different programmes of the UGC for *ad hoc* grants, research support and special assistance. These centres are to be concerned with the curricular requirements of under-graduate teacher training institutions.

C.7. *A Statutory Body for Natonal Curriculum Development* in Higher Education with sub-committees in each discipline to function under the aegis of the UGC.

10

REPORT OF NATIONAL SEMINAR ON VOCATIONALISATION OF EDUCATION, (1990)*

Objectives of the Seminar

The Seminar was organised with a view:

- to review the progress of the vocational education programme implemented under the centrally sponsored scheme.
- to share the experiences amongst the participating States/UTs and exchange ideas.
- to find out constraints and deficiencies.
- to suggest remedial measures to realise policy goals.

Agenda of the Seminar

The Seminar had the following agenda:

1. Presentation of Status Reports of the Vocational Education Programmes by the participating States/UTs.
2. Deliberations on the challenges, constraints and problems faced in the implementation.
3. Disussion on NCERT'S input in the Programme and the requirement of the States /UTs.
4. Suggestions and Recommendations.

---

* NCERT, *Vocationalisation of Education: Achievements in the Seventh Plan (1990)*, NCERT, New Delhi.

Participation

The Seminar was attended by 20 high level delegates from 15 States and 11 Union Territories, 3 delegates including the Secretary of the Deptt. of Education from MHRD, the Director, NCERT, 2 delegates from Regional Boards of Apprenticeship Training (Northern and Southern Regions), and 19 NCERT persons, field advisers and 12 faculty members of the Department of Vocationalization of Education. The seminar was held from December 12 to 14, 1989.

RECOMMENDATIONS OF THE SEMINAR ON VOCATIONALIZATION OF EDUCATION, 1989

1. **Creation of Management Systems**

Most of the States/UTs have not yet created the management system as envisaged in the CSS. This, in fact, is coming in the way of proper and early implementation of the programme. It is, therefore recommended that:

> The MHRD should emphasize and effectively influence the State/UT governments for early creation of the proposed management system in their States/UTs.

2. **Sharing Pattern of Expenditure**

Under the existing Centrally Sponsored Scheme of sharing pattern of expenditure between the Centre and the States/UTs varies from item to item. Moreover, during discussions this sharing pattern was not found to be much conducive especially in view of the scarce resources in majority of the states. Hence the seminar recommended that:

> The sharing between the Centre and the States should be in the ratio of 80 : 20 for the items of recurring nature whereas the funding pattern with regard to items of non-recurring nature should remain unchanged.

3. **Financial Provision for Language and General Foundation Course (GFC) Teachers**

The CSS in its present form does not have provision for expenditure incurred on teaching of language and General Foundation Course. This was perhaps done with the understanding that the services of the existing academic staff will be utilized for the purpose. But today there are States where vocational courses have schools where there are no language or other subject teachers. In order to overcome this difficulty it is recommended that:

> The CSS should also make financial provisions for language and General Foundation Courses teachers for those schools/junior colleges where there is no academic stream.

It is also recommended that:

The grant for the purchase of books for the library should be separately mentioned in the CSS.

4. **Allocation for Construction of Shed**

It was observed during the presentation of state reports that the cost of construction in certain parts of the country, e.g., in hill areas is quite high. In view of this factor it is recommended that:

> The allocation of workshop/laboratory building under CSS should be enhanced by one and a half times that of the present rate.

5. **Attractive Institutional Set-up**

In order to catch the attention and imagination of parents and students to opt for the vocational alternative in larger numbers it is recommended that:

> The institutional set-up should be made fairly attractive by substantially increasing allocation for infrastructural facilities partly because of the realisation that the funds allocated thus for the purpose are quite inadequate.

6. **Course Design**

Vocational courses by and large, are so designed that they failed to prepare students for employment, either self or wage. But it is felt that in view of the difficult wage employment situations generally prevailing in the country most of the vocational products may have to settle themselves in self-employment ventures. In view of the need for developing entrepreneural skills for such ventures it is recommended that:

> The General Foundation Course comprising entrepreneurship, rural development and environmental studies designed and developed by the NCERT should be introduced by all the States/UTs.

7. **Course Structure**

It was observed during the discussions that there are States which are deviating from the course structure given in the CSS thereby invariably diluting the vocational content and practice. It is, therefore, once again recommended that:

> Each vocational course should have the following three components and the percentage of total time for them:

– Language(s)	30%
– General Foundation Course – Vocational Theory and Practice	70%

8. **Revision of Curriculum Design**

The curriculum design as recommended at the national level tends to develop desired level of competency in vocational products in their respective areas of specialization. However, during presentations of state reports, it was observed that curriculum design in at least some of the States is out of focus. Hence, it is recommended that:

> There is definite need to scrutinize and revise curriculum pattern of some of the States, including those prescribed by the Central Board of Secondary Education to bring them in tune with the national pattern as also to ensure development of desired level of competency in their vocational products.

9. **Standardization and Uniform Norms**

In order to bring about certain amount of uniformity and standardization in the various vocational courses offered in different States it is recommended that:

> A group or body of professionals at the national level should go into the question of standardization of vocational courses and setting up certain uniform norms with a view to bringing in uniformity, rigour and equivalence among these courses.

It is further recommended that NCERT should examine this question in detail so that an appropriate authority is created at the national level on the pattern on of AICTE, NCTE or NCVT.

10. **Nature of Certification**

In order to maintain homogeneity in the format and nature of certification as also to facilitate inter-state mobility of vocational products the seminar recommended that:

> While the states accrediting bodies, viz., secondary and higher secondary boards, intermediate councils and other such agencies should accredit the vocational students by issuing a certificate similar to that issued to academic stream students, the vocational certificate should, in addition, highlight the name of the vocational course and subjects offered. A mark sheet and a sheet indicating competencies acquired by the student should also accompany it.

11. **Training of Teachers**

Non-availability of suitable trained and qualified teachers is one of the stumbling blocks in the way of proper implementation of vocational education programme. In order to overcome this situation it is recommended that:

> Each state should identify one or two existing teacher training colleges having adequate infrastructural facilities which could be converted into vocational teacher training colleges by supplementing them with additional facilities through Central assistance.

12. **Orientation and Training of Vocational Officers and Teacher Educators**

As at present the vocational education programme in the States/UTs is being managed by the existing officers of the education departments who neither have the background nor have been specifically trained for the purpose. It is, therefore, recommended that:

> The NCERT should organize orientation programmes of 10-15 days duration for such newly inducted officers.
>
> It is further recommended that NCERT, in due course of time, should offer a specially designed diploma course of nine months duration for the managers and supervisors of vocational education programmes in the States/UTs.

The seminar also recommended that:

> The Four Regional Colleges of Education of NCERT should design and offer programmes for the preparation of teacher educators in major vocational areas of Agriculture, Business and Commerce, Home Science, Technology and Humanities and others.

13. **Inter-State Exchange Programmes**

It is strongly recommended that exchange programmes for various levels of vocational functionaries should be organized from time to time on an inter-state basis which will go a long way in motivating, clarifying, convincing and innovating in addition to bringing in uniformity and national integration.

14. **Coverage Under Apprentices Act**

As at present only 20 vocational courses have been notified as designated subject fields for the purpose of training under the amended Apprentices Act. The list is grossly inadequate looking at the large number of vocational courses, being offered throughout the country. It is, therefore, recommended that:

> The coverage of designated subject fields should be greatly enhanced to bring within its fold all possible vocational courses so that almost all the vocational products can avail of, if they so desire, training under the amended Apprentices Act.

15. **Modification of Recruitment Rules**

Modification of recruitment rules in favour of vocational products will greatly enhance their chances of finding an employment. With this in view the seminar recommended that:

> The State Education Department or the department concerned with implementation of vocational education programme should take urgent steps to get rules of recruitment in the government, quasi-government institutions, the public and the private sector suitably amended to provide a clear performance for the graduates of the vocational stream.

16. **Self-Employment Support**

Keeping in view the limited opportunities in the wage employment side the scheme of vocationalization of education should primarily address itself to the development of entrepreneurship and self-employment capabilities in vocational products. It is, therefore, recommended that:

> In order to effectively enhance self-employment and entrepreneurship amongst vocational graduates properly devised mechanisms should be organized at the state levels for effective delivery of self-employment support to the vocational products.

17. **Restructuring of First Degree Courses**

During the last few years UGC has been emphasising the need for restructuring of the first degree courses in favour of practical and vocational inputs. In this context it is recommended that:

> The MHRD and UGC on the one hand and respective State Governments on the other hand should impress upon the universities to keep in view the specific needs of the vocational education programmes being run by the different States while restructuring their first degree courses.

18. **The Bridge Courses**

The National Policy on Education, 1986 has suggested the introduction of a variety of bridge courses. It states, "Graduates of vocational courses will be given opportunities, under pre-determined conditions, for professional growth, career improvement and lateral entry into courses of general, technical and professional education through appropriate bridge courses." It is, therefore, recommended that:

> Appropriate bridge courses should be designed by the examining boards in the States in collaboration with the tertiary level agencies/institutions to facilitate professional courses. However, the concept of vertical mobility here should not be of unlimited nature rather, as far as possible it should be in corresponding specialization. Direct mobility of vocational products to restructured university level .courses should also be examined and extended to them.

19. **Publicity**

In order to popularise the programme and to highlight its potentialities, possibilities and characteristics to people in general and students and teachers in particular it is recommended that:

> The State/UT Governments should make adequate use of mass media like radio, TV, newspapers, journals etc. to educate the masses regarding vocational education programme in schools and colleges.

20. **Creation of Centralized Facilities**

Considering the difficulties experienced in providing intensive practice to vocational students and on-the job training it is recommended that:

> Wherever possible centralized facilities should be created for a set of vocational courses to be utilized by a group of neighbouring Higher Secondary Schools.

21. **Non-Formal Vocational Courses**

Keeping in view the general lack of skill base among the labour force in the unorganized sector and also the fact that the facilities created in vocational schools remain idle for certain periods of time it is recommended that:

The scope of the present scheme of financial support for Higher Secondary Vocationalization should also be extended to non-formal out-of-school population.

It is further recommended that non-formal vocational programmes of varying durations could be offered to out-of-school population like the drop outs from the general system, unemployed and partially employed labour force, small entrepreneurs and such other unskilled in-service workers to raise the skill base in general and to utilize the created facilites to the optimum in particular.

11

EDUCATION FOR ALL BY 2000 (1990)*

Introduction

Universalisation of elementary education has been one of the most important goals of educational development in India since Independence. The goals of free and compulsory education for all children up to age of 14 years as stipulated in Article 45 of the Constitution should have been fulfilled within a period of 10 years i.e. by 1960. On account of various constraints it has been revised several times; first by 1970, then by 1976, and later to 1990. The present date according to the National Policy on Education, 1986 is 1995. The document under reference does not subscribe to the problem and attempts to indicate possible directions and broad resource requirements.

EXTRACTS

Goals and Targets

Unrealistic Targets in the Past

A review of the progress of basic education shows that goals and targets were fixed in the past on the basis of an inadequate understanding of the significance of education. These targets did not take into the account the problem of availability of resources, and the conflicting

---

* *Education for all By 2000: Indian Perspective* National Institute of Educational Planning and Administration, New Delhi, 1990.

Notes: 1. Serial numbers and captions inserted.
2. Figures in the parentheses indicate Chapter number and page number of the publication.

claims of social and economic planning. (3.26)

Realistic Targets

If right from the beginning, it is apparent that goals are unrealistic and unachievable, they do not lead to the kind of motivation and resource mobilisation required. The right approach, therefore, is to set realistic targets – realistic not defined as easily achievable, but as achievable with conceivable maximum input of meticulous planning and resources – financial as well as human.

We shall, therefore, proceed to propose realistic targets that we believe can be achieved by the year 2000, keeping in view the past trends, the contemporary situation, and the future prospects of availability of resources and other favourable environment, as also the constraints. The targets will be presented in more precise and specific terms. Although it is a plan for ten years, it would be useful to set separate targets for the first five and the second five years to enable mid-term appraisal and corrective action. This will also coincide with the Eighth and the Ninth Five Year Plan periods. (3.26-27)

Identification of Educational Inputs

For ideal planning, educational inputs provided by other sectors should also be taken into account.

Limited Specificity and Disaggregation in Target Fixing

Different targets for different states and areas could be attempted, but this would make the whole exercise too cumbersome to be meaningful. It is, therefore, proposed that the national targets may have limited specificity and disaggregation with the further requirement that more detailed disaggregated targets will be set for each state, each district, each development block and each unit of microplanning. In this disaggregated target-setting at various levels, the following important considerations will be kept in view:

(1) Separate targets for rural and urban areas should be fixed.
(2) Separate targets for the disadvantaged sections of the society will be fixed genderwise.
(3) The low participation in education of girls and women is the

most significant factor to be taken into account. Any target for a group may be achieved with continued inequity between males and females of that group, so long as the targets do not clearly indicate the levels to be achieved separately for both genders. That is why it has been suggested that the groupwise disaggregated target will also be genderwise.

(4) Access to educational facilities, participation in education and achievement in education are distinct, though interrelated. These aspects should be separately considered for fixing targets and appropriate planning.

National Leval Targets

The mechanism of micro-level planning will result in separate targets for each planning unit – state, district, block, and village. In a truly decentralised approach of planning, realistic targets fixed by all the villages of the block should lead to the target of the block, the targets of all the blocks in a district should lead to the target of the district and so on. However, such a process will not only be time-consuming, it would also lack a national goal reference. By expecting certain national level targets on the basis of disaggregation, we are also hoping to oblige the national and state level planners to pay higher attention to areas and groups and within them to girls/women, receiving special attention.

A. *Access*

1. By the year 1995, primary schools or their alternatives will be provided to every child in the rural areas with a distance of one km.

2. By the year 2000, upper primary schools or their alternatives will be provided to every child in the rural area within a distance of three km.

According to the All-India Educational Survey (1986), conducted by the NCERT, 94 per cent of the rural population is being served by a primary school within one km and 85.39 per cent of the rural population is being served by an upper primary school within a distance of three km. In view of this, it should not be difficult to provide a school or an alternative education centre in the next 5 years to the remaining 6 per cent of the rural population for primary education, and the remaining 14.61 per cent for upper primary education in the next 10 years. In this we are assuming a growth rate of slightly above one per cent, which is not very high.

B. *Participation*

3. Primary education through schools or alternatives will be provided to:

(a) Eighty per cent of all children up to the age of 11 years by 1995, which will necessarily include at least 70 per cent belonging to every identified disadventaged group; and
(b) Ninety-five per cent of all children up to the age of 11 years by the year 2000, which will necessarily include 85 per cent girls belonging to every identified disadvantaged group.

Taking into account the current lower participation rate of the children of disadvantaged groups as compared to the total participation of children, different levels of participation are proposed for children of disadvantaged groups and for the overall participation.

4. Upper primary education through schools or alternatives will be provided to:

(a) Sixty per cent of all children up to the age of 14 years by 1995, which will necessarily include at least 65 per cent of girls belonging to every identified disadvantaged group; and
(b) Seventy-five per cent of all children up to the age of 14 years by 1995, which will necessarily inculde at least 65 per cent of girls belonging to every identified disadvantaged group. (3.28.29)

The dropout rate is extremely high in the early stages of primary education and is considerably less between the conclusion of primary and the start of the upper primary education. Of those who complete primary education roughly 75 per cent continue studies for upper primary education. Most of the children who continue studies for upper primary education usually complete that stage. Keeping this in view, the targets for participation in upper primary education have been kept at approximately 75 per cent of those for primary education. An assumption implicit is that if the existing transfer rate for primary to upper primary is 75 per cent, it is likely to go up and similarly the dropout rate at the upper primary stage would also be reduced. The effect of the level achieved in 1995 at the end of the primary stage will usually be seen at the end of the upper primary stage after three years. However, in view of the improved environment for education, it has been visualised that improved transfer to and retention in upper primary education will not be sequential but partly contemporaneous with improvement in primary education. (3.29)

C. *Achievement*

(a) Seventy per cent of children, including at least 60 per cent girls of every disadvantaged group, pursuing elementary education, will achieve the minimum levels of learning by the year 1995; and

(b) Eighty per cent of children, including at least 70 per cent girls of every disadvantaged group, pursuing elementary education, will achieve the minimum levels of learning by the year 2000.

These targets highlight the new approach and thrust in the plan for Education for All by the Year 2000. Minimum levels of learning will be clearly defined and laid down for the end of primary education and upper primary education. To enable the monitoring of progress of children towards these levels, the teachers will be suitably oriented to appreciate the concept of minimum levels of learning, to work towards their achievement, to design and administer tests, and to ensure progress. (3.59)

The Future Requirements and Resources for Education

Targets of Elementary Education

According to population projections, the target population for elementary education, i.e., of the age-group 6-14, will be 163 million in A.D. 2000; 102 million of the age-group 6-11, and 61 million of the age-group 11-14. How much would it cost to provide primary education to 95 per cent of children of the age-group 6-11, and upper primary education to 80 per cent of children to the 11-14 age group, as pragmatically suggested in this document? It is proposed that 70 per cent of the children will be provided formal education. Further, it is felt that the number of over and under-age children in elementary education would come down gradually, to levels of 25 per cent in primary education and 15 per cent in upper primary education. (13.99)

Resources for Elementary Education

A. *Salary of Teachers*

In the absence of recent estimates on expenditure per student, we shall consider here the salary of teachers in estimating the requirement of resources. After all, teachers' salaries constitute about 95 per cent of the total recurring expenditure. The average salary of teachers in primary schools is found to be Rs. 24,000 per annum and in the upper primary schools Rs. 36,000 per annum. Assuming teacher-pupil ratios of 40 and 35 in primary and upper primary schools respectively, the total number of teachers required in A.D. 2000 is estimated at 2.1 million in primary and 1.1 million in upper primary schools. Accordingly the teacher costs worked out to Rs.91.2 thousand million – Rs. 50.9 thousand in primary schools and Rs. 40.3 thousand million in upper primary schools. To this, we add 5 per cent non-teaching recurring cost, i.e. Rs. 0.46 thousand million. Thus the total recurring cost amounts to Rs. 91.7 thousand million.

Now, this is only recurring expenditure, and it does not cover expenditure on capital items; it also does not make any allowance for improvement in the quality of education. This is the level of resources required for elementary education by A.D. 2000.

B. *Additional Finance Requirements*

One may briefly note that the additional resources required, in the context of several measures of improvement in quality as suggested in the present document, would be quite substantial. The Working Group on Resources for Education for the Eighth Five Year Plan (1990-95) has estimated the requirements for a few such items. The Group estimated the indirect expenditure on administration and supervision, quality improvement, stipends, scholarships and other incentives, at Rs. 2067 million, the cost of construction of classrooms for additional children at Rs. 11,095 million, and the cost of construction of the backlog of schools, based on the Fifth All-India Educational Survey, at Rs.38,561 million. In addition, for Operation Blackboard, an additional amount of Rs.15,139 million was estimated as the requirement, and in all Rs.88 thousand million. It is assumed that during 1995-2000 an additional amount of Rs.23 thousand million would be required. Thus on an average, Rs.11.2 thousand million would be required for formal elementary education as non-recurring expenditure every year during 1991-2000. These estimates exclude normal recurring expenditure in the form of teacher cost etc., that we have estimated separately. (13.100)

C. *Total Expenditure*

Thus, in all putting recurring and non-recurring expenditures together, elementary education requires about Rs.800 thousand million during the next ten years; in other words the total expenditure should gradually increase to Rs.103 thousand million in A.D. 2000 at 1989-90 prices. (13.100)

Resources for Non-formal Education at the Elementary Stage

It is being planned that 30 per cent of the children of the age group 6-14 would be provided education through the non-formal channel.

We believe that the non-formal system of education should be comparable with formal system as far as the quality and content are concerned. Then only vertical mobility of the students into the formal system of education would be possible. This obviously requires more resources.

At present it is estimated by the Ministry of Human Resource Development (Department of Education), that a centre for non-formal education costs about Rs.12,000 per year and it provides education to 20 students. Within two years of non-formal education, one is expected to have acquired an education equivalent to compulsory elementary education. The unit costs of non-formal education for two years per student works out to Rs.1200 (at current 1989-90 prices). Accordingly it is estimated that non-formal education will require Rs.52.6 thousand million in A.D. 2000 at 1989-90 prices. It amounts to about Rs.500 thousand million for the 10 years until A.D. 2000.

Total Financial Requirements of Elementary Education Including Non-Formal Education

In all, the requirements of elementary education, including non-formal edcuation, in A.D. 2000 would be of the other of Rs.156 thousand million at 1989-90 prices. Given the earlier trends, it seems to be a gigantic task. Between 1960-61 and 1970-71, the real expenditure on elementary education was doubled; and between 1970-71 and 1980-81 it increased by about 40 per cent. The present estimates suggest that these trends would be substantially reversed: the total expenditure should be doubled by thé turn of the century. (13.101)

Minimal Level of Resources

Thus the requirement of resources for a few major programmes is estimated here. It should also be noted that the estimates are based on some crude and quick calculations. More importantly, these estimates allow for mere enrolment in the system by A.D. 2000. Hence they should be viewed as the minimum level of resources required.

It is clear that, the estimates made here do not cover several programmes and policies suggested in this document, such as training of teachers, administrators, voluntary agencies, mothers, community leaders, public provision of incentives to school children, particularly, of the weaker sections, establishment of special organisations like National Testing Service, central, state, and district boards of education, village education committees, school complexes, and mechanisms of monitoring, etc. These are only illustrative. If one were to cost each item, assuming that reliable estimates of unit costs of the items are available, it is likely that the actual level of requirement of resources would be of a very high order. (13.102)

Generating Non-Conventional Resources

While every effort should be made to generate additional resources for education, it is also required that non-conventional strategies need to be devised in mobilising and effectively utilising monetary, physical, and human resources. As an example, a few strategies relating to human resources are out-lined below. However, it may be noted that these strategies do not necessarily mean that the level of resources required for education could be substantially lowered. (19.102)

Human Resources

The stupendous task of Education for All will require massive human resources. For this, we have to diversify the sources. Some of them are as follows:

Local Community

The local community is a tremendous fund of human resources, if imaginatively used. Our present approach of looking towards outside sources will have to change to enable us to properly identify and utilise the local human resources. The teachers and instructors for NFE and adult education can be drawn from the community. They will have a greater motivation and involvement. Volunteers from the community can be identified and their assistance obtained. Persons in the community with special skills and expertise can be identified and used as a resource persons for development of those specified skills. (13.102)

The concept of Village Education Committee also reflects the utilization of local human resources for management and supervision, which the existing hierarchical and bureaucratic system is unable to perform satisfactorily. In framing curriculum and preparation of textual materials, we are adopting a decentralised approach and also desire that the local needs and environment should be properly linked.

Support of Voluntary Organisations

The support of voluntary organisations and social action groups may be enlisted for motivating and enabling the community to get fully involved in EFA, working as a catalyst for changing the culture of educational management in which community and teachers will have a more central role and to identify, promote and encourage more voluntary groups and social activists in areas where they are required. A well-designed policy to approach the human resources in colleges, universities, research institutions, and other institutions of higher learning, national laboratories, etc., and to motivate them to spare their free time and knowledge for elementary education is required. There is a number of other important sources from which valuable human resources can be drawn for educational effort, including educated people. (13.103)

Concluding Observations

It will be against the spirit of the Constitution to allow elementary education to suffer from inadequacy of resources. As far as funding elementary education and literacy programmes is concerned, it should be viewed in the framework of the Constitution. It is not just the

Department of Education, but all the government departments which should be made to allocate substantial resources for elementary education, as no sector can develop significantly with illiterate masses. In fact, the whole nation should feel responsible for the development of education in the country.

In the system of central planning we are used to in this country, only the resources required from the government or public sector agencies are taken into account. However, for an activity like education, there are considerable costs borne by the children and their parents. Individuals have to spend on books, stationery, uniform, transport, etc. These costs are not included in the financial implications presented here, except for the provision of incentives like books and uniforms to the weaker sections. The Constitution has directed that education for children in primary and upper primary levels of education should be free. This has been so far taken, in practice, to mean that schools should not charge any fees. The cost incurred by parents for education of their children has been ignored and has not been considered as a violation of the directive of free education. In view of the paucity of resources, it may be pragmatic to continue this approach and let the parents bear costs of this nature, while underscoring that ideally these costs should be borne by public funds. (13.103)

We may also have to move from the concept of exclusive responsibility of the government for education to shared responsibility between the government and the community. This would not be difficult, keeping in view the tradition in India of community support to education from ancient times. The scope for better utilisation of non-financial resources available within and outside the education system should be explored, and the provision for meeting the costs to utilise them, which would obviously be small, should be made. (13.103-104)

Serious efforts should be initiated to encourage individuals and organisations through task incentives and other measures to make large endowments and donations to the education sector. However, given the earlier experience, mobilisation of cheap local resources, revision of the fee structure in higher education, and voluntary donations and endowments, etc., should be viewed only as peripheral sources of mobilisation of additional resources for marginal improvements in the system. After all, they cannot become primary and reliable sources of revenue for large-scale improvements in the system. The Government cannot but continue taking more responsibility for elementary education. (13.104)

For safeguarding democracy and strengthening the foundations of the integrated nation, it is necessary not to compromise with the requirements of these basic needs in education. It should be noted that without adequate resources, financial, physical, and human, our target of Education for All will remain unachieved even by the turn of the country. If we have to enter the twenty-first century without the burden of the unfulfilled goals originally proposed by the Constitution-makers of India, substantial resources should be allocated to elementary and adult education programmes. (13.104)

12

GUIDELINES FOR UNIVERSITY SCIENCE INSTRUMENTATION CENTRES (1990)*

Need for University Science Instrumentation Centres (USICs)

Experimentation forms a major component of training and research in Science and Technology; hence accurate observations and measurements assume considerable importance in science education and research. For the training of experimental scientists of high calibre and for sustaining the continuous interest of students in an environment of rapid advance in science and technology, the University departments and colleges need to be continuously provided with highly reliable sophisticated instruments for teaching and advance research. The UGC has recognized such needs and has provided funds whenever possible to procure such instruments from indigenous and foreign sources. It is natural that this would also call for an activity related to their maintenance since maximum and proper utilisation of instruments depends to a large extent on whether they are kept in working condition and the user is well versed with them. Unfortunately, like many other areas where maintenance has been given low priority, instruments in university and colleges have also often remained underutilised and in some cases even unutilised for want of technicians to look after them. It has also been observed that instrumentation as a culture has not yet taken roots in our higher educational system which manifests itself in a number of ways. One observes overdependence on imported instruments and general reluctance on the part of teachers and research workers to innovate through design and fabrication or through improvisation of instruments as teaching aids. Efforts on their part to design instruments

* *Guidelines for University Science Instrumentation Centres*, University Grants Commission, New Delhi, 1990.

even for their own research are not much in evidence. Students generally do not get much needed 'hands-on' experience with instruments in the course of their studies.

Modern instruments are becoming more and more sophisticated and hence expensive. With limited resources available for the higher educational system, liberal purchase of instruments is not possible and hence the need for bringing them in a common pool in the university for their better use. All this requires a well planned structure with appropriate facilities and technicians to help the academic staff of the university and colleges in all aspects of instrumentation and above all, needs close cooperation among all academic staff members and the staff of the Centre.

The UGC has, therefore, taken a major step by introducing a scheme of University Science Instrumentation Centres (USICs) in individual universities. Under this scheme the UGC will assist universities to create essential support facilities where all major instruments in the university could be centralised for their maximum utilization, with workshops supported by well qualified personnel for fabrication, repairs and maintenance of all types of instruments. In addition, the Commission has also established Regional Instrumentation Centres in Bombay and Bangalore for supporting the USICs.

Standing Committee on USICs and its Functions

The Commission will be assisted, to achieve these objectives, by a Standing Committee which will frame detailed programmes, and will monitor and evaluate the USICs established under this scheme in the universities.

Objectives of the USIC Programme

The overall objectives of the USIC programme shall be as follows:

1. To encourage Universities to establish and develop USICs with a view to strengthen their technological infrastructure if required through collaborative efforts of the academic community of the University.
2. To provide adequate infrastructural resources as developmental inputs to the universities.
3. To undertake programmes with a view to nurture and spread the

culture of instrumentation in the higher educational system.

4. To maximise use of expensive equipments in universities through training and suitable pooling mechanism.
5. To generate manpower at different levels to enable the country to face the challenges of modern instrumentation.

13

REPORT OF UGC COMMITTEE: Towards New Educational Management (1987-90)*

Introduction

The Committee appointed in January 1987 submitted its report in January 1990. The Committee made a detailed study of the observations made by several Commissions and Committees on university management. It also took note of the NPE 1986 and the Programme of Action. It made an extensive study of Acts of Indian Universities. It constituted five Sub-Groups to make an indepth study of the various issues relating to university management. The Committee is popularly known as Gnanam Committee after the name of its Convener.

Broad Terms of Reference

(i) To review the management patterns including the structure, roles and responsibilities of various university bodies in the light of the new demands on the university system to develop effective alternate models; and

(ii) To set criteria for assessment of performance of educational institutions.

Committee Composition

Convener

1. Professor A. Gnanam, Vice-Chancellor Bharathidasan Univer-

* University Grants Commission, New Delhi, 1990.

sity, Tiruchirapalli, and afterwards Vice-Chancellor, University of Madras.

Members

2. Profesor C.N.R. Rao, Director, Indian Institute of Science, Bangalore.
3. Professor R.P. Bombah, Vice-Chancellor, Panjab University, Chandigarh.
4. The Secretary, Association of Indian Universities, New Delhi.
5. Dr. D.P. Sinha, Principal, Administrative Staff College of India, Hyderabad.
6. Prof. R.S. Nigam, University of Delhi, Delhi.
7. Prof. P.K. Dongre, M.S. University of Baroda, Baroda.
8. Professor S.K.R. Bhandari, Former Vice-Chancellor, A.P.S. University, Rewa, later on Management Consultant, based at Jaipur.
9. Professor Mitra G. Augustine, Principal, Madras Christian College, Madras.
10. Shri R.C.P. Sinha, Registrar, Banaras Hindu University, Varanasi.

Member-Secretary

11. Dr. M.L. Mehta, Additional Secretary, U.G.C.

Summary of Recommendations (Extracts)

Higher education has an important role to play not only for academic pursuit and augmenting knowledge but also towards national development. University management has a crucial role to play in order to enable the system to discharge the role. We have deliberated upon several aspects of the management of Universities in our report, with particular reference to challenges which the National Policy on Education, (1986) and the Programme of Action in this regard, have posed for the university system. In the following paragraphs, we have given a summary of our major recommendations.

The main emphasis has been to provide a sound scientific framework for governance of Universities which will make them efficient, result oriented and averse to politicisation.

General

1. Universities are the centres of excellence as also of regional/national development. In the light of current changes and challenges also the National Policy on Education, Universities must come centre stage. The objective of the Universities and their modes of funding should be reviewed and redefined accordingly.

2. The students, teachers, administrators and the society's representatives must be involved in setting the new goals and objectives of the Universities.

3. In deciding the Management pattern of Universities it should be recognised that the academic administration is very different from that in vogue in the governmental or in the corporate system and it should be based on the principle of participation, decentralization, autonomy and accountability.

4. The managerial patterns of a University System must necessarily have an in-built flexibility to adapt itself quickly to the changing needs of the country and the region it serves and to carry out innovations and experiments. Any effort, therefore, to bring the bodies of the Universities, and managements of colleges strategies are a further step from recommendations to specific courses of action in the direction of realising the organisational objectives. Union legislation in this regard needs to be the foremost to set in motion strategies for implementation by the different constituencies of the system as shown hereunder:

1. *Government of India*

(A) (i) The Parliament may enact a law (Model Act) setting out the basic structure of the University governance and ensuring that all related legislations by the State Governments conform to the core provisions of this law;

(ii) To review the Acts of Central Universities to effect changes in the nomenclature, size and composition of their governing and other bodies and in the modes of appointment of members thereof and that of officers;

(iii) To make a statutory stipulation in the Acts of Universities that it be obligatory for the Universities to follow the regulations issued by the UGC from time to time;

(iv) To require that new legislations (including amendments) in respect of State Universities be referred to the University

Grants Commission prior to their enactment; and

(v) To provide for a Council of Central Universities.

(B) *The UGC Act to be reviewed and revised:*

(i) To empower the Commission for greater improvement in the overall development of higher education in the country;

(ii) To make prior concurrence of the Commission obligatory for opening new Universities; and

(iii) To provide for concurrence with the State level machinery.

2. *University Grants Commission*

To establish 4-5 regional offices for effective implementation and monitioring of the Commission's programmes and its funding to universities and colleges.

3. *State Governments*

(i) To constitute the State Council for Higher Education to assist and coordinate the functioning of the universities and for effective liaison with the State Government and the UGC; and

(ii) To review the Acts of the State Universities to effect changes in nomenclature, size and composition of their governing and other bodies and in the modes of appointment of members to these bodies as also officers of the Universities in accordance with the recommendation made by the UGC.

4. *Universities*

(i) To initiate action to create new positions – bodies as suggested by the UGC;

(ii) To periodically review the working of its governing bodies – the Board of Management, the S.S.C. and the Academic Council;

(iii) To recommend to the State Council for Higher Education and the State Government changes considered helpful in the modes of governance of the University as envisaged by the UGC;

(iv) Large Universities, with 40 or more colleges affiliated to it, to establish regional centres to compensate for the infrastructural deficiencies in colleges in the rural and semi-urban areas; and

(v) To start building up endowment funds so that total dependence on government grants is reduced.

5. *Colleges*

(i) To constitute a Planning and Evaluation Committee to formulate the specific/distinctive goals of the institution, periodically review its personnel and material resources, administrative patterns, overall accountability and to propose developments phased over a period to qualify at the earliest for the autonomous status.

(ii) To review and revamp its administrative structure.

Making the System Work Better

We have made conscious efforts, inter-alia, to ensure:

- clarity of role and functions of University Authorities and reduction in their over-lapping functions;
- introduction of decentralised or self-management at different levels linked with accountability;
- enlargement of the scope of Universities' linkages with National Research Laboratories, as also for the establishment of Regional/National Facilities/Autonomous Institutes on University campuses;
- clarity in the role and working of different functionaries to remove prevailing confusion and to meet the new demands on the University System and also suggest new functionaries to meet new demands;
- a more effective role for the collegiate system to meet the demands for Higher Education;
- better Management of Research and Extension; and
- grievances re-dressal machinery.

We hope that implementation of the recommendations made by the committee will improve the efficiency of University Management and lead to more effective achievement of the objectives of the Universities.

AIU Seminar

The Association of Indian Universities (AIU) had organised a National Seminar on the Theme of "Making the System Work Better." (7th December 1988 at Benaras Hindu University). The Summary of recommendations of the Seminar are given below:

1. It is necessary that each University clearly spells out the objectives which it intends to pursue.

2. The role of the University as a centre of creation and dissemination of knowledge must be preserved and protected.

3. The social standing and image of the University and/or that of its Vice-Chancellor, who symbolises the University, is to be preserved and not denigrated by anybody for any reason whatsoever.

4. Norms for appointment of and for transacting business with Vice-Cancellors and preserving their social prestige and for taking any action against them by the Government/Chancellor should be evolved and respected by all.

5. It is to be ensured that only people of the highest level of competence, integrity, morals and self-respect are appointed as Vice-Chancellors and that conditions are created so that once appointed they receive cooperation of all including the Government/Chancellor to discharge their duties satisfactorily until the end of their full tenure.

6. It must be ensured that appropriate modalities and norms are developed by the Central and State Governments, the UGC and other funding agencies so that adequate funds are allocated to the Universties/Colleges and that they are also released in time.

7. Suitable procedures and norms must be evolved to overcome delays in decision-making by the Central and State Governments, the University Grants Commission and other parallel agencies.

8. The Ministries, Government Departments of Education, the UGC, other parallel bodies, and the University System must enable the teachers and students to play a meaningful and constructive role in planning and implementation of "Making the System Work Better" by setting up consultative forums at various levels.

9. Strategies should be devised to improve the motivation of the entire community of teachers, who form the backbone of the University System.

10. A System of the assessment of teachers' performance must be evolved and implemented by Universities, ensuring modalities for

recognition of creative and innovative work.

11. Appropriate machinery for quick redressal of grievances (Teachers, Students and Non-Teaching Staff) must be created/ improved in all Universities and Colleges.

12. The maintenance of discipline amongst the students and to keep the undesirable elements under control is the responsibility of the Vice-Chancellor and the University adminstration, and no interference should be allowed in this field.

13. The political parties should work out for themselves and adhere to a code of conduct, ensuring that the student community is left completely free to engage itself in study, research and other cocurricular and related activities, and is not drawn into active politics.

14. The administration of universities needs to be modernised and the procedures rationalised so as to ensure that delay in admission, conduct of examinations and declaration of results etc. are finally eliminated.

15. "Performance Audit" within the institution must be instituted forthwith, to appraise the institution of its own shortcomings and possibilities of its improvement.

We are of the view that recommendations made by the Committee in this Report, and in the seminar of the A.I.U. would certainly help in "Making the System Work Better".

14

ELEMENTARY TEACHER EDUCATION CURRICULUM (1991)*

Introduction

Developments in the educational system especially after National Policy on Education, 1986 suggested overhauling the teacher education. In this context the Department of Teacher Education of NCERT undertook a project entitled 'Development of Guidelines and Syllabi based on the Teacher Education Curriculum Framework for Elementary and Secondary Teacher Education. In April 1989 a draft document was developed and was sent to various teacher educators and content experts for their comments and observations. Alterations/modifications were incorporated in the light of the feed-back. The present document is the outcome of this exercise.

EXTRACTS FROM THE DOCUMENT

Elementary Stage (Primary and Upper Primary)

Elementary education generally extends over standards I to VIII, ordinarily covering the age-group 6 to 14 years. It comprises two distinct stages, referred to as the primary stage (standards I to V) and the upper primary stage (standards VI to VIII). Generally, the class teacher system, which requires a teacher to teach almost all the academic subjects, is followed in the primary stage while special interests and proficiency of the teacher are taken in view for teaching at the upper primary stage. Each teacher must also be able to impart health and physical education, art education and work experience with adequate knowledge. He

---

* *Elementary Teacher Education Curriculum: Guidelines and Syllabi*, National Council of Educational Research and Training, New Delhi, 1991.

should be able to handle handicapped children and be acquainted with at least one area like adult education, non-formal education, women education or library service, etc. The curriculum components have been designed keeping these requirements in mind.

	Curriculum Components	Weightage in terms of time	
A.	*Foundation Courses*		20%
i.	Education in Emerging India (Philosophical and socio-cultural perspective)	10%	
ii.	Elementary School Students Learning Processes, Adjustment (Educational Psychology)	10%	
B.	*Stage Relevant Specialization*		30%
iii.	Elementary Education and Teacher Functions	5%	
iv.	Language Teaching (Mother Tongue and English)	5%	
v.	Mathematics Teaching	5%	
vi.	Environmental Studies Teaching (as related to stds. I to V)	5%	
vii.	Health and Physical Education	5%	
viii.	Arts Education and		
ix.	Work Experience	5%	
C.	*Additional Specialization*		10%
x.	Science Teaching and Social Studies Teaching/ Pre-School Education	5%	
xi.	Elective-one : (Adult Education/Non-Formal Education/Social Education/Tribal Education/Multiple Class Teaching/Population Education/Special Education, Educational Technology, etc.)	5%	
D.	*Practicum*		40%
xii.	Practical work	20%	
xiii.	Internship in Teaching (in Primary and Upper Primary/ Pre-school systems	20%	

The above course offerings have been divided and spelt out in the revised NCTE Draft Curriculum into the following four major components as (1988).

(a) Foundation Courses
(b) Stage Relevant Specialization
(c) Additional Specialization

(d) Practicum/Fieldwork

Foundation Courses

The Foundation Courses component of the teacher education curriculum may provide the prospective teacher necessary theoretical insights into the understanding of aims and objectives of education in the context of national development with reference to socio-cultural, political and economic imperatives. Another objective is that the student teacher may acquire knowledge and develop understanding of the process of human development and learning.

Stage Relevant Specialization

This component may include historical background and scope of education at the stage concerned e.g. elementary or secondary level and functions of the teacher with reference to curriculum planning, instructional strategies and skills, evaluation, management, guidance and counselling and co-curriculum activities etc.

Additional Specializations

The subject areas like art education, adult education, non-formal education, special education and population education etc., have been included in the teacher education curriculum to provide professional area of his interest and to equip him with higher knowledge, understanding and skills in that area. A few areas have been discussed in this document.

Practicum/Field Experiences

This component deals with the central objective of teacher education viz., development of professional competencies in areas like evaluation, managing classroom learning, organizing co-curricular activities, guiding students and other similar activities which are 'beyond' the classroom.

Guidelines and Syllabi

The guidelines and syllabi included in this document for the following curricular subjects at the elementary level have been developed through a series of workshops held in 1989 and 1990.

A. *Foundation Courses*

1. Education in Emerging India
2. Educational psychology

B. *Stage Relevant Specialization*

3. Teacher Functions
4. Teaching of Mother Tongue
5. Teaching of English
6. Teaching of Mathematics
7. Teaching of Environmental Studies (Science)
8. Teaching of Environmental Studies (Social Studies)
9. Teaching of Health and Physical Education
10. Teaching of Art Education
11. Teaching of Work Experience

C. *Additional Specialization*

12. Non-Formal Education
13. Multigrade Teaching
14. Girls Education
15. Education for Disabled

D. *Practicum-cum-Field Work*

15

SECONDARY TEACHER EDUCATION CURRICULUM (1991)*

Introduction

The National Policy on Education, 1986 suggested an overhauling of teacher education at all levels, National Curriculum Framework for Elementary/Secondary School stages was developed by NCERT keeping in view the major thrusts of NPE. All these significant developments had an impact on teacher education programme relating to setting up District Institutes of Education and Trainings (DIETs) at the elementary stage and upgrading some colleges of education as Institutes of Advanced Studies in Education (IASEs) and strengthening of Colleges of Teacher Education (CTEs). These institutes are expected to contribute their mite in improving the quality of teacher education. It is now felt that to provide effective training experiences to the teacher trainees, different components of teacher education curriculum specially at the secondary level need to be reviewed and revised.

The present document containing detailed outline of the teacher education curriculum at the secondary level is based on NCTE (National Council for Teacher Education) curriculum framework especially revised draft version of framework (1988) developed by the Department of Teacher Education (NCERT).

Suggestive Curriculum at the Secondary Stage

The secondary stage extends over standards 9 and 10 and is meant for general education for all with proviso of a common curriculum for all.

---

* *Secondary Teacher Education Curriculum: Guidelines and Syllabi*, National Council for Educational Research and Training, New Delhi, 1991.

All subjects except languages have to be taught as disciplines. The core curriculum aiming at national identity, cultural enrichment and concerns of environment etc., must be given due emphasis. Secondary school teachers have to be specialized in teaching one or two subjects and are expected to possess reasonable level of mastery in respect of content and pedagogy. Furthermore, the teacher of today is expected to play the multiple roles of a teacher. The special needs of exceptional children of different categories and activities related to in or outside the secondary school, such as Population Education, Education Technology, Adult Education, Non-formal Education, etc., are some of the activities which may be included in the secondary teacher education curriculum. The curriculum components have been designed keeping these needs in mind.

Curriculum Components	Weightage in terms of time	
A. *Foundation Courses*		20%
(i) Education in Emerging India (philosophical and socio-cultural perspectives)	10%	
(ii) Educational Psychology (with focus on learner development and stages, learning adjustment)	10%	
B. *Stage Relevant Specialization*		30%
(iii) Secondary Education and Teacher Functions	10%	
Specialisation in methodology of:		
(iv) A secondary school subject with prior specialisation	10%	
(v) A second secondary/Higher secondary/ primary school education subject	10%	
C. *Additional Specialization*		10%
(vi) An elective from areas like : Adult Education, Secondary Education, Population Education, Distance Education, Library Services, Tribal Education, Special Education (Integrated and one category), Health and Physical Education, Art Education, Educational Technology, Action, Research, Computer Education, etc.	10%	
D. *Practicum/Field Work*		40%
(vii) Internship in teaching including field assignments	20%	
(viii) Practical work including working with community, social service and work experience	20%	

The above course-offerings have been divided into the following four major components as spelt out in the revised NCTE Draft National Curriculum Framework (1988):

(a) Foundation Courses
(b) Stage Relevant Specialization
(c) Additional Specialization
(d) Practicum/Field Work

Foundation Courses

The foundation courses component of the teacher education curriculum may provide the student teacher necessary theoretical insights into the understanding of aims and objectives of education in the context of national development with reference to socio-cultural, political and economic imperatives. Another objective is that the student teacher may acquire knowledge and develop understanding of the process of human development and learning.

Stage Relevant Specialization

This component may include historical background and scope of education at the stage concerned e.g. elementary or secondary level and functions of the teacher with reference to curriculum planning, instructional strategies and skills, evaluation, management, guidance and counselling and co-curriculuar activites, etc.

Additional Specializations

The subject areas like educational and vocational guidance, educational technology, special education and population education, etc. have been included in the teacher education curriculum to provide professional education to the student teacher in an educational area of his interest and to equip him/her with higher knolwedge, understanding and skills in that area.

Practicum/Field Experiences

This component deals with the central objective of teacher education viz., development of professional competencies with reference to the evaluating, managing classroom learning, organising co-curricular activities, guiding students and several other activities which may be 'beyond' the classroom.

Guidelines and Syllabi

The guidelines and syllabi developed in this document for the following curricular subjects at the secondary level have been developed through series of workshops held in 1989 and 1990.

Foundation Courses

1. Education in Emerging India
2. Educational Psychology

Stage Relevant Specialization

3. Teacher Functions
4. Language Teaching

   (a) Teaching of English
   (b) Teaching of Hindi

5. Teaching of Mathematics
6. Teaching of Science
7. Teaching of Social Studies/Social Sciences
8. Teaching of Health and Physical Education
9. Teaching of Art Education

Additional Specialization

10. Educational and Vocational Guidance
11. Population Education
12. Educational Technology
13. Work Experience
14. Special Education

Practicum/Field Work

(i) School Experience Programme
(ii) Practical work including working with community, social service and work experience.

The detailed guidelines and syllabi alongwith suggested weightages in terms of time are given in the chapters that follow. It is also suggested that while evaluating the student's performance, 40 per cent weightage may be given to internal assessment.

Thus, the guidelines and syllabi given in the present document are based on the Teacher Education Curriculum Framework for Elementary and Secondary Levels. These guidelines/syllabus outlines are suggestive and not prescriptive in nature. These may not neecessarily be applicable in all situations due to constraints of time and resource facilities. It is also suggested that teacher educators may make use of appropriate modalities for transacting different units of the suggested syllabi. Furthermore, the Council has plans to develop instructional materials based on these suggested guidelines/syllabi. Therefore, we have not incorporated suggested readings in this document. Practicum/ field work component has been discussed in the school experience and work experience components of this document.

16

EDUCATION IN ELECTION MANIFESTOES OF POLITICAL PARTIES (1991)

Bharatiya Janata Party (BJP)

The party views with concern that with the rising cost of education, the existing social economic disparities will be perpetuated in the field of education. The BJP believes in equalisation of educational opportunities and building up a system worthy of the genius of our heritage and undoubted capacities of our youth. Towards the end, we will :

1. Implement Article 45 of the Constitution to give free education to all children who are in the 6-14 age group to enforce the principle of universal primary education.
2. Give education a vocational and technical content, establish a complex of agro-industrial polytechnics in each district.
3. Ensure academic freedom and the autonomy of universities, raise the emoluments and status of teachers.
4. Progressively increase the allocation to education till it reaches the six per cent of the GNP.

Languages

The BJP supports the principle that people have a right to be educated and run their administration in their own language. The BJP will:

1. Engage adequate number of linguists all over country to translate standard literature of other languages into Indian languages.
2. Strictly implement the three language formula.
3. Give credit in the matter of admission to institutions of higher

education and in job recruitment to persons knowing more than three languages, Indian or foreign.

4. Encourage study of Sanskrit.

Communist Party of India (CPI)

Implementation of compulsory primary education, mid-day meals for children in primary schools, free education up to secondary stage; stipends and hostel facilities for students coming from low income groups; abolition of illiteracy, adequate funds for the job; radical reorganisation of the education system to make it vocation-oriented.

Communist Party of India (Marxist) (CPI-M)

Free and compulsory education must be ensured by the state by law for all children, free education up to secondary level; full state support to mass literacy campaigns to eradicate illiteracy; end the new education policy still being pursued since the Rajiv Government introduced it which is elitist and weighed against the common people acquiring education. Syllabus and curriculum to strengthen scientific temper, secularism, national unity and integrity.

Indian National Congress (Congress-I)

The Congress attaches the highest priority to education as the instrument for the material, physical and spiritual development of society.

The Congress formulated a New Education Policy in 1986 which emphasised scientific, technological, professional and distance education, education for girls, continuing and adult education and education for cultural and spiritual development.

The policy envisages equality in education, universal education and national integration through a common core curriculum. A key element of the NPE was the establishment of Navodaya Vidyalayas designed to extend the best available education to boys and girls of merit living in mainly rural Indian, however poor their parents.

The policy was sabotaged by the National Front Government which neither implemented the NPE nor brought forward any alternative policy.

The Congress will vigorously implement the New Education Policy. Priority will be given in implementing the Policy, to wiping out illiteracy and significantly expanding investment in primary and secondary education. Operation Blackboard will be intensified and the completion of the scheme accelerated. Special measures will be undertaken to reduce the drop out rate at the primary level. The Congress will faithfully implement the three-language formula. The mother-tongue of the child shall be the medium of instruction in primary schools and the first language under the three-language formula. This will include Urdu for which teachers will be trained in adequate numbers.

Institutions of higher education with Urdu as the medium of instruction will be progressively built up and upgraded, on the analogy of other language.

Middle-level technical education will be multiplied, with a view to expanding unemployment and self-employment. A National Midday programme will be launched to cover every child in every primary school. It will be implemented as a mass movement with the full participation of the community, teachers, social service organisations, local authorities and the State Governments.

A special drive will be undertaken to expend education for girls, including the provision of special facilities for hostels, transportation and uniforms to needy students.

All benefits and facilities now available to students of SCs and STs and Backward Classes will be continued.

Assistance for the provision of textbooks and educational materials will be provided to SC and ST and Backward Class students.

Congress will set up one Navodaya Vidyalaya in every district with reservations for SC and ST and Backward Class students and with reference to poor sections. A special drive will be launched to enroll SC and ST and Backard Class students in schools.

Training, working conditions wages and career development opportunities for teachers will be improved.

Policies will be formulated for expanding the adult education programme targeted towards the rural and urban poor. The programme of ensuring at least one 100 per cent literacy districts in each State will be vigorously pursued. Electronic media will be used increasingly for this purpose.

New schemes will be formulated and new Open Universities established to further expand Distance Education.

Investment in education will be progressively increased so as to reach the targeted figure of 6 per cent of GNP.

Janata Dal (Socialist)

The foundations of a democratic policy lie in the assumption that the electorate are conscious of their rights and obligations as citizens of the country. In a large country like India (with a majority of illiterate population) the educational system will need to be re-structured at the primary, middle and higher levels. Youth and educated in India owe an obligation to the society and should be mobilised for a nationwide programme of adult education and illiteracy eradication.

National Front

The National Front regards education as an activity that must contribute to social justice, promote knowledge and excellence in society with equity, and accelerate economic progress.

The National Front will accord the highest priority to education both as human right and as a means for bringing about a transformation towards a more humane and enlightened society.

We will make education an effective instrument for securing equality and justice for women, the Scheduled Castes and Scheduled Tribes, other socially, educationally and economically backward classes, and minorities. At the same time, by making social service and productive work an ingredient of the curriculum, we will strive to inclucate social consciousness and a spirit of service, sacrifice and co-operation among the students, across the various sections of society.

The National Front is committed to raise the level of investment in education to at least 6 per cent of the Gross National Product, as recommended by the Kothari Commission. It will aim to achieve this target by 1995. At least 50 per cent of the funds allocated to education shall be invested in elementary education. Half of all the funds allocated to education at different stages, shall be utilised for promoting girls' and women's education.

The Constitution enjoined on us to provide free and compulsory education to all children up to the age of 14 years by 1960. However, less than half of our children receive primary education today and only about one-fourth complete the middle school. The National Front regards this failure to fulfil the Constitutional directive during the last 43 years as the fundamental cause of the high rate of illiteracy prevailing in the country. Therefore, the National Front commits itself to fulfil the goal of universal elementary education within the decade by reorganising education in the following ways:

(i) devolving the responsibility to plan, administer and to develop elementary education to block-level or sub-block level autonomous school complexes, with full participation of the community, teachers and voluntary organisations;

(ii) giving autonomy to the school to adjust its annual calendar, timings and locale for holding classes, textbooks and curriculum, and even staffing pattern to the needs of children, particularly the working children, with special reference to girls' needs;

(iii) transforming education to empower people for the Right to Work by relating academic activity to productive work and environment from primary stage onwards;

(iv) imparting primary education in the mother tongue;

(v) integrating early childhood care and pre-primary education with primary education; and

(vi) introducing school meals or any other incentive scheme for pre-primary and primary level children.

The Neighbourhood school concept shall be introduced and universalised by stages in order to correct elitist aberrations in education. Special programmes shall be started to develop excellence and talent without discrimination on the grounds of creed, caste, gender and economic status.

Building upon the foundation laid down through productive work-orientation to education at the elementary stage, the secondary level curriculum (i.e., after eighty years of schooling) shall provide for only a common stream of vocationalised education for all students, with provision for additional vocational and technical courses for those who desire to seek employment immediately after completing secondary education. Recognising the need to relate vocational and technical courses with the employment market and pattern of production in different regions, both public and private sector organisations (including the tiny and the small sector) shall be associated with planning and organisations would thus be expected to contribute towards the cost of education too. Similarly, both the government and the voluntary agencies involved in rural development, agriculure, afforestation, cottage industries, health services and such other activities in the rural areas shall also be involved in organising vocational courses.

The content and process of education at different stages, i.e., primary, middle and secondary, shall be worked out on the basis of the needs of the children at that stage, rather than being determined by the requirements of the higher secondary or college levels, as is the case at present.

Admitting the failure of the present annual examination system as a means for just and reliable assessment of the students' capacities and aptitudes, the National Front commits itself to take the courageous step to replace the present system by a carefully monitored continuous and comprehensive assessment system at all stages of education. For each next stage of education, a system of entrance test by the concerned institution would be worked out.

The National Front undertakes to review the entire curriculum with a view to reduce the proverbial load of the school bag and to create an enjoyable learning environment.

The National Front shall replace the system of capitation fee by loan-linked education.

The National Front commits itself to review and raise the status of the teaching community and provide it with all due facilities in order to attract and train the highest quality of talent.

The National Front shall strive to help bring a new spirit to our campuses of higher education and foster a commitment to creative knowledge, national service and social cohesion. For this, the entire curriculum in languages, sciences and humanities shall be reviewed and amended in stages.

Measures will be taken to promote adult education for awareness of human rights and duties, integrity of the environment, scientific temper, fight against communal and casteism division and promotion of national unity, secularism and democracy.

The National Front considers the education of the minorities both religious and linguistic to be a national responsibility and will take vigorous steps to see that the constraints on their educational progress are removed as speedily as possible through planned and conserted action.

The Acharya Ramamurti Committee Report (1990) on the review of the 1986 National Policy on Education shall be carefully considered and taken up for early implementation.

17

MINIMUM QUALIFICATIONS OF TEACHERS (1991)*

In pursuance of the revision of scales of pay of University and College teachers as notified by the Governmant of India, Ministry of Human Resource Development, Department of Education, vide letter No. F.1-21/1987-U.I. dated 22nd July, 1988, the University Grants Commission had under its consideration the revision of minimum qualifications required for recruitment of teachers (Lecturers, Readers and Professors) in subjects other than Fine Arts, Management, Engineering and Technology in Universities and Colleges. These qualifications have since been finalised and approved by the Commission in consultation with the Ministry of Human Resource Development, Department of Education, New Delhi and are circulated vide Commission's letter No. F.1-11/87 (CPP) dated 28th October, 1991.

The Regulations framed by the Commission for qualifications required of a person to be appointed to the teaching staff of a University and Institution(s) affiliated to it and contained in Commission's circular letter No. F.1-11/87 (CPP) dated 19th September, 1991 have been Notified in the *Gazette of India* on 5th October, 1991. These shall apply to every University established or incorporated by or under a Central Act, Provincial Act or a State Act, every institution including a constituent or an affiliated college recognised by the Commission, in consultation with the University concerned under Clause (f) of Section 2 of the University Grants Commission Act, 1956 and every institution deemed to be a University under Section 3 of the said act.

The revised qualifications take effect from 19-9-1991.

Minimum Qualifications for the posts of Professors, Readers and

---

* UGC Circular September 19, 1991, University Grants Commission, New Delhi, 1991, as published in *University News, January 6, 1992*, Association of Indian Universities, 1992.

Lecturers in subjects other than Fine Arts, Management, Engineering and Technology in Universities and Colleges for appointment of persons through open advertisement and for promotion of persons as Reader and placement in Selection Grade Lecturer and Senior Scale Lecturer.

1 *Professor*

An eminent scholar with published work of high quality actively engaged in research with 10 years of experience in postgraduate teaching and/or research at the University/National Level Institutions, including experience or guiding research at doctoral level

OR

An outstanding scholar with established reputation who has made significant contribution to knowledge.

2(A) *Reader* (Open Selection)

Good academic record with a doctoral degree or equivalent published work. Candidates from outside the university system in addition shall also possess at least 55 per cent marks or an equivalent grade at the Master's degree level.

Eight years experience of teaching and/or research including up to 3 years for research degrees and has made some mark in the areas of scholarship as evidenced by quality of publications, contribution to educational renovation, design of new courses and curricula.

2(B) *Reader* (Promotion)

(a) As regards the promotion to the post of Reader in accordance with the scheme of revision of pay scales of teachers in universities and colleges notified by the Government of India vide Notification No. F. 121/87-U.I. dated the 22nd July, 1988, the guidelines are circulated by the University Grants Commission vide its letter No. F.1-6/90 (PS Cell) dated the 29th January, 1990.

(b) Every Lecturer in the Senior Scale will be eligible for promotion to the post of Reader if he/she has:

(i) completed 8 years of service in the Senior Scale, provided that the requirement of 8 years will be relaxed if the total service of the lecturer is not less than 16 years;

(ii) obtained a Ph. D. degree or an equivalent published work;

(iii) made some mark in the areas of scholarship and research as evidenced by self-assessment, reports of referees, quality of publications, contribution to educational renovation, design of new courses and curricula;

(iv) participated in two refresher courses/summer institutes of approved duration, or engaged in other appropriate continuing education programmes of comparable quality as may be specified by the UGC after placement in the Senior Scale; and

(v) consistently good performance appraisal reports.

(c) Promotion to the Post of Reader will be through a process of selection by a Selection Committee to be set up under the statutes/Ordinances of the University concerned or other similar committes set up by the appointing authorities.

2(C) *Lecturer* (Selection Grade)

Lecturers in the Senior Scale who do not have Ph.D. degree or equivalent published work and who do not meet the scholarship and research standards, but fulfil the other criteria prescribed in (2)B(b) above to the post of Reader and have a good record in teaching and/or participation in extension activities, will be placed in the Selection Grade subject to the recommendation of the Selection Committee for promotion to the post of Reader. They will be designated as Lecturers in the Selection Grade. They could offer themselves for fresh assessment after obtaining Ph.D. and/or fulfilling other requirements for promotion as Readers, and if found suitable, could be given the designation of Reader.

3(A) *Lecturer*

(a) *Arts, Sciences, Social Sciences, Commerce, Education, Physical Education, Foreign Languages and Law*

Good academic record with at least 55 per cent marks or an equivalent grade at Master's degree level in the relevant subject from an

Indian University or an equivalent degree from a foreign University.

Candidates besides fulfilling the above qualifications should have cleared the eligibility test for Lecturers conducted by UGC, CSIR or similar test accredited by the UGC.

(b) *Journalism and Mass Communication*

Good academic record with at least 55 per cent marks or an equivalent grade at Master's degree level in communication/mass communiation, journalism from an Indian University or an equivalent degree from a foreign University.

Candidates besides fulfilling the above qualifications should have cleared the eligibility test for Lecturers conducted by UGC, CSIR or similar test accredited by the UGC; OR

At least 55 per cent marks or an equivalent grade at Master's degree level in Social Sciences/Sciences/Humanities with at least second class bachelor's degree or Post-graduate diploma in communication/mass communication or journalism from a recognised Indian University/ National Institute.

Candidates besides fulfilling the above qualifications should have cleared the eligibility test for Lecturers conducted by UGC, CSIR or similar tests accredited by the UGC.

(c) *Music*

Good academic record with at least 55 per cent marks or an equivalent grade at Master's degree level in relevant subject or an equivalent degree from an Indian/Foreign University.

Candidates besides fulfilling the above qualifications should have cleared the eligibility test for Lecturers conducted by UGC, CSIR or similar test accredited by the UGC; OR

A traditional or a professional artist with a highly commendable professional achievement in the subject concerned.

3(B) *Lecturer* (Senior Scale)

Every lecturer will be eligible for placement in a senior scale of Rs. 3000-5000 through a procedure of screening/selection laid down by the University in accordance with guidelines of UGC referred in Para 2B(a) above, if he has:

(i) completed 8 years of service after regular appointment with relaxation as provided in Notes (2) and (3) below;
(ii) participated in two refresher courses/summer institutes, of approved duration or engaged in other appropriate continuing education programmes of comparable quality as may be specified by the UGC; and
(iii) consistently satisfactory performance appraisal reports.

Notes

(1) For placement of Lecturers in Selection Grade as well as for promotion to the post of Reader, the required number of positions would be created by upgrading the posts held by the incumbents concerned.
(2) In order to encourage research in continuation of Postgraduate studies, candidates who at the time of recruitment as Lecturers, possess, Ph.D. or M.Phil. Degree (called jointly as the 'research degrees') will be sanctioned three and one advance increments respectively in the Scale of Rs. 2200-4000 alongwith the benefit of the corresponding years of service for the purpose of promotion. The exisiting Lecturers without research degrees, and those similarly situated, recruited in future will be eligible for a similar benefit in service for the purpose of promotion as and when they acquire research degrees, but will not be eligible for advance increments. Existing Lecturers with research degrees will also be eligible for similar benefit.
(3) Counting of previous service for the purpose of placement in Senior Scale/Selection Grade will be in accordance with UGC Guidelines issued vide circular No. F. 1-6/90 (PS Cell) dated November 27, 1990.

It may however be noted that the instructions as contained in UGC letter No. F. 4-12/86 (NET) dated 30th January 1990 stand without any change.

Pay Scale of PVCs/Rectors in Central Universities

The Government of India, in consultation with the University Grants Commission, after taking into consideration the revised pay scales of teachers in universities and colleges, the pay of Vice-Chancellors and various other factors, have decided vide their circular No. F. 10-65/88-Desk (U) dated 3rd July, 1991 that the Pro-Vice-Chancellors/Rectors in Central Universities may be granted the revised scale of Rs. 5900-200-7300 subject to a minimum of Rs. 6500 per month.

The above scale of pay will be effective from 1-1-1986.

The Pro-Vice-Chancellors will be entitled for such allowances as are admissible under the Rules of the concerned university.

18

REPORT OF CABE WORKING GROUP ON ADULT EDUCATION AND LITERACY (1991)

We declare that the attainment of mass literacy is linked to the attainment of the national objectives of eradication of poverty, the achievement of full employment and realisation of the values of national concern, namely national integration, women's equality and employment, small family norm, protection and conservation of environment.

1.1 *Magnitude of the problem of illiteracy*

The number of illiterate adults should be shown on the basis of the Census of 1991 instead of projecting them on the basis of 1981 Census.

1.2 Factors contributing to the phenomenon of rising illiteracy in the country.

These include :

* Inadequate coverage of children of school going age in schools due to poor infrastructure and unwillingness of parents.
* Majority of the children, particularly belonging to the underprivileged and in educationally backward areas, not staying long enough in the school to acquire the minimum levels of learning on account of social and economic compulsions caused by poverty and deprivation.
* Adult Education/Literacy programmes not being able to counter the pulls and compulsions resulting in large scale drop-out of adult learners before achieving minimum levels of literacy.
* Inadequate and unsatisfactory arrangements failing to enthuse neoliterates to take up post-literacy and continuing education

programmes and preventing them from relapse into illiteracy.

* Growth in literacy (both in rate as well as in absolute number) not keeping pace with rise in population (both rate of growth as well as in absolute number).
* Educational backwardness of specific areas (desert areas, slum areas, tribal and forest areas and other interior and inaccessible areas), poverty, social deprivation, economic exploitation, unemployment, irrelevance of the educational system to the larger needs of life, absence of a positive and conducive learning environment and general absence of a society which values and prizes literacy.

1.3 *Strategy for reduction in illiteracy*

This would include the following measures :

* Universal enrolment and retention of children in schools up to 14 years of age.
* Improvement of socio-economic conditions including creating conditions for ameliorating the plight of socially and educationally disadvantaged groups and creating an environment which will facilitate learning and reinforce the teaching-learning process.
* Improvement in the quality of education imparted in the formal school system.
* Provision of non-formal education of good quality to those who cannot join regular primary school.
* Provision of opportunities to illiterate adults in 15-35 age group to enable them to become functionally literate.
* Overriding priority to female literacy.
* Provision of opportunities and facilities for post-literacy and continuing education.
* Outlining a special strategy for areas which are actually disadvantaged from the point of infrastructure, communication, transport, etc. as also other educationally deficient areas.

1.4 Findings of Institutes of Social Science, Research and Management on evaluation of the impact of the Adult Education Programme conducted by them.

The summary of the findings of evaluation studies as brought out in the agenda was noted. These include the following :

* Lack of stress on time-bound plan for eradication of illiteracy.
* Lack of adequate planning and preparation with special reference to environment building prior to actual commencement of the Centre-based programme.
* Wrong selection of staff.
* Lack of back-up support by training and continuing education of functionaries.
* Delayed supply of teaching-learning materials.
* Deficient physical teaching-learning environment.
* Excessive emphasis on quantitative rather than on qualitative achievement.
* Lack of credible and effective management information system.

It was emphasized that while these deficiences be made good in the current programme, they should not be allowed to repeat themselves in the future Centre-based programmes.

1.5 *Shift from institutionalised Centre-based approach to Campaign approach*

Determination and unqualified support of State Govts. and UTs to literacy campaigns

The welcome shift which is taking place from the traditional Centre-based approach to the Campaigns approach, which is area-specific-time specific, volunteer-based, cost-effective and result-oriented, is endorsed. For this, there is need for total political will, commitment and unqualified support of the State Govts. and UTs as preconditions for the success of these campaigns and suggested that such involvement and support may be secured in the following manner:

In respect of districts where campaigns have already been launched.

* An energetic and committed district administration will have to be the focal point of mobilisation of social forces as well as coordination of all such forces to act in synergy for the success of the campaign. The State Government, in addition to creating conditions for such a synergy, will also have to ensure continuity of tenure of the functionaries at various levels of district administration who are closely involved with the campaign and

particularly of the District Magistrate who provides the principal driving and coordinating force for the campaign in the district.

* Voluntary Agencies are grassroot level organisations which have flexibility of structure and operations and have volunteers who have intimate knowledge of and contact with field conditions. They have, therefore, a very special role to play in a campaign for total literacy. The State Government and the District Administration will have to create conditions in which the VAs can make their voluntary contribution to the campaign more meaningfully and effectively. Such involvement and support of VAs can be secured in a number of ways such as giving them representation at various committees, assigning specific responsibilities such as resource support through training, evaluation and conducting of literacy programmes, etc.
* Involvement of State Government would also mean total emotional involvement of development functionaries in the campaign. Such an involvement is also necessary to convert the campaign for total literacy into a campaign for immunisation, maternity protection, child health care, protection and conservation of environment, small family norm, etc. In addition to issuing instructions in clear and unambiguous terms to secretaries to Govt., Heads of Development Departments, Revenue Divisional Commissioners, Collectors and all other independent bodies (including statutory and corporate bodies) regarding release of personnel and provision of logistic support to the campaign, the State Government also needs to monitor the pace and progress of such involvement.

In selection of new districts for launching campaigns afresh

* Campaigns can become a part of our strategy for total eradication of illiteracy only if State Govts. develop faith in the efficacy of the campaigns approach and create conditions for their success. One of the factors which can contribute to this process is selection of TLC districts with imagination and far sight. The following broad criteria may be kept in view for selection of the TLC districts:

  – A rich folk culture and tradition which can be harnessed for

environment building.
- A confluence of creative forces and energies which can be harnessed for providing resource support such as training, monitoring and evaluation of the campaign.
- A team of energetic and committed officials and non-officials at all levels.

Campaigns for total literacy have, as their clientele, persons in different age-groups such as 6-60, 9-35, 9-45, 15-35, 14-45 etc. Of these, children belonging to the age-group of 6-8 and 9-14 will have to be covered in the NFE programme, which has a duration of two years for achieving the minimum levels of learning as against the duration of 6 months or 200 hours for adults. While children in these age-groups can be covered in the campaigns by providing separate curriculum instructional materials, training and separate teaching-learning places for them, the State Govt. will have to take a policy-decision in regard to extension of the NFE programme (Centre-based) beyond the campaign period with a view to ensuring minimum levels of learning for children covered in the campaign.

Ensuring adequate media coverage and support to the developments in campaign districts

While sizeable media coverage and support will have to come from the Ministry of I&B and the autonomous bodies thereunder, such as AIR and Doordarshan the State Govt. can contribute a lot in (a) preparing and disseminating success stories of ongoing campaigns in districts; (b) identifying creative thinkers, writers and artists and encouraging them to contribute by way of regular writeups in the local press to disseminate the message of literacy in its correct perspective as well as to dispel the mistaken notions about such campaigns for total literacy, and (c) placing the services of the District Information and Public Relations set up at the disposal of the campaign authorities for intensive publicity and propaganda for reporting the pace and progress of the campaign as well as the outcome thereof.

Mass Mobilisation

It was noted that significant achievement has been made both in regard to coverage as well as creation of a positive environment for literacy by *Bharat Gyan Vigyan Jatha* as well as *Paidal Jatha* of Gandhian and Sarvodaya workers in October-November 1990. It was also noted that a large number of area-specific concrete action plans for total literacy have been formulated as a result of the positive environment which has been created and total literacy campaigns are being implemented in a number of districts. In view of the imperative need for reinforcing and sustaining, it is suggested that similar initiative may be launched on a large scale all over the country. It is also suggested that necessary measures be taken to secure large scale involvement of students and teachers in the environment building as well as campaign effort by designing apropriate motivation strategies for them.

The new initiative taken by Prof. Yash Pal, former Chairman, UGC and a number of like-minded persons on the subject of Mass-Action for National Regeneration by large scale involvement of students in schools, colleges and universities for one year to deal with the problems of illiteracy and mal-development was welcomed. It was noted that for the current year, a beginning is to be made by extending the summer vacation during which students and teachers will work intensively for literacy on the one hand and by integrating literacy as an integral part of the curriculum in the school, collegiate and university system on the other. It was further noted that this has been endorsed by the Council of the National Literacy Mission Authority in its recent meeting held on 15th February, 1991.

Priority to women's literacy

Keeping in view the close linkage between the female literacy and the status of the women in society, maternity protection, child health care and its impact on reduction of infant mortality rate and birth rate and also in view of the abysmally low rate of females literacy in several parts of the country, the Group suggested a number of measures for giving an effective boost to female literacy (both in terms of rate as well as absolute number), such as involvement of women functionaries in adult education and literacy programmes in large number, designing curriculum (both teaching-learning and training) as well as conducting the programme in a manner which will enthuse and motivate women to participate in the programme in large numbers, etc. It was noted with satisfaction that a good deal of linkage has been established between the campaign for total literacy in some of the districts and the new programme for women's equality and empowerment, known as

'Mahila Samakhya'. The functionaries of Mahila Samakhya in these districts, in addition to helping in creation of a positive environment for literacy have also acted as resource persons in training and mobilisation of women. While recommending extension of the Mahila Samakhya project to larger number of districts, reinforcement of the nexus between Mahila Samakhya and Campaign mode for total literacy was also emphasised.

Involvement of Voluntary Agencies

The voluntary agencies will also have to be persuaded to adopt the new approach which is area-specific, time-bound, volunteer-based, cost-effective and result-oriented as far as possible and practicable. This would require considerable efforts on the part of the Central and State machinery in-charge of implementation of the programme in (a) organisation of workshops for VAs for their large scale familiarisation with the area-approach and IPCL techniques; (b) assisting the VAs in formulation and reformulation of action plans for total literacy in specified areas; and (c) extending continuous encouragement, support and help to VAs to enable them to run the programme in a climate of total freedom and spontaneity.

The Director-General, National Literacy Mission stated that in the wake of the *Paidal Jatha* undertaken by a large number of Gandhian and Sarvodaya workers in the 5 States of Assam, Orissa, Bihar, UP and MP a good number of good and reliable VAs have been mobilised and motivated to come up with concrete action plans for total literacy in specific areas. A workshop was held at Sevapuri near Varanasi with representatives of 30 such voluntary groups, which was attended by him and the Education Secretary Govt. of India, and the need for creating a decentralised set up and mechanism for processing of such proposal from the VAs, with utmost speed and expedition on the one hand and also to provide continuous encouragement guidance, leadership and support on the other, was felt. It is in this context that need for constituting a State level body to assist the VAs in formulation and reformulation of action plans, sanction and release of funds, monitoring and all other promotional activities related to the VAs, was felt. He indicated for information of the Group the consensus which had emerged from the workshop about the broad composition of such a state level body. The composition would be as below:

Chairman : a distinguished civil servant serving or retired, of sufficiently high seniority in the hierarchy who has empathy and sensitivity to the voluntary sector and who is acceptable as such; OR

an otherwise eminent person in public life.

Secretary : Should be full time to be taken on deputation from the State Govt. (Dev. Deptt.). Should be acceptable to the VAs.

Members : 3 local VAs of whom atleast one should be a woman.

1 VA from outside the State.

1 representative from GOI.

The state level body would be registered as a Society under the Societies Registration Act and may be named as "Sampoorna Sakshrata and Gram Swarajya Samiti" or by such other name as may be considered locally appropriate. In addition to scrutiny and sanction of proposals of VAs, this body would also function as a promotional and development body vested with mobilisation and leadership development functions. While endorsing the suggestion regarding constitution of such a State level body for the specific purpose as indicated above, it was recommended that Director, Adult Education of the State and Director, State Resource Centre should also be made members of the society.

1.6 *Flexibility in Approach*

The new thrust, initiative and awakening in the direction of mass campaigns for total literacy was noted and the following suggestions made:

* Mass mobilisation and campaigns for total literacy should be taken up wherever possible. A campaign for total literacy would mean mass mobilisation, voluntarism and learning outcome according to NLM norms as its cardinal principles. This would also require for its success designing good training modules, an effective Management Information System (MIS) and an effective system of evaluation of the learning outcome.
* The traditional Centre-based programme should be totally frozen in those districts where mass campaigns for total literacy have been launched.
* The traditional Centre-based programme should be progressively phased out even in districts where mass campaigns for total literacy have not been launched but by adopting other alternative approaches like involvement of women coordinators,

prerak/instructor centred approach etc.

* In areas, such as border areas, desert areas, tribal and forest areas, inaccessible areas and other disturbed areas where it is not possible to go in for mass campaigns for total literacy, a more flexible approach or mixed approach (both Centre-based and Volunteer-based) could be adopted, as may be relevant to the specific needs of that region (it being noted that in the same area, the Centre-based approach and the Volunteer-based approach should not be adopted).
* The Group noted that we should be a little guarded and cautious about the continuance or replication of the scheme of payment for results, as has been introduced in the 20 CD Blocks of West Bengal and the Ex-servicemen projects in the States of Tamil Nadu, U.P., MP and Rajasthan.

2.1 *Post-Literacy*

In districts where mass campaigns for total literacy, have been launched, it was suggested that alternative mechanisms could be designed for an effective post-literacy and continuing education programme, which would take into account :

(i) Continued Non-Formal Education of children in the 9-14 age group until they achieve the minimum levels of learning;
(ii) Retention and strengthening of literacy skills of those persons (neo-literates) who have achieved the NLM levels of literacy with a view to making them permanent;
(iii) Continued basic literacy skills for those persons who have during the course of the campaigns, not quite achieved the NLM levels of literacy; and
(iv) A programme of literacy for those persons who were for various reasons not able to participate in the basic literacy campaign.

It was felt that adequate steps should be taken to design graded post-literacy materials and making available these materials in sufficient quantity for the neo-lierates through libraries and other institutionalised avenues. It was felt that priority in organising the post-campaign and post literacy strategies should be given to continuing education for women. It also noted that a series of meetings/workshops are being planned with a view to evolving strategies for post-literacy and continuing education in the campaign context. It was also felt that it may be necessary to organise training programmes in skills including vocational skills in which opportunities for self-employment as well as wage-employment are locally available. Illustratively simple and short duration training could be organised on health and nutrition, common ailments and inexpensive remedies, information about proper upkeep and maintenance of productive assets, measures of safe storage of water, growing and storage of vegetables, introducing devices which can minimise hardships and drudgeries, particularly in the lives of rural women (smokeless *chullahas*, bio-gas, solar cooker, etc.). Such training could also be organised to provide access to legal literacy, such as provisions of labour, tenancy laws and welfare laws, etc.

We, the students, teachers, working people in Govt., business concerns, firms and factories, men and women of all ages pledge to devote ourselves wholly beginning this year for the attainment of total literacy which is the hallmark of progress and development.

Participants in the Group on Adult Education and Literacy

Chairman

1. Dr. Malcolm S. Adiseshiah
   Chairman,
   Madras Institute of Development Studies.

Rapporteurs/Members

2. Shri A.J. Shukla
   Director (AE and PE)
   Government of Gujarat.
3. Shri Mohd. Abdul Bari
   Minister-in-Charge
   Mass Education and Extension
   West Bengal.
4. Shri Prem Bhai
   Secretary, Banwasi Seva Ashram
   Govindpur, Sonbhadra, Uttar Pradesh.
5. Shri Vijendra Kabra
   Director, Indian Institute of Rural Works
   Aurangabad.

6. Shri Harivallabh Parikh
   Chairman, Anand Niketan Ashrama
   Rangpur, Baroda, Gujarat.
7. Smt. Sarva Sridevi
   Sitaphalmandi
   Secunderabad.
8. Shri J.C. Ranganayakulu
   Director of Adult Education
   Government of Andhra Pradesh.
9. Smt. Tilottama Barooah
   Additional Director, Adult Education
   Government of Assam.
10. Shri S.G. Amonkar
    Director, State Literacy Mission
    and Adult Education,
    Government of Goa.
11. Shri M. Madan Gopal
    Director, Mass Education
    Government of Karnataka.
12. Shri P.K. Sivanandan
    Secretary (Local Administration) and
    Secretary, Kerala Saksharata Samiti
    Government of Kerala.
13. Shri R. Kar
    Director, Teacher Education
    Government of Orissa.
14. Shri M. C. Mathur
    Director, Education
    Government of Sikkim.
15. Shri G.P. Upadhayaya
    Deputy Director, Education Department
    Government of Sikkim.
16. Miss Gauri Dhar
    Additional Director SW and Social Education
    Government of Tripura.
17. Dr. K.A. Pandey
    Director, Adult Education
    Government of Uttar Pradesh.

18. Shri M. Roy
    Director, Mass Education and Extension
    Government of West Bengal.
19. Shri Narendra Prasad
    Commissioner-cum-Secretary (Education)
    Delhi Administration.
20. Shri Lakshmidhar Mishra
    Joint Secretary (AE)
    and Director General (NLM)
    Department of Education
    Ministry of H.R.D.

Recommendations and Observations of CABE on Adult Educations

The report of the Working Group on Adult Education and Literacy was presented by the Chairman of the group Dr. Malcolm Adiseshiah. The following points were made in course of discussion:

(a) The initiative taken by Prof. Yash Pal, former Chairman, UGC and a number of like-minded persons to involve school and college students in national issues like eradication of illiteracy was welcome;
(b) Concrete steps should be taken to revive the Vidyapeethas set up in Karnataka under the auspices of Karnataka Adult Education Council;
(c) There is need for greater linkage of the adult education programme with the system of libraries. Systematic programmes need to be undertaken for ensuring that neo-literates do not relapse into illiteracy; and
(d) In the planning of literacy and post-literacy programmes special attention should be paid to habitations with SC/ST concentration.

With these observations the CABE adopted the working group report.

19

REPORT OF CABE WORKING GROUP ON ELEMENTARY EDUCATION (1991)*

The Group on Elementary Education was chaired by Dr. (Smt.) Komala Das, Minister of State for Education, Orissa.

In view of the vast subject for discussion and the limitation of time, the Group decided that it would concentrate on discussing Minimum Levels of Learning, Micro-Planning and Non-Formal Education.

Minimum Levels of Learning

Recognising that Universalisation of Education does not mean universal enrolment only, but also universal achievement of all children in the school going age, the Group discussed the strategy of Minimum Essential Level of Learning in this context. Dr. R.H. Dave, the Chairman of the Committee set up to lay down the Minimum Levels of Learning for the primary stage and to recommend a procedure for comprehensive learner evaluation sketched in brief the reaons why it was necessary to draw up minimum levels of learning as performance goals for universal achievement and for measuring progress towards UEE. The major concern behind the need to have minimum levels of learning was to reduce the existing disparities and improve the level of achievement in rural areas, socially and economically backward areas and thus work towards the establishment of equity and social justice. It is in this context that the Minimum Essential Levels of Learning were proposed.

It was seen that one of the factors which affected the quality of primary education was an over-ambitious and excessively heavy curriculum that had little relevance to the lives and needs of the majority

* Ministry of Human Resource Development, New Delhi.

of students and had compelled a joyless rote memorisation and over-emphasis on text-books. What was required was a curriculum that equipped children to acquire mastery over competencies and skills essential for them to function as literate adults in their communities even if they do not get the opportunity for further studies. The Minimum Levels of Learning, therefore, emphasise relevance and functionality. Another important feature of the MLL is achievability. Reduced quantum of learning will enable children to learn to mastery levels, even while permitting the teacher to relate text-book information and objective reality into a meaningful process of understanding and application through experimentation, exploration and activity-based teaching. The reduced quantum will thus not only permit a greater joyousness in the class-room but also by virtue of a good mastery over the earlier learning units, the ability to progress faster through later stages of education.

The strategy of Minimum Levels of Learning will provide the common basis for both formal and non-formal modes of imparting primary level education. This strategy can, therefore, be effectively utilised for establishing comparability and equivalence of achievement between the formal and the non-formal system, at least in the essential subjects of study such as Language and Mathematics.

An important aspect of the MLLs was that it took into account the existing disparities between regions, districts, and States in achievement levels. The strategy for introducing MLLs therefore, envisaged that each region would examine the MLLs in relation to its existing conditions and achievement levels and modify them suitably before accepting them as expected goals of performance. Thus in areas with significantly lower achievement levels, intermediate levels of MLLs could be set with time-bound targets. Different regions could thus have differentiated MLLs. The endeavour of this strategy would be to direct better results where levels of learning were lower and to consciously accelerate the pace of development in the interior regions thereby reducing disparities and equalising the minimum standards over the entire country.

Continuous and comprehensive evaluation forms an important part of the strategy of MLLs. Having set MLLs as the performance goal, continuous and comprehensive evaluation would ensure the attainment of competencies and skills through continuous and periodical evaluation and corresponding recedial measures as well as summative assessment of performance from stage to stage.

In the discussion that ensured, several viewpoints were highlighted. The opinion was expressed that there was nothing new in the subject, and that the work on defining the Minimum Levels of Learning had been done in this country as early as 1978.

Instead of 're-inventing' the wheel each time, the Government should be advised to take earlier experiments and studies into account. While recognising that the need to specifying MLLs was long overdue some members expressed concern for the learning needs of gifted children and said it should also be given some thought. Others felt that the better achieving schools should be allowed to progress ahead at their own pace. Since a majority of children grow up in bilingual or multilingual environment, their home language should be used as the strategy for learning the school language. The view was also expressed that there was danger in taking the MLLs prescribed by the R.H. Dave Committee as the final word on the subject and as the basis for deciding the progress of UEE. Some members expressed the view that crux of the matter lay in making the teachers perform their duties and not only in re-defining the curriculum. It was stated that measures such as continuous in-service teacher training, provision of Early Childhood Education, convergence of services, provision of facilities such as transportation, etc., aimed at reducing drop-outs and improving the functioning of the schools would also need to be given continued importance.

Overall, however, the Group accepted that fixing the minimum levels of learning as an achievable, relevant, functional and measureable goal for the school system was a significant move forward. It was seen that measuring the progress of the educational system by the number of children who attained MLLs would be a distinct improvement over measuring the progress by the additional enrolments into the system. The Group felt that MLLs, taken together with a continuous and comprehensive evaluation system, would help the teachers to control the pace of learning and get an insight into the learning difficulties and learning achievements of children and thereby help them to structure their pace, method and success of teaching. A proper analysis of the evaluation results would also indicate to the educational planners the kind of inputs that are necessary to improve conditions, facilities and the quality of teaching in schools. Thus, the programmes for teacher training, improvement in facilities, supervision of schools, etc., would all be guided by a proper understanding of classroom processes and structure towards a well-defined goal.

The Group saw the MLLs as an effective solution to the vexing question of comparability of standard between formal and non-formal systems. It was felt that the question no longer remained one of NFE conforming to the primary school standards but became one of the viability of a different model and methodology to attain a prescribed level of learning.

Some concern was expressed by the Group that the MLLs might result in imposing a centralised curriculum on the system. It was clarified by Prof. R.H. Dave that, in fact, the move would encourage flexibility, innovation and experimentation, and greater involvement of teachers with the teaching-learning processes and materials taking into account the local realities and resources. It was also clarified that the recommended levels were not prescriptive and that each State or any other unit would be advised to measure the present levels of learning of children, and on that basis, decide the quantum of skills and competencies it would wish to keep as the minimum for mastery by all children as the goal for the system.

After the detailed discussion, the Committee recommends as follows:

(i) The strategy of Minimum Levels of Learning (MLL) should be accepted as an important component of all educational planning for universalisation of elementary education, including non-formal education;

(ii) Steps should be taken to widely disseminate the strategy and concept of MLL, highlighting its inbuilt flexibility and the active involvement in a decentralised manner of teachers, educationists, parents, etc.;

(iii) Concrete measures should be initiated as early as possible to implement the whole strategy in order to improve the quality of achievement coupled with equity and social justice;

(iv) The State Governments and Voluntary Organisations, universities and other institutions should be provided assistance, financial and academic, to operationalise the strategy; and

(v) Since the ultimate objective is universalisation of elementary education, a similar exercise should be initiated for the upper primary level so that improvement in attainment together with social justice and equity is ensured at the upper-primary level also.

Micro Planning

At the outset, the Working Group wanted to be fully apprised of the main parameters of micro-planning. These were explanined as follows:

Efforts have been made in the past to bring elementary education system closer to the community. The modalities created over the years have continued to serve the well-to-do sections of the society, which co-opted into their fold, the influential teachers and other persons concerned with delivery of basic education services. This powerful section has protected the disfunctionality of the school system and has not made much contribution to enhancing the participation of children in the elementary educational system. The disfunctionality of the elementary education system has consequently reached an alarming stage. In large parts of the country, schools are running in an unsatisfactory manner, children drop-out in large numbers, and the levels of their learning are well below the expected norms. A significant percentage of children has remained altogether deprived of the benefits of elementary education.

The situation has to change. A widespread mobilisation has to be generated to energise the hitherto deprived sections in the countryside. Mobilisation could be generated with the help of mass-media, traditional and folk forms of communication and person to person contact by committed activists. Such a communication strategy should highlight the present status of elementary education and indicate areas in which useful intervention can be made. The mobilisation which has got generated in several parts of the country under the National Literacy Mission, should also be harnessed in this behalf. Simultaneously with the creation of an environment, large-scale programme of training and orientation should be taken up for village youth and women. The purpose behind this should be to explain the responsibility of the village community towards elementary system and engendering a confidence among them to secure accountability of the elementary system to the Village Education Committee. The trained women and youth will need to work in rapport with the local level Panchayati Raj structure as well as with teachers and AE/NFE instructors. The latter viz. elementary school teachers and AE/NFE instructors, should be given confidence that the process of micro-planning is not a confrontation with them but a new kind of mutually beneficial partnership. This group (comprising oriented women and youth) could take the shape of Mahila Samooh (as has happened in several hundred villages in Rajasthan where the

Women's Development Programme is being implemented), or Village Education Committee (VEC). This Mahila Samooh or VEC will not be a structure only in name as in some States. This organisation will have its own inner strength. It must take the form of Lok Shakti/Stree Shakti. This group (MS or VEC) will need to be provided a support system in the form of school complexes or a block level education organisation which is permeated by a similar spirit.

The elementary education system (Primary and upper primary school as well as the NFE Centre) will be accountable to this kind of a village education structure. In concrete terms, accountability will imply an effective say (without interference in academic aspects) in the running of elementary education programmes. While on the one hand, this MS/VEC will secure accountability of the elementary education system, it will, on the other hand, help the schools and NFE centres in their work. The group will undertake school mapping to ensure that practically every child of the village has access to elementary education; it will monitor from day to day and week to week the rate of participation of children in the elementary education system to ensure retention and active participation; and, it will also take interest to see that the shortcommings and difficulties, found by teachers are resolved and the children have satisfactory achievement in cognitive as well as non-cognitive areas.

The Working Group endorses the micro-planning approach for improvement of elementary education programmes and calls upon all State Governments to take steps for its careful implementation. It requests the Central Government,NIEPA and NCERT to actively associcate themselves with the State Govts. in effective implementation of this approach as early as possible. In doing so, the State Govts. may have to incur a good deal of expenditure, which should be built into various schemes of the Central and State Govts. and the additionality required should be separately provided as a Centrally-sponsored Scheme. The Working Group is also of the view that the monitoring of the present status of elementary education and in particular of micro-planning, NFE programme, achievement related progress of pupil's etc. should be effectively monitored.

School Calendar

The Group felt that School Calendar should match the major agricultural activities, socio-economic factors of the region. This would improve attendance of children in schools on the one hand and control teacher absenteeism on the other.

Non-formal Education

The Group noted that in the present socio-economic condition of the country, all children cannot take advantage of school and therefore, non-formal education will have to continue to play a significant role in providing learning opportunities to children (i) of small and remote habitations, and (ii) who because of economic compulsions or social constraints cannot attend the schools, being pre-occupied with a variety of economic activities including sibling care, domestic chores, work in agriculture, etc. The Group also noted with regret that the Non-Formal Education system in many parts of the country is not working satisfactorily. It stressed the need to make a success of Non-Formal Education and to operationalise effectively a system of Non-Formal Education to meet the needs of the out-of schools children in such a manner that the achievements of the learners are comparable to those in the schools. Analysing the factors contributing to the present unsatisfactory performance of the system, the Group recommended the following measures for revitalising the Non-Formal stream of education:

(i) Greater financial allocations are necessary both from the Central Government and the State Governments. To begin with, the Central share for co-educational centres should be enhanced from the existing 50 per cent to 75 per cent;

(ii) Honorarium to Instructors should be enhanced suitably keeping in mind parallel structures;

(iii) Adequate teaching learning material should be provided to the learning centres somewhat on the lines of material supplied under the Operation Blackboard;

(iv) Children in NFE programme should be provided free text-books and stationery. The NFE Centre should emphasise activities which are relaxing and joyful for the participants;

(v) Attention should be paid to improve all text-books and learning material adopting to the extent possible the Improved Pace and Content of Learning approach followed for the primers of Adult Education;

(vi) The pedagogy should be improved to emphasise learning rather than rote memorisation of texts and to condense the courses to the extent possible;

(vii) The training of Instructors should be strengthened with a provision for recurrent continuous training through periodic -monthly or quarterly-meetings and other modes;

(viii) The transferability of children between Formal and Non-Formal system should be made common, easy and convenient. A system of certification having equivalence with primary schools should be provided. This should be possible as both Formal and Non-Formal Centres will aim at attaining the same minimum levels of learning; and

(ix) Management system should be improved to ensure timely payment to Instructors, effective supervision, regular and timely supply of teaching learning materials.

The Group also recommended that the existing Scheme of Non-Formal Education should be revised, taking into account the above suggestions. It also felt that the revisd scheme should be discussed with the representatives of the State Governments and Voluntary Organisations before finalising it.

The Group also strongly felt that the States should be given a clear assurance that Central assistance for the programme would be available at least during the Eighth Five Year Plan, if possible till the year 2000 A.D.

Teacher Education

1. The Group stressed that a proper system of teacher preparation is essential for improving standards of education. It discussed and endorsed the features of the proposed NCTE Bill which were circulated for the Board's consideration, with the observation that all States of a region should be represented on the Regional Committee and these Committees should be enabled to take care of regional and state-to-state variations.

2. The Group noted with concern the current status of implementation of the Centrally-sponsored Scheme of Teacher Education, especially the District Institutes of Education and Training (DIETs). It felt that the scheme needed much greater attention by State Governments – especially in the matter of induction of willing, committed and competent persons in these institutions, and their proper orientation. It is now three years since the scheme began. The Group felt that all-out

efforts need to be made by State Governments to operationalise the maximum possible number of DIETs etc. within the next few months. It also strongly recommended that Central Government should continue assistance for salaries, programmes, etc. for all institutions sanctioned during the Seventh Plan for the entire Eighth Plan period, besides meeting commitments of non-recurring nature.

3. The Group also noted with concern that Teacher Education Institutions which are sub-standard and/or indulging in malpractices continue to exist in some States, and in a few of them, even continue to grow. It urged State Governments to urgently take effective steps to curb such institutions.

4. The Group stressed the crucial importance of SCERTs as a support system for ECE, School Education, Non-Formal Education and Teacher Education and urged that these bodies be suitably strengthened for the purpose at the earliest, with adequate assistance from the Central Government.

Teachers' Representation in Legislative Councils

Under Article 171 of the Constitution, voting rights in Legislative Council elections from teachers' constituencies are at present limited to teachers working in institutions 'not lower in standard than that of a secondary school'.

The issue of non-inclusion of elementary teachers was discussed by the Group. It noted that these Councils at present exist in only four States. A number of views were expressed on the subject. One view was that discrimination between different types of teachers was unreasonable. Another view was that elections from teachers' constituencies resulted in considerable politicisation of teachers and affected the smooth functioning of the education system. Yet another suggestion was that teachers, including elementary teachers, should be represented on the Councils-but through nomination of meritorious teachers rather than through elections.

Most members in the Group felt that the issue needed in depth and comprehensive consideration. The Group accordingly suggested that CABE constitute a Committee to quickly go into all aspects of the matter and make its recommendations for the Board's consideration.

Educational Management

Although the Group was not able to discuss educational management, it recognises the critical importance of an effective, properly functioning and people oriented decentralised system of educational administration. It is, therefore, recommended that in the next meeting of the CABE the matter should be placed for in-depth consideration particularly to galvanise and revitalize the system to meet the needs of the kind of micro planning approach, we have recommended in which the communities, the people and decentralised functioning would be the main features.

Participants in the Group on Elementary Education

Chairperson

1. Dr. (Mrs.) Kamala Das
   Minister of State for Education
   Orissa

Rapporteurs/Members

2. Dr. L.P. Pandey
   Director, Basic Education
   Government of Uttar Pradesh
3. Dr. Ramchander Purve
   Education Minister
   Bihar
4. Shri Ashoka Bajpai
   Minister of Education
   Uttar Pradesh
5. Shri K. Kandaswamy
   Councellor (Education)
   Andaman and Nicobar Islands
6. Dr. S. Anandalakshamy
   Senior Fellow, MCRC
   Madras.
7. Dr. Syad Hasan
   Director, Insan School/College
   Kishanganj, Purnea
8. Dr. (Smt.) Radhika Herzberger
   Director, Rishi Valley School
   Chittor, Andhra Pradesh
9. Dr. D.P. Pattanayak
   Bogadi Road
   Mysore

10. Dr. Suman Sahai, President
    T.C.S., Tilhar
    Uttar Pradesh
11. Shri Kertikaya V. Sarabhai
    Centre for Environment Education
    Ahmedabad
12. Dr. (Smt.) J.H. Trivedi
    Bombay.
13. Prof. R.H. Dave,
    Chairman, MLL Committee
14. Shri K. Penchallaiah
    Director of School Education
    Government of Andhra Pradesh
15. Shri Phool Singh
    Director, Primary Education
    Government of Bihar
16. Shri A.K. Joti
    Director, Higher Education, Government of Gujarat
17. Shri S.S. Kaushal
    Director, Primary Education
    Government of Haryana
18. Shri M.L. Chandra Keerthi
    Commissioner, Public Instruction
    Government of Karnataka
19. Smt. Lizzie Jacob
    Secretary (General Education)
    Government of Kerala
20. Shri Lalit Kumar Joshi
    Secretary, School Education
    Government of Madhya Pradesh
21. Shri S.P. Srivastava
    Director, State Institute of Education
    Government of Madhya Pradesh
22. Shir S.S. Salgaonkar
    Director, MSERT, Pune
    Government of Maharashtra
23. Prof. (Dr.) Mahapatra
    Director, SCERT
    Government of Orissa

24. Shri Talitsuba
    Director of School Education
    Government of Nagaland
25. Shri P.S. Bhupal
    Director, SCERT
    Government of Punab
26. Shri Damoddar Sharma
    Director, Primary and Secondary Education
    Government of Rajasthan
27. Shri T. Natchimuthu
    Director of School Education
    Government of Tamil Nadu
28. Shri H.S. Dhar
    Hindi Education Officer
    Dte. of School Education
    Government of Tripura
29. Shri D. Ghosh
    Director, School Education
    Government of West Bengal
30. Shri S.C. Behar
    Consultant, NIEPA
31. Shri S.D. Roka
    Professor, NCERT
32. Shri R.P. Singh
    Professor, NCERT
33. Prof. P.N. Dave
    NCERT
34. Dr. C.J. Daswani
    Head, Deptt. of NFE and Education of SC and ST, NCERT.
35. Prof. J.S. Rajput
    Joint Educational Adviser
    Department of Education
    Ministry of H.R.D.
36. Shri K.M. Acharya
    Director
    Department of Education
    Ministry of H.R.D.
37. Ms. K. Dhingra
    Director (EE)
    Department of Education
    Ministry of H.R.D.

38. Shri Amitabh Mukhopadhyay
    Deputy Secretary
    Department of Education
    Ministry of H.R.D.
39. Shri A.K. Mehra
    Deputy Secretary (NFE)
    Department of Education
    Ministry of H.R.D.

Recommendations and Observations of CABE on Elementary Education

The Working Group Report on Elementary Education was presented by Dr. L.P. Pandey, the Rapporteur of the group.

Education Minister, Karnataka said the CABE should recommend adoption of mid-day programme for improving enrolment and retention. He said that the experience of the States which had adopted such a programme had been very positive. In response to this, Shri Anil Bordia explained that CABE had always endorsed the idea of provision of mid-day meals to children but had also consistently taken the stand that the responsibility for this should not lie with the school system, as the work relating to procurement of foodgrains, their storage, cooking, distribution, accounting, monitoring, etc., greatly interfered with the task of teaching/learning in schools.

Prof. D.S. Kothari said that while he fully agreed with the MLL approach and concept, there was need for a re-examination of the recommendations of the R.H. Dave Committee in regard to specific skills and competencies before adopting them. He also advised that inclucation of values and other non-cognitive and affective areas should also be emphasised.

Some other members also made observations on different aspects of the report of the working group. CABE adopted the Report of the working group with the following additional observations :

(a) The specific levels of skills and competencies recommended by the R.H. Dave Committee should be got thoroughly re-examined by the Ministry before accepting the Report;
(b) Operation Blackboard should continue in the Eighth Plan and expanded to the upper primary stage. Funds for appointment of teachers provided by the Central Government during the

Seventh Plan should continue to form part of the Centrally-sponsored Scheme during the Eighth Plan. A timebound programme should be taken up for provision of infrastructure and basic facilities for primary education based on well-laid down norms; and

(c) The Central and State Governments should be called upon to fully implement the law relating to child labour while efforts are made to provide education to all working children.

20

REPORT OF CABE GROUP ON SECONDARY EDUCATION (1991)*

Chairperson
Shri Kanti Biswas
Education Minister
Government of West Bengal

Rapporteur
Km. Sushma Choudhary
Education Secretary
Government of J and K

The Group of the CABE which met to discuss issues connected with Secondary Education resolved to place on record its concern that Secondary Education was not getting its rightful importance both in terms of financial allocations and physical facilities. It was stressed that secondary education, which includes higher secondary education, is the vital link between elementary education and higher education and therefore, it deserves appropriate importance *vis-a-vis* the other stages of education.

Vocationalisation of Secondary Education

The scheme of vocationalisation of secondary education was taken up for discussion first. At the end of an interesting and thought provoking discussion, the following recommendations were made:

1. The scheme of vocationalisation of secondary education should

* Ministry of Human Resource Development, New Delhi.

continue as a Centrally-sponsored Scheme at least till the end of the 8th Plan. The financial ceilings of various components under the existing scheme need to be revised upwardly in view of cost escalation.

2. The Group recommended that vocational education at the +2 level may continue as a distinct stream.
3. Keeping in view the need of a large number of students who do not study beyond class X, pre-vocational education at the lower secondary stage, in lieu of work experience, should be introduced in a phased manner. The group agreed in principle with the draft scheme circulated and suggested that the details should be finalised in consultation with the State Governments/U.T. Administrations.
4. The group welcomed the suggestion to set up separate vocational schools, particularly in the North Eastern States and also in certain rural areas of other States. Initially, a few schools may be started on an experimental basis and thereafter based upon the evaluation of the scheme, further expansion could be considered. As in the case of the Pre-Vocational Scheme, it was suggested that the details of this scheme also be finalised in consultation with the State Governments/U.T. Administrations.
5. The Members of the group felt that the proposal to involve the community in helping the vocational students to achieve self-employment/wage-employment through the scheme entitled 'Each One Place One' was interesting and had tremendous potential. It recommended its wide circulation throughout the country and called upon all State Govts./U.Ts. and NGOs to give it appropriate publicity.
6. The programme of vocationalisation of secondary education needs to be consolidated and the quality improved. While it is desirable that the programme should be expanded, this expansion should be undertaken in a selective manner after providing the necessary inputs.
7. The group considered the recommendation of the Acharya Ramamurti Report, which has accorded a very high priority to Vocationalisation of Education. There was unanimity among the group that sex-stereotyping in courses should be carefully avoided and that access for Scheduled Castes and Scheduled Tribes should be enhanced. It also agreed that there should be a meaningful linkage between the courses in schools and the

world of work and that there should be greater decentralisation in decision-making and implementation with more involvement of the Heads of Institutions. The suggestions for introduction of Vocational Courses before Class XI and the modular approach to these courses have in a modified manner, been incorporated in the scheme of Pre-vocational Education with which the group has already agreed in principle.

8. The Group noted that many of the States have made a lot of progress in introducing vocational courses at the plus 2 level but that some States are still lagging behind. Some of the areas in which particular attention needs to be paid by the State Governments are the following :

(i) The setting up of adequate management structures at all levels;
(ii) Construction of worksheds;
(iii) Procurement of equipment before commencement of the course;
(iv) Appointment of qualified teachers;
(v) Development of instructional material and text-books;
(vi) Development of appropriate linkages for practical training during the courses and later for wage/self-employment;
(vii) Avenues for vertical mobility to higher professional courses in certain vocational areas and horizontal mobility should be facilitated;
(viii) Modification of recruitment rules;
(ix) Strengthening of training institutes for pre-service and in-service training of vocational teachers. Financial assistance from the Central Government was requested for this purpose;
(x) Selection of courses to be guided by the developmental activities of the States and the labour market profile, for which Surveys should be completed and periodically updated; and
(xi) The States should work in close collaboration with the Regional Boards of Apprenticeship Training to facilitate maximum placement of vocational students.

Novadaya Vidyalayas

The majority of the Group recommended that the existing imbalance in the pattern of coverage of Districts in a few States/UTs may be reduced, by bringing the percentage of coverage of Districts to the National percentage of 65. This will enable students of those particular States/UTs to compete for admission in Novadaya Vidyalaya on a comparatively equitable basis. The majority of the Group suggested that corrective action be taken by opening a few Novadaya Vidayalayas in those States/UTs where the present percentage of coverage is less than that of the national average figure i.e. 65.

Programmes for Qualitative Improvement in Secondary Education

(i) *Elevation of the status of the Principals/Headmasters of High and Higher Secondary Schools*

The Group recognises the need for granting greater delegation of authority-administrative, financial and academic to the Principals/ Headmasters of high and higher secondary schools and commensurate accountability on their part. However, it was suggested that the specific delegations listed in the Agenda note may be considered by each individual State Government. It was also suggested that the proposed scheme may be adopted first in the school systems directly under the control of the Central Government.

(ii) *Examination Reform*

The Committee noted that inspite of several recommendations that have been made for examination reforms there are many State Boards of Secondary Education which have yet to take necessary steps to reform their examination systems.

The Group felt that there is need to monitor the implementation of examination reform in the various States, and that this task could be effectively done by the Conference of Boards of Secondary Education (COBSE) and NCERT which are already involved in this activity.

(iii) *Curricula Development*

The group noted that this is an on-going activity and recommended that State Government should continue to strive for upgradation of the curriculum.

Improvement of Specific Subject Areas

It was recommended that the schemes aimed at improvement in the quality of school education such as science education, environmental orientation to school education and educational technology should be continued with central assistance during the Eighth Plan. It was suggested that for teacher training programmes, provision of TA/DA should also be made since the State Governments are unable to meet this financial commitment.

CLASS Project

Recognising the importance of imparting computer education in Government and Government aided schools in order to reduce disparities of access in this area, continuation of the CLASS Project and its phased expansion is recommneded. Schools should be selected carefully to ensure that basic facilities such as building and electricity are available.

Other Items with Permission of the Chair

(a) The attention of the group was invited to a communication received from the Ministry of Welfare and the Department of Women and Child Development regarding unique problems being faced in admission of destitute, orphaned, abandoned children and recommended that the following may be done:

(i) The form for admission may be amended to provide for the name of the parent/guardian. The name of the father need not be insisted on.

(ii) The date of birth as declared by the parent/guardians of the child should be accepted by all educational institutions without insistence on birth certificate.

(b) It was acknowledged that handicapped children such as deaf, dumb and blind find it difficult to learn more than one language. The Government of India had earlier recommended to all States/UTs to permit children with hearing and vision disabilities to learn one language only and other subjects in lieu of the second or third launguage. In some States/U.Ts this is still not being done. To facilitate the education of the handicapped, it was recommended by the Group that provision of this facility may be considered by the States/U.Ts where it is yet to be provided.

(c) The group recommends that the norms regulating the establishment and upgradation of schools in reference to roll factor and teacher-student ratio for hilly and in-accessible areas should be relaxed.

Participants in the Group on Secondary Education

Chairman

1. Shri Kanti Biswas
   Education Minister
   West Bengal

Rapporteur/Members

2. Km. Sushma Choudhary
   Education Secretary
   Government of Jammu and Kashmir
3. Shri Arun Kumar Kar
   Education Minister
   Tripura.
4. Shri Ashoka Bajpai
   Education Minister
   Uttar Pradesh
5. Shri H.S. Singha
   Chairman,CBSE.
6. Shri G. C. Yadava
   Director of Public Instruction
   Government of Arunachal Pradesh
7. Shri S.D. Sharma
   Additional Commissioner (HRD)
   Government of Bihar
8. Shri Shakti Sinha
   Secretary (Education)
   Government of Goa
9. Shri R. C. Sharma
   Dy. Director (VE)
   Department of Industrial Training
   and Vocational Education
   Government of Haryana

10. Dr. S. Kumar
    Dy. Director, Secondary Education
    Government of Haryana
11. Shri Narain Dass
    Dy. Superintendent
    Vocational Education
    Government of Haryana
12. Shri Ashok K. Angurana
    Director of Education
    Government of Jammu and Kashmir
13. Shri K.P. Hamza
    Director, Vocational Education
    Government of Kerala
14. Shri R. Bhargava
    Commissioner, Public Instruction
    Government of Madhya Pradesh
15. Dr. H.L. Malsawma
    Dy. Director, Higher Education
    Government of Mizoram
16. Shri Jaswant Singh
    Director of Public Instruction
    Government of Punjab
17. Shri T. Natchimuthu
    Director of School Education
    Government of Tamil Nadu
18. Shri S.B. Biswas
    Director, School Education
    Government of Tripura
19. Shri B.P. Khandelwal
    Director of Education (Secondary)
    Government of Uttar Pradesh
20. Shri B. Ganguly
    Professor and Head
    Department of Education in Science and Maths.
    and Dean (Academic), NCERT
21. Shri Ashok K. Mishra
    Head, Deptt. of Vocational Education,
    NCERT
22. Shri Arjun Dev
    Professor, NCERT

23. Shri P. M. Patel
Professor, NCERT
24. Shri K. S. Sarma
Director
Navodaya Vidyalaya Samiti
25. Dr. (Mrs) D. M. de Rebello
Joint Secretary (S)
Department of Education
Ministry of H.R.D.
26. Smt. S. Brar
Deputy Secretary (ET)
Department of Education
Ministry of H.R.D.
27. Ms. P. Bolina
Deputy Educational Adviser
Department of Education
Ministry of H.R.D.
28. Shri A. Banerji
Deputy Secretary (Schools)
Department of Education
Ministry of H.R.D.
29. Smt. R. Mehra
Deputy Education Adviser
Department of Education
Ministry of H.R.D.

Observations and Recommendations of the Board on Secondary Education

Ms. Sushma Chaudhary, Rapporteur presented the report of the working group on secondary education. While considering the Report, Prof. Ramlal Parikh was of the view that the vocational education should not continue as distinct stream at the +2 level. The consensus, however, was that the report as prepared by the Group may be adopted. It was also pointed out that in any case this matter will again come up for consideration in the context of examination of Acharya Ramamurti Committee Report. Dr. Anandalakshmi suggested that in the report the terms 'deaf', 'dumb' and 'blind' should be replaced by the terms persons suffering from 'auditory' and 'visual' handicaps. This suggestion was accepted. With this modification the report was adopted.

21

REPORT OF CABE WORKING GROUP ON HIGHER EDUCATION (1991)*

The Working Group on Higher Education under the Chairmanship of Shri Vikram Verma, Hon. Minister of Education, Madhya Pradesh met on 8-9 March, 1991 and deliberated on various issues concerning Higher Education in India.

Gnanam Committee Report

The Group first took up discussion on the Gnanam Committee Report. The Group felt that although the report is too voluminous to be considered in a short meeting, it should benefit from the presence of Prof. Gnanam who was requested to give a brief resume of his recommendations. Prof. Gnanam explained that the management structure of most Indian Universities was based on the pattern of traditional British Universities and this structure was not adequate to meet with the requirements of present-day University in India. He stated that the report emphasised the principle of academic autonomy of universities and decentralisation of their management structure. The Report made detailed recommendations about the powers and functions of various officers and Authorities of Universities and the role of teachers, students, politicians and others in its management structure.

The Group felt that the recommendations made by the Gnanam Committee are of far reaching importance and should be very carefully considered by all State Governmants. The Group, therefore, recommended that the State Governmants should formulate their views on the report in three months time and send their recommendations to the UGC which should process the same and place them before the next meeting of the CABE.

* Ministry of Human Resource Development, New Delhi.

Academic Calendar

The Group expressed serious concern at the disruption of academic schedule in several Universities in the country. Examples were quoted of delay in admissions, examinations, declaration of results and disruption of class-room teaching due to agitations and several other reasons. The Group felt that restoration of academic calendar was of utmost importance to restore the credibility of our higher education system. Secretary, UGC explained that UGC had prepared a model academic calendar which was circulated to all Universities and State Governments for implementation from the academic year 1990-91. The UGC guidelines also provide for setting up a three-tier machinery for monitoring the implementation of the academic calendar. The Group resolved that the calendar prescribed by the UGC with appropriate modifications to suit local conditions, and without reducing the prescribed minimum number of teaching days, should be adopted and implemented by all the Universities. The Group also resolved that for the above purpose necessary statutory provisions may also be made by the universities before the beginning of the next academic year.

Quality of Higher Education

The Group felt that there are several reasons for deterioration in the quality of education, particularly at the college level. Serious concern was expressed at the opening of colleges which did not have adequate facilities. It was mentioned that out of nearly 7000 colleges in the country, 3000 colleges have not been found fit for assistance from UGC, as they do not possess necessary infrastructure facilities like buildings, class-rooms, laboratories, libraries and some do not even have the required number of teachers and students. Taking this into account the Group recommended that new colleges shall not be permitted if they do not conform to certain basic requirements in terms of population, buildings and other infrastructural facilities. The Group also felt that political will needs to be mobilisd to prevent proliferation of colleges without necessary facilities.

The Group felt that quality of higher education could be improved if the minimum qualifications prescribed by UGC for recruitment of teachers are strictly followed by all Universities and Colleges. The Group also recommended that facilities for inservice training for University and College teachers which are not adequate should be further strengthened.

University Finances

The Group observed that while there has been a general decline in the share of higher education in the overall budget of education, the requirements of funds in the education sector have increased substanially because of increase in number of institutions, students and teachers, and cost of providing education facilities. The Group expresed its concern at the financial condition of several Universities which do not have necessary resources to pay even salaries and have often to depend on bank over-drafts for their day-to-day expenditure. The Group felt that the State Governments should take a serious note of this situation and allocate adequate resources and release them on time to enable the Universities to function smoothly. The Group felt that the UGC and the Government of India should make a reappraisal of the threshold level of financial assistance to Universities and colleges and enhance it, taking into account the developmental needs of each University and college. While making the above recommendations the Group also observed that there is a need to bring about financial discipline in the Universities and curtail wasteful expenditure. The Group also rcommended that the University system should reduce its dependence on Government grants and raise resources on their own. The Group felt that to encourage universities to do so, they may be allowed to retain the additional resources raised by them.

Promotion of Sports in Universities and Colleges

The Group strongly felt that adequate attention is not being given to promotion of sports and youth activities in our colleges and universities. At present U.G.C. does not provide any resources for development of sports but only acts as an agency for Department of Youth Affairs and Sports which provide limited funds for development of sports infrastructure and promotion of sports activities. The Group recommended that the sports facilities in colleges and universities should be substantially upgraded and to begin with at least one institution in each district should be provided with minimum sports infrastructure and facilities for coaching and training.

Distance Education

The Group recognised the growing importance of distance education in the system of higher education and recommended that each State should establish an Open University. The Group recommended that the States can utilise the course material prepared by the INGOU by having it translated into local languages. The Group also recognised the need of re-orientation of correspondence courses into distance mode by increasing use of audio and video material and counselling facilities. The Group emphasised the need to provide for mobility between conventional and open university systems.

Participants in the Group on Higher Education

Chairman

1. Shri Vikram Verma
   Education Minister
   Madhya Pradesh

Repporteurs/Members

2. Shri C.T. Benjamin
   Commissioner and Secretary, Education
   Government of Karnataka
3. Dr. D.P. Singh
   Minister of Higher Education
   Bihar
4. Prof. A. Gnanam
   Vice-Chancellor
   Pondicherry University
5. Prof. Izhar Hussain
   Aligarh Muslim University
6. Prof. Mrinal Miri
   Deptt. of Philosophy
   NEHU
7. Smt. A. Shukla
   Professor and Principal
   Mahila Mahavidyalaya
   Banaras Hindu University
8. Prof. R. Balasubramanian
   Chairman, ICPR
9. Prof. S.K. Khanna
   Vice-Chairman, UGC
10. Shri T.V. Reddy

Director, Collegiate Education
Government of Andhra Pradesh

11. Shri B.P. Chaudhery
Joint Secretary (HRD),
Government of Bihar
12. Dr. M.L. Tayal
Director, Higher Education
Government of Haryana
13. Shri B.K. Gowel
Director, Education (Secondary and Higher)
Government of Himachal Pradesh
14. Shri Kuruvilla John
Director of Collegiate Education
Government of Kerala
15. Shri K.K. Vijayakumar
Director, Higher Secondary Education
Government of Kerala
16. Smt. M.V. Garde
Principal Secretary
Government of Madhya Pradesh
17. Ms. Alka Sirohi
Commissioner, Higher Education
Government of Madhya Pradesh
18. Dr. N.K. Patole
Director of Higher Education
Government of Maharashtra
19. Shri Lalawia
Director, Higher and Technical Education
Government of Mizoram
20. Dr. L.K. Das
Director, Higher Education
Government of Orissa
21. Dr. Ujagar Singh Banga
Director of Public Instruction (Colleges)
Government of Punjab
22. Smt. A.K. Ahuja
Secretary, Education
Government of Rajasthan
23. Dr. B.M.L. Tiwari
Director, Higher Education

Government of Uttar Pradesh

24. Dr. P.K. Chaudhuri
DPI and Ex-officio Secretary
Government of West Bengal
25. Shri Y.N. Chaturvedi
Secretary, UGC
26. Dr. P.B. Tripathy
Joint Director, UGC
27. Shri S.G. Mankad
Joint Secretary
Department of Education
Ministry of HRD
28. Shri M.P.M. Kutty
Director
Department of Education
Ministry of HRD

Recommendations and Observations of the CABE on Higher Education

The Report of the Working Group on Higher Education was presented by Shri C.T. Benjamin, Rapporteur of the group. In the course of discussion, the following decisions were taken:

(a) In regard to the Gnanam Committee Report, the State Governments should formulate their views and send them to the Ministry within three months. The Chairman, CABE should set up a CABE Committee to consider the recommendations of the Gnanam Committee Report keeping in view the comments of the State Governments, and have the Report of the Committee placed before CABE at the next meeting.

(b) The Chairman may also set up a CABE Committee on Distance Education to examine steps to be taken for promotion of distance education in the country, including the role of IGNOU *vis-a-vis* the State Open Universities, as well as the need for greater use of radio and TV for promotion of distance education.

The CABE approved the Report of the working group with the additional decisions as above.

22

REPORT OF CABE WORKING GROUP ON TECHNICAL EDUCATION (1991)*

Prof. D. Swaminathan, Member, Planning Commission, chaired the meeting of the Working Group.

Prof. B. B. Chopane, Director of Technical Education, Maharashtra acted as Rapporteur.

In his introductory remarks, Prof. Swaminathan emphasised the need to view technical education system in the total perspective of the socio-economic and environmental development of the country, integrated with the production system and service sectors and with active participation of all sections of the society. In this context, he identified a few parameters with which technical education development is to be viewed. They are:

- Treating Technical Education as a continuum.
- Access and equity to all sections of community including SC/STs and women.
- Relevance of the programmes and courses.
- Employability including self-employment.
- Cost effectiveness – minimising the cost and maximising the result.

He further stressed the importance of reducing the subsidy from the exchequer to the higher and technical education system to the extent possible, enhancing the scope for generating internal resources through appropriate resource mobilisation. For this purpose, he enumerated the different approaches such as profitable exploitation of research findings and pooling, sharing and optimising available facilities in institu-

* Ministry of Human Resource Development, New Delhi.

tions as well as research organisations and industry. There was also a need for up-dating the infrastructure and information system. The Chairman also highlighted the necessity for strengthening/providing facilities for training and re-training of teachers of higher technical institutions and also for adequate and active linkages among institutions, industries, universities and research organisations through a system of symbiosis. He also stressed the need to develop and expand part time education and distance education for the employed, who missed such opportunities earlier. In this connection appropriate courses at diploma, degree and postgraduate levels need to be developed.

After a general discussion on the issues facing technical education, the Working Group took up the three items on the agenda for consideration:

Item No. 11. Regulation of fees and admission (Prohibition of capitation fee), self-financing, provision of financial support to needy and talented students.

The Group discussed the item in detail and also the present position in various States. The Group recognised the need for adequate resource mobilisation to reduce the high level of subsidy being given from the Government ex-chequer towards recurring cost of Technical Education and for further developments. To this extent, it was felt necessary that the fee structure in various (State institutions) need upward revision. However, this enhancement may be done suitably depending upon and as decided by concerned States and if necessary in stages. In the case of self-financing and non-aided institutions, a realistic maximum limit may be prescribed by the AICTE, keeping in view, elimination of malpractices like collection of huge sums of money as donation, capitation fee, etc. The Group also emphasised the need for AICTE to incorporate/invoke punitive provisions to prevent such malpractices altogether. Hence the Group recommended that —

- Fee structure in Government, Government aided and University institutions should be enhanced and, if necessary, in stages, so as to augment resources.
- A realistic maximum limit of fees should be prescribed by AICTE for self-financing Engineering Colleges and Polytechnics, keeping in view the elimination of collection of capitation fees in any form altogether.

- Punitive measures may be enforced by AICTE/State Governments for curbing malpractices such as collection of capitation fee, etc.
- With regard to admissions, the norms prescribed by AICTE should be followed by all institutions so that quality of standards could be improved. This will also eliminate the malpractice of giving admission to undeserving students.
- Institutions should strive to mobilise resources, generated internally through sponsored research, consultancy, technology transfer, continuing education programme, testing, etc. which should meet at least 10 per cent of the recurring costs.
- To encourage private investment to the Technical Education System; the amount invested/donated, may be exempted from income-tax.

Item No. 12. Making AICTE more effective

Shri I.B. Sangal, Additional Secretary, AICTE explained the various steps taken during the past one year to make the AICTE effective. Dr. K. Gopalan, Member-Secretary, AICTE supplemented the points. The Group noted with satisfaction, the progress in this regard and also the steps taken by AICTE and its Regional Committees, Universities and the State Governments for the effective implementation of the AICTE Act.

Further in order to make AICTE's role more effective, the Working Group recommended that:

- The Chairman, Vice-chairman and the Member Secretary should be appointed on full-time basis at the earliest.
- The staff structure at the Headquarters of the AICTE and at the Regional Committees should be adequately strengthened without any further delay.
- In order that the States are able to control and develop technical education in the changed circumstances the State Boards/ Councils of Technical Education should be made autonomous/Statutory.
- The AICTE should take over the various schemes which are at present being handled by the Bureau of Technical Education.

Item No.13. Review of implementation of the World Bank Assisted Project on Technical Education

Prof. S.K. Shrivastava, Joint Educational Adviser (T) and National Project Director of the Project enumerated various aspects of the project and the present position in this regard. He highlighted the need for the State to optimally utilise the resources provided under the World Bank Project. It is expected that States and Union Territories which are not covered at present in phases I and II, will be covered after the first annual review of the project, taking advantage of the built-in flexibility.

The Group deliberated on the item and recommended that the States should ensure the following:

(1) Scarce and valuable resources made available are optimally used.
(2) Construction programmes are completed in the stipulated time and with quality as planned.
(3) Purchase and installation of equipment is completed in time and quality ensured.
(4) Staff is appointed in time and training is arranged adequately and effectively.
(5) A proper monitoring system is developed and ensured to get accurate feed-back for taking corrective measures in time.
(6) Special attention is paid to increase enrolment of women students so as to double the intake from the present level by the end of the project.

Participants in the Group on Technical Education

Chairman

1. Prof. D. Swaminathan
   Member Planning Commission

Rapporteurs/Members

2. Prof. B.B. Chopane
   Director of Technical Education
   Government of Maharashtra
3. Shri A. K. Padmapati
   Director of Technical Education
   Government of Assam

4. Dr. P. Baskaran
   Director of Technical Education
   Government of Bihar
5. Shri A. K. Srivastava
   Director of Technical Education
   Government of Goa
6. Shri Balwant Singh
   Secretary (Sc. and Tech.)
   Government of Gujarat
7. Shri D. M. Talwar
   Additional Director
   Technical Education
   Government of Haryana
8. Dr. R. Jayaraman
   Director of Technical Education
   Government of Kerala
9. Shri C.A. Keswani
   Joint Director of Technical Education
   Government of Madhya Pradesh
10. Shri Lalawia
    Director
    Higher and Technical Education
    Government of Mizoram
11. Shri S.K. Handa
    Director
    Technical Education and Industrial Training
    Government of Punjab
12. Shri G.P. Upadhyaya
    Deputy Secretary
    Department of Education
    Government of Sikkim
13. Shri Sudhir Sharma
    Secretary, Education
    Government of Tripura
14. Shri L.N. Mishra
    Joint Secretary
    Technical Education (West Zone)
    Government of Uttar Pradesh
15. Shri D.C. Das
    Director, Technical Education

Government of West Bengal

16. Shri V.S. Malhotra
Director, Technical Education
Chandigarh Administration
17. Shri V. Narayanan
ADTE
Delhi Administration
18. Shri D. Taneja
Registrar, B.T.E.
Delhi Administration
19. Shri M.S. Krishna Murthy
Additional D.T.E.
Government of Pondicherry
20. Dr. K. Gopalan
Member-Secretary, AICTE
Department of Education
Ministry of H.R.D.
21. Prof. S.K. Srivastava
Joint Educational Adviser (T)
Department of Education
Ministry of H.R.D.
22. Shri I.B. Sangal
Joint Educational Adviser (T)
and Additional Secretary, AICTE
Department of Education
Ministry of H.R.D.
23. Shri S.D. Awale
Additional Apprenticeship Adviser
Department of Education
Ministry of H.R.D.
24. Shri S. Tayal
Director
Department of Education
Ministry of H.R.D.
25. Shri M.L. Gilautra
Assistant Educational Advisor (T)
Department of Education
Ministry of H.R.D.
26. Shri S.K. Jindal
Assistant Educational Advisor (T)

Department of Education
Ministry of H.R.D.

27. Dr. C.T. Mahajan
Assistant Educational Adviser (T)
S.R.O.
Ministry of H.R.D.
28. Prof. A. Ramakrishnan
Director
Board of Apprentice Training
Department of Education
Ministry of H.R.D.
29. Prof. G.S. Chandran
Prof. TTTI, Bhopal
Department of Education
Ministry of H.R.D.

Recommendations and Observations of the CABE on Technical Education

The Report of the Working Group on Technical Education was presented by its rapporteur, Prof. B.B. Chopne. In the course of discussion some members drew attention towards the urgent need to attract and return qualified teachers in engineering. Steps need to be taken to improve the general quality of engineering teachers and to provide them better avenues for career advancement. The Board noted that the All India Council for Technical Education was already seized of this matter and that necessary action is being taken by it. The report of the working group was adopted by the CABE.

23

REPORT OF CABE WORKING GROUP ON EDUCATION OF WOMEN AND OTHER DISADVANTAGED GROUPS LIKE SC/ST/MINORITIES ETC. (1991)*

The Group on Education for Women and Other Disadvantaged Groups like SC/ST/Minorities, etc. constituted by Central Advisory Board of Education to consider items of the agenda on the subject, namely Item No. 18 met on 8 March, 1991 under the Chairmanship of Shri H.S. Lyngdoh, Education Minister of Meghalaya. Shri A.K. Mishra, Secretary, Education, Government of Orissa acted as rapporteur.

The Chairman of the Group highlighted the issues to be considered. He stated that the education for weaker sections must occupy highest priority in any programme of education. He further stated that this was the right time to make concrete and practical recommendations so that they can be included in the Eighth Five Year Plan. He referred to the Acharya Ramamurti Committee Report and also other reports on Scheduled Castes and Scheduled Tribes and Minorities. In the light of the discussions and in the background of the available reports and data on the subject, the recommendations of the Group were finalised.

While discussing the specific problems of women, scheduled castes and scheduled tribes and minority communities some common recommendations emerged in order to improve their access to education. They are:

- An area intensive approach needs to be adopted in order to focus on extremely backward regions and pockets where literacy rate is very low.

---

* Ministry of Human Resource Development, New Delhi.

- Certain sub-castes, tribes, communities need special attention because literacy rate among them is extremely low. Women in such communities are more disadvantaged. The Group, therefore, recommends special community focus.
- The Group took note of the fact that due to shortage of funds, most State Governments are not in a position to introduce special programmes for disadvantaged groups. The need to continue and to expand centrally sponsored schemes for women, SC/ST, minorities was emphasized.
- Specific measures need to be taken for the empowerment of backward communities and women. Total literacy campaigns and other campaigns for education should begin with awareness generation. The need to create a demand for education from the community was emphasized.
- Participatory planning where village education committees are actively involved in monitoring educational activities in villages and micro-level planning, especially taking the block as a unit was emphasized by the Group.
- Recommendations (1) – (102) of the Report of the Committee for Review of National Policy on Education 1986 was endorsed by the Group.
- On-going schemes for women, SC/ST and minority communities have to be evaluated and closely monitored. The impact of such schemes in ensuring access to education needs to be studied and on-going schemes suitably modified to reach the goal of universal/elementary education.

It was noted that any investment in education of women, SC/ST and minority communities should be seen as an investment in the development of the country. Educational opportunities should be geared as far as possible, towards employment, for this will encourage increased participation in the educational process. Positive discrimination in favour of such communities could be explored.

Women's Education

At the outset, the Group discussed the reasons for low literacy among woman in the country and focused on the problems which prevent young girls from attending schools. Among other reasons, special emphasis was laid on the social attitudes of people, responsibility shouldered by the girl-child specially in collecting water, fuel and in looking after her siblings. The regional variations especially between areas like North East on one hand where the position of women is different from regions like Uttar Pradesh and Bihar were noted. Therefore, the first recommendation of the Sub-Group was that special efforts should be made to understand the region's specific problems of women and girls in order to design special inputs. All recommendations should thus be seen in area and culture specific context.

2. The position of women in minority communities was an important focus of the Group. It was noted that literacy rate among Scheduled Castes and Scheduled Tribes and other minorities was much lower than the literacy rate among forward areas/communities. In some areas, the literacy rate among Scheduled Castes women is lower than one per cent. The Group, therefore, recommended that the problems of girls education among these communities should receive special attention and area/community specific strategies may have to be devised.

3. Most young girls, especially in poor families share a very large burden of household responsibilities. In this context, the need to provide child care facilities and ECCE centres alongwith primary schools was emphasised.

4. Focusing on problem of high drop-out rates among girls and their non-participation in the formal school system the Group was of the opinion that the formal system needs to be non-formalised. Possibility for operating different shifts for girls and working children could be explored, along with reduction of school hours, wherever necessary. In order to achieve universal elementary education a special Action Plan may have to be prepared for addressing the problem of girl's education. If necessary special funds could be earmarked for such an initiative.

5. The Group strongly recommended the need to evaluate the impact of special provisions, schemes and projects made for women over the past 40 years. An understanding of the impact of the Scheme could help policy-makers to make specific recommendations. Area specific special programmes will have to be devised after a thorough study of those regions where female literacy is extremely low.

6. The Group was of the opinion that a Council to monitor women's education should be set up under the Chairmanship of the Chief Minister with senior officers as members. This Council should have a Chief Executive who could systematically monitor progress of different schemes, ensure target is achieved and above all ensure

resources are allocated for women's education.

7. The Group recommended the need to have awareness generation programmes which could create a demand for education for women and also encourage parents to send their girls to schools. Additional facilities or infrastructure alone cannot ensure increased participation. In this context, the Group took note of the pilot programme initiated by the Department of Education, Ministry of Human Resource Development – Mahila Samakhya.

8. The Group endorsed the recommendations made in agenda item No. 18 on Women's Education. The Group noted that the specific recommendations of the NPE-1986 are still relevant. Special mention was made on the following items:

- Increased women's access to vocational, technical and professional education.
- Preference for women in recruitment of teachers.
- Special Polytechnics for women.
- Special hostel facilities for women.
- 100 per cent assistance for NFE centres for girls.
- Schemes of freeships and scholarships.
- Special focus on the campaign approach to encourage women's participation in adult literacy programmes.
- Mahila Samakhya Programme as an important pilot programme.

9. The Group also took note of the main recommendations of the Report of the Committee for Review of National Policy on Education, 1986. Special mention was made to the following recommendations of that Committee :

- Need to link girls access to elementary education with ECCE facilities.
- Decentralised and participative mode of planning to address policy measures to region and community specific problems.
- Need to encourage vocational and technical education.
- Increase the number of women teachers in schools to at least 50 per cent and provide necessary facilities to them.
- Awareness generation programmes as an important input in the Adult Education.
- Earmarking funds for girls' education.

10. Rounding off the discussion, the Group reiterated the need to focus on areas and region specific problems especially to encourage women's education. Culture attitudes and practices vary from region to region. Therefore, planning for education should be sensitive to the above context.

Education for Scheduled Castes and Scheduled Tribes

Profile

According to 1981 Census, Scheduled Castes and Scheduled Tribes constitute 23.67 per cent of the total population of the country. Majority of the SC/ST population is still backward not only socially, economically but also educationally. The experience of the development planning as undertaken over the successive Five Year plans has been that the overall development of Scheduled Castes and Scheduled Tribes cannot be achieved only through economic development. Their educational development is of foremost importance to bring them into the main stream of national life. For them, education is an input not only for their economic development but also for promoting in them self-confidence and inner strength to face the new challenges. They have been the targets of economic exploitation and social oppression. They have fallen victims to the exploitation of the middlemen, merchants and money-lenders on account of their illiteracy, ignorance and superstition. The need for their educational development, therefore, assumes importance to save them from all types of exploitation and to help them in their all-round development. Although the spread of education in the country has been quite fast during the last decades, the gaps in the educational development of Scheduled Castes and Scheduled Tribes still persist.

The literacy rate amongst Scheduled Castes has though gradually increased and it is now 21.38 per cent, yet this is not a significant success. The literacy rate in STs is 16.4 per cent. The literacy rates in the females in SCs and STs are very low being 11 per cent in SCs and 8 per cent for STs. The literacy gaps between SC/ST and the rest of population as may be seen from Table 23.1 have rather been widening.

TABLE 23.1: Literacy Gap between SC/ST and the Rest of Population

Year	SC	ST	Rest of Population	Gap SC	Gap ST
1	2	3	4	5	6
1961	10.27	8.53	27.86	18	19
1971	14.67	11.30	33.80	19	22
1981	21.38	16.35	41.22	20	26

The literacy rate amongst Scheduled Castes in Bihar is the lowest (10.40%) according to 1981 census. This is followed by Rajasthan (14.04%). The position is extremely unsatisfactory in the case of females, which is 10.9 per cent as against 29.4 per cent for others. There are 48 districts in the country where the Scheduled Castes female literacy rate is less than one per cent, stooping to as low as 0.48 per cent in Barmer district of Rajasthan (as against 4.75 per cent amongst others). There are some communities which have hardly any literate persons amongst them. Among the recognised educationally backward States are Andhra Pradesh, Orissa, Assam, Bihar, Jammu and Kashmir, Madhya Pradesh, Rajasthan, Uttar Pradesh and West Bengal. In respect of literacy rate, enrolment ratio and drop-out rate, SCs and STs are far worse than the non-SCs/STs.

The main causes of wastage in education among SCs/STs have been identified as their social disability, persistent poverty, poor nutritional standards, poor home conditions with unhealthy environments and inadequate accommodation, apprehensions of rejections on account of perpetual exploitation and failure, internalised feelings of disappointing experiences in life and as a consequence the overall apathy towards education, especially when children in their families are treated as economic assets.

The State Governments are seized of the magnitude of the problem and have launched many schemes to improve the educational standards of Scheduled Castes and Scheduled Tribes. Bulk of the schemes at pre-matric stage are with the respective State Governments. These schemes include pre-matric scholarship, boarding grants, hostel facilities, free supply of books, stationery and uniforms, mid-day meals and attendance scholarships. The contents of the schemes vary from State to State.

Apart from these State sector schemes, there are some Centrally

Sponsored Schemes being handled by the Ministry of Welfare. These schemes include post-matric scholarships for SCs/STs, pre-matric scholarships to those children whose parents are engaged in unclean occupations, book banks to SC/ST students in medical and engineering colleges, construction of buildings for SC/ST boys and girls hostels, coaching and allied schemes for SC/ST candidates and national overseas scholarships scheme. The Department of Education have also taken up a scheme of remedial coaching for SC/ST students in subjects like Maths and Sciences in which they are generally weak for classes IX to XII to enable them to face examinations confidently and also to prepare them for entering into the professional courses like medical and engineering.

Recommendations

In order to ensure speedy and overall educational development of SC/STs, following steps are suggested:

1. All out efforts should be made to build up a strong educational base of SC/ST children at the primary and pre-primary level. To achieve this, adequate funds should be earmarked for the education sector under Special Component Plan/Tribal Sub-plan of the States. UTs and also of the Department of Education.

2. Special drives should be organised at the beginning of every academic session to enroll all school-age male and female children belonging to Scheduled Castes and Scheduled Tribes. For this purpose, the official agencies outside the regular Education Department and also the voluntary organisations preferably with larger representation of these communities may be associated.

3. In all the SC and ST habitations with viable population of school-age children there should invariably be a primary school. For school-age children of poor and destitute scattered SC population there should be Ashram schools. Ashram schools for STs that are already in existence should be further expanded. To supplement these efforts. 'Literacy Centres' should also be established. All such Ashram schools should fit into the environment of the habitations in linguistic/ethnic/community lines. Wherever teachers belonging to these communities are available they should be posted in these Ashram schools and also other schools situated in areas with concentration of SC and ST population.

4. The schools in SC and ST habitations should be equipped with

all infrastructural facilities.

5. There should be provision of adequate incentives in the form of scholarships, uniforms, text-books, stationery and midday meals. All the Scheduled Caste and Scheduled Tribe children studying in pre-matric classes should be given scholarships.

6. The above facilities are particularly necessary for the children of the vulnerable groups among Scheduled Castes such as sweepers, scavengers, flayers, tanners, bonded-labourers, nomadic/semi-nomadic and denotified tribes.

7. The indigent families among SCs/STs should be given some incentives as a compensation for opportunity cost to send their children (particularly girls) to schools rather than engaging them in some gainful employment to earn their subsistence income. This would also avoid drop-outs of these children at the primary and elementary levels.

8. The Centrally Sponsored Scheme of pre-matric scholarships for the children of those engaged in unclean occupations should be extended to cover the students in classes I to VI and the day scholars also. It should be extended to children of all vulnerable groups.

9. Under the Scheme of post-matric scholarships, the rates should be revised periodically keeping in view the increase in the cost of living index.

10. The restriction of providing scholarships only to two children of SC/ST parents should be removed in view of the lower levels of education in them. Income ceiling of parents prescribed for parents in this regard should be enhanced to be Rs. 50,000 per annum as per the present cost of living index.

11. A merit scholarship scheme for students who secure 60 per cent and above marks in the last annual examination should be introduced.

12. Arrangement for sanctioning and disbursing scholarship should be reviewed to ensure their prompt payment etc.

13. Under the scheme of book banks for SCs/STs it would be advisable to give a set of books to each of SC/ST student.

14. As has been done by Mizoram Government, local educated youth should be made to participate in the literacy programmes and they should be provided adequate remuneration for doing this work.

15. The recommendations on the common school system of Education Commission reiterated by Ramamurti Committee should be given weightage.

16. As far as possible, adult literacy centres should be established in SC/ST habitations so as to attract more and more illiterate adults to

these communities. There should be adequate post-literacy centres to follow up the results achieved.

17. Adequate reservation for SCs/STs should be provided in the public and private convents and the expenditure involved in admitting SC/ST poor children in these schools should be met by the Government.

18. There should be earmarked opportunities for SCs and STs in all courses and at all levels of education in proportion to SC and ST population percentage. Wherever necessary, there should be special attention on them and adequate measures should be taken to ensure that these recomendations are fulfilled.

19. There should be Advisory Bodies to review and oversee the implementation of the education programmes for SCs/STs at block district, State and Central levels. SC/ST people should be adequately represented in these bodies.

20. Wherever there are tribal communities in adequate number, there should be attempts to make them learn in their mother tongue at primary levels.

21. Whereas teachers are not available in schools located near SC/ST localities, crash programme under a Centrally-sponsored Programme should be given to eligible persons from SCs and STs and the eligible among them should be appointed in these schools.

22. The delivery system should be streamlined and made effective.

23. In sports activities, it should be ensured that in those sports and games which are an integral part of the tribal way of life such as archery and javeline, the ST boys and ST girls from amongst students should be given additional incentives and encouragements.

24. The existing Central or Centrally-sponsored Schemes should be continued and also expanded wherever possible to ensure effective implementation of all recommendations found above.

25. The philosophy of Dr. Ambedkar should form part of school and college curriculum.

Minorities Education

The Group reviewed the Report of the action taken on the recommendations of the 45th Conference of the CABE held at New Delhi on July 6-7, 1989. The Group is firmly of the view that a well coordinated, fully funded, time-bound and a closely monitored programme specifically designed and to bring the backward minority communities into the educational mainstream should be evolved and implemented. On the basis of available data and reports on the subject the Group has made the following recommendations.

1. Special Plan for Backward Minorities (SPBM)

A Sub-Plan should be formulated for the educational uplift of the educationally backward minorities on the lines of Special Component Plan and Tribal Sub-Plan.

2. Data Relating to Educational Status of Minorities

The Group observed that in the absence of reliable data with regard to educational status of minorities realistic planning has not been possible. It accordingly recommends that community-wise data in this regard should be made available to the public.

3. Centrally-sponsored Schemes for Educationally Backward Minorities

The Central Government should make use of the concurrency provision in education and play a vital role to make its recommendations incumbent on the State Governments to implement the programmes on uniform basis throughout the country. There should be some Centrally-sponsored Schemes for minorities.

4. Educational Mapping of Minority Concentration Areas

The list of 41 minority concentration districts should be reviewed and those districts, particularly in the East and North-East, which were left out should be included. Detailed educational mapping should be carried out in minority concentration districts to identify the deficiencies in educational infrastructure and to draw time-bound action plan.

5. Women's Education

Schools and hostels for women should be given first priority in all future programmes of opening of schools. Arrangements for subsidised transport in towns and other incentives like uniforms, mid-day meals should be given to the girls in minority concentration areas.

6. Incentives to Poor Students

The alarming rate of drop-out among the minority students should be checked by specially designed measures. Incentives should be given to poor minority students in the shape of freeships, stipends and uniform. They should also be given pre-matric and post-matric scholarships.

7. Remedial Coaching

Most of the student drawn from the backward minority communities are grievously handicapped because many of them are first generation learners with the result that they get neither academic environment nor academic support at home. The Group, therefore, feels that provision of remedial coaching at class VI and above to the weaker students of minority communities is absolutely essential in lifting these communities out of the morass of education backwardness.

8. Crash Programme

A time-bound crash programme of school improvement with an in-built mechanism for covering minority concentration areas with the on-going programmes of Operation Blackboard, Non-Formal Education and District Institute of Education and Training should be implemented on priority basis.

9. Instruction in Mother-tongue

(a) Primary Education: The Group observed that the present arrangements for instruction in the mother-tongue at the primary stage are grossly inadequate. The Group, therefore, recommends that the States and Union Territories and the Local Bodies should make all necessary arrangements for imparting instruction in the Mother-tongue at the primary stage. The Group also recommends that the recommendations of Gujral Committee for promotion of Urdu on primary education be accepted for Urdu and extended to other minority languages.

(b) Secondary Education: The Group recommends that the recommendations of the Gujral Committee on promotion on Urdu in respect of Secondary Education should be also accepted for Urdu and extended

to other minority languages.

(c) Training of Teachers: The Group also felt that it is absolutely necessary to ensure on a continual basis the training of teachers in minority languages and their utilisation for the purpose for which they had been trained. A Centrally-sponsored Scheme for appointment of language teachers, fully funded by the Government of India, should be launched in the Eighth Five Year Plan.

(d) Timely Availability of Text-Books: By suitable arrangements it should be ensured that text-books are made available to the school students on time in their own language along with text-books in English/Hindi.

(e) Three Language Formula: No programme for educational development among minorities can succeed unless adequate and effective arrangements are made not only for providing instruction to children from minorities in their first language (mother-tongue) at the primary level but also at the secondary level under the Three Language Formula. The distortions that have crept into the Formula over the years to the disadvantage of Urdu speaking people and speakers of other minority languages should be straightened.

10. Continuous Evaluation of School Text-Books

This Group is of the view that the evaluation of text-books should be a continuous programme both at the Centre and the States. It should be effectively monitored periodically and members of minority communities should be associated with the process of evaluation and review.

11. Improvement of Education in Traditional Institutions

Traditional institutions like Madrasas should be encouraged and assisted to include Science, Mathematics and English in their curriculum. This is necessary to bring them into the educational mainstream of India. A Centrally-sponsored Scheme in this regard should be launched.

12. Training in Crafts

As provided for in the Programme of Action, 1986 technical institutes should be opened in areas predominantly populated by artisans. The latter's children should be allowed to upgrade their inherited skills by availing of these facilities to the extent of 80 per cent. Similar preferences may operate in case of admission to polytechnics.

13. Community Polytechnics

The Group observed that the Department of Education has already established 20 community polytechnics in minority concentration areas but they do not cover all the 41 districts of minority concentration identified in the POA of which only 16 districts have been covered so far. The remaining 25 districts which have not yet been covered under the scheme of Community Polytechnics should also be brought under their coverage before the end of the Eighth Five Year Plan.

14. Coaching for Competitive Examinations for Minorites

The Group observed that the scheme for pre-examination coaching operated by the UGC through universities/colleges has not made a dent into the problem so far primarily because of certain weakness in the scheme. The implementation of the scheme needs to be reviewed effectively on continuing basis and remedial action taken from time to time with a view to ensuring that the benefit of the scheme goes to the target group.

The Group also observed that the Ministry of Welfare has recently launched a scheme for setting up of pre-examination coaching/training centres through minority voluntary organisations. It is necessary that the pitfalls observed in the implementation of this scheme, and the implementation should be closely monitored.

The Group further recommends that Open Universities including the IGNOU should establish distance education programmes for imparting special coaching to the minorities.

15. Recognition and Encouragement of Voluntary Efforts

Recognition and encouragement of voluntary effort for education of backward minorities is essential. Government can, in this context, act as a catalyst. Socially-oriented and public spirited persons in the communities should receive due recognition and impetus; for in the ultimate analysis, it is the voluntary effort that can bring about a real educational and social transformation. Federations and Associations of

Minority-managed institutions should be encouraged and actively associated with the functioning of minorities education and implementation of programmes of educational uplift.

16. Monitoring

A strict and vigilant monitoring of the recommended programmes for minorities education is absoluetly essential if these are to make a real impact.

17. Amendment of Prime Minister's 15-Point Programme for Minority Welfare

The Group noted that at present the 15-Point Programme does not incorporate any point relating to general education for minorities. Accordingly it recommends that the Programme may be recast so as to include a specific point of general education so that it gets necessary impetus.

Other Backward Classes

The Group recommends that facilities extended to SC and ST communities in the matter of promotion of education should be *mutatis-mutandis* extended to the children of socially, educationally and economically backward classes. A suitably formulated Centrally-sponsored Scheme in this regard should be implemented.

Specially Disadvantaged Groups
(Most needy and most neglected)

This group consists of:

(1) Working Children
(i) Children engaged in family jobs/Mostly rural.
(ii) Children in small menial unskilled jobs/Mostly Urban Slum.
(iii) Children in industries/Rural and Small Towns.

(2) Handicapped Children
(i) Physically handicapped;
(ii) Socially handicapped like street children, children of beggars and prostitutes' children in custody, children of migrant labour, etc.

Recommendations

(i) Reaching children through alternative modes of education, flexible hours etc.

(ii) All facilities extended to the children of SC/ST should be provided to these children at least up to the level of primary education.

(iii) Coordination with other Ministries like Labour, Industry, etc. for–

(a) Compulsory provision of teaching and learning time during children's work hours;

(b) The centres should be located in the place of work;

(c) Expenses should be borne by the employer and the State; and

(d) Close monitoring of the system.

(iv) Strong links between functional literacy/non-formal educational programmes with mainstream educational programme. Multiple entry point in the mainstream education.

(v) Strengthening of voluntary efforts and enabling them to play their watch-dog and conscientization role effectively.

(vi) Employment/Income guaranteed linkages with education.

(vii) Provision of vocational guidance and counselling.

(viii) Role of mass media and traditional media to highlight the educational problems of these groups.

(ix) In-depth study of this problem for effective understanding and intervention by the State.

Participants in the Group on Education of Women and Other Disadvantaged Sections Including SC, ST, Minorities etc.

Chairman

1. Shri H.S. Lyngdoh
Education Minister
Meghalaya.

Rapporteurs/Members

2. Shri A.K. Mishra
Secretary, Education
Government of Orissa,
3. Shri Ram Dayal Munda
Professor, Ranchi University

4. Dr. (Smt.) Saraswati Swain
   Kalyan Nagar, Cuttack
   Orissa.
5. Shri K.V. Madanan
   Director of Public Instruction
   Government of Kerala
6. Shri R.N. Datta
   Additional Secretary of Public Instruction
   Government of Meghalaya
7. Dr. H.L. Malsawma
   Secretary (Scholarships and Higher Education)
   Government of Mizoram
8. Dr. M.L. Sachdeva
   Deputy Director (Vocational Education)
   Government of Punjab
9. Shri V. Venkatachalam
   Special Secretary, Education
   Government of Uttar Pradesh
10. Shri S.C. Behar
    Consultant, NIEPA
11. Shri T. Munivenkatappa
    Joint Secretary
    Ministry of Welfare
12. Shri M.S. Pandit
    Joint Secretary
    (Minorities and Backward Classes)
    Ministry of Welfare
13. Shri Ram Singh
    Director
    Ministry of Welfare
14. Shri G. Balachandran
    Deputy Secretary
    Ministry of Welfare
15. Dr. Manjula Chakravarty
    Deputy Director
    W.D. Division, NIPCED
    Department of Women and Child Development
    Ministry of H.R.D.
16. Smt. V. Lakshmi Reddi
    Director (Planning)

Department of Education
Ministry of H.R.D.

17. Shri K.K. Khullar
Consultant
Department of Education
Ministry of H.R.D.
18. Smt. Vimla Ramachandran
Project Director (MS)
Department of Education
Ministry of H.R.D.
19. Shri Jai Ram Singh
Deputy Educational Adviser (P)
Department of Education
Ministry of H.R.D.
20. Shri G. Balachandran
Deputy Director
Department of Education
Ministry of H.R.D.

Observations and Recommendations of the CABE on SC, ST, Minorities and Women

Report of the Working Group on Women's Education and on Disadvantaged Groups like SC, ST, Minorities etc., was presented by Shri A.K. Misra, Rapporteur of the Working Group.

Dr. Adiseshiah criticised the clubbing of Women with SCs, STs and other disadvantaged groups. It was agreed that in future women's education would be deliberated upon by a separate working group. The CABE noted that the report of the working group had endorsed several recommendations (1 to 102) of the Report of the Acharya Ramamurti Committee. As the Board had not yet considered the Acharya Ramamurti Committee and a CABE Committee is being set up to go into the recommendations of Ramamurti Committee, it was considered inappropriate at this stage to endorse the recommendations of the Review Committee and thereby pre-empt due consideration of the Report. Hence the working group's report was adopted with the deletion of those portions which endorsed the recommendations of the Ramamurti Committee.

24

REPORT OF CABE WORKING GROUP ON POLICY AND PLANNING (1991)*

The Group was chaired by Shri K. Chandrasekharan, Minister of Education, Kerala. Shri Ashok Saikia, Secretary and Commissioner of Education, Government of Assam acted as Rapporteur. The Group considered Agenda items 3, 19, 20 and 21.

2. The Group considered the manner in which the report of the NPE Review Committee is to be processed. The Group noted that there is a certain degree of uncertainty in regard to the educational policy and is of the view that this uncertainly needs to be dispelled at the earliest. The Group recommends the constitution by the Chairman of the CABE of a sub-committee to study in depth the report of the NPE Review Committee. The Group also recommends that the State Governments and other related bodies be given time till the end of April to send their comments on the NPE Review Committee report. The CABE committee should take into account these views in formulating its proposals.

3. The Group considered in depth the resource requirements of the education sector. The Group welcomes the proposition set out in the Eighth Plan approach document that the developmental pattern and process should be explicity reoriented so as to enable everyone, *inter alia*, to have access to education and strongly urges that this proposition be adequately reflected in the Plan allocations. Ever since the Kothari Commission made a fervent plea for progressively raising the level of expenditure on education to 6 per cent of the national income, the 6 per cent norm has become a national goal reiterated again and again in many policy documents, including the NPE, 1986. The Group strongly pleads the immediate implementation of the 6 per cent norm.

* Ministry of Human Resource Development, New Delhi.

Keeping this in view, significant increase in allocation for the education sector should be made by the States and the Centre in the Eighth Five Year Plan. Without a sizeable infusion of additional resources it would not be possible to translate into practice the laudable objective of reorienting and restructuring the educational pattern and process. The Group strongly feels that this would be a timely step against the backdroup of the stirring developments in the field of adult literacy and the nation-wide resolve to universalise elementary education in order to accelerate social transformation in the shortest possible time.

4. The Group discussed the question of mobilising additional resources for education by increasing fees, efficient management of resources, reduction of subsidies, by greater community participation and through appropriate tax incentives through amendments to the Income Tax Act. For example, the scope of deductions under the Income Tax Act can be extended to cover donations to educational institutions on 100 per cent basis; incentives can be provided to support research in science and technology, humanities and social sciences on par with R & D. The Group also recommends that adequate incentives should be provided by the State and Central Governments to educational institutions to raise resources through consultancies and similar services. The present practice of deducting such income from the block grants acts as a severe disincentive. The Group also notes that while these resources can supplement to some extent they do not detract from the strong need for adequate budgetary support by the States and Centre for the education sector as envisaged in the earlier paragraphs. To supplement Government effort, corporate bodies should also undertake educational promotion activities from their own resources.

5. The Group takes note of the attempt of the Department of Education, Government of India, to tap external funds in the field of basic education from bilateral sources as well as multilateral agencies. While endorsing this effort the group is of the view that external funding should be an additionality to the resources for education, that the projects must be in total conformity with national policies, strategies and programmes, that the project formulation should be the responsibility of the Central/State Governments/other national agencies, that project formulation should be a process of capacity building, that the projects must be drawn up on innovative lines, emphasising people's participation, improvement of quality and equality of education and a substantial upgradation of facilities. The Group notes that in the implementation of the externally aided projects the State Governments

are handicapped by the stipulation requiring the States to first incur expenditure from their own resources and claim reimbursement subsequently. The Group would recommend a specially earmarked ways and means advance to the States for the implementation of the externally aided projects including the World Bank assisted Technician Education Programme. Further the outlay on externally aided projects should be additionality to the State Plan in the Education sector.

6. The Group would recommend that district be the unit for determining educational backwardness, and the benefits accruing to the educationally backward States should be extended to the educationally backward districts. Moreover, the hill, desert, remote rural areas, urban slums as well as tribal areas should be provided special Central Assistance.

7. The Group appreciated the support provided by the Central Government for the wide-ranging HRD activities for the western border areas under the Border Area Development Education Programme (BADEP). The Group was apprised of the serious resource constraint being faced by the States of the north-eastern region and Sikkim and also of the need to enhance investment in HRD activities in these States. As the objectives of BADEP are equally applicable to the North-Eastern States and Sikkim, the Group strongly recommends extension of BADEP to these States with necessary enhancement of outlays or to start with immediate effect, another Scheme for the North-Eastern States and Sikkim taking into consideration their difficulties.

8. On a review of the Centrally-sponsored Schemes, the Group came to the conclusion that the Schemes in the education sector mainly relate to extension of the facility of education to the deprived sections and improvement of quality of education. Considering that education is a concurrent subject and concurrency entails sharing of responsibility between Centre and States the Group is of the view that strong Central support to major programmes in priority areas of education is a categorical imperative. The States need to be reassured that adequate and sustained support from the Centre would be forthcoming. The Group strongly recommends that the Centrally-sponsored Schemes should not only be continued but also strengthened and widened in the Eighth Five Year Plan. The Group would suggest that the Department of Education, Government of India should review, in consultation with the States, the existing Centrally-sponsored Schemes with a view to improving their effectiveness. The Centrally-sponsored Schemes should have an element of flexibility to fulfil the individual needs of

the States. Moreover, the Group would suggest that in consultation with the States the Central Govt. should initiate new Centrally-sponsored Schemes in areas which have remained uncovered during the Seventh Plan. These schemes should be started in 1991-92.

Participants in the Group on Policy and Planning Report

Chairman

1. Shri K. Chandrasekharan
   Minister (Education and Law)
   Government of Kerala

Rapporteurs/Members

2. Shri Ashok Saikia
   Secretary and Commissioner
   Education, Government of Assam
3. Dr. D.P. Singh
   Minister of Higher Education
   Bihar
4. Shri Arun Kumar Kar
   Minister (Education)
   Tripura
5. Prof. Syed Khaleefathullah
   President
   Central Council of Indian Medicine
6. Prof. Ramlal Parikh
   Vice-Chancellor, Gujarat Vidyapeeth
   Ahmedabad
7. Prof. K.L. Chopra
   Director IIT
   Kharagpur
8. Dr. Jyotibhai Desai
   Gandhi Vidyapeeth, Vedachhi
   Surat
9. Shri B.C. Jhaveri
   Technical Director
   M.N. Dastur and Co. Ltd.
10. Prof. Satya Bhushan
    Director, NIEPA

11. Shri R.K. Srivastava
Secretary, Education
Government of Bihar
12. Shri A.N. Mathur
Secretary, Education
Government of Haryana
13. Shri D. Eswarappe
Director of Collegiate Education
Government of Karnataka
14. Shri J.S. Badhan
Commissioner and Secretary, Higher Education
Government of Kerala
15. Dr. Vasant Nagpure
Director of Education
Government of Maharashtra
16. Shri Lalhums
Commissioner and Secretary Education
Government of Nagaland
17. Smt. Gurbinder Chahal
Secretary, Education
Government of Punjab
18. Shri V. Sankarasubbaiyan
Secretary
Government of Tamil Nadu
19. Shri Sudhri Sharma
Commissioner (Education)
Government of Tripura
20. Shri Shardindu
Joint Secretary, Education
Government of Uttar Pradesh
21. Shri Hari Prasad Pandey
Director, SCERT
Government of Uttar Pradesh
22. Shri A.K. Chatterjee
Secretary, Higher Education
Government of West Bengal
23. Dr.J.B.G. Tilak
Senior Fellow, NIEPA
24. Dr. M. Mukhopadhyaya
Senior Fellow, NIEPA

25. Dr. Manjula Chakravarty
    Dy. Director (Women's Development Division)
    NIPCCD, Deptt. of Women and Child Development
    Ministry of HRD
26. Shri Kalyan Roy
    Assistant Director (ECE), NIPCED
    Deptt. of Women and Child Development
    Ministry of HRD
27. Dr. R.V. Vaidyanatha Ayyar
    Joint Secretary
    Department of Education
    Ministry of HRD

Observations and Recommendations of CABE on Policy and Planning Report

The Report of the Working Group was presented by Shri Ashok Saikia, Rapporteur of the group. In the course of discussion, Education Minister, Karnataka said that the Central Government should set up some specialised institutions in the States as deemed universities. He added that he would send a detailed note on the subject to the Union Education Minister. Education Minister, Bihar pressed for a CABE Resolution in favour of establishment of a Central University in Bihar. It was decided that a group may be set up by the Chairman, CABE to go into the whole matter of setting up of Central Universities. Dr. Saraswati Swain expressed disagreement with the recommendations of the group in regard to securing external funds for basic education. Education Minister, West Bengal (Shri Kanti Biswas) and Dr. M.S. Adiseshiah also expressed reservation in this behalf. CABE took note of these observations but adopted the report of the working group on policy and planning as presented.

25

MID-TERM APPRAISAL OF THE SEVENTH PLAN DEVELOPMENT PROGRAMMES OF THE STATE UNIVERSITIES (1991)*

Introduction

In pursuance of the decision with regard to conducting the mid-term appraisal of the Seventh Plan Development schemes/programmes of the Universities, University Grants Commission constituted Expert Visiting Committees to visit various Universities and their colleges.

The Expert Committees visited 90 State Universities and 243 affiliated colleges during July 1988 and December 1989.

Objectives of the Expert Visiting Committees

The broad objectives of the UGC Expert Visiting Committees to the universities were essentially the following:

(i) To assess the performance of the universities during the Seventh Plan period and highlight the achievements and shortfalls regarding targets and objectives;

(ii) To recommend a policy frame and guidelines for the quality development of higher education during the Eighth Plan period within the framework of the New Education Policy of 1986 and the Programme of Action in this regard;

(iii) To identify specific tasks and programmes to be implemented

---

* *Reports of the Seventh Plan Visiting Committees for Mid-Term Review*, University Grants Commission, New Delhi, 1991.

by the universities and/or colleges either individually or in a coordinated manner with the assistance of the UGC, State Governments etc., for the maintenance of standards and improvement of quality of education in universities and colleges; and

(iv) To suggest measures for ensuring universities to become not only centres of excellence but also centres of regional and national development.

Common Problems of Colleges (Extracts)

(i) Under the Faculty Improvement Programme, the UGC, besides the delay in approving the proposal, takes considerable time in releasing the salary of the substitute teacher appointed in place of teacher who has proceeded elsewhere for this research work for M.Phil/Ph.D. degree. The UGC reimburses the minimum in the scale of Lecturer and not the additional and other allowances permissible to the substitute. This causes hardship and financial loss to the substitute teacher and the college.

(ii) The recruitment of the substitute teacher under the Faculty Improvement Programme according to the prescribed procedure, takes considerable time and during that period the teaching work in the college suffers. In the case of the Government Colleges, the Director of Collegiate Education (especially in Kerala) insists that the entire amount of the emoluments of the teacher who has proceeded on study leave be got reimbursed from the UGC, otherwise the Principal is held responsible for the shortfall.

(iii) Following the UGC guidelines has become impracticable in many ways in the light of the Constitution of Andhra Pradesh College Service Commission which is the sole competent body to select and appoint the college teachers. Appointment of full-time substitute is a long process and many fellowships remain unutilised. The procedure involved hampers rather than help the purpose in view.

(iv) As per recent directive of the Director of Higher Education, Andhra Pradesh, the release of FIP candidate approved by the UGC also needs the prior consent of the Director of Higher Education.

(v) In Bihar also the appointment of College Teachers is made by the Bihar Teachers Service Commission which has its own difficulties and has not made any appointment for the last 5 and 6 years. The substitutes in place of FIP selected teachers may be allowed to be appointed on *ad hoc* basis for claiming FIP grants. Similarly the Principals of Colleges in Madhya Pradesh were reluctant to depute teachers for FIP due to shortage of staff, as the Government sends a substitute teacher after a long time and the teaching in the college suffers.

(vi) More slots be allowed for undertaking research leading to M.Phil/Ph.D. awards under the Faculty Improvement Programme, so that the maximum number of teachers are enabled to improve their qualifications in shortest possible time.

(vii) The institution of matching contribution by the management of the college/State Government leads to widening the gaps between a well developed and developing college with poor financial resources The not well-to-do colleges without internal resources cannot, therefore, take the benefit of UGC schemes, especially for the construction extension of building projects. It was pleaded that starting from the Eighth Plan, the UGC may give 100 per cent assistance for building projects and other schemes, especially for women's colleges and those situated in rural/backward areas.

(viii) The UGC should allow sufficient flexibility in the utilisation of grants for any approved purpose, viz. building grants may be allowed to be used for the purchase of books and equipment, and inter-se utilisation of grants meant for books and equipment. This may be allowed from the Eighth Plan period.

(ix) Financial limit of grants to colleges should be increased substantially. The provision of library grant for appointment of temporary library staff is inadequate. This should be increased. It was desired that the UGC stipulation that equipment grant should not be used on consumables, should be removed.

(x) In some cases, the colleges are unable to utilise the UGC grant for want of sanction/concurrence of the State Government in time.

(xi) The Principals of the colleges, by and large, supported the grant of autonomy to eligible colleges. There were, however, reservations on the part of teachers' associations in some cases on political non-academic considerations. The UGC should initiate a dialogue with the State Governments and teachers associations in this regard.

(xii) The institution of redesigning of courses in the colleges was supported by the Principals of the colleges. It was, however, expressed that redesigning of courses depended much on initiative and cooperation of the academic community as also on continued support from the UGC beyond 1990, for additional expenditure on infrastructure. Some mis-givings and fears were, however, expressed in as much as the ap pointment of fresh teachers to teach restructured and redesigned courses might render some of the existing teachers surplus. Such misgivings needed to be removed by holding discussions with academic community and the existing teachers trained for redesigned courses through summer/winter institutes, workshops, refresher/orientation courses.

(xiii) The colleges were not in a position to make much headway in introducing new courses/combination as the State Government of Andhra Pradesh did not provide assistance nor allow surplus staff to be utilised for these programmes.

(xiv) COSIP and COHSSIP programmes are generally not taken up in Government colleges due to frequent transfer of staff.

(xv) The guidelines for assistance to colleges for the Eighth Plan may be finalised a year before the start of the next plan and circulated to the colleges by the UGC well-in-advance so that the colleges could derive the maximum benefit by sending proposals to the UGC at the earliest opportunity and are enabled to utilise the approved grant within the plan period itself, so that there is no spill over to the next plan.

(xvi) The UGC should provide special assistance for library, laboratories and class-rooms and staff quarters as also auditorium (for a college with an enrolment of 1000 students and above), in the colleges outside the plan ceilings for the colleges under development schemes.

(xvii) Adequate publicity should be given to UGC schemes directly by the UGC, as also through the Universities and College Development Councils so that the faculty in the colleges could derive maximum benefits of UGC schemes.

(xviii) The buildings of some of the old colleges were in very dilapidated conditions. Their hostels lacked necessary amenities for the students. Residences were provided to very insignificant proportion of teachers. The UGC may provide special grants for the extension, repair and rehabilitation of building facilities in such colleges.

(xix) As a consequence of remaining on temporary affiliation for a long time, the colleges affiliated to Bangalore University cannot take the advantage of UGC assistance until such time they are granted permanent affiliation.

(xx) A large number of Constituent Colleges are Constituent Units of the Universities in Bihar, and as such they also suffer from serious financial crises. The colleges do not get salaries of staff and other contingency grants through the University in time and regularly. The PG classes were allowed to be started in these colleges without any State financial assistance. Teachers are transferred from the colleges to the University Teaching Departments irrespective of their qualifications and PG teaching experience.

(xxi) The UGC grants to Government Colleges in Orissa have to be deposited into government treasuries and it created difficulties to draw amounts as and when required from the treasuries. It was suggested the Principals of Government Colleges should also be allowed (as in the case of non-government colleges) to utilise the grants as per UGC norms.

(xxii) Teachers in Government Colleges, should be transferred, only if absolutely essential, at the end of the session. Teachers engaged in research and development activities should be encouraged to continue their work without disruption and not transferred as a general rule.

(xxiii) In the States such as, Bihar, Maharashtra, etc., where the colleges provide teaching facilities for intermediate/junior college classes, alongwith UG and PG studies, the development of UG and PG education has been seriously affected. The large enrolment at the intermediate classes entails a heavy burden on the limited resources of the colleges in terms of administration, finance, space and academic personnel. It has adversely affected discipline and healthy academic environment. The correct place of intermediate classes is at the Higher/ Senior Secondary stage.

26

REPORT OF NATIONAL SEMINAR ON DECENTRALISATION OF HIGHER EDUCATION SYSTEM (1991)*

Introduction

On the occasion of the 66th Annual Meeting of the Association of Indian Universities, a National Seminar on 'Decentralisation of Higher Education System' was organised on 8 October, 1991, at the University of Kerala, Thiruvanthapuram. As many as 100 Vice-Chancellors/ Directors of other University level institutions of higher learning participated in the seminar. Following were the sub-themes:

1. Decentralisation in the University Grants Commission – Regional Officer and State Councils of Higher Education.
2. Decentralisation within the University System – Academic, Administrative and Financial.
3. Decentralisation in the Relationship of the Universities with the Colleges and that of the Colleges with the Government.
4. Decentralisation : Financial Autonomy and Accountability.

Consensus and Recommendations (Chapter I of the Report)

Recognising that a decentralised system of higher education will be more conducive for enriching human resources by promoting scientific temper and inculcating the values of universalism, humanism, egalitarianism, tolerance, and democracy in a cross-section of the

---

* *Decentralisation of Higher Education System : A Report on the Proceedings of the Vice-Chancellors' Conference held on October 8, 1991, at University of Kerala, Thiruvanathapuram*, Association of Indian Universities, New Delhi.

society;

Hoping that vertical delegation of well-defined powers in respect of administrative, and financial matters will generate a better sense of responsibility and accountability among various constituents and functionaries of the system;

Anticipating that a decentralised system of higher education will be able to better address the specific requirements of different geographic regions for promoting balanced regional development;

Noting that in view of multi-cultural characteristics, and vastness of the country, a decentralised system is imperative for raising efficiency by way of introducing socially useful and economically relevant programmes.

1. Decentralisation of the University System at National Level

1.1 Administrative Decentralisation

1.1.1 The University Grants Commission (UGC) should establish at least four regional offices – one each in the North, South, East and West, and possibly a separate fifth one for the north-eastern region, with a view to ensuring effective implementation and monitoring of its programmes throughout the country. The regional offices should be vested with well-defined powers to take decisions, issue sanctions and pass orders at their levels and should not become mere processing units of the UGC in which final decisions continue to be taken at the central level.

1.1.2 The National Policy on Education (1986) stipulated the establishment of State Councils of Higher Education (SCHE) and consequently various Committees have further upheld this recommendation by laying down the specificities for its constitution. Necessary steps should, therefore, be taken to expeditiously establish the proposed Councils in each State.

1.2 Academic Decentralisation

1.2.1 The mis-match between the supply of and demand for university graduates has got aggravated due to the increasing pressure of enrolment on the system of higher education. In order to ameliorate such conditions, substantial number of students are required to be diverted, preferably at the stage of Class X and Class XII towards vocational streams; and only those who have the real motivation and relevant aptitude to benefit from higher education should be admitted to the universities. To this end, effective manpower planning should be initiated keeping in view the requirements of the agricultural, industrial and service sectors at the regional and national level.

Besides, the concentration of enrolment in universities and colleges in certain regions is found to have been highly disproportionate in terms of total working population or the ratio of students in higher education in the relevant age-group. Appropriate policy measures, therefore, need to be initiated at the national level for ensuring more even distribution of enrolment across different regions so that the benefits of higher education could be extended to all parts of the country in a balanced manner.

1.2.2 The degree and nature of relationship between the extent of decentralisation and academic and administrative performance at various levels should be studied and evaluated so as to obtain necessary feedback from the experience of the existing institutions/departments for policy formulation. To this end, a high level committee may be constituted.

1.3 **Financial Decentralisation**

1.3.1 The Central and State Universities should receive uniform treatment from the funding agencies as far as the creation of facilities and provision of finances are concerned.

1.3.2 (a) The prevailing system of block-grant, which is fixed for a period of 3 to 5 years, is perferable for providing maintenance grants to the universities; (b) Suitable norms and formula need to be evolved for determining the financial requirements of these institutions; and (c) the grants should be released in time.

1.3.3 Universities should have full autonomy to decide upon the manner in which block grants are to be utilized for realising their specific objectives.

1.3.4 The UGC should do away with the 'matching grant' system and provide 100 per cent development grants to the universities.

1.3.5 With a view to reducing excessive dependence upon governmental grants and to finance the new programmes, the universities should be encouraged and empowered to mobilise revenues from such sources as fees, donations and contract research. Such increase in revenue should be treated as expenditure for development and the grant should not be reduced rupee for rupee. The grants released should be as per criteria.

1.3.6 Financial autonomy of universities is to be jealously safeguarded. The funding agencies must exercise restraints in interfering in the functioning of the universities. By the same token, it is incumbent on universities to ensure accountability with regard to their financial performance and cost–effectiveness of the educational programmes.

2. Decentralisation within the University System

2.1 Administrative Decentralisation

2.1.1 In order to relieve the Vice-Chancellor from work of routine, it is necessary to make arrangements for proper devolution of powers within the university system. The Vice-Chancellors should be able to devote more time for reviewing and monitoring of ongoing, as well as for planning of developmental programmes of their respective institutions. Their focus should be on academic development and not on institutional administration.

2.1.2 With a view to overcoming the problems of overlapping responsibilities and concentration of powers in the hands of the apex authorities/officers, it is necessary to make arrangements for clearcut divisions and separations of powers *vis-a-vis* responsibilities among the authorities and officers of the university.

2.1.3 For efficient supervision of undergraduate education and closer liaison with the colleges, Administrative Sub-Centres (ASC) should be set up for a unit of 20 to 25 Arts, Science, Commerce and multi-disciplinary affiliated colleges, in the case of large universities. An ASC, to be headed by an officer of the rank of a Pro-Vice-Chancellor, should be given sufficient administrative and financial autonomy for all the works connected with evaluation, inspection, conduct of examinations as well as co-ordination of various developmental programmes available for colleges.

2.1.4 Every affiliating or federating university should have a Collegiate Wing to be governed by a Collegiate Council, for maintenance of standards of education in college, including curriculum development and selection of teachers for colleges. The Council should be presided over by the Vice-Chancellor, and should include such members as pro-Vice-Chancellors of different campuses/ASCs and a few members from each sub-campus, some Professors from the university teaching departments whose subjects are taught in the colleges, besides experts from industry, research institutions, etc.

2.2 **Academic Decentralisation**

2.2.1 Each faculty should have a Faculty Council, which should have the representation of all the concerned departments as well as other functionaries so as to ensure participation of faculty members. The Faculty Council should play a co-ordinating and supervisory role by fixing guidelines for teaching, research and extension programmes of the department. The Faculty Council should also act as a channel of communication between the departments and the highest authority of the university system.

2.2.2 Every academic department should have a Departmental Council and its composition should offer adequate opportunities to all the members of the department. Within the broad policy guidelines laid down by the Academic Council and the Faculty Council, the Departmental Council should have the freedom to frame their syllabi, courses of study, examination schemes, and research and extension programmes.

2.2.3 The individual Schools/Departments should be made both administratively and financially self-contained, so that academic programmes and other related activities could be freed from undue bureaucratic controls. Therefore, once the budgets of the individual Schools/Departments are sanctioned by the appropriate authorities, the Directors/Heads of the Departments should be entrusted with the powers to manage funds and co-ordinate academic programmes. In turn, they should be responsible for realising their set objectives of teaching and research.

2.2.4 Each Centre of Advanced Studies should be autonomous and responsible for all administrative, financial and academic matters of the Centre.

2.2.5 The moves towards granting academic autonomy to colleges should be further declared and the objective of making all colleges autonomous should be realised within a definite time-frame.

2.3 **Financial Decentralisation**

2.3.1 The Finance Committee of each university should be made move effective in allocation and management of funds and also for proper procedural review of its utilization.

2.3.2 Financial powers of the university (Syndicate) should be delegated to the Vice-Chancellor and to other officers like the Registrar, Registrar (Evaluation), the Deputy Registrars, Assistant Registrars, Finance Officers, Deputy Finance Officer, the Librarian, the Deputy Librarian, the Dean of Students' Welfare, Director of Publications, Director of Printing Press, Director of Correspondence Courses, Principals of Colleges managed by the University, Director of College Development Council and the like.

2.3.3 The structure and composition of the Finance Committee should be suitably changed to allow for major participation of academics in it.

2.3.4 Distinctive provisions should be made to delegate financial powers of the university to the Heads of the Departments, and from them down to those in charges of the sub-units of the Departments engaged in different specialisations. They should be reasonable for utilizing funds on approved projects and in the manner laid down by the appropriate authority.

2.3.5 The university and its fraternity of academics should try to display better financial accountability to make the system of decentralisation a financial administration a success.

27

IMPORTANT COURT JUDGMENTS RELATING TO EDUCATION (1991-1993)

Minority Educational Institutions: Supreme Court Judgment on Reservation

In a 4:1 judgment delivered in the *St. Stephen's College case*, by a five Judge constitution bench held that under Article 30(1) of the Constitution, the minority-aided educational institutions are entitled to prefer their community candidates to maintain the minority character of the institutions subject of course in conformity with the university standard.

The court said that "the state may regulate the intake in this category with due regard to the need of the community in the area which the institution is intended to serve. But in no case such intake shall exceed 50 per cent of the annual admission".

The majority judgment delivered by Mr. Justice M.H. Kania, Mr. Justice K. Jaganatha Shetty, Ms. Justice M. Fathima Beevi and Mr. Justice Yogeshwar Dayal, said that minority institutions shall make available at least 50 per cent of the annual admission to members of communities other than the minority community. The admission of other community candidates shall be done purely on the basis of merit.

However, Mr. Justice N.M. Kasliwal delivered the dissenting judgment.

Mr. Justice Kania who delivered the majority judgment observed that "the minorities have the right to admit their own candidates to maintain the minority character of their institutions. This is a necessary concommitment right which flows from the right to establish and administer educational institution in Article 30 (1) of the Constitution."

He said, "there is also a related right to the parents in the minority communities. The parents are entitled to have their children educated in institutions having an atmosphere congenial to their own religion."

The judges said that "the collective right is required to be made functional and is not to be reduced to useless lumber. A meaningful right must be shaped, moulded and created under Article 30(1), while at the same time affirming the right of individuals under Article 29(2) which says that no citizen shall be denied admission into any educational institution maintained by the state or receiving aid out of State funds on the ground of religion, race, language or any of them.

The court allowed the plea of St. Stephen's College affiliated to the Delhi University that it was entitled to have its own admission programme since it was a minority institutions. The similar plea was made by the Allahabad Agricultural Institute at Naini. The validity of the admission programme and the preference given to Christian students were the issues before the court.

The court rejected an argument that St. Stephen's College after being affiliated to the Delhi University has lost its minority character.

The judges said "we find no substance in the contention. The state or any instrumentality of the State cannot deprive the character of the institution founded by a minority community by compulsory affiliation."

The judges said "The minority institution has a distinct identity and the right to administer with continuance of such identity cannot be denied by coercive action. Any such coercive action would be void being contrary to the constitutional guarantee".

The right to administer is the right to conduct and manage the affairs of the Institute. This right is exercised by a body of persons who the founders have faith and confidence. Such a management body of the institution cannot be displaced or reorganised if the right is to be recognised and maintained, the judges said.

The judges said "reasonable regulations, however, are permissible but regulations should be of regulatory nature and not of abridgement of the right guaranteed under Article 30(1) of the Constitution.

The judges further said that there was no provision in the Delhi University Act with overriding powers precluding the management of the college from exercising its right to administer the college as a minority institution.

Referring to a circular issued by the Delhi University on 5 June, 1980 directing the college to admit students solely on the basis of merit, the judges said that the University cannot direct the college to dispense with its admission programme in the absence of proof of maladministration of the college. The judges concluded that St.

Stephen's Colleges is not bound by the impunged circulars of the University.

Referring to minority rights and balancing interests, the judges said the Constitution establishes secular democracy. The animating principle of any democracy is the equality of the people. But the idea that all people are equal is profoundly speculative.

The judges said "we have to recognise a fair degree of discrimination in favour of minorities. But it is impossible to have an affirmative action for religious minorities in religious neutral way. In order to get beyond religion, we cannot ignore religion".

The judges said that it is now an accepted jurisprudence and practice that the concept of equality before the law and the prohibition of certain kinds of discrimination do not require identical treatment. The equality means the relative equality, namely the principle to treat equally what are equal and unequally what are unequal. To treat unequals differently according to their inequality is not only permitted but required.

Source: *Hindustan Times*, December 7, 1991.

Delhi High Court Judgment on Examination Reform by Central Board of Secondary Education, Delhi

The Delhi High Court reluctantly gave green signal to the Central Board of Secondary Education's experiment of multiple sets of question papers in the same hall for class XII and X examinations in Delhi only from March 3, 1992 onwards.

The two judges, Mr. Justice D.P. Wadhwa and Mr. Justice R.L. Gupta, said they were "inclined to agree" with the complaints that the board's decision "was arbitrary and discriminatory" but added they were helpless in restraining the Board, as the examination was only three days away.

"It is impossible to prepare question papers all over again at such short notice", they stated. "The petitioners have come too late in the day" they added.

However, Mr. Justice Wadhwa and Mr. Justice Gupta admitted the petition for detailed scrutiny and even recalled their earlier order of dismissal of a similar writ questioning the new system of examination issued on January 21, 1992. "The points now raised were not fully agitated at that time and the petitioner (then) also did not file any further appeal" they observed.

The present petitioners, two class XII students had applied saying that the Board's decision of introducing multiple sets of question papers in the ensuing CBSE examination for only Delhi schools was arbitrary and discriminatory. So it be restrained from doing so.

In their order the judges held, "we are, *prima facie*, inclined to agree with the petitioners that the decision to introduce multiple sets of question papers is arbitrary, unreasonable and it has no rational relationship with the object sought to be achieved". The Board said they were doing this experiment in Delhi, as it had the maximum cases of mass cheating during past CBSE examinations. And multiple sets of question papers was one method to combat this. The judges were, however, not convinced with this argument.

The judges even said they will have certainly stopped the Board from going ahead with such an examination but there were even graver considerations at this time.

"There are about 96,000 students appearing for examination for XII class and over 1.5 lakh for X class. Their dates of examination had been announced much earlier. All preparations for the conduct of the examination have been taken... to hold an examination for such a large number of students is a Herculean task. The question papers all ready are lying in sealed packets to be sent to various centres."

Source: *Times of India*, February 29, 1992.

Court Judgments on Capitation Fee (1992-93)

1. Andhra Pradesh High Court Judgment

In a significant judgment, a full bench of the Andhra Pradesh High Court struck down as unconstitutional the recent amendment to the Andhra Pradesh Educational Institutions Prohibition of Capitation Fee Act under which private managements of medical and engineering colleges were allowed to fill up 50 per cent of the seats on their own.

Consequently, the bench also quashed the two Government orders permitting 12 private and eight dental colleges.

The controversial orders had caused uproar in the State Assembly for several days and a section of ruling Congress had also come out against it.

The floor leader of the CPM in the Legislative Assembly, B. Venkateswara Rao, said the State Government had now lost the moral right to govern the State. "The court verdict is a clear victory to people's agitation and a slap on Government policies."

CPI leader P. Nageswara Rao said the State Government had no right to continue in office and the High Court judgment had come on the lines of people's expectation.

Meanwhile the students youth united struggle committee which led the nearly two-month long anti-capitation fee stir in the State also said the Janardhana Reddy Government had lost moral right to continue after the High Court had outrightly struck down the Government order.

Spokesman of the committee, D. Venkateswara Rao, said the High Court had clearly indicted the Government for violating the Constitution.

Referring to certain *mala fides* alleged against the State Government and Mr Janardhana Reddy, the bench said "we do not propose to enter this controversial region for the reason that we are not basing our decision on allegations and mala fides".

However, while dealing with the validity of permission granted to the medical and dental colleges, especially to the one given to Janapriya Educational Society, Nellore, the bench observed that the file disclosed "the Chief Minister gave finality to the decision to grant permission to the society for which his close relatives – his brother and wife-were the moving spirits".

The bench observed the Chief Minister in fairness should have avoided associating himself with the decision. He could have it under rule 5 and rule 7 of the rules of business. His association with the decision cannot but have effect of violating the decision for unfairness due to bias.

The bench pointed out the State Government had abdicated its power completely to the expert committee and the committee had not applied its mind to relevant matters nor discharged duties in an appropriate manner with seriousness the situation demanded.

The bench also considered in detail the events from the day on which the amendment was issued and pointed out that there was hardly any time for applications for private colleges to comply with several onerous conditions.

The bench declined leave to the State Government to apply to the Supreme Court against the judgment.

Source: *Hindustan Times*, September 19, 1992.

2. **Suprement Court Judgment**

In a historic judgment the Supreme Court struck a body blow at the commercialisation of higher education abolished arbtrary admissions through "management quotas" and evolved a scheme which provides more opportunities to meritorious students who can pay a higher fee while imposing a ceiling to be fixed by the State.

In a majority 3:2 verdict, a five-judge Constitution bench headed by Chief Justice L.M. Sharma ruled that admissions to all recognised private educational institutions, particularly medical and engineering shall be based on merit, but 50 per cent seats in all professional colleges be filled by candidates prepared to pay a higher fee.

Mr. Justice B.P. Jeevan Reddy who delivered the 127-page majority judgment, made it clear that hereafter there shall be no quota reserved for the management or for any family, caste or community which may have established such college.

The criteria of eligibility and all other conditions shall be the same in respect of both "free seats" and "payment seats" and the distinction shall be the requirement of higher fee by the payment students.

The judges said that the scheme evolved by the apex court would apply to only those institutions which were either recognised or affiliated to appropriate authorities and would not apply to either Government or university colleges.

The judges observed that "our idea in devising this scheme has been to provide more opportunities to meritorious students, who may not be able to pay the enhanced fee prescribed by the Government for such colleges."

"The system devised by us would mean correspondingly more financial burden on affluent students whereas in the aforesaid system (in vogue in Andhra Pradesh) the financial burden is equally distributed among all the students", the judges said.

Mr. Justice Reddy and M Justice S. Ratnavel Pandian delivered the majority view. Mr. Justice S. Mohan agreed with the conclusions given by Mr. Justice Pandian but gave different reasonings.

The judges made it clear that children up to the age of 14 had a fundamental right to free education but thereafter this right was subject to the economic capacity of the State to provide such free education.

Mr. Justice Reddy made it clear that "citizens have a fundamental right to education under Article 21 of the Constitution but this right is not an absolute right.

The judgment came on a batch of petitions by some managements of medical and engineering colleges and some of their students challenging a judgment by a full bench of the Andhra Pradesh High Court striking down Section 3(1) of the AP Educational Institutions (Prohibition of Capitation Fee and Regulation of Admissions) Act, 1992.

The Act enabled the managements of capitation fee-based unaided private medical and engineering colleges to fill 50 per cent of the seats irrespective of any ranking of the candidates in the common entrance test.

The High Court also quashed two orders issued by the State Government on July 27, 1992 granting permission for starting 12 new medical colleges and eight dental colleges. The State Government had also filed special leave petitions against the judgment of the High Court.

The five-judge Constitution bench had been constituted to reconsider an earlier two-judge bench decision of the apex court in the *Mohini Jain's case* (also known as the "capitation fee" case) where the two-judge bench ruled that collection of "capitation fee" by whatever name called by educational institutions in consideration for allotment of seats was arbitrary and unconstitutional.

The two-judge bench also took the view that education at all levels was a fundamental right of citizens and fees charged by any institution should not be higher than what was collected by an institution.

The judges said that no Government, university or any other authority was competent to grant recognition except specified under the scheme evolved by the apex court. Such institutions receiving aid from the Government would be subject to the terms and conditions laid down by the aid giving authority.

The court, however, ruled that students admitted to State medical or engineering colleges on capitation fee for the academic year 1992-93 would continue in their studies.

Mr. Justice Sharma and Mr. Justice S.P. Bharucha in their separate judgments said that they were in agreement with the majority view except that the finding given by the apex court in *Mohini Jain's case* on the question of fundamental right to education was not necessary in that case.

They said that the question whether the right to primary education as mentioned in Article 45 of the Constitution, was a fundamental right under Article 21 did not arise in *Mohini Jain's case* and no finding or observation on that question was called for.

Mr. Justice Sharma said that this question would need a thorough consideration, if necessary by a larger bench, in a case where the question squarely arises.

The judges said that "it is enough to state that there is no fundamental right to education for a professional degree that flows from Article 21 of the Constitution.

Source: *Hindustan Times*, February 5, 1993.

APPENDICES

Documents not Included in Second Survey

A.I.1. National Curriculum for Teacher Education: A Framework (1989)*

Specific teacher education programmes for all stages of school education has been conceived of as the most crucial input for improving the quality of school education. The framework is mainly concerned with specific curriculum design for each of the stages of school education.

Introduction

An appropriate linkage among educational policy, school curriculum and teacher education must be established to achieve optimum results. The National Curriculum for Teacher Education: A Framework prepared by NCERT in the context of the National Policy on Education (NPE), 1986 and National Curriculum Framework for Elementary and Secondary Education (NCERT, 1988), provides broad directions in which the desired changes could be brought about in the content and process of pre-service and in-service teacher education programmes by the concerned agencies like the State Departments of Education and the Universities. It may also be broadly interpreted as the framework for institutional reform in teacher education through the process of curriculum renewal. The salient features of the framework are presented here.

EXTRACTS

Changing Role of the Teacher

The teacher's role is relative to our perception of education. It has,

---

* *NCERT Bulletin, Curriculum Special*, Vol. I, No. 1, June 1989, National Council of Educational Research and Training, New Delhi.

Note : Not included in the Second Historical Survey of Educational Documents in India.

therefore, kept changing. Contemporary compulsions have led to a review of our educational objectives and priorities. These should give shape to the new role teachers would play. Thus the future teacher will be a competent, professional, skilled teacher like the one he always has been expected to be but this would now mean that he will be an effective communicator, a designer and user of learning resources, a learning facilitator and an active participation in community life.

Objectives of Teacher Education Programmes

A teacher in our society is called upon to do a variety of things. In order to plan teacher education curriculum and training strategies, it is necessary to recall the multi-dimentional nature of the teacher's roles and functions:

- Organise learning resources
- Plan effective curriculum transaction strategies
- Conduct interactive classroom teaching
- Evaluate outcomes of learning
- Implement compensatory education programmes
- Cater to special needs of disabled children
- Organise and guide a variety of co-curricular activities
- Train students in problem solving
- Participate in complementary education
- Develop in students qualities of democratic citizenship and promote environmental consciousness
- Organise and participate in programmes of community service and development.

The Curriculum Framework sets out in detail general and specific objectives for pre-service teacher education programmes for levels starting from the pre-primary. These objectives provide the basis for designing teacher education programmes for these stages, in its content, organisation, etc.

Pre-service Teacher Education Curriculum Designs

Some basic principles and considerations for developing teacher education curriculum designs are:

- Teacher education programmes are the programmes for professional preparation of teachers and they should provide for a comprehensive coverage of professional knowledge, values and skills and have a strong functional orientation.
- Pre-service teacher education is to be considered as an induction and initiation process. It is an open ended design fostering initiative for further growth.
- The programme should be flexible to accommodate local and regional needs.
- The programme design should have built-in provision for vertical and horizontal mobility of professionals from stage to stage.
- The curriculum should emphasize integration of theoretical understanding with their practical applications.
- The programme should provide for comprehensive and continuous evaluation.
- The programme should foster research outlook and the desire to experiment and innovate.

Structural Aspects

The pre-service teacher education programme for any level should have a duration of at least one academic year if it is suffixed to or built on an adequate, long and sound base of general education, e.g.

- Ten years' school education for the pre-primary level,
- 10+2 years for the primary/elementary level,
- Bachelor's degree for the secondary level,
- Master's degree in relevant subjects for the higher secondary level.

Apart from this, alternative integrated teacher education programmes have been suggested which should be tried by some of the upgraded Institutes for Advanced Studies in Education (IASEs).

Curriculum Components and their Organization

A programme of teacher education is essentially an enterprise of initiating one to a profession, and provides for theoretical learning and development of professional competencies and skills. For organizational convenience, however, the whole programme could be divided into four major components:

(a) *Foundation Courses*

The foundation courses have to be designed as core courses. The foundation component should fulfil two important functions. The first is to provide the trainee with necessary theoretical insights into and understanding of the meaning and aims of education and its role in national development. The second objective is to develop knowledge and understanding of the process of human development and learning. Accordingly, the component may be organised around two courses. The first course should present the student with an integrated understanding of education, social structure and teacher's role. The content for this course is to be derived from the basic objectives of teacher education, which cuts across all contributing disciplines to the study and understanding of education. The organizing principle of this course will be to highlight the crucial role of education in an evolving and contemporary society and the course accordingly may be tried as 'Education in Emerging India'. The second course, based on psychology, will mainly focus on the development and nature of learners at the stage concerned, the principles of different kinds of learning relevant to the stage, individual differences and the psychology of adjustment.

(b) *Stage Relevant Specialization*

The stage relevant specialization component will have two parts. The first part highlights the special objectives, features, historical background and the scope of education at the given stage. The second part deals with subject specific learning concerning different methods, techniques and strategies of teaching different school subjects. These have been hitherto organized as content-cum-methodology course.

(c) *Additional Specialization*

In addition, provision is made for additional specialization in areas like health education, physical education, etc.

(d) *Practical Field Experience*

This component is of crucial importance in the entire design of teacher education curriculum as it is concerned with the fulfilment of the central objective of development of professional competencies with respect to the different functions of a teacher. Some of the important activities to be covered under this component are:

- Observation and critical analysis of lesson and unit planning.
- Preparation of instructional material.
- Using education technology and media resources.
- Construction and administration of evaluation tools.
- Organization of and participation in curricular activities.
- Carrying out special assignments like case study, action research and work experience.
- Carrying out health and physical education activities.

Programme Designs

The following sections present structured outlines of teacher education programme designs for the different levels:

Early Childhood Education Level (Pre-Primary)

Duration: One year.
Pre-primary or pre-school education generally covers the age group of 3 to 5 years. This period is considered to be the most crucial for maximization of cognitive development. Pre-primary education has, therefore, to be fully development-oriented to cater to all inter-related dimensions of development-physical, cognitive and language, social, moral, aesthetic etc., and unify them through an integrated approach.

TABLE A-1: Curriculum Components at the Bi-Elementary Teacher Training

Curriculum Components	Weightage in terms of time	
A. *Foundation Courses*		20%
(i) Education in Emerging India (the socio-cultural content of education)	10%	
(ii) Child Development and Adjustment (focus on age group 3 to 7)	10%	
B. *Stage Relevant Specialization*		35%
(iii) Early Childhood Education Systems (Montessori, Froebel, etc.) and Integrated Child Development Services (ICDS) in India.	5%	

Curriculum Components	Weightage in terms of time
(iv) Cognitive Development Activities (Piagetian and such other lines of treatments).	5%
(v) Language Development Dimension and Activities (Spoken language sounds, vocabulary, sentence patterns)	5%
(vi) Personal-Social Development/ Dimensions and Activities.	5%
(vii) Reading, Writing and Arithmetic (Scientific treatments)	5%
(viii) Readiness and Initiation-Physical and Major Development, work skills, and Health Care.	5%
(ix) Aesthetic and Culture Development Activities.	5%
C. *Practicum/Field work*	45%
(x) Practical Work (with children and homes/community).	20%
(xi) Internship in Teaching (in Pre-primary and Primary Schools).	25%
(xii) Cocurricular Activities.	

Elementary Stage (Primary and Upper Primary)

Duration: Two years.

Elementary education extends over standards 1 to 7/8, ordinarily covering the age group 6/6 to 12/13/14 years. It comprises two distinct stages, referred to as the primary stage (standards 1 to 5) and the upper primary stage (standards 6 to 8). Generally, the class teacher system, which requires one to teach almost all the academic subjects, is followed in the primary stage while special interests and proficiency of the teacher may be taken in view for teaching at the upper primary stage. Each teacher must also be able to contribute to health and physical education, art education and work experience with adequate knowledge to handle handicapped children and be acquainted with at least one area like adult education, non-formal education, women education or library service, etc. The curriculum components have been designed keeping the needs in mind.

TABLE A-2: Curriculum Components at the Elementary Teacher Training

Curriculum Components	Weightage in terms of time	
A. *Foundation Courses*		20%
(i) Education in Emerging India (Philosophical and Socio-cultural Perspective)	10%	
(ii) Elementary School Students - Learning Process, Adjustment (Educational Psychology)	10%	
B. *Stage Relevant Specialization*		30%
(iii) Elementary Education and Teacher Functions	5%	
(iv) Language Teaching (Mother tongue and English)	5%	
(v) Mathematics Teaching	5%	
(vi) Environmental Studies Teaching (as related to Students I to V)	5%	
(vii) Health and Physical Education	5%	
(viii) Arts Education, Work Experience	5%	
C. *Additional Specialization*		10%
(ix) Science Teaching and Social Studies Teaching/Pre-School Education	5%	
(x) Elective-one: (Adult Education/Non-formal Education/Social Education/ Multiple Class Teaching/Population Education/Special Education, Educational Technology etc.		
D. *Practical/Field Work*		40%
(xi) Practical Work	20%	
(xii) Internship in Teaching (in primary and upper primary/pre-school system)	20%	

Secondary Stage

Duration: One year

The secondary stage extends over standards 9 and 10. All subjects except languages have to be taught as disciplines with their logical structure and inherent methodology taking the content to a reasonably high level of understanding. The core components of the curriculum, aimed at national identity, cultural enrichment, citizenship qualities and awareness of environment, etc., must be duly emphasized at this stage. The teacher education curriculum should provide scope of vertical and horizontal mobility of teachers. The curriculum components for this programme have taken care of the special needs of this stage of teacher education.

TABLE A-3: Curriculum Components at the Secondary Stage Teacher Training

Curriculum components	Weightage in terms of time	
A. *Foundation Courses*		20%
(i) Education in Emerging India (Philosophy and Socio-cultural Perspectives)	10%	
(ii) Educational Psychology (with focus on learner development and stages, learning adjustment)	10%	
B. *Stage Relevant Specialization*		30%
(iii) Secondary Education and Teacher Functions	10%	
Specialization in Methodology of:		
(iv) A secondary school subject with prior specialization	10%	
(v) A second secondary school subject/ higher secondary education/primary education	10%	
C. *Additional Specialization*		10%
(vi) An elective from areas like Adult Education, Secondary Education, Population Education, Distance Education, Library Services, Tribal Education, Special Education (Integrated and one category) Health and Physical Education, Art Education, Work Experience, Educational Technology, Action Research, Computer Education, etc.	10%	
D. *Practicum/Field Work*		40%
(vii) Internship in Teaching including Field Assignments	20%	
(viii) Practical work including working with community and social service and work experience	20%	

Higher Secondary Stage

Duration : One year

The higher secondary stage has certain special characteristics, different from other stages in respect of aims, curriculum, learners and teachers. The curriculum at this stage is organised under two broad streams – academic and vocational, and sub-stream areas under each stream. At this stage, besides thorough knowledge of adolescent psychology, a teacher should possess the mastery of the subject matter. The one-year B.Ed. programme for teachers of +2 stage may comprise (a) foundation courses, (b) stage relevant specialization, (c) additional specialization, and (d) practicum/field work. The curriculum components reflect all these requirements of this stage.

TABLE A-4: Curriculum Components of the Higher Secondary Stage Teacher Training

Curriculum Components	Weightage in terms of time	
A. *Foundation Courses*		20%
(i) Education in Emerging India (with special reference to Higher Education)	10%	
(ii) Educational Psychology (with special emphasis on adolescence/learning, adjustment and personality)	10%	
B. *Stage Relevant Specialization*		30%
(iii) Higher Secondary Education and Teacher Functions	10%	
(iv) Communication Technology and Media Resource	10%	
(v) Curriculum Transaction Strategies (one subject related to +2 stage)	10%	
C. *Additional Specialization*		10%
(vi) One from among Curriculum Development, Instructional Strategies and Designs, Evaluation, Educational and Vocational Guidance, Education of the Gifted, Institutional Planning and Management, etc.	10%	
D. *Practicum/Field Work*		40%
(vii) Practical Work	20%	
(viii) Internship Teaching (at the +2 stage)	20%	

Integrated Teacher Education Programme for Secondary Stage
(Four Years)

The basic assumption underlying the integrated programme of teacher preparation is that it will break the isolation between content and pedagogy. The student will make a conscious decision to join the teaching profession at a young age and thus will get more time to develop and stabilize positive attitudes towards the profession.

Different structural designs are presented based on requirements of special type. The curriculum includes general education, content courses and professional education with 25, 50 and 50 per cent weightage respectively.

Like the one-year programme, the four-year programme is also recommended to have the following components:

(a) General Education,
(b) General courses, and
(c) Professional Education.

Curriculum Transaction

The stage next to visualising the curricular outline is specifying it in terms of various courses with their details. It is the ability, sincerity and motivation of the persons responsible for transaction which largely determines the extent to shich curriculum objectives are realised. This would mean carrying out those educational activities in teacher education institutions which would develop in students the required qualities and a comprehensive view of educational experience.

Although the Curriculum Framework, its components, guidelines and methodologies would be made available to each teacher education institution, yet freedom and flexibility of approach to transaction of curriculum will rest with individual institutions. The areas of stress shall be:

(a) to generate a climate conducive to the development of desired attitudinal make-up of student teachers;
(b) to develop competencies in methods of teaching, and techniques of evaluation; and
(c) to train for adoption of self-learning technologies.

The systematic development of instructional material, revision through trial and feedback, developing modes of its effective use and designing evaluation procedures require high degree of expertise couple with initiative and sustained work. This calls for instituting research fellowships and sponsoring relevant research projects in teacher education institutions which might go a long way to make the programme of teacher education more scientific and more meaningful.

A.I.2. Report of the Curriculum Development Centre in Education: M.ED. (1989)*

Introduction

The University Grants Commission (UGC) has taken up a programme of developing Curriculum in different subject areas through Curriculum Development Centres located in the University system. These centres undertake the task of developing and modernising the curricula and courses. This exercise is at the National level through many experts drawn from all over India.

The University of Kerala set up the National Curriculum Development Centre in Education, in its Department of Education, Trivandrum. A Committee of Experts drawn from various universities and institutions was set up with Prof. Vasantha Ramkumar, Professor and Head, Department of Education, Dean, Faculty of Education, University of Kerala to suggest curriculum at the post-Graduate Level in Education.

4.3 Terms of Reference of the Committee: U.G.C. Guidelines

1. The Committee will examine the existing curriculum in the respective subjects of different Universities in the country in terms of quality as well as workload.
2. The Committee will examine how the new curriculum would promote human resource development and identify areas which are crucial to make education meaningful in the task of national development.

---

* Published by University Grants Commission, New Delhi.

Notes: 1. Not included in the *Second Historical Survey of* ***Educational Documents***.

2. Paras numbers refer to para numbers of the Report.

3. The Committee will devise a model curriculum which will be relevant to the requirements of the country.
4. The Committee will suggest textual materials which would be required to follow the new curriculum.
5. The Committee will suggest ways and means for preparing textbooks, teaching aids, library as well as laboratory equipments in implementing the proposed curriculum.
6. It should also indicate how the teachers are to be trained in order to impart education according to the revised curriculum.

4.4 Constitution of Committee for Post-Graduate Level

Eleven specialists in the discipline from different Universities were invited to be members of the Committee on the basis of their long experience and expertise in the field of education. Two members were co-opted from the Curriculum Development Centre.

4.5 Curriculum Development Committee : Post-Graduate Level

1. Prof. A. Sukumaran Nair, Pro-Vice Chancellor, University of Kerala, Trivandrum. (Former Professor and Head, Department of Education and Dean, Faculty of Education, University of Calicut).
2. Prof. D.B. Desai, Centre of Advanced Studies in Educatior M.S. University of Baroda, Vadodara-390002.
3. Prof. R.N. Mehrotra, Central Institute of Education, University of Delhi, 33, Chhatra Marg, Delhi 110 007.
4. Prof. P.R. Nayar, Department of Education, University of Mysore, Manasa Gangotri, Mysore-570 006.
5. Prof. Lokesh Koul, Department of Education, Himachal Pradesh University, Shimla-5.
6. Prof. K.L. Pandit, P.G. Department of Education, Nagpur University, Law College Campus, Amravati Road, Nagpur-1.
7. Prof. S.N. Singh, Department of Education, Banaras Hindu University, Varanasi.
8. Prof. S.C. Sharma, Department of Education, Andhra University, Waltair, Andhra-530 003.
9. Prof. Ramjee Prasad Singh, Professor and Head and Dean of the Faculty of Education, Patna University, Patna-800 004.
10. Prof. L.C. Singh, Department of Teacher Education, NCERT,

Sri Aruobindo Marg, New Delhi-110 016.

11. Prof. (Miss) M.D. Bengalee, Vice-Chancellor, University of Bombay, Bombay.*
12. Mr. P.I.A. Karim, Reader, Department of Education, University of Kerala, Trivandrum-695 012.
13. Dr. M.S. Gomathy Ammal, Reader, Department of Education, University of Kerala, Trivandrum-695 014.
14. Prof. Vasantha Ramkumar, Department of Education, University of Kerala, Trivandrum-695 014 – Co-ordinator, Curriculum Development Centre.

4.6 Committee Meetings

The Committee met five times at the Department of Education, University of Kerala.

First meeting	:	3rd to 6th Dec., 1986.
Second meeting	:	3rd to 6th March, 1987.
Third meeting	:	20th of 27th June, 1987.
Fourth meeting	:	3rd to 8th August, 1987.
Fifth meeting	:	14th to 19th Dec., 1987.

The second meeting was a joint committee meeting with the under-graduate committee to discuss modes and problems of articulation of the two courses.

4.7 Experts Consulted

The draft syllabi were sent to the following experts for their comments:

Prof. M.Abu Baquer, Jamia Millia Islamia, New Delhi; Prof. S.T.V.G. Acharulu, Regional College of Education, Bhopal; Prof. Y.P. Aggarwal, Kurukshetra University; Prof. S.P. Ahluwalia, Sagar University; Prof. Arati Sen, Viswabharati University; Prof. Hemelatha Swaroop, Kanpur University; Prof. Iswara Reddy, Osmania University; Dr. D. Joshi, Jamia Millia Islamia, New Delhi. Prof. J.N. Joshi, Punjab University; Prof. C.L. Kundu, Kurukshetra University; Dr. Lokesh K. Verma, University of Jammu; Prof. S.S. Mathur, Punjab University;

---

* Dr. (Miss.) Bengalee was not able to attend the meetings of the Curriculum Committee due to unavoidable circumstances.

Prof. V.S. Mishra, Gorakhpur University; Dr. H.N. Majoo, Lucknow University; Prof. S.K. Pal, Allahabad University; Prof. K.C. Pande, Regional College of Education, Bhuvanesar; Prof. S.N. Panda, Regional College of Education, Orissa; Prof. H.N. Parimoo, Kashmir University; Prof. Pushpita John, Retd. Professor of Education, University of Kerala; Prof. J.K. Pillai, Madurai Kamaraj University; Dr. P.N. Rai, R.B.S. College of Education, Agra; Prof. Renudevi, Gauhati University; Dr. S.Roy, M.S. University of Baroda; Prof. S.P. Ruhela, Jamia Millia Islamia; Prof. C. Seshadri, Regional College of Education, Mysore; Prof. A.S. Sethi, Sri Sathya Sai Institute of Higher Learning, Andhra Pradesh; Prof. G.B. Shah, South Gujarat University; Prof. J.C. Sharma, Maharashi Dayanand University, Haryana; Prof. M.K. Sharma, Dibrugarh University; Prof. S.N. Sharma, Patna Training College, Bihar; Prof. T.R. Sharma, Punjabi University; Dr. R.J. Singh, Lucknow University; Dr. K.Sivadasan Pillai, University of Kerala; Prof. Sivarudrappa, Karnatak University; Prof. K. Soman, Calicut University; Prof. T.S. Soundara Raja Rao, Coimbatore; Prof. R.P. Varma, Banaras Hindu University; Prof. C.L. Vashin, University of Kashmir; Prof. E.G. Vedanayagam, Madras University; Dr. Venkatarama Reddy, S.V. University; Prof. M.S. Yadav, CASE, M.S. University, Baroda.

4.8 Participation of Faculty of Department of Education, University of Kerala

The syllabi of all the Universities were analysed and exhaustive draft syllabi for the four core papers were prepared by the Faculty Members of the Department of Education, University of Kerala.

The following faculty members were also involved in the preparation of modules:

1. Dr. K.R. Sivadasan, Reader, Department of Education, University of Kerala.
2. Dr. K.N. Lalithamma, Reader, Department of Education, University of Kerala.
3. Dr. Mercy Abraham, Reader, Department of Education, University of Kerala.
4. Dr. P.M. Jaleel, Lecturer, Department of Education, University of Kerala.
5. Dr. R. Sujatha Rani, Lecturer, Department of Education, University of Kerala.

7.0 Suggested Models for Master's Course in Teacher Education

A. *Structure of Postgraduate Course (Master's Course) in Education*

The Committee was of the opinion that the structure of the present programme needs to be revised and changed prior to the preparation of model curriculum. The Committee also obtained the opinions of educationists through a questionnaire sent out by the Centre for the purpose.

The Committee analysed the existing structure of the M.Ed. and M.A. Education course.

7.0.1 *Existing Models*

M.Ed.

Model - I - 1 Year
Core papers - 3
Optionals - 2
Model - II - 1 Year
Core papers - 4
Electives - 2
Dissertation -

M.A.

Model - I - 2 Years
Core papers - 10
Elective - 5
Practical Work
Internal Assessment
Model - II - 4 Semesters
Core papers - 4
Electives - 4
Practical work
Internal Assessment

7.0.2 *Suggested Models*

The Committee was of the opinion that in a large country like ours with the rich diversity and pluralities, developmental, regional and sectoral imbalances and discrepancies, *one uniform model may not be desirable*.

Keeping in mind the present three degree programmes viz., **B.Ed.**,

M.Ed. and M.A. (Education) the need to avoid anomalies and confusions, the complementary nature of the 'liberal' and the 'professional' in education and strengthening and enriching the foundations, specialisation and research component of the educational studies, the Committee was of the opinnion that the *duration of the M.Ed. programme be lengthened to 2 years.*

The Committee was also of the opinion that *the objectives of M.Ed. course could be increased.* In addition to (a) develop leadership in the field of education, (b) produce worthy teacher educationists, (c) produce good administration in education, (d) promote innovation practices, and (e) the objective of producing trained teachers at the different levels of education would be also added.

The Committee suggests two different Models for the M.Ed. programme for consideration and adoption by different universities keeping in view their local conditions, needs, requirements and resources.

Model I : A. 2 years M.Ed. programme with seven core papers and three electives.

1st Year

1. Philosophical Foundations of Education
2. Sociological Foundations of Education
3. Psychological Foundations of Education
4. Methodology of Educational Research
5. Development of Educational Thought and Systems

II Year

6. Curriculum Instruction and Evaluation
7. Contemporary Indian Education in Comparative Perspective
8. Elective I
9. Elective II
10. Elective III (from another group)/Dissertation based on any group.

7.0.3 *Electives*

Educational Management and Change

0.0.1.1 Principles of Educational Management, Administration and supervision.
0.0.1.2 Resource Management in Educational Institutions.
0.0.1.3 Educational Planning and Financing.
0.0.1.4 Educational Leadership and Change in Education.
0.0.1.5 Economics of Education

Educational and Vocational Guidance

0.0.2.1 Principles and Procedures of Guidance in Education
0.0.2.2 Information Services in Guidance
0.0.2.3 Organisation of Guidance Services.
0.0.2.4 Career Development and Vocational Guidance

Adult Education

0.0.3.1 Foundation and Methods of Adult Education
0.0.3.2 Adult Education System and Management of Adult Education
0.0.3.3 Problems and Practices in Adult Education

Teacher Education

0.0.4.1 Principles and Systems of Teacher Education
0.0.4.2 Teaching : Theories, Models and Effectiveness
0.0.4.3 Advanced Methodology of Teaching any one School subject

Technology

0.0.5.1 Fundamentals of Instructional Technology
0.0.5.2 Computer in Education
0.0.5.3 Educational Technology
0.0.5.4 Hardware and Software in Instructional Technology
0.0.5.5 Printmedia for Instruction

Curriculum and Instruction

0.0.6.1 Curiculum : Foundations, Patterns and Processes
0.0.6.2 Teaching : Theories, Models, Analysis and Assessment
0.0.6.3 Measurement and Evaluation.

Comparative Education

0.0.7.1 Principles and Methods of Comparative Education
0.0.7.2 Education in Developed World
0.0.7.3 Education in Developing World

Special Education

0.0.8.1 Special Education : Principles and Practices
0.0.8.2 Education of the Gifted
0.0.8.3 Education of Children with Hearing and Speech Handicaps
0.0.8.4 Education of Children with Neuro Muscular, Orthopaedic and Multiple Handicaps
0.0.8.5 Education of the Socially Disadvantaged and Maladjusted

Early Childhood Education

0.0.9.1 Child Development and Guidance
0.0.9.2 Mental Health and Child Guidance
0.0.9.3 Principles and Practices in Pre-Primary Education
0.0.9.4 Principles and Practices in Primary Education

Educational Research

0.10.1 Research Methods
0.10.2 Statistical Analysis
0.10.3 Dissertation

Measurement and Evaluation

0.11.1 Test Construction
0.11.2 Management of Examinations
0.11.3 Educational Statistics
0.11.4 Measurement and Evaluation in Education

Higher Education

0.12.1 Principles and Practices in Higher Education
0.12.2 Innovations in Higher Education
0.12.3 Measurement and Evaluation in Higher Education
0.12.4 Management of Higher Education

Special Studies

0.13.1 Women's Education
0.13.2 Rural Education
0.13.3 Population Education
0.13.4 Art and Culture Education
0.13.5 Distance Education
0.13.6 Social Education
0.13.7 Basic Education
0.13.8 Non-formal Education

The Model increases the duration of the present B.Ed. and M.Ed. degree programme for 2 to 3 years. The present M.Ed. and M.A. (Education) get merged into one degree only and the B.Ed. remains.

A graduate with or without a B.Ed. degree is eligible for admission to this 2 year M.Ed. programme. In this model, a degree for school teaching, say B.Ed. continues to exist, and be the necessary and sufficient condition for the job of school teaching. That is, a person with this degree will need to have a B.Ed., before or after the M.Ed., to be eligible for school teaching.

This M.Ed. may be a basic requirement for the various (other than school teaching) personnel in education.

7.0.4 *Rationale for Suggested Model - I*

M.Ed. seems to be the only one year master's degree course in Universities, apart from M.P. Ed. in the same faculty and M.Lib. Sc., M.P.Ed. usually adopts the general pattern of the M.Ed. Library Science, expanded and enriched as Information Sciences, is likely to propose a two-year master degree programme shortly. Another comparable professional area, Law, has/had a three-year full time bachelor degree course, which is now being replaced by a five year integrated course. Of this, more than three years time would be devoted to the study of law. This is followed by a two year master degree course for the LLM degree. Medicine and Engineering, as more exacting professional areas, may not be comparable and would continue to be larger and richer courses than in law, education, library science, etc. Most Master's Degree programmes like those in Arts, Social Sciences, Science and Commerce are all of two years' duration. They come after three years of Bachelor degree level study in the subject, over and above, earlier levels.

A one year M.Ed. course or the equivalent component in any integrated course in teacher education, has to become increasingly functionally oriented and emphasise the 'Training Function' rather than the study of education as a discipline, with an adequately broad and strong theoretical foundation and it can be built up only at the master degree level. The one year M.Ed. course, with serious limitations of time, and consequent overcrowding with 6 papers or 5 papers and dissertation (generally, as against 4 or 5 papers/practicals in each year of other master degree courses) cannot do adequate or reasonable justice in this respect. Even if the course outlines indicate a broad and rich coverage and the written examination papers appear adequate with ready-made answers, the strength is only apparent and deceptive and real learning with understanding not to speak of mastery–is very limited and that too, to a small percentage of the increasingly larger and weaker M.Ed. student population. This learning can be strengthened and enriched if the programme is not so overcrowded and they are given more time to study.

Further, the ocean of literature in the professional discipline of education, is expanding at a fast pace. Even if we select, sequence and structure the relevant and useful content very economically, there is no escape from greater coverage and enrichment of what goes into a master degree course, if such a degree is to have meaning and justification. And if these essential have to be learnt adequately, the teachers and students will need more time. All these facts point to the need to make M.Ed. a two year course.

Even if, B.Ed. is made a strong two year professional course, there would still be need and justification to make M.Ed. a rich two year programme. It should be easier to convert M.Ed. into a two year course, than the B.Ed. course, which can perform a reasonable good job of teacher training and introduction to the discipline even in one year, if it is structured and organised in a better way, and the year is used fully. A two year M.Ed. would also discourage B.Ed.'s who are mainly waiting for a job and joining M.Ed. just to mark time till they get it, without any serious interest in the study of the discipline at a higher level from joining it and causing wastage by dropping out, due to indifference.

This two year course will provide a course of study for all those who wish to work in Education in capacities other than school teaching e.g., researchers, knowledge-generators, theorists, policy-makers, planners, administrators, teacher educators, etc.

The course will comprise the various elements of 'Education as a Discipline' and 'Education as a Profession'.

The admission to the course will be open to those who have secured Bachelor's/Master's degree (B.A./B.Sc./M.A./M.Sc. etc.) in any subject of the various faculties of the Universities.

If a person after studying this course and obtaining the Master's Degree wishes to teach in a school, he/she will have to secure the one year B.Ed. degree.

A B.Ed. intending to take up other kinds of work in the field of education (other than teaching) will be required to study for the 2-year master's course.

The implications of the above proposal are :

1. There will be increase of one year in B.Ed. + M.Ed.
2. One year course will remain the necessary and sufficient requirement for school teaching.
3. The only one Master's Degree course of two years will be a re-

quirement for the various liberal and professional personnel in Education.

Model II : A two-year multi-stream integrated M.Ed. programme.

1st Year : A. Compulsory Papers

1. Philosophical Foundations of Education
2. Sociological Foundations of Education
3. Psychological Foundations of Education
4. Curriculum - Instruction and Evaluation
5. Educational Thought and Systems – a Seminar Course

2nd Year : A. Compulsory Papers

6. Education in India in Historical and Comparative Perspective

B. *Specialisation Papers*

Methodology of Teaching School Subject will be one of the Specialisations.

7.
8.
9.

The suggested 2-year course will form a sound base for all types of responsibilities and functions in the theory and practice of education.

The Committee was also of the opinion that the objectives of M.Ed. course could be increased to include in addition to (a) developing leadership in the field of education, (b) producing worthy teacher educators, (c) produce good administrators in education, (d) promoting innovation practices, the objective, (e) producing trained teachers at the different levels of education. This suggestion is based on the following arguments.

This Model implies that the present B.Ed., M.Ed. and M.A. (Education) get abolished and be substituted by a single post-graduate course of study of education of 2 years' duration. After a common first year course of study, the students will opt for different specialisations (including school teaching at different levels). The second year will provide multi-stream programmes catering to different areas like, school teaching, teacher education, guidance and counselling, expertise in philosophy of education and so on.

The present duration of B.Ed. and M.Ed. (1+1 = 2) does not increase.

7.0.5 *Rationale for Model II*

At present one year B.Ed. course is the common programme for different types of personnel and specialisations in Educational Technology, Primary School Training, Teacher Education, Educational Administration, Educational Planning, Financing etc. In the present programme after offering a core study of the bases of Education different courses for different types specialisation course will be provided.

It is therefore said with some justification that the present B.Ed. neither prepares a good technician nor a good academic, that is, it is neither adequately skill-based nor has a rigour in its theory, and the M.Ed. course appears to be mere extensions of the B.Ed. They do not give any depth of understanding of Education nor do they properly prepare a professional.

The M.Ed. (Education) course offered by certain Universities claim to offer study of education as a discipline, a liberal knowledge in the realm of social sciences–as different from the M.Ed. course which is considered to be a professional programme. The present attempt at integrating the two programmes for teacher education at the Bachelor's and Masters degree while continuing to keep the total period for teacher training as 2, provides the different personnel in education with a stable foundation of theory and adequate opportunities for developing specialised skills which include teaching and research. A two year duration should enable the student to acquire a sound basis in the discipline and also the specialised skills and improved capacities required in the faculty of Education. The possibility of improving the professional nature of the programme is very high.

Semester Programmes

The course has been so designed that it can be converted to semester programme. The first year programme could be split to be included in Semesters I and II. The second year programme would be split to be included in Semesters III and IV.

11.0 **Recommendations**

Curriculum change is a complex process which involves the interaction of objectives, methods, materials and personnel. Its effectiveness is characterised by movement from one position to another for each of these components singly and as an integrated whole. A conscious effort at change has to follow the preparation of the new curriculum; to prevent the stagnation which is often seen in the implementation process, the misplaced emphasis on a few activities that results in gaps, the gradual dilution of standards when the curriculum is handled by a large body of personnel with varying interests, capabilities and expertise and who are not direct participants in the process of curriculum development and the unpredicability of institutional conditions for implementation.

The recommendations for the implementation of the curriculum are intended to :

(1) enable the implementation process to be initiated and carried out smoothly, with adequate support and close monitoring at the State, Regional and National levels.
(2) provide a stable framework for Curriculum Development as an ongoing process, incorporating preparation, implementation and evaluation as continuing activities.
(3) raise the standard of post-graduate teaching in education for which Curriculum Development is a critical but not the only requirement with curriculum development as the starting point for action.
(4) develop curriculum development as an important area of inquiry within the discipline of education.
(5) initiate discussion and debate at the National, Regional and State levels on the curriculum.

Categorisation of Recommendations

The recommendations are presented as :

A. steps to be taken to finalise the curriculum and recommendations for effecting them.
B. actions to be initiated to implement the curriculum and recommendations for carrying them out.
C. details of structure required to initiate, co-ordinate and evaluate the implementation of the curriculum and to do further studies in the area and recommendations concerning agencies, institutions and bodies needed.

A. Finalisation of the Curriculum

A. 1. *Steps to be taken to Finalise the Curriculum*

The following tasks remain to be completed before a final curriculum can emerge.

1. The modules of the four core papers need to be refined.
2. The basic and further reading have to be categorised modulewise, from the total bibliography.
3. Elective papers have to be presented as modules.
4. Bibliography for elective papers need to be completed.
5. Basic books for core papers require to be written.
6. The content of specific teacher training programmes need to be further detailed.
7. The reactions of teacher educators to the curriculum have to be obtained and the curriculum modified on this basis.

A. 2. *Recommendations for Finalisation of the Curriculum*

To complete the above-mentioned tasks for finalisation of the curriculum, it is recommended that :

1. The U.G.C. Curriculum Development Centre at the Department of Education, University of Kerala, be requested to continue functioning for another one year with a fresh budget allocation and change in manner of functioning.
2. The present national committees be permitted to continue and to meet at least four times to complete the curriculum for the different specialisation papers.
3. Six workshops to be organised of ten days duration to translate the curriculum for the specialisation papers into modules with experts identified in terms of the particular expertise required.
4. The curriculum prepared by the Curriculum Development Centre to be discussed and modifications made before it is accepted and implemented.

To enable focused discussion on the Curriculum the following suggestions are made :

(a) *National Meeting*

The draft curriculum should be discussed at a National Meeting of U.G.C. officials, the Curriculum Committee Members and twenty invited teacher educators (Deans and Professors of Education) from all over the country.

(b) *Regional Seminars*

Six regional seminars, organised by U.G.C. in collaboration with six Departments of Education, at which teacher educators, administrators, research workers and other personnel in the field of teacher education, including those involved with the undergraduate programme, are to be given the opportunity to discuss and react to the draft curriculum.

(c) *State Level Seminars*

State Level Seminars organised by the U.G.C. and the University Departments of Education at which concerned teaching fàculity of Master's course in education discuss and give their reactions to the curriculum.

B. Action to be Initiated to Implement the Curriculum

B.1. *Understanding the Context for Implementation*

To implement the new curriculum certain background information is required. The Curriculum Committee has provided a status survey of the existing curriculum in terms of structure, papers, and scheme of evaluation, but has not provided information on facilities in institutions and particular competencies required for teacher orientation as it lay beyond its scope.

To obtain this information it is recommended that :

1. A National Survey on existing conditions in teaching departments to be conducted and a report prepared.
2. A National Committee to be entrusted with this task, with the necessary sponsorship facilities and finances provided by U.G.C.
3. National Regional and State agencies to be represented through:

   (a) memebership in committees; and
   (b) participation in the survey

B. 2. *Dissemination of Information on the Curriculum*

The curriculum requires a large number of personnel for its actual implementation and the involvement of both active and passive members of a wider community for its acceptance and use. The rationale for the changes have to be spelt out and debated to establish the relevance for the changes. The curriculum has to be understood before it is translated and one of the important tasks for effective implementation is discussion of the ideas and materials of the curriculum. The rationale, objectives, structure and other elements have to be clearly explained particularly when the changes have been very significant. The present curriculum has given a changed structure to the course and the duration of the course has been lengthened. The full implications of these changes need to be analysed and communicated. The curriculum has also been presented through modules. The use of modules is not widerspread as yet, particularly in certain disciplines of which education is one. An understanding of the principles and procedures involved in the modular approach, and of the requirements for implementation have to be built-up.

The following recommendations are made for exposure of the curriculum;

1. Publication of a Curriculum Bulletin which would provide the required information on the characteristics of the curriculum and its weidespread circulation through a network of State, Regional and National agencies.
2. Organisation of local based small group discussions/seminars with national resource persons for clearing doubts and identifying particular hindering factors.
3. Arrangement of National level lectures on the curriculum to place the curriculum in a wider perspective.
4. Publication of articles in the media by eminent educationists on the existing conditions, indicating the need for change and presenting the possibilities of the new curriculum.
5. Specific literature to be prepared and seminars to be organised on the modalities for use of modules in teaching to orient teachers with the requirement for effective teaching through modules.

B. 3. *Development of Materials to Support the Curriculum*

The materials required have been spelt out earlier
They include :

1. comprehensive and annotated bibliographies.
2. different papers of the prescribed curriculum.
3. reports of curriculum analysis of papers which would serve as Handbooks.
4. basic texts and translations.
5. supportive audio-visual materials.
6. educational technology, hardware and software
7. test materials
8. comprehensive Question Bank.

To provide these materials the following actions are suggested :

1. Compiling and collating tasks are to be completed at the existing Curriculum Development Centre as part of finalisation of the curriculum.
2. Materials required are to be prepared at creative workshops with specially invited participants.
3. Systematic curriculum analysis to be initiated at the identified national centre.

To initiate and complete these actions the following recommendations are made.

1. Agencies, institutions and bodies at the State, Regional and National levels are to be set up for the tasks.
2. Departments of Education have to be provided the capability to utilise the materials prepared through adhoc grants for the purpose from the U.G.C.

B. 4. *Development of Curriculum as an area of Inquiry*

Curriculum Development has grown as an area of inquiry and it now requires focused attention both in terms of theory and practical applications. To reflect this development and to enable the departments of education to provide leadership in the area of curriculum development in other disciplines as well the following recommendations are made:

1. Systematic curriculum analysis has to be undertaken and the results reported by National and Regional Curriculum Development Centres established for the purpose.
2. Research in curriculum related areas has to become the focus of concern of research scholars and the teaching faculty.
3. To enable a large number of research workers to be engaged in the work it is recommended that :

    (a) UGC allot research scholarships specifically for research in curriculum at the doctoral and post-doctoral levels. Research Associates and Research Assistants for Curriculum research to be appointed in all University Departments of Education;
    (b) Curriculum research to be included in the Research agenda of national agencies; and
    (c) Experts in curriculum studies from foreign universities be invited as visiting professors in Departments of Education.

B. 5. *Strengthening of Departments of Education in Terms of Physical Facilities, Teaching Personnel and Scope of Functioning*

Strengthening of Departments of Education

To enable Departments to implement the curriculum meaningfully certain vital requirements need to be provided. They include:

1. adequate library
2. reprographic facilities
3. computer and video units
4. testing materials
5. adequate staff structure

Based on the status survey findings as suggested earlier the requirements for each Department need to be worked out.

To enable this task to be completed it is recommended that UGC Commission for different regions be set up with six members to inspect each department, in the identified area and analyse its requirements and report to the U.G.C.

C. *Agencies, Institutions and Bodies for Implementation of the Curriculum*

A systematic structure for implementation of the curriculum is required if the initiative taken in the curriculum development is to have the follow through.

The agencies, institutions and bodies of the structure could (1) disseminate information on the rationale of the curriculum developed, on the capabilities and resources required on the part of the education system, and on the new approaches needed in inservice training, (2) provide the support system required in terms of direction, materials and personnel, (3) engage in field-data collection which would serve as a framework for assessing effectiveness; and (4) sponsor all the actions recommended in an integrated manner. Careful continuous monitoring of the implementation of the curriculum requires a process of constant communication and feedback. The suggested structure is outlined here:

1. A NATIONAL CURRICULUM DEVELOPMENT CENTRE to be established by U.G.C.

This Centre will :

(a) integrate the different activities for finalising the development and implementation of the curriculum;
(b) disseminate information on the descriptive characteristics of the new curriculum through its various publications;
(c) publish the results of research in Curriculum Development through the Journal of Curriculum Studies;
(d) arrange guest lectures at the National level on Curriculum related areas;
(e) identify experts in the area of Curriculum Development and provide resource personnel;
(f) organize National seminars on the different issues in Curriculum Development and Implementation;
(g) prepare resource materials, including textbooks, through group and individual efforts to support the new curriculum;
(h) develop programmes for teacher training in collaboration with regional centres and teacher training institutions;
(i) develop tools and materials for evaluation of curriculum outcomes;

(j) organise a curriculum materials library to serve as the nodal centre for curriculum research and studies;
(k) carry out research studies in the area of curriculum; and
(l) edit and publish the Journal of Curriculum Studies.

Note : The present UGC Curriculum Development Centre at the Department of Education, University of Kerala which has also been identified for Special Assistance by the University Grants Commission with Curriculum Development as an important thrust area has the potential to be organized into the National Curriculum Development Centre.

2. SIX REGIONAL CURRICULUM DEVELOPMENT CENTRES to be identified by UGC with networking arrangements with the National Centre to provide leadership in Curriculum Development in defined areas. Departments of Education in six universities could be identified by the UGC for this purpose.

Regional Centres will :

(a) co-operate with the national centre in all its activities;
(b) publish and distribute curriculum bulletins to teacher education institutions in the region;
(c) organize regional seminars;
(d) disseminate information on the curriculum;
(e) provide leadership for teacher training activities in the area;
(f) carry out research studies in the area of curriculum;
(g) organise libraries in identified areas of specialisation within Curriculum Development; and
(h) arrange lectures on curriculum related areas.

3. TEN TEACHER TRAINING INSTITUTIONS to be established in the Universities by the U.G.C.which work in close collaboration with Regional and National Centres.

Teacher Training Institutions will:

(a) organise different types of in-service programmes for teachers of Post-graduate Courses in the area;
(b) distribute curriculum bulletins to the teachers;
(c) obtain feedback from teachers and communicate to Regional and National Centres;

(d) co-operate with Regional and National Centres in all their activities; and

(e) carry out action research studies.

4. CURRICULUM IMPLEMENTATION CELLS to be established in at least one University Department of Education in each of the States not covered by the National and Regional Curriculum Development Centres.

Curriculum Implementation Cells will:

(a) monitor the implementation of the Curricula at the state level; and

(b) provide feedback information to teacher training institutions, regional centres and national centres.

5. CURRICULUM MATERIALS UNITS to be an integral part of the National and Regional Curriculum Development Centres for the preparation of resource materials for development and implementation of the new curriculum.

Curriculum Materials Units will :

(a) collect curriculum materials and resource materials from different institutions for study;

(b) prepare materials according to local requirements;

(c) disseminate information on materials available; and

(d) prepare new materials.

6. DEPARTMENT OF CURRICULUM STUDIES Certain Departments of Education which have the interest and the capability are to be identified and assisted for teaching and research in specialisation within the area of Curriculum, through the different programmes of the UGC for *ad hoc* grants, research support and special assistance.

7. A STATUTORY BODY FOR NATIONAL CURRICULUM DEVELOPMENT IN HIGHER EDUCATION with sub-committees in each discipline to function under the aegis of the U.G.C.

The Statutory Body will :

(a) monitor the total process of curriculum evaluation;

(b) provide initiative and new directions in curriculum development;
(c) identify and maintain a list of experts in curriculum development;
(d) select guest lecturers to deliver lectures on curriculum related areas;
(e) initiate action for national level seminars on curriculum development; and
(f) provide a forum for discussion and debate on curriculum issues.

A.I.3 UGC Guidelines Regarding the Minimum Number of Actual Teaching Days, Programme of Examination Reform and Working Load for Teachers in Universities and Colleges (1989)*

(A) Working Days

The number of actual teaching days in an academic year in a university/deemed to be university/constituent/affiliated colleges of the university should not go below 180 days excluding the preparation days and examination days. These are days on which classes such as lectures, tutorials, seminars, laboratories are or may be conducted. Holidays cannot be counted although students may be studying in their homes or hostels or may even be informally consulting teachers. The time taken up for admission i.e. when the classes are not formed, to start work; time meant for examinations or for preparing for examinations cannot be counted. It would be desirable for universities to make an effort to raise the number to 200 or more. The Universities should budget their time in regard to work and holidays. For example, admissions should be completed by the last day of the long vacation. Ex-

* Published by University Grants Commission, New Delhi

Notes 1. Not included in the *Second Historical Survey of Educational Development in India.*

2. First circulated by the UGC vide D.O. letter No. F. 1-117/83 (CP) dated 17/18th January, 1984.

3. These guidelines now form part of regulations under notification No. F. 1-117/83 (CP) dated 25-11-1985.

aminations results should also be compiled and announced during the vacations to enable admissions to take place. In a semester pattern, examinations should not be so prolonged as to take away more working days – there could be more reliance on internal assessment, examiners of first semester could be internal so that the short vacation can be utilised for evaluation. The universities should also see that a working day in a department or faculty does not become just a few hours of the forenoon. The time-table should be spread to accommodate the various academic activities over at least on 8 hours working day.

The University should also insist that the manner of conducting a course is also spelled out. The number of lectures, tutorials, seminars, lab-sessions etc. normally adequate for each course should be worked out and preferably made known in a handbook of courses. If students cut classes, or if working days are otherwise disrupted it should be made clear that only when the norm is reached will there be examinations. This also involves disciplined regular work on part of the teachers – which should be ensured. Every item in a given syllabus may not have to be taught in the class as a pre-requisite for the examination, but on the other hand it would be counter productive to hold examinations on reduced courses because the number of working days has been curtailed in a particular situation. If this happens, examinations will lose their credibility, students will perform poorly in competitions and interviews, and if they are admitted to the next class its standards will also suffer.

(B) **Minimum Programme of Examination Reform**

Every university/deemed to be university shall have to adopt the following minimum examination reform.

Syllabus/Question Paper:

(a) The syllabus in each paper should be demarcated into well defined units areas of content alongwith a topicwise breakdown. The units may be numbered;

(b) Examiners should be free to repeat questions set in a previous examination. This is necessary in order to ensure that students do not leave out important portions of the syllabus. Instructions to paper setters should be amended accordingly;

(c) There is often a very wide choice given to students for answering questions, say 5 out of 10. Such overall choice restricts the area of knowledge with which a student can pass an examination and is therefore undersirable. If there is choice, it may be provided by alternate questions in each unit of the syllabus;

(d) No examination should be held without fulfilling the requirement of a minimum number of lectures/tutorials/laboratory sessions etc. which should be clearly laid down by the university; and

(e) Examinations should be conducted in fair and impartial manner. Cheating in examinations is a cognizable offence. Universities must take steps for the proper conduct of examinations such as effective security measures, proper supervision and invigilation, cordoning off the examination centres from the range of loudspeakers and other interference, flying squads and stern action in all cases involving copying and use of unfair means.

(C) **Work Load of Teachers**

The work load of various activities should be not less than 40 hours a week for a teacher who is in full time employment. (Any good teacher, particularly one who is involved in creative activity and who has a spirit of challenge towards giving his best to the students, would certainly spend much more than 40 hours a week in academic pursuits).

The break up of work load shown below is for the sake of example. It is not a rigid breakup. But, every teacher could be given duties according to some such general pattern and no one should have a significantly reduced load:

1. *Undergraduate College:*

(a) Lecturers in Non-laboratory/Field work subjects:

	Activity	*Average No. of hours per week*
(i)	Teaching	16
(ii)	Testing/Exams	2
(iii)	Tutorials	4
(iv)	Preparation of Teaching	10
(v)	Supervision of extracurricular work	4
(vi)	Administrative Work	4
	Total	40

Where extra-curricular work or administrative work is not assigned or unfortunately tutorials do not take place, teaching work may be slightly increased, but as far as possible a teacher should not have to teach or lecture more than three hours per day.

(b) *Lecturers in Science Subjects or where field work is necessary :*

	Activity	*Average No. of hours per week*
(i)	Teaching	16
(ii)	Lab. work	4
(iii)	Testing/Examinations	2
(iv)	Teaching preparation and lab-setting	12
(v)	Administrative activities	4
(vi)	Extra curricular activities	2
	Total	40

2. *Lecturers in PG Colleges/Universities*

(a) *Lecturers in non-laboratory/Field work subjects*

	Activity	*Average No. of hours per week*
(i)	Teaching	10
(ii)	Testing/Exams.	1
(iii)	Tutorials	4
(iv)	Preparation for Teaching	10
(v)	Research	10
(vi)	Own Reading/Studies	5
	Total	40

(b) *Lecturers in Science Subjects or where field work is involved :*

	Activity	*Average No. of hours per week*
(i)	Teaching	10
(ii)	Testing	1
(iii)	Laboratory work	4
(iv)	Teaching preparation and lab-setting	10
(v)	Research	10
(vi)	Own Reading/Administrative work	5
	Total	40

Teaching combining Undergraduate and Postgraduate teaching will have a position in between (1) and (2) above.

(c) Senior teachers like Readers and Professors, in addition to their own research work guide and supervise a fairly large number of students for M. Phil./Ph.D. Degrees. They have also to attend consultative meetings of various organisations, sometimes related to teaching and sometimes to research. Therefore, it is felt that their direct teaching responsibilities may be slightly curtailed allowing them a greater portion of time for guiding and supervising research work. However, to the 10 hours of research per week on the average, it should be possible to add not more than 4 hours, bringing the total of research to 14 hours per week. This again implies that the number of students to be supervised should be limited to perhaps 4 to 6, and that senior teachers should be able to assign specific time to each scholar whose work they are supervising.

It is also felt that with 14 hours for research and 5 or 6 hours for reading and study and perhaps another 5 hours for extra-curricular or administrative work, senior teachers should be able to put in about 8 hours of teaching and laboratory work including testing and about 8 hours for preparation of teaching work. Teachers not having such extensive research responsibilities should put in more teaching work. Ordinarily a teacher may not have more than two postgraduate theory courses to teach with some laboratory or tutorial responsibility.

It is further observed :

(i) That young people are given enough time to help in their professional growth and achievement of academic excellence particularly in the initial years of their service.

(ii) that teachers guiding research students have adequate time to look after them; and

(iii) that 'pleasant' as well as 'unpleasant' work is shared by all teachers. In case a certain teacher likes to have an extra load at a particular time in the year and compratively less teaching work at some other time during the total academic year this should be accommodated if it does not cause any serious difficulty in the teaching programme of the department. Where teaching is organised in semesters and terms such adjustments could be made in the corresponding period provided the teacher has given adequate notice to the university.

The underlying principle being that the maximum work load should be the same in all departments and for all teachers. In postgraduate centres where considerable research activity is envisaged it is obvious that the direct teaching of the staff will be reduced and the staff will accordingly devote the remaining time for active research.

Teachers should spend a certain amount of time everyday in the department/college whether or not they have direct teaching duties on certain days. If facilities are provided, preparation for teaching can mostly be done in the department/college. This is so as to ensure that a teacher is available for his students if they need his help and that a teacher is also available when he is needed for consultation or discussion on various matters that come up in institutions.

APPENDIX-II

Diverse Matters : Short Notes

A.II.1 **CBSE Decision on Marks for Literacy Work**

The Central Board of Secondary Education (CBSE) has decided to award marks to students for literacy work under a Special Drive on Adult Literacy. The scheme launched on October 2, 1991 will cover class IX and XI during the current session and will be extended to class X and XII from 1992-93 session.

Under the scheme, five marks will be awarded to a student for each person made literate in a year, 8 marks for two persons and 10 marks for three or more persons made literate in one year. The marks will be awarded by schools in class IX and XI and by the CBSE in class X and XII.

Apart from the students, the Board has also worked out a package of incentives for teachers as well as institutions. With the expected target of one literate per student per year in Secondary and Senior Secondary classes, schools will be entitled to Golden Certificate with achievement of 90 per cent and above and Silver Certificate with achievement between 80 per cent and 90 per cent. The Board will award every year Special Trophy for three best schools on the basis of best average of persons made literate.

Similarly teachers will be honoured by the schools with certificates or trophies for commendable work in literacy.

Besides the incentive of marks, certificates will also be awarded to students who make five or more illiterates literate in a year. It is expected that more than 8 lakh illitrates would benefit every year under the special drive for Adult Literacy Launched by CBSE.

Source : *Yojana*, December 15, 1991.

A.II.2 **Janardhan Reddy Committee on Education**

A meeting of the Central Advisory Board on Education had been convened to discuss the recommendations of the Janardhan Reddy Committee report on education submitted to the Government recently.

The Reddy Committee reviewed the Ramamurthy Committee report which went into the 1986 New Education Policy.

A.II.3 **Committee to Study Performance of Government Schools in Delhi**

A committee has been constituted by the Directorate of Education to study the performance of Government schools. The Committee is headed by a senior Deputy Director of Education, assisted by other officials of the Education Department.

A.II.4 **Committee to Prepare Staff Training Plan in NCERT**

In order to prepare a comprehensive training plan for administrative personnel in the National Council of Educational Research and Training (NCERT), a high level Committee has been constituted by the Director.

The terms of reference for the Committee are :

(a) to assess the training needs of each category of administrative staff keeping in view the job requirements and the promotional channels etc.,
(b) to consider and suggest modalities for giving orientation/induction training to new entrants,
(c) to suggest details of training programmes specifically tailored for each category, and
(d) to give due weightage for introducing the basics of computers/Word Processing etc. for the appropriate categories of staff.

It is expected that the training plan so evolved will help in the career development of these categories of staff, besides increasing their efficiency. The Committee has been constituted in order to streamline the existing training facilities for the staff.

The four-member Committee consists of : (i) Shri S.C. Vajpai, IAS (Retired), Ex-Chief Secretary, Delhi and Ex-Pro-Vice Chancellor, IGNOU, (ii) Shri O.P. Gupta, Ex-Director, Training, Deptt. of Personnel and Training and presently Executive Director (Non Gazetted), Railway Board, (iii) Shri S.N. Swarup, Officer on Special Duty

(Training), Department of Personnel and Training, and (iv) Dr. K.J.S. Chatrath, Secretary, NCERT (Member Convener).

A. II. 5 **Early Schooling : Survey Report**

A survey of 250 parents, whose children were attending the "preparatory schools", was conducted, to know the extent of health problems, life-styles and other aspects of the pre-school children.

The survey categorised the age group of the children in percentage. The percentage of 24 to 36 months old children who were going to preparatory schools was 21.3 per cent, 37 to 48 months old children were 36.9 per cent and six year old children were only 0.1 per cent.

Highlighting the reasons for sending the children to school, the survey showed that 83.6 per cent children were sent to pre-school by parents for preparing them for admission to the pre-school of a big formal school, 61.4 per cent were sent to give company, 53.2 per cent to learn alphabets, 18.85 per cent to follow just the general practice, 17.2 per cent because the child is a nuisance at home and 9.84 per cent because there was nobody at home to take care of the child.

There was an increased incidence of recurrent respiratory infections, fever, pains and temper tantrums among the pre-scholars which could be related directly or indirectly to early schooling.

The present system of admission causes a lot of tension and trauma to young children if they face rejection at the entry stage and it instils a sense of loss in their mind thereafter.

Introduction of formal instructions too early can lead to adverse consequences not only in terms of intelligence but also motivational and socio-economical development. It has been observed by paediatricians that there is increasing incidence of stress-related medical problems in children due to hazards of early formal schooling.

Moreover, during early age, the children's muscles are still in the process of developing and their muscle co-ordination, particularly of the wrists and fingers needs strengthening. Hence they do not have the capacity to hold and use a pencil in a well-coordinated way.

Further, their attention span is limited to a maximum of seven to 15 minutes, that too in an activity in which they are physically and mentally involved. Their vocabulary is limited and listening comprehension is as yet not adequate to take group instructions.

Considering the consequences involved in early schooling, it has been suggested in a charter of recommendations that school admissions for children below six should be stopped and instead they should be sent to licensed neighbourhood play centres.

Source : *Hindustan Times*, February 5, 1992.

A. II. 6 **Educational Projects**

The Government proposes to take up a series of multi-million basic education projects in Uttar Pradesh, Orissa and Madhya Pradesh with funding by external resources.

These will be in addition to similar projects at present under implementation in Andhra Pradesh, Rajasthan and Bihar among others.

The Uttar Pradesh basic education project with World Bank assistance proposes to cover 10 districts. The State Government has prepared a project which is with the Bank for appraisal. The draft project envisages an outlay of about Rs. 550 crore during 1992-97.

Possibility is being explored to mobilise external resources for a project in the four most backward tribal districts of south Orissa, according to an official announcement.

It seeks to impart education oriented to the problems of the local environment as well as promote development of skill and entrepreneurship.

In Madhya Pradesh an education for all project entitled "Roopantar" is proposed to be taken up with assistance from the EEC and another educational project for tribal areas entitled "Dhumkuria" with UNESCO assistance.

"Roopantar" proposes to cover fully the four districts of Mandsaur, Sidhi, Raisen and Raigarh and partially the two districts of Satna and Dhar in the first phase. The outlay for the first phase is Rs. 64 crore.

The second phase, to be spread over from July 1994 to June 1999, will cover one hundred blocks with an estimated outlay of Rs. 403 crore.

The project "Dhumkuria" is under preparation with UNESCO assistance. It proposes to cover the five districts over a period of three years at an estimated outlay of Rs. 60 crore.

The earliest of the basic education projects with external assistance currently under implementation is the Andhra Pradesh primary education project assisted by the overseas development administration of the U.K.

It is being implemented since April 1983 with an outlay of 31 million pounds. Its objective is to improve the quality of primary education by providing school buildings and enhancing the professional competence of teachers and supervisors of primary schools.

The first phase of the project covering 330 schools in 11 districts of Andhra Pradesh was over in 1987. Under the second phase from 1989-90 to 1995-96, all the primary schools in the State would be covered.

In Rajasthan, the "Shiksha Karmi" project is being implemented with the assistance of the Swedish International Development Authority (SIDA) to tackle teacher absenteeism. Voluntary education workers, called 'Shiksha Karmis', are engaged in place of primary school teachers under the project.

Shiksha Karmis are selected by the local community and given intensive training. About 1,050 remote villages in 70 blocks of Rajasthan are proposed to be covered under the project with an outlay of Rs. 41 crore.

Another project "Lok jumbish" – people's movement for basic education for all – is being taken up in Rajasthan also with SIDA's assistance. The goal of the project is to achieve education for all in the State by the year 2000.

The total project outlay is estimated to be Rs. 500 crore to be shared by SIDA, the Central Government and the State Government. Twenty-five blocks are being covered in the pilot phase (1992-94).

Mahila Samakya, or education for women's equality programme was launched with Dutch assistance in 10 districts of Gujarat, Karnataka and Uttar Pradesh in April 1989.

The programme is addressed to the poorest women in rural areas and over the last three years it has had a visible impact in the villages covered. Women have been able to tackle problems like access to drinking water, payment of minimum wages, access to health services, functioning of the village school, domestic and social violence.

The Bihar education project is to cover all aspects of basic education and will be expanded in phases to cover 150 blocks in 20 districts. Project activities have begun in seven districts.

An outlay of Rs. 360 crore is envisaged for the project during 1990-95. Of this, the UNICEF will contribute Rs. 180 crore, the Union Government Rs. 120 crore and the State Government Rs. 60 crore.

(Source : *Hindustan Times*, September 28, 1993.)

A. II. 7 **Government Decision on Chattopadhyay Commission**

The Government did not find the demand of various teachers organisations for a single running pay scale acceptale as it would affect standards and efficiency. Medical allowance at the rate of 7.5 per cent of the basic pay irrespective of actual need, did not seem appropriate, in view of the repercussions it could have on other Government employees.

A. II. 8 **High Powered Committee on Computer Education**

The high powered committee set up by the Government regarding orientation to computer education has recommended that about Rs. 1,000 crore be provided over a period of three years for setting up five new advanced information system institutes like IIT's, upgradation of about 15 existing main centres in the educational institutions to centres for information technology and for providing minimum computer facilities in about 100 universities and other teaching centres.

The Committee was set-up to suggest the measures to augment computer education and training in the country.

Stating that the investment of Rs. 1,000 crore should be recovered from the beneficiaries over five years, it has suggested that tax benefits could be granted to encourage private investments in computer facilities.

It feels that there is a need for setting up an autonomous apex body to set guidelines for the growth of computer manpower development.

Recommending that all formal computer education facilities be under the purview of the Human Resource Development Ministry, it suggests that private institutions, with local or NRI participation, should be encouraged.

The Government is stated to be considering how the committee's recommendations could be implemented.

A. II.9 **Jafri Committee to Examine Gujral Committee Recommendations on Promotion of Urdu**

Centre set up the Gujral Committee for the Promotion of Urdu in 1972. The Committee gave its report in 1975 which was tabled in Parliament in 1979. In February 1990, a Committee of Experts was set up under the chairmanship of Ali Sardar Jafri to examine Gujral Committee recommendations on the promotion of Urdu.

The 15-member Jafri Committee was asked also to assess the present status of Urdu and advise the Government on the ways to implementing the Gujral Committee recommendations. It was given a three-month period from the date of its first meeting to submit its report. Its tenure was, however, subsequently extended by three months.

In September 1990 it gave its report to the Education Minister.

The Gujral Committee's main recommendations included the amendment of the three-language formula, use of Urdu for official purposes where there are 10 per cent or more speakers and adequate safeguards for the Urdu-linguistic minority. The Ali Sardar Jafri Committee has endorsed these.

The Jafri Committee has recommended that the Cabinet take a definite decision on each and every one of the Committee's recommendations, incorporate these in a comprehensive Resolution and get this endorsed by Parliament. Thereafter a time-bound procedure should be followed.

A. II. 10 **Mahila Samakhya**

An innovative project entitled 'Mahila Samakhya' (Education for Women's Equity) was launched on a pilot basis in April 1989 in ten districts in the States of Karnataka, Uttar Pradesh and Gujarat. It will continue up to 1995. It is built around the empirical observation noticed in many programmes for women's development that a group of motivated women can be an effective focal point for mobilisation. The project receives 100 per cent assistance from the Government of the Netherlands. The programme is currently operational in 1500 villages in ten districts and is likely to expand to 20 districts in a phased manner.

A. II. 11 **Educational Technology (ET) Programme**

As a measure of widening access to education and towards bringing about qualitative improvement in education, an Educational Technology Programme was started as a Central Sector Scheme in 1972 and has been continuing as such till 1987-88 when it became a Centrally-sponsored Scheme. However, the Government of India continue to bear 100 per cent expenditure on most of the components of the scheme.

A. II. 12 **National Population Education Project (NPEP)**

The Project was launched with effect from April 1980 designed to introduce population education in the formal education system. The underlying objective is to create in the younger generation adequate awareness of the population problems and realisation in this regard of their responsibilities towards the nation. The programme has been developed in collaboration with the United Nations Population Fund (UNFPA) and with the active involvement of Ministry of Health and Family Welfare which is nodal Ministry for the project. The NCERT provides technical assistance. The expenditure incurred by the implementing agencies in States/UTs and NCERT on this project is reimbursed by UNFPA.

In order to facilitate effective integration of population education elements, the conceptual framework of population education has been revised and Minimum Essential Contents have been identified. A compendium of Lessons on Population Education for selected subjects that are being taught in different classes from I to XII has been developed. A number of prototype curricular and instructional materials including textual and audio-visual materials and also evaluation tools, have been developed at the national level and circulated to States/UTs for their use. Four hundred titles of different kinds of material available in 17 Indian Lanuages have been developed. An evaluation study of curricular and textual materials was conducted. Instructional and training materials, including audio-visual material of 9 Hindi--speaking States and Union Territories were reviewed and screened. About 600 posters and charts prepared in different themes and content of population education were reviewed as also some video cassettes and slide sets. Meaningful guidelines for preparing effective and qualitative audio-visual materials have been developed. The States/UTs developed audio-visual materials which are used primarily in teacher training programmes. Orientation programmes for textbooks authors, curriculum developers and teacher educators are organised. In States/UTs over a million teachers, teacher educators, key persons, educational administrators and other functionaries have been trained during the last eight years. Painting competition and essay writing competition have been organised at the national level. States/UTs also organise debates, declamation, essay writing and painting competitions, exhibitions, youth parliament and *kavi darbars* on this subject.

A. II. 13 **Computer Education in Schools**

A Pilot Project on Computer Literacy and Studies in Schools (CLASS) was initiated in 1984-85 in 248 selected Secondary/Higher Secondary Schools jointly by the Department of Electronics and the Department of Education to acquaint students and teachers with the range of computer applications and its potential.

A. II. 14 **National Advisory Committee on History**

Government had constituted an eight-member National Advisory Committee to help prepare a contemporary history of post-independence India and transform it in an appropriate curriculum.

It was thought desirable to prepare an objective and impartial historical narrative and convert it into a syllabus for the curriculum at the school and college levels by the end of the century.

The Committee, chaired by Dr. S. Gopal, a noted historian, will have its term till August 15, 1997, the day India will complete 50 years of Independence.

Besides Dr. Gopal, the other members of the Committee will be Prof. Sabyasachi Bhattacharya, Prof. Ravinder Kumar, Dr. Bipan Chandra, Dr. (Mrs.) Dharma Kumar, Prof. Ram Guha, Prof. Sumit Sarkar and Prof. Neeladri Bhattacharya.

The nominees of the UGC, the ICHR and the NCERT will be permanent invitees to this Committee. It will evolve its own procedures and submit its recommendations to the Government.

The suggestion to constitute the Committee emanated from Shri M.J. Akbar, the then Advisor to the Human Resource Development Minister.

The years since Independence had been full of tribals and tribulations, tumult and sometimes turmoil, but in this crucible of time, the earnest endeavours of the people from all walks of life had been able to fashion the destiny of modern India.

Government had no proposal to review the work of the National Advisory Committee set up to prepare the curriculum on the history of post-independent India for school and college levels, and the Committee was free to determine its own procedure and methodology of work.

A. II. 15 **National Institute of Adult Education (NIAE)**

On 4 January, 1991 the Government of India adopted a resolution establishing a National Institute of Adult Education (NIAE) as an autonomous national institution. The main purposes of this Institute are: (1) to provide açademic and technical resource support for the National Literacy Mission (NLM) and adult education programmes of every description; (2) to organize training courses designed to meet the needs of the adult education programmes; (3) to work at the improvement of the contents of those programmes and the methods used; (4) to prepar material for the media and to make use of traditional and folk media; (5) to undertake research, evaluation and monitoring activities; (6) to establish links with the different types of institutions and other agencies concerned and co-ordinate their efforts; and (7) to establish develop and administer an institution with these purposes in view.

Although set up in an academic context, NIAE will draw its strength from its close links with field programmes and cultivate team work rather than a bureaucratic hierarchical system.

A. II. 16 **Indian Institutes of Technology**

The five Indian Institutes of Technology (IITs) at Bombay, Delhi, Kanpur, Kharagpur and Madras were established as premier centres of education and training in engineering and applied science at the under-graduate level and to provide adequate facilities for post-graudate studies and research. These are Institute of National Importance. They admit nearly 2,000 students every year to the Post-Graduate courses and research scholars. Their annual provision for under-graduate courses is about 1,600 students.

The IITs conduct four-year under-graduate programmes leading to Bachelor's Degree in Technology (B. Tech.) in various fields of engineering and technology. They also offer integrated Master's Degree Courses in many disciplines.

A. II. 17 **Literacy**

The failure to achieve UEE makes it inevitable to take up Adult Literacy Programme. The National Adult Education Programme was introduced in 1978. As of 30th June, 1990 about 2.7 lakh adult education centres were being operated, in which about 80 lakh illiterate adults are enrolled every year. However, 40 per cent of these enrolled drop out due to a variety of compulsions, about 20 per cent relapse into illiteracy. The remaining 40 per cent who go through the cycle of learning can be said to have acquired some literacy and numeracy though not necessarily of the desired level.

The National Literacy Mission (NLM) was launched in 1988; one of the six technology missions NLM sought to impart functional literacy to about 800 lakh illiterate adults in the age group of 15-35 by 1995. Another landmark was the introduction in 1988 of Jana Shikshan Nilayams (JSNs); the network of JSNs provides an institutional framework for post literacy and continuing education and would help ensure that neoliterates do not relapse into illiteracy. At present, there are over 2.50 lakh AE centres being run through the Rural Functional Literacy Projects, the State Adult Education Programme and voluntary agencies. Out of about 32 thousand JSNs sanctioned so far over 22 thousand have already become operational. During 1990-91 it is estimated that 84 lakh adults would be enrolled.

A. II. 18 **Panel on School Curricula**

The Government has appointed a National Advisory Committee under former UGC Chairman, Prof. Yash Pal to recommend how the school curricula could be modified to reduce the workload on students at al levels, particularly the young ones.

The other members of the committee are Prof. Krishna Kumar of Delhi University, Prof. T.S. Saraswathy of the Baroda-based MS University, Ms Dina Guha, a Psychologist from Bombay, Mrs. V. Parthasarathy, Principal of the Sardar Patel School, Delhi, Dr. V.G. Kulkarni of the Homi Bhabha Science Centre and Prof. Poromesh Acharya of the IIM, Calcutta. Dr. G.L. Arora, SCERT director, would act as member-secretary.

A.II.19 **University Grants Commission Committee on UGC Act (Amendment) Bill and Grievances Redressal**

UGC report covers the grievance redressal matter in detail. Beginning with dispute settlement involving teachers and non-teaching employees of a university and its colleges, the report suggests a Tribunal of Arbitration which shall be constituted as and when a complaint is received by the authorities against the final determination by the university governing body. These tribunals shall have jurisdiction over all service matters including initial appointment, promotion and seniority.

Since these are tribunals of arbitration, their decisions shall be binding on the parties concerned and no appeal would be permissible to any other court or authority including the High Court. Thus special leave to appeal under Article 136 of the Constitution or a writ petition under Article 32, to the Supreme Court would only be possible.

For the resolution of all other disputes in a university and its colleges, a committee of three members be constituted which excludes any person holding office of authority in the university or college. This committee will be primarily for those aggrieved persons who do not want to take recourse to arbitration. In any case, the decision of this committee shall be final and not appealable before any court or tribunal.

In order to enable the dispute settlement machinery at the grassroots level to act effectively, it is necessary that the jurisdiction of the civil courts in these matters be completely excluded. Such a provision in university enactments, if it does not already exist, needs to be legislated upon.

The report states that "disputes are not the same thing as grievances" therefore the machinery for the settlement of the two should not be identical. The report suggested that only minimum additions be mae to the existing university structures, and does not favour the creation of an additional office of Ombudsman.

The UGC Committee, recommends that there ought to be a grievance redressal cell for the university which would receive representations in case the complainant has failed to have the grievance redressed by the existing units. The cell should be put in charge of a senior deputy registrar and it shall submit a brief report to the Vice-Chancellor every month regarding the nature and number of representations received, the method adopted for redressing them and the final outcome.

On group grievance a joint consultative machinery would be most appropriate. Each university, in the context of the existing arrangement in this regard, should consider and decide as to who may be the head of these committees so as to ensure their functionality.

The recommendations of each joint consultative committee shall be considered by the executive council of the university or managing committee of the college as the case may be at its next meeting.

Reasons for rejecting any recommendation shall be stated by these bodies in writing.

If the Executive Council feels that it can not implement the recommendations since they are outside their powers or because of inadequate finance, it may refer them to the State Government with its clear opinion indicating whether it supports the recommendations of the joint consultative committee concerned or opposes them. The State Government, in turn, shall dispose them of within reasonable time in the overall interest.

The UGC report takes into account the major shortcomings of the existing dispute settlement machinery and provides suggestions from the legal angle to stengthen the outfit and introduce changes or evolve a new structure.

Source : Arup Ghosh, *Hindustan Times*)

APPENDIX-III

Backgrounders

1. *Annual Report* (s), *1990-91* and *1991-92*, Department of Education, Ministry of Human Resource Development, Government of India, New Delhi.

2. *Development/Digression Diary of India: 3D Companion to information India, 1990-91* and *1991-92*, by S.P. Agrawal, Concept Publishing Company, New Delhi, 1993.

3. *Development of Education in India, 1990-1992*, National Institute of Educational Planning and Administration, New Delhi, 1992.

4. *Educational Planning in India: With a Slant to Educational Financing and Administration, Vol. 1, Reports of Committees and Commission, Five Year Plans, Statististical Tables*, by J.C. Aggarwal and S.P. Agrawal, Concept Publishing Company, New Delhi 1992.

5. *Educational Policy in India*, by J.C. Aggarwal, Shipra Publication, Delhi, 1992.

6. *Eighth Five Year Plan*, by J.C. Aggarwal, Shipra Publications, Delhi, 1992.

7. *Information India, 1990-91* and *1991-92: Global View*, by S.P. Agrawal and J.C. Aggarwal, Concept Publishing Company, New Delhi, 1992 and 1993.

8. *Landmarks in the History of Modern Indian Education*, by J.C. Aggarwal, Vikas, 1992.

All other Documents/Publications cited in this volume.

CICIL LIST

CONCEPTS IN COMMUNICATION, INFORMATICS & LIBRARIANSHIP

(CICIL)

General Editor: **S.P. AGRAWAL**

CICIL-1 Development of Library Services in India: Social Science Information
S.P. Agrawal Rs. 150

CICIL-2 Development of Documentation in India: Social Science Information
S.P. Agrawal Rs. 250

CICIL-3 UNESCO and Social Sciences: Retrospect and Prospect
S.P. Agrawal and **J.C. Aggarwal** Rs. 250

CICIL-4 INDIANA : A Bibliography of Bibliographical Sources
M.K. Jain Rs. 200

CICIL-5 Dimensions of Library and Information Science: Kaula Festschrift
V. Venkatappaiah (Eds.) Rs. 600

CICIL-6 Book Numbers: Some Indian Methods
M.P. Satija and **S.P. Agrawal** Rs. 100

CICIL-7 National Policy for University Libraries in India: Problems and Perspectives
N.B. Inamdar and **L.S. Ramaiah** (Ed.) Rs. 250

CICIL-8 Media Utilisation for the Development of Women and Children
B.S. Thakur and **Binod C. Agrawal** Rs. 150

CICIL-9 Terrorism: An Annotated Bibliography
Susheela Bhan (Ed.) Rs. 275

CICIL-10 Transnational Library Relations: The Indo-American Experience
M.B. Konnur Rs. 175

CICIL-11 Geography of Marketing and Commercial Activities in India (Documentation on Research Information)
R.S. Dixit Rs. 130

CICIL-12 Information India 1988: Global View
S.P. Agrawal and **J.C. Aggarwal** Rs. 200

CICIL-13 Women's Education in India: Historical Review, Present Status and Perspective Plan
S.P. Agrawal and **J.C. Aggarwal** Rs. 360

CICIL-14 Cultural Communication in India: Role and Impact of Phonograms
J.M. Ojha Rs. 220

CICIL-15 Second Historical Survey of Educational Development in India: Select Documents 1985-1989
S.P. Agrawal and **J.C. Aggarwal** Rs. 490

CICIL-16 Documentation Encyclopaedia of UNESCO and Education
J.C. Aggarwal and **S.P. Agrawal** Rs. 800 (set of 2 parts)

CICIL-17 Attitude Towards Information: A Study of Post-Graduate Teachers and Researchers in Social Sciences
N.G. Satish (in press)

CICIL-18 Librarianship and Bureaucratic Organisation: A Study in the Sociology of Library Profession in India
P.K. Jayaswal Rs. 175

CICIL-19 Literature Search
K.A. Isaac Rs. 150

CICIL-20 Child Education in India: Index to Scholarly Writings in Indian Educational Journals and Newspapers since independence
S.P. Agrawal and **Naresh Kanta** Rs. 100

CICIL-21 Lok Sabha and Vidhan Sabha Elections in India 1989 & 1990: Process and Results with Comparative Study of Manifestos
S.P. Agrawal and **J.C. Aggarwal** Rs. 250

CICIL-22 Islamic Studies in India: A Survey of Human, Institutional and Documentary Sources
Mohamed Taher Rs. 180

CICIL-23 Panchayati Raj: An Annotated Bibliography
N.B. Inamdar, N.G. Satish and **Anil Takalkar** 290

CICIL-24 Information India 1989-90: Global View
S.P. Agrawal and **J.C. Aggarwal** Rs. 500

CICIL-25 First Handbook of Psychological and Social Instruments
Udai Pareek and **T. Venkateswara Rao** Rs. 500

CICIL-26 Educational and Social Uplift of Backward Classes: At What Cost and How? Mandal Commission and After
S.P. Agrawal and **J.C. Aggarwal** Rs. 275

CICIL-27 Mass Media and New Horizons: Impact of TV & Video an Urban Milieu
H.R. Trivedi Rs. 180

CICIL-28 Indian Writings on Education : An Indicator to Indian Educational Journals Grouped by Subject Deseriptors 1979 to 1986 (in two parts)
S.P. Agarwal Rs. 900 (per set)

CICIL-29 Nation in Crisis
S.P. Agrawal and **J.C. Aggarwal** Rs. 200

CICIL-30 Information India 1990-91: Global View
S.P. Agrawal and **J.C. Aggarwal** Rs. 500

CICIL-31 Development of University Libraries in India after Independence
O.P. Gupta Rs. 270

CICIL-32 Handbook on Child : With Historical Background
Pramila Pandit Barooah Rs. 320

CICIL-33 Weaker Section in Indian Society : Undiscovered Past, Uncertain Present and Unpredictable Future : Index to Writings in Indian Scholarly Journals and 10 National Newspapers Classified under 1500 Descriptors 1886-1990
S.P. Agrawal and **Rajeev Kumar Sharma** Rs. 600

CICIL-34 Communication Informatics and Librarianship in India : An Introductory Guide to Publications Based on a Survey of Libraries in Capital City of India
S.P. Agrawal and **Pushpa Rani Sharma** Rs. 720

CICIL-35 Problems of Collection Development in Special Libraries
M.S. Sridhar Rs. 225

CICIL-36 National Information Resources for Social Sciences in India : Mobilisation, Dispersal and International Enhancement
S.P. Agrawal Rs. 225

CICIL-37 Modern History of Punjab : A Look Back into Ancient Peaceful Punjab Focusing Confrontation and Failures Leading to Present Punjab Problem, and a Peep Ahead : Relevant Select Documents
J.C. Aggarwal and **S.P. Agrawal** Rs. 400

CICIL-38 India Information Sources : Economics and Business
Kyllikki Ruokonen and **Manohar Lal** Rs.

CICIL-39 Educational Planning in India : With a Slant to Educational Financing and Administration, Vol. 1, Reports of Committees and Commissions, Five Year Plans, Statistical Tables
J.C. Aggarwal and **S.P. Agrawal** Rs. 650

CICIL-40 Integrated Library System : Two Case Studies : Latin America and India
Maria Luiza Rigo Pasquarelli, Rosaly Favero Krzyanowski, Ines Maria M. Imperatriz and S.P. Agrawal Rs. 160

CICIL-41 Social Science Information in India: Effort towards Bibliographical Control
S.D. Vyas Rs. 300

CICIL-42 Higher Education in India Since Independence: U.G.C. and Its Approach
O.P. Gupta Rs. 360

CICIL-43 Government and Politics in India: A Bibliographical Study of Contemporary Scenario Chronicling Rajiv Gandhi Era
S.P. Agrawal and **Rajeev Kumar Sharma** Rs. 500

CICIL-44 Second Handbook of Psychological and Social Instruments
D.M. Pestonjee Rs. 300

CICIL-45 Development/Digression Diary of India; 3D Companion Volume to Information India: 1990-91
S.P. Agrawal Rs. 200

CICIL-46 Development/Digression Diary of India; 3D Companion Volume to Information India: 1991-92
S.P. Agrawal Rs. 300

CICIL-47 Information India 1991-92: Global View
S.P. Agrawal and **J.C. Aggarwal** Rs. 500

CICIL-48 Committees and Commissions in India 1974, A Concept's Project, Compiled by a team of professionals guided by **Virender Kumar** (Vol. 12) Rs. 450

CICIL-49 Committees and Commissions in India 1975, A Concept's Project, Compiled by a team of professionals guided by **Virender Kumar** (Vol. 13) Rs. 450

CICIL-50 Committees and Commissions in India 1976, A Concept's Project, Compiled by a team of professionals guided **Virender Kumar** (Vol. 14) Rs. 450

CICIL-51 Committees and Commissions in India 1977, A Concept's Project, Compiled by a team of professionals guided by **Virender Kumar** (Vol. 15) (in four parts) Rs. 450 each

CICIL-52 Committees and Commissions in India 1978, A Concept's Project, Compiled by a team of professionals guided by **Virender Kumar** (Vol. 16) (in two parts) Rs. 450 each

CICIL-53 Subject Guide to Communication, Informatics and Librarianship in India (Based on a Survey of Library Holdings in Capital City of India)
S.P. Agrawal and **Pushpa Rani Sharma** Rs. 400

CICIL-54 Restructurring of Library and Information Science Curriculum
A. Tejomurty Rs. 250

CICIL-55 Committees and Commissions in India 1979, A Concept's Project, Compiled by a team of professionals guided by **Virender Kumar** (Vol. 17) (in two parts) Rs. 450 each

CICIL-56 Committees and Commissions in India 1980, A Concept's Project, Compiled by a team of professionals guided by **Virender Kumar** (Vol. 18) (in two parts) Rs. 450 each

CICIL-57 Third Historical Survey of Educational Development in India
S.P. Agrawal and **J.C. Aggarwal** Rs. 700